Bioresources for Development

Pergamon Policy Studies on Energy and Environment

Diwan Alternative Development Strategies and Appropriate Technology
Kidd Manpower Policies for Use of Science and Technology
King/Cleveland/Streatfeild Bioresources for Development
Morgan Renewable Resources for Development
Morgan Science and Technology for Development
Segafi-nejad/Belfield Transnational Corporations, Technology Transfer, and Development
Standke Science, Technology, and Society
Thomas/Wionczek Integration of Science and Technology with Development

Related Journals*

Habitat International
Socio-Economic Planning Sciences
World Development

*Free specimen copies available upon request.

PERGAMON POLICY STUDIES ON ENERGY AND ENVIRONMENT

Bioresources for Development

The Renewable Way of Life

Edited by
Alexander King
Harlan Cleveland
with the assistance of
Guy Streatfeild

Published in cooperation with the
World Academy of Art and Science,
American Division, and the
Center for Integrative Studies,
State University of New York
at Buffalo

Pergamon Press
NEW YORK • OXFORD • TORONTO • SYDNEY • FRANKFURT • PARIS

Pergamon Press Offices:

U.S.A.	Pergamon Press Inc., Maxwell House, Fairview Park, Elmsford, New York 10523, U.S.A.
U.K.	Pergamon Press Ltd., Headington Hill Hall, Oxford OX3 0BW, England
CANADA	Pergamon of Canada, Ltd. Suite 104, 150 Consumers Road, Willowdale, Ontario M2J 1P9, Canada
AUSTRALIA	Pergamon Press (Aust.) Pty. Ltd., P.O. Box 544, Potts Point, NSW 2011, Australia
FRANCE	Pergamon Press SARL, 24 rue des Ecoles, 75240 Paris, Cedex 05, France
FEDERAL REPUBLIC OF GERMANY	Pergamon Press GmbH, Hammerweg 6, Postfach 1305, 6242 Kronberg/Schönberg, Federal Republic of Germany

Library of Congress Cataloging in Publication Data

International Conference on Biopotentials for
Development, University of Houston, 1978.
Bioresources for development.

(Pergamon policy studies in energy and environment)
Papers presented at the International Conference
on Biopotentials for Development held Nov. 5-11, 1978
at the University of Houston.
Includes index.
1. Biochemical engineering—Congresses.
I. King, Alexander. II. Cleveland, Harlan.
III. Streatfeild, Guy. IV. Title. V. Series.
TP248.3.I57 1978 660'.63 79-28229
ISBN 0-08-025581-7

Printed in the United States of America

Contents

Preface

The last major task to which John McHale turned his extraordinary integrative mind was, typically, what had not been done before: to pull together from around the world a critical mass of thinking about renewable resources. He and Magda Cordell McHale - his partner in a symbiosis of love and work - had moved their Center for Integrative Studies to the University of Houston not long before. The International Conference on Bio Resources for Development was hosted by the university and scheduled for November 5 to 11, 1978. It was our privilege to join with Professor Roger Porter, of the University of Iowa, one of the world's leading microbiologists and president of their international association, in chairing a week crowded with exciting perspectives and truly integrative thought.

On November 2nd, John McHale died of a sudden and wholly unexpected heart attack. Magda urged us to go ahead with his plans, and we did so. We opened the conference in celebration of John's life and work,* which had touched most of the participants in one way or another. And his plan for the conference worked so well that the whole occasion turned out to be the best kind of living memorial to a bright and lively spirit.

The purpose of the conference, John McHale had written, was

> to contribute to an integrative and long-range assessment of the potentialities of the bioresources field - with specific emphasis on the overall development process, particularly for the lesser developed countries. Economic and environmental constraints upon the present and future uses of the "capital" resources of fossil fuels

---

* A tribute to John McHale, spoken at the opening session of the Conference, will be found in the Appendix. It was published in The Futurist 13, no. 1 (February 1979): 22.

and nonfuel minerals underline the need for more coordinated approaches to renewable "income" resources. These range, principally, from the direct use of solar and solar-related energies to the indirect aspects of solar resources such as enhanced bioproductivity and bioconversion, the greater utilization of organically renewed materials and the bio-transformation of agro-industrial wastes. Although there is a wide interest in this renewable resource range, due to recent concern over supplies of depletable fuels and materials, the larger socio-economic implications of its more intensive use have not been fully clarified.

The McHale initiative was certainly timely. The subject is still at a very early stage of development. Contributions towards its advancement come from very many disciplines - agriculture, forestry, soil science, microbiology, oceanography, thermodynamics, molecular biology, physical chemistry, systems engineering, to mention only a few. There is as yet little coherent literature; links between the disciplines are tenuous where they exist at all.

The Houston Conference, therefore, brought together individuals from a wide diversity of disciplines and a wide range of cultures and countries, scientists who would not normally meet at the traditional international gatherings of professionals in closely related fields. The cosponsorship of the conference represented a wide gamut of organizations and interests: the World Academy of Art and Science, the International Federation of Institutes of Advanced Studies, the Aspen Institute for Humanistic Studies, the Bio Energy Council, and the University of Houston's Energy Laboratory all joined with the McHales' Center to bring people and ideas together in Houston that week.

The very variety of the contributions made it a difficult week to organize, but John and Magda McHale had designed around the difficulty. The first half of the week consisted of a series of discussions of submitted papers, arranged as logically as their diversity would permit. The second half of the week was devoted to discussions in three working groups, meeting simultaneously, the smaller numbers of participants permitting in each case a more thorough examination of the crosscutting topics entrusted to them.

These working groups were concerned essentially with questions of policy, the management of resources, and a deeper analysis of how the biomass could be organized to help meet human needs. The first working group, chaired by Roger Porter, focused on the inherent characteristics of the bioresource, man's interaction with it, and the governance of this interaction so as to maintain and enhance the resource for the use of future generations. The second group, chaired by Alexander King, zeroed in on the implications, immediate and long-term, of the new possibilities of bioresource development for the countries of the Third World. The third group, chaired by Harlan Cleveland, considered the systemic impact of the wide variety of bioresource potentials on the future development of societies of all kinds, with more emphasis on the implications for the more industrialized societies.

The notions collected in our introductory essay have been gleaned from the interdisciplinary freewheeling these arrangements made possible.

The papers presented thereafter are arranged in a somewhat different order than was used at the conference. Once the material could be seen as a whole, it fell into more logical baskets, and the definition of those baskets came partly from the discussion of the papers at the conference itself. We are profoundly grateful to Guy Streatfeild of the Center for Integrative Studies, whose skillful editing converted so diverse a collection of papers into a book.

As the three cochairmen prepared to assemble these rich and renewable materials into a coherent volume, the community of creative thinkers about bioresources suffered another loss with the sudden death of Professor Roger Porter. More than any others, John McHale and Roger Porter were responsible for this volume. It is, naturally, dedicated to them.

Introduction: The Renewable Way of Life

Bioresource is a new word in our vocabulary, and for good reason. The subject is as old as hunting, fishing, and cultivating. But the 1970s have seen a wholesale shift in perspective that makes renewable processes suddenly seem fresh, attractive, and much more important in our immediate future than in our recent past.

The biological resources have been out there all the time, often ignored or exploited or wasted yet somehow durable in their seasonal reincarnations. There is the three-fifths of the biomass that is green plants, from the slenderest ferns to the sturdiest sequoias; the one-fifth that is animals, (including man, the only animal that theorizes about biology or resources); and the one-fifth that is microorganisms or microbes. But to think about all of this, in an integrated way, as a resource - that is new.

It is a resource with characteristics strikingly different from things like minerals or soils or sands of the earth, the waters of the oceans and lakes and rivers, or the atmosphere and magnetism and radiation all around us. These resources of the age of geophysics may be combustible or energetic or turbulent; they can certainly be terribly dangerous and mightily useful. Combined in fruitful ways - bringing water to the land, floating vehicles in the water, modifying the very air we breathe - they are indeed essential to life. But they are not alive. The bioresource is alive.

Since his emergence, man has lived in an always uncertain and sometimes precarious symbiosis with organic nature, obtaining his nourishment and the small amounts of energy he needed from plants and animals personally accessible to him. During the early phase of hunting and foraging for roots and berries, his numbers were, no doubt, limited by the supplies of wild foodstuffs. But with settled agriculture and the domestication of animals, bioresource availability expanded very greatly - and, encouraged by the added elbow room, the human population gradually expanded too.

The management of agriculture was the central engine of civilization. Long before the dawn of scientific agriculture, trial and error by farmers had continuously improved the breeding and selection, and hence the quality and yield of both plants and animal products. Systems we now know to be scientifically sound, such as the rotation of crops to allow nitrogen fixation through the root bacteria of legumes, were discovered by laborious practice and handed down by oral tradition.

Until quite recently, therefore, all humanity existed (and part of humanity flourished) mainly on the basis of renewable resources: agricultural products, firewood, simple devices for the generation of wind- and waterpower. The majority of the human population still does so today. But with the impetus of the Industrial Revolution two centuries and more ago, the life support systems began to transform the very nature of society in many parts of the world.

The new industrial societies developed by the accumulation of scientific knowledge and the spread of technological innovation. They were fed, not as in the past essentially by the annual bounty of nature, but also by the consumption of vast amounts of nonrenewable resources - especially minerals which yielded all the chemical elements, and fossil fuels, at first coal and then oil, which had stored up the solar energy trapped by photosynthesis over the aeons.

The use of these new (and eventually exhaustible) sources of energy influenced human development not only through industrial processes; they also modified the way bioresources were used. The traditional vegetable and animal fibers, for example, were increasingly replaced or extended by synthetics manufactured from coal and petrochemicals, altering in fundamental ways the patterns of consumption, land use, international trade, and the distribution of wealth. Exotic foods from around the world were transported to metropolitan centers in ships, trains, and trucks powered by fossil fuels. Even in agriculture, profound changes have resulted from the use of oil-driven tractors and other farm machinery, synthetic fertilizers, and a wide range of agricultural chemicals derived, once again, from fossil fuels; these now contribute a considerable proportion of the total energy input to food production in the most productive parts of the world. And parallel with these developments - made possible in part by them - expansion of world population has been extremely rapid, calling for ever greater quantities of foods and goods of all kinds, entailing the use of still further quantities of nonrenewable resources and energy.

But this pell-mell human intervention in the use of natural resources was often the opposite of beneficial. Through ignorance, thoughtlessness, and the lack of a sense of responsibilty for the future, early practices - clearing land by slash and burn, overgrazing, and damaging agricultural techniques of many kinds - led to desertification and environmental deterioration in many places. Today, with the great increase in the quantum of human activity, danger to the natural environment is more serious than ever.

Manufacturing industries, with their effluents of heat and toxic substances, many of them nonbiodegradable, and the outflow from modern agriculture based on chemical fertilizers, have grown so great as to raise a question without historical precedent: can the earth, the rivers, the oceans, and the atmosphere provide an infinitely capacious sink to absorb the waste products of industry, agriculture, and urban living? Moreover, there are strong recent indications that the increasing carbon dioxide content of the atmosphere, arising both from the combustion of fossil fuels and from the profligate cutting of tropical rain forests, may cause both general and regional temperatures to rise, with possibly irreversible climatic effects that might be disastrous to humanity.

During the decade of the 1970s, four new perceptions have become pervasive enough to make the decade a kind of watershed - a moment of major change in the direction of human development that spotlights the bioresource potential. One new perception was the risk to the natural environment of staying in the groove of more-is-better economic growth. A second perception was the need for a more "ecological" way of thinking about the social, economic, and political impact of science and technology. A third was the promise of bioresources for development in the less developed areas of Asia, Africa, and Latin America. And a fourth was the sharper focus on the inherent characteristics of the bioresource itself - and their implications for its purposeful management.

At the beginning of the decade, people in very large numbers in many parts of the world were questioning both the possibility and the desirability of continuing to stimulate "growth" in the directions which had become traditional - growth of the economic product, human populations, urban development, numbers of automobiles, and size of bureaucracies. The environmental risks and the threat of resource depletion were only part - an important part - of this disillusion with material growth. The doubts about growth were intensified by the petroleum crisis with its sudden and massive increase in the cost of energy, its wholesale shift in the world balance of payments and pattern of investment, and its demonstration of the vulnerability of industrialized, oil-importing countries to disruption of supplies that could threaten their economic health and styles of life. Most of the less developed countries likewise suffered from the greatly increased cost of the fuels and fertilizers they needed if their exploding populations were to be adequately fed. In both "developed" and "developing" countries, the realization was coming in a rush: that oil resources could run out, and that new energy sources had to be found or invented, and developed, before the oil wells dried up.

The natural conclusion of this line of thinking was to reassess economic needs and the ways of meeting them in such a way as to reduce reliance on resources which might be near exhaustion, or at least would predictably become more and more costly during the generations to come. On the positive side, the same reasoning led naturally to working with nature. Maybe humankind should modify its economic practices so as to improve its use of the bioresources provided, and continuously regenerated by a bountiful nature. Maybe the bioproductivity of the planet could be preserved, and indeed enhanced, to ensure this eternal renewal.

The arguments supporting such an approach seemed clear enough:

- Present and foreseeable increases in world population will call for increases in materials and energy which are unlikely to be met if present practices, policies, and life-styles persist.
- Provision of basic physical needs (especially of food, clothing, shelter) of existing and foreseeable populations is politically and humanly urgent; so is a fairer chance for deprived peoples to participate in a life of modest prosperity and human dignity.
- The limits to the carrying capacity of the planet, and its toleration of human intervention and waste, are at best uncertain.
- The interest of future generations - and perhaps even of our own - requires us to reduce our reliance on nonrenewable resources such as minerals and fossil fuels, to adopt conservationist and recycling practices and to encourage a much more effective use of the continuous inflow of solar radiation, notably the photosynthetic mechanism of the green plant.
- Humankind will need to maintain and increase the bioproductivity of the planetary soil, and mold agricultural policies and practices so as to ensure a full and regenerative use of the biomass available to man, recycling "wastes" as a new form of raw material.

The 1970s have thus been a turning point in our perception of man's relation to his natural environment, the biosphere. The same decade has also seen a shift in man's relationship to the man-made environment, the technosphere.

In the short 300 years of the Scientific Revolution, and the even hastier history of its offspring, the Industrial Revolution, widely held views about man and society have stemmed quite directly from the discoveries and innovations of science and technology. The harmonious universe of Newtonian physics somehow made it easier to believe in Adam Smith's "invisible hand," or the natural balance of separated powers in the politics of Jefferson and Madison. Darwin's doctrine of evolutionary struggle made it almost respectable to believe that if the poor did not survive it must be because they were unfit. The development of industrial technology and mass production led to efforts to make the management of people a kind of science too - efforts doomed to failure by the glorious cussedness of the human animal.

A comparable social fallout is in evidence now, from the flowering of the life sciences and the spreading enthusiasm for biological and genetic engineering. The new world view is ecological, powered by the conviction that everything is related to everything else, that organizations are not hierarchical pyramids but systems of interaction, that each segment of humanity depends in some degree on each other segment of humanity, and that the interconnections are of the essence. If the key words in the earlier cosmologies were harmony, struggle, and planning, the key word in the ecological world view is interdependence.

But the traffic patterns of ecology do not form a one-way grid: the causes and effects travel in both directions. If science and technology can drive society, society - by taking thought and taking action - can drive science and technology. Society need no longer treat the science-and-technology enterprise as autonomous, with an "inner logic" or "invisible hand" of its own. People and their governments began in the 1970s to say out loud that science and technology should consciously be aimed at the meeting of human needs and the fulfillment of human purposes.

The ecological worldview provides the justification, and the bioresource provides the means for doing just that.

The bioresource approach, especially in some of its more primitive manifestations, is often seen by scientists and others in the industrial countries as a "countercultural" technology, interesting especially for the alleviation of poverty in the Third World. We do not view it so; the proper perspective, we think, is that of the total biomass. Bioresources should be developed with full knowledge of the significance for their development of new discoveries in molecular biology and other disciplines. But because the need is greatest in the developing regions, and because the physical environment in the tropical zones is more inviting, bioresource development may indeed evolve more quickly in the more remote, the more rural, and the more tropical areas of the globe.

Planet Earth is heterogeneous, with wide variations in the distribution of its mineral and energy resources, its fertile lands and its deserts, its concentrations of population, and the levels and types of development in its societies. Cultural diversity is doubtless enriching and biologically sound. But the disparities of material levels of development and of income distribution are now generally held to be excessive, and intolerable.

Multinational and bilateral aid programs have tried hard to reduce the disparities between the world's richer and the poorer regions; much has been achieved, but the gaps are still wide, and in some ways are still widening. Economic growth in the Third World has, in recent years, been faster on the average than that of the industrialized countries. But it started from a very low base line; its benefits have been partly absorbed by population increase; too much of it has been used for the purchase of military equipment, and some of that represents a counterflow of wealth from the poor to the rich; and much of the development achieved has served mainly the minority modern sectors of developing countries, and has not alleviated the misery of those who live largely outside the money economy.

In considering how the bioresource might be used to brighten this picture, it may be helpful to recall those problems, situations, and opportunities which are generally present in, and are special to, the world's less developed regions:

- Most of them are in tropical or semitropical zones and have exceptionally reliable input of solar radiation.
- Many of them - though not all - are already overpopulated, are experiencing endemic unemployment and underemployment, and have abnormally high rates of current population increase - adding to demands for food, housing, water, and energy in places where hunger and poverty are already the major problems.
- They generally suffer from a scarcity of conventional energy resources - and in regions where energy resources may occur in nature, exploration for them has barely begun.
- Many less developed countries have a high rainfall, but this is often seasonal and there are many very arid lands.
- Many of the tropical soils are extremely fragile and particularly vulnerable to unwise agricultural and other practices.
- Transportation and communication is often difficult and many villages are virtually isolated.
- Poverty, disease, and malnutrition - interacting on each other - are widespread.
- In many places agricultural residues are insufficiently and inefficiently used. The spoilage of stored foods by rodents and insects is enormous.
- In tropical lands, however, the temperature, radiation and water supply favor a much quicker growth of the biomass than in temperate climates.

The aid programs have not, for the most part, grasped and modified the pattern of poverty they were established to tackle. For too long they took as their starting point that growth in the gross national product, as in the industrialized countries, was the unique and inevitable path to development everywhere; that the benefits of such growth would rapidly "trickle down" to the masses of the poor; and that the technologies on which northern prosperity is based could be quickly, easily, and relevantly transferred to quite different social and cultural environments. The first two assumptions simply proved to be wrong as a matter of history and economics. The transfer of technology turned out to be extremely tricky, and its assimilation and extension fragile and uncertain in the absence of scientific and technical competence inside each country, organically related to the educational system on the one hand, and the productive sectors of agriculture and industry on the other. The aid programs learned the hard way that it was not enough for the national scientific and technological competence to develop just to serve the interests of particular individuals, groups, or even nations if it was not part of a wider infrastructure which, in some sense, was serving humanity as a whole.

The promise of bioresources is its role, not as a southern "counter culture" but as a complement to northern technology. Each country will need, within its overall social and economic planning, to encourage a mix of different types of technology, to match its unique environment, traditions, existing level of development, and availability of relevant resources. Within this mix, bioresource development promises much - and has until now been greatly underestimated. The dangers of linear technological pathfinding have been illuminated by much analysis, and illustrated by many examples, in the decade of the 1970s. The bioresource approach opens a promising array of alternative paths to world development.

Science and systems have already clothed the promise with some visible raiment. First, much empirical experience has accumulated, mainly in rural and peasant economies, about new methods of using wastes and recycling materials so as to increase the bioyield. Examples are the widespread use of biogas generated from human and animal waste now common in China and parts of Southeast Asia; inland pond fish cultivation; the use of algae as an intermediate in food production; the speeding up of plant growth (notably in rubber); and the use of quick-growing leguminous trees which can provide organic nitrogen, cattle fodder, and wood.

There is also much promise in contemporary biological research, for example in enzyme technology, genetics, and a variety of methods for the production of fixed nitrogen from plants other than the traditional legumes. Behind the many lines of applied research, there seem to be great potentials in fundamental work in molecular biology and cytology. Nonbiological developments in the use of solar energy are also going forward, if somewhat slowly; they can complement the photosynthetic path in many applications.

A third line of advance comes from the application of systems science to problems of total or integrated bioresource management. The conventional approach has been to examine the possibilities of particular crops, wastes, devices or processes in isolation from each other, with rather little attention given the management problems of resource utilization, the economic balance, or the energy flow. The systems approach tends to focus on the whole utilization of the biomass available to a particular community, including the interactions of the constituent processes, with the central objective of providing optimum output of food, energy, and fertilizers in an indefinitely sustainable system.

Many new lines of development are illustrated in the richly varied papers brought together in this volume. Among many other suggestions, the reader will find microbiological methods of nitrogen-fixation to reduce or eliminate the use of chemical fertilizers, a call for better understanding of the mechanism of photosynthesis, biological methods of creating humus, the use of bacteria as catalyst in the biological fuel cell, a fish culture chain involving human effluents and algae, and microbiological techniques for the use of agricultural residues.

But the most important idea of all inheres not in the plants or animals or microbes, but in our own minds; the increasing and encouraging awareness of the interdependence of nations, of problems, of functions, of scientific disciplines, and of objectives.

The adjectives "holistic" and "integrative" are already bordering on the cliche, but they have a very special significance in the use and management of the bioresource. They mean, quite literally, that the problems of a nation, of a city, of a village are to be seen as interconnected and, therefore, to be tackled simultaneously and as a complex, not separately or sequentially. The community's future comprises economic, social, cultural, and political, as well as technical facets; these cannot be dealt with by the politician alone, or by the economist, the engineer, or the scientist in isolation. When it comes to the use of resources, it is necessary to consider them all: agricultural, forest, soil, water, microorganisms, plants, animals, men and women. In a particular development scheme, only an integrated approach can make optimum use of the resources, consider food and energy requirements together, arrange for full use to be made of "wastes" and "residues," include traditional agriculture in the community's planning, maintain soil fertility and humus content, explore food addition possibilities through fermentation and the use of plants not commonly consumed, use plant, animal, and human wastes to generate biogas for cooking, lighting, refrigeration, and distillation, develop algal and fish culture, invent or adopt simple solar and windpower devices, and so on almost without end. An integrated plan will include a careful appreciation of the carrying capacity of the soil, so that its fertility can be maintained indefinitely, as well as of methods for augmenting it, for example by inoculation with nitrogen-fixing bacteria. It will consider the energy balance to ensure that the net energy balance is positive. And it will look to the preservation of the environment, locally and globally, in recognition of the place of man in the ecosystem, living in mandatory symbiosis with all the species of creation.

The dangers of indiscriminate "growth," the opportunities for human benefit, and the special needs of developing countries have, thus, in the decade of the 1970s brought the bioresource to center stage. Suddenly we are examining it anew - and finding in its inherent characteristics an intriguing new sense of direction for the processes we call "modernization," or "development," or even "civilization."

What are the inherent characteristics of the bioresource? How can it be perceived by man, who is part of it? What direction signals can we discern in the bioresource for the development of purposeful technologies, the construction of an appropriate analytical system to guide policy choices, and the management of a "modernization" that makes the best and the most of the only biosphere we have?

Think first about the essence of the bioresource:

- The bioresource is "alive."
- The bioresource is a "ubiquitous," "continuous storehouse."
- The bioresource is "resilient" (or adaptive), "versatile," and "renewable."
- The bioresource is "self-balancing," full of feedback mechanisms.
- The bioresource is, however, "bulky" (there is no way to miniaturize a forest), "limited by natural cycles" (each kind of organism will grow only so fast), "variable" (each plant or microbe is different just as people are), and "finite" (unlike another recently rediscovered resource called information).
- The bioresource is "interconnected." (No one has said it better than Lewis Thomas, who writes of the earth as an "immense organism" where chemical signals "serve the function of global hormones, keeping balance and symmetry in the operation of various interrelated working parts, informing tissues in the vegetation of the Alps about the state of eels in the Sargasso Sea, by long interminable relays of interconnected messages between all kinds of other creatures.")
- Above all, the bioresource is "essential to human survival."

Does this inventory of characteristics suggest the changes in concepts, assumptions, and definitions - that is, the changes in man's perceptions - which the new emphasis on the bioresource may bring about? We think it does.

Because it is alive and man is immanent in it, the bioresource requires human cooperation with the environment.

Because it is spread so widely throughout the world, the bioresource has a potential for promoting equity - for responding constructively to the "global fairness revolution." The same cannot be said of oil wells or uranium deposits. Its ubiquity also carries a potential for disaggregation and decentralization, and also perhaps a potential for reordering the urban-rural balance, which industrial civilization as we have known it has done so much to distort.

Because the bioresource is resilient and self-balancing, mistakes need not be irreversible. In managing the biomass for human purposes, we might become better able to learn from trial and error than is safe in, say, the realm of nuclear physics.

Because it is continuous, the bioresource requires us to think harder about the interest of future generations, to include sustainability in our concept of "progress."

Thinking of the bioresource as a continuous storehouse helps us see "waste" as just another form of raw material, waiting to be recycled some productive process.

The nature of the bioresource's limits - limits to pace, to concentration, to consistency - points to ways to increase the limits through breeding and selection, and other synonyms for bioproductivity.

These conceptual changes, in turn, permit and even require individuals to exercise more choice. And because all choices are interconnected, in dealing with the bioresource the responsibility for outcomes is spread more widely. On a farm, productivity is a function of numberless small personal efforts, often unsupervised; these efforts cannot be optimized at the point of a gun, but only by the willingness of the farmer himself to enhance his efficiency in dozens of private and unstandardized ways.

The wider the spread of personal responsibility for outcomes, the more each participant in the management of the bioresource has to try to understand "the situation as a whole," of which his efforts can only be a very small part.

Man's revised perceptions of the bioresource are presented here with their positive implications. But they all imply change. That means the very nature of the bioresource is a threat to existing beliefs, concepts, institutions, and power structures.

The technological choices implied by these revised perceptions leap to the eye. In the spectra of technologies by which resources are molded to purpose, the bioresource (as compared to nonliving resources) inherently favors polyculture rather than monoculture, self-sustaining systems rather than systems requiring more and more energy input from the outside; "extensive" rather than "intensive" systems (in terms of geography, capital, or labor); economic, social, and cultural patterns that encourage independence rather than dependence (for nations, for groups, for individuals); the spreading of benefits rather than the concentration of wealth; the maximization of choice rather than the suppression of diversity; and the diffusion of individual responsibility rather than hierarchical command and control.

In a bioresource-conscious world, therefore, management will have a different "feel" to it: cooperation not coercion, horizontal not vertical structures, nobody in general charge but everybody partly in charge, multiple-objective preferred to single-purpose organizations.

More participatory decision-making implies a need for much feedback information widely available. That means more openness, less secrecy - not as an ideological preference but as a technological imperative.

In such a management environment, "planning" cannot be achieved with detailed blueprints. Planning has to be improvisation by the many on a general sense of direction which is announced by "leaders" only after consultation with those who will have to improvise on it.

Preparing people to participate responsibly in the kind of management appropriate to the bioresource will evidently require a wholesale review of existing educational systems. A dedication to the separateness of specialties may have to give way to an emphasis on integrative, interdisciplinary, interprofessional, and international modes of analysis since only these can be plugged in directly to action on an interconnected resource.

Indeed, one casualty of the new emphasis on bioresources is likely to be traditional analytical systems, especially economics; in a laudable effort to be more rigorous, economics has succeeded in being too narrow. A new analytical system, one with a wider lens, is going to be needed to illuminate the technological choices and guide the pluralistic management, which the new perceptions of the bioresource make both possible and necessary.

There can be no place in the new analytical system for a purposeless "equilibrium" that supplies demands but not needs, and treats any form of growth, constructive or cancerous as "progress." There is certainly a place for some conventional professional tools and concepts: cost-benefit analysis, profitability, "efficiency." But the bioresource pushes us to expand the analytical fremework to include considerations that have been treated in economics as "externalities," or as the primary business of some other (and equally separate) discipline: equity and fairness (among nations, among groups, among individuals); the energy balance, which may be quite as important as the balance of payments or the profit-and-loss calculation; environmental impact; employment impact; long-term sustainability; flows of information, and access to information; implications for the distribution of personal and political power; the interests of future generations; and (when the scale of the problem to be analyzed demands it) a global perspective.

A wider frame of thinking, a wider participation in management, a wider range of technological choice - to take seriously these implications of the bioresource will certainly mean changes in our minds and our habits. But, precisely because we are ourselves part of the bioresource, we may find that adjusting our minds in the directions just indicated is much more "natural" than our efforts in this century to adjust to space travel or telecommunications - or to urban congestion, thickening air, desertification, and the daily threat of global nuclear war.

I

The Rationale of Renewability

Introduction to Part I

The first group of five papers gives, collectively, a general survey of the overall situation on bioresource possibilities and needs. The first, by Russell W. Peterson, provides the most general overview of needs and possibilities. Its text is a quotation from Georgescu-Roegen which says, "In a different way from the past, man will have to return to the idea that his existence is a free gift of the sun." This paper stresses the interdependence of the human and natural worlds, discusses the significance of bioresource potentialities for energy production, and gives a number of interesting examples of novel applications.

Roger Porter's masterly overview of the significance of microorganisms in the total biomass economy cites many examples of the use of microorganisms, and especially enzymes for practical purposes. This essay is important in itself and deserves wide attention.

W.G. McGinnies and J.D. Johnson open up quite a different line in their survey of possibilities of using and developing native plants for the improvement of life in arid environments, for food, fibers, rubber and other products, as well as for the concentration of water to assist the growth of other crops. They make a plea for the carrying out of a thorough survey of worldwide range in different environments.

Ingmar Falkehag again accepts the need for new approaches to the use and management of bioresources, and sees the probability of a great deal of industrial development resulting from substitution of fossil fuel by biomass utilization. He warns of the need to foresee and take account of ecological consequences in advance of widespread application.

The final paper of the section, by Bertrand Chatel, gives another broad survey of the potentialities of bioresource development, this time from the point of view of the less developed countries. He describes the work of the United Nations family of organizations in this field, and stresses the need for international cooperation in research.

1 Green Energy: Problems and Prospects

Russell Peterson

In his remarkable little book, The Lives of a Cell, Lewis Thomas observes that humans, throughout their recent history at least, have liked to think of themselves as standing astride the earth in supreme and solitary splendor - as the tough and enduring species in a world of fragile and fleeting life forms. But that, he says, is simply a lot of romantic rubbish and things are, in fact, the other way around. "The life of the earth," he says, " is the toughest membrane imaginable in the universe." "We," on the other hand, "are the delicate part, transient, and vulnerable as cilia." "The biologic science of recent years" has increasingly underscored "just how interlocked we are" with the life and laws of the natural world. "Man," he says, "is imbedded in nature," and nature is imbedded in man.

This deep interdependence between the human and the natural worlds remains a fundamental fact of life - some would say the fundamental fact of life. Lately, we have begun to realize what the industrialized world has all too often seemed to have forgotten: that today as in the dawn of human life the health and growth of human society are intimately linked to those of natural systems.

Interest in bioresource potentials reflects our growing awareness that the sun is the source of nearly all energy and that, even in the industrialized world, we are by no means as removed as we once imagined from relying on the sun to sustain us and on earth's original, enduring, and most ubiquitous energy factory - photosynthesis.

In terms of making efficient, effective use of the sun and that vast storehouse of solar energy we call biomass, we are still, relatively speaking, in the dark ages. We have been so bedazzled by what once appeared the lavish abundance of fossil fuels and the incredible things we could accomplish with them, that we have done little - other than the major and successful efforts in agriculture - to develop the technologies for making the most of the radiant energy sent by the sun, and the green energy stored by plants.

At the same time, there is an enormous amount of activity going on in the bioresources field. Indeed, so much is happening so fast that we lack anything that remotely resembles an adequate inventory of what is occurring. And if the technologies for tapping biomass for various forms of energy - such as food, fuel, and fertilizer - lack the relative sophistication of our fossil and other fuel technologies, they are, at least on a small scale level, less priimitive and more practically available than most people realize.

Through the work of conferences such as this, through the studies and assessments that the Office of Technology Assessment (OTA) and others are undertaking, through the activities of groups such as the Bio Energy Council, the expert and interested public is rapidly learning more about the importance and availability of various biomass technologies.

For example, as part of a planned "world of tomorrow" demonstration, Walt Disney World in Florida, under a grant from the U.S. Environmental Protection Agency, intends to research, design, and operate a water hyacinth system to treat and utilize wastes generated at Disney World. The hyacinths will serve as a tertiary filtration device for stripping nutrients from the waste water and thus reclaiming that water for reuse. The enriched hyacinth crop will be harvested and processed for fertilizer and fuel. This project is described as "the first total research and development effort to tie all the elements" involved in using hyacinths for waste water conversion, and fuel and fertilizer production. If such a system proves to be practical, it could be used widely in small communities with similar climates in this country and elsewhere in the world.

ENERGY POTENTIAL OF BIOMASS

The amount of raw energy stored up in bioresources is simply staggering. In a single day the sun sends more energy to earth than the world consumes in an entire year. Although plants capture only 1 percent or less of that energy, they store some 20 times as much energy in a year as the world uses. It has been estimated that, used efficiently, 10 percent of the world's current yearly production of biomass could readily meet the entire projected year 2000 requirements for food and energy. Biomass remains the main source of fuel for half the world's people.

In this country, biomass accounts for about 2 percent of our total annual energy consumption. This is equivalent to all the hydroelectric power delivered annually by that vast network of reservoirs, dams, and hydroelectric plants all across the country. It is equivalent to about 7 percent of imported oil and about 65 percent of the heat released by nuclear fission to generate electricity in this country.

If the sheer energy potential of biomass is enormous, so are the difficulties and obstacles to taking advantage of anything like a significant fraction of that potential. Much of the biomass that we could tap for energy is far more valuable to us as food or lumber. Moreover, green plants support not only humans, but the entire spectrum of living creatures. Some biomass must eventually be returned to the soil. And there are formidable technical and economic and ecological barriers to putting much of that huge, renewable reservoir of biomass to practical use. On the other hand, until recently we have done very little on developing plant species specifically for efficient energy production, or about modifying or developing biomass collection and conversion processes for economic energy production. For these and other reasons, we have only the haziest idea of the potential practical contribution of biomass to the United States or world energy supply.

Our most urgent task is to find out what the practical potential of biomass is for energy that humans can use - to determine what the real problems and prospects for bioenergy are. This is the purpose of several studies that OTA has underway or in the offing.

OTA BIOMASS STUDIES: SOME EXAMPLES

Two studies at the Office of Technology Assessment are exploring the agricultural potential of plant resources. One - a study of alternative pest management strategies for food production - includes an assessment of the development and use of pest-resistant crops and plants. The other - on the impact of applied genetics - includes an assessment of the applications of genetic technologies to agriculture. In this second study, we are taking an especially close and a comprehensive look at the impact and implications of developing new strains of crops capable of fixing their own nitrogen.

Nitrogen makes up some 80 percent of the earth's atmosphere. To the degree that we can find ways of converting that nitrogen to fertilizer that crops can use and farmers can afford - through such efforts as the breeding of plants that fix their own nitrogen, and thus, in effect, manufacture their own fertilizer - we can reduce the cost, avoid the harm and hazard caused by the 80 percent of chemical fertilizers we now lose to the environment, and save nonrenewable natural gas now going in substantial amounts into the production of commercial fertilizer.

There are some exciting developments going on in this field. For example, on a visit to Sri Lanka about a year ago, I had the opportunity to observe the work of the Central Research Laboratory at Perydenia in using solar energy and biological processes to produce nitrogen fertilizer. This work builds on the work by D.W. Rains, at the University of California at Davis, who elucidated the centuries-old practice of the Vietnamese. Yields are markedly increased by seeding rice paddies with a blue green algae that grows in irrigation ditches.

What is involved here is a symbiotic relationship between a blue green algae and a miniature fern which, biologically, does an excellent job of fixing the air's nitrogen into a useable fertilizer. It reduces the need for chemical nitrogen fertilizer in rice paddies by 50 percent.

Dr. Sylvan Wittwer, of Michigan State University, has stated that by further research on biological nitrogen fixation it should be possible to select some super strains of rhizobium that would improve the nitrogen fixing of legumes. Dr. Wittwer estimates that we could reduce by at least 50 percent the amount of chemical nitrogen needed for corn and wheat crops by rotating these crops with the legumes.

Today, in the United States, the equivalent of about 11 million metric tons of nitrogen fertilizer is produced by biological fixation. Forty years ago, that was the only source of nitrogen fertilizer. During the years since, we have rapidly increased our use of chemical fertilizer to the point where we now use 11 million tons of it at the annual cost of 2 billion dollars. We have thus far achieved little in developing the alternative of biological nitrogen-fixation.

Another especially important area of genetic research involves the discovery and development of new strains of bacteria, which could increase the efficiency of human and animal waste digesters in the production of methane, especially at lower temperatures. Today, in the developing world where large numbers of these digesters are used, their efficiency falls off markedly in the winter months. Nor should we forget that the key to the Green Revolution was the development by more conventional genetics of strains of wheat and rice that led to major increases in yields, and that further research in this field is very much in order.

Genetic technologies not only have enormous potential for meeting human needs and improving the quality of our life, but pose such potential problems as the inadvertent creation of harmful life forms, and they raise an array of ethical, legal, and political questions. For example, General Electric has developed a new strain of bacteria which is extremely effective in breaking down oil in oil spills to products which can be readily absorbed by the natural processes of the ocean. The Court of Customs and Patent Appeals granted General Electric a patent on that new strain. Yet, in another case, the Supreme Court has asked the Court of Customs and Patent Appeals to reconsider its grant of a patent to the Upjohn Corporation for a pure strain of organisms which produces an antibiotic. The critical and unresolved issue in these cases is whether, and under what conditions, living organisms can be patented. Beyond this issue are even larger ones. For example, if American corporations cannot secure patents on the results of their genetic research, then research in recombinant DNA and other areas will inevitably move overseas, and our balance of payments will eventually suffer along with the entire innovative effort in this country.

OTA has nearly completed another study on bioenergy resources - on materials and energy from solid waste. Every year the United States generates 135 million tons of municipal solid wastes. We now have commercially-proven technologies for converting the organic matter in these wastes into fuel for burning with coal, or converting into compost. However, substantial uncertainties remain concerning the health of workers at resource recovery facilities, as well as possible air and water pollution resulting from such facilities. In addition to using the biomaterial in waste, we now know how to recover - with low capital investment - high quality glass, aluminum, paper and iron, and steel from municipal wastes.

On energy recovery from solid waste, we find that about one quad or

10^{15} BTU (10^{18} joules), could theoretically be recovered in the United States from municipal solid waste, but that in many cases the economics would be more favorable if separation of the solid waste into burnable and unburnable fractions were accomplished at the source. Several pilot projects in at-source separation are underway and the results look promising.

The world's forests are one of the richest and most sorely abused bioresources. OTA is currently considering launching an assessment of forest resources technologies in this country and around the world. Forests are dynamic systems that are vital to the life-sustaining capacity of the global environment. They are living factories which serve as renewable sources of energy. They generate food and oxygen through photosynthesis, and ensure the continued productivity of land and water by filtering degradable wastes, storing CO_2, regulating water flow, and protecting erosion and flooding. Although outwardly impressive and apparently enduring, forests are - as we are belatedly discovering - fragile ecosystems.

Forests cover nearly one-third of the earth's land area; yet trends in forest exploitation have reduced the global forest area by 15 percent since 1963. The global demand for wood and forest products is estimated to be increasing at a yearly rate of 3 percent. The demand may grow even more rapidly in the future. In the developing countries, 90 percent of wood consumption is for firewood. Existing forest areas are being rapidly depleted through overcutting, overgrazing and clear-cutting for crop and pasture lands. The failure to reforest depleted areas has led to erosion, flooding, siltation, and in some cases, desertification of once fertile land.

An OTA study of the future of forests and forest resources would focus on the increasing pressures from population growth and economic development on forests of the world. It would explore the interaction among the various aspects of forest growth, the harvesting, processing, and use of woods, and analyze the impact of technology on all parts of the system.

It takes from 20 to 100 years for a tree to grow to maturity. The policy decisions we make today will affect the availability of forest resources in the twenty-first century. For that reason, it is essential that we make a thorough assessment of the impacts impinging on our future forest resources available to our decision-makers today.

Finally, OTA is involved in a major assessment of energy from biological processes. One of the major aims of this assessment is to determine what the practical resource base is for energy from biomass in the United States. Deciding what the practical base is must, of course, involve a careful look at such aspects as the costs of competing fuels, the status of production and conversion technology, and acceptable kinds of levels of environmental and social impact.

This study covers far more ground than can be adequately described here. The following is a brief description of some of the OTA's current interests.

There has been a great deal of interest and controversy concerning the use of methanol or ethanol as at least a partial substitute for oil-derived gasoline for automobiles. Because of present gasoline prices in the United States, this substitution will have an uphill fight, and it is not clear whether the energy balance for producing ethanol from biomass is favorable or not. Experts disagree about the effect of alcohols and alcohol-gasoline blends on engine performance and life, and on emissions. In general, the future of biomass alcohol as a petroleum substitute looks bright or gloomy depending on the assumptions one makes about oil prices, the biomass sources to be used, the pace of development in conversion technology and the values that are assigned to such factors as reducing oil imports, increasing income in the agricultural sector, and the decreasing use of all fossil fuels including coal.

Promising research on the cultivation of plant species that produce hydrocarbons directly has commenced. One can envision eventually growing trees on currently submarginal land, and tapping them for hydrocarbons, just as we tap the rubber tree and the maple tree today for latex and syrup. In this case, we would not have to harvest the whole biomanufacturing plant as we do for producing other biofuels such as wood and alcohol. This is an exciting long-term possibility, but is unlikely to help us in the midterm or near future.

There are a number of other bioenergy products and uses which are clearly technically and economically feasible now or on the verge of feasibility. We are exploring the possiblity of minimal, low-cost incentives designed to remove some institutional barriers and overcome some of the social inertia that prevent us from taking fuller advantage of such products and uses. Minimal incentives and near term technical advances may be especially effective in encouraging the greater use of wastes which have already been collected, especially the dirty wastes such as municipal solid waste and feedlot residues.

Biomass products and processes, which may not be ready for widespread use in the United States, may be appropriate and effective in some developing countries. For example, the climate, the integrated technology for sugar/molasses/alcohol production, and the price of gasoline in Brazil combine to make ethanol production from sugarcane economically competitive now. Already digesters, for producing methane gas from organic wastes, are making a real contribution to living standards in the rural areas of many poor countries. We are examining the most effective roles the United States might play in helping these countries develop and deploy technologies that do not require expensive petroleum or electrical transmission grids. We are also exploring the so-called reverse technology transfer that might eventually benefit the United States.

Like everything else under the sun, there are real limits and hazards to the use of biomass for energy, and we need to make certain we know what those limits and hazards are. But, as we do determine what they are and take steps to ease or avoid any adverse impacts, I have no doubt that in the years ahead, we will make far greater and better use of our vast bioresources for energy in its various forms.

Several years ago, the economist, Nicholas Georgescu-Roegen, predicated that: "In a different way than in the past, man will have to return to the idea that his existence is a free gift of the sun."

This conference and the burst of activity that has occasioned it are ample evidence that we may be returning to that old and enduring idea a lot sooner than anyone thought.

2 Microorganisms as Bioresource Potentials for Development

J.R. Porter

Microorganisms are most frequently thought of in a restricted sense as the cause of disease in human beings, animals, or plants. There are, in fact, many more types that are beneficial than harmful to higher forms of life. Microbes should be recognized for their ecological significance in the earth's biosphere, as a source of food and energy, as as producing many useful and profitable substances.

A recent ecological estimate indicates that higher plants make up over half the biomass (kg bound carbon) of our planet, whereas the remainder is composed almost equally of animals (including human beings) and microorganisms (6 to 11 x 10^{12} kg bound carbon and 2.3 to 10.8 x 10^{12} kg bound carbon, respectively). This raises the following question: Is mankind taking full advantage of a natural resource in biomass that is almost equal to the animal kingdom and is largely untapped? If the answer is in doubt, then how can microbes be used to improve the welfare and quality of people's lives, while maintaining a balance between the environment and the changing demands of society?

A microbiologist can give a fresh perspective to the following of world problems in terms of the usefulness of microorganisms:

1) Growth of the world population and its significance.
2) Need to improve human nutrition.
3) Degradation and erosion of fertile land as related to feed and food production.
4) Need for increased sources of energy and new products for adequate development.
5) Protection of the environment, including the air, water, and other natural resources
6) Development of some form of economic stability and justifiable trade among nations.

MICROORGANISMS AND THE GROWTH OF THE HUMAN POPULATION

First, consider the microbiological implications of the recent rapid growth of the world population, and the plight of many people. By controlling the agents that cause some of the most serious killing infectious diseases, microbiology is partly responsible for the world's population growth from about 2,600 million people in 1945 to over 4,300 million today.

Unfortunately, with this growth in population there has not been a corresponding increase in satisfying the basic human needs of people, as so well described by McHale and McHale (1978); in fact living standards have declined for many people, and their plight remains deplorable (table 2.1). Microbiology can contribute more than most people realize to solving certain of the conditions listed in the table.

Some of our well-known diseases, that a few years ago we thought were controlled, are again on the increase or need constant surveillance to forestall epidemics. Other serious infectious diseases of human beings, animals, and plants remain to be conquered. For example, diarrheal diseases caused by various microbes are the leading cause of death among poor children in Third World countries. Six so-called tropical diseases (malaria, schistosomiasis, the filariases, trypanosomiasis, leishmaniasis, and leprosy) still affect some 700 million people. Furthermore, certain diseases kill millions of head of livestock, and ravage food crops. These losses of life due to microbes can and should be reduced.

As far as noninfectious diseases are concerned, we may be on the verge of certain interesting breakthroughs that involve microorganisms. The recent finding that the genes for human insulin, and for the brain hormone somatostatin, may be manufactured by microbial genetic engineering holds exciting possibilities for development. Other speculations for using microorganisms to improve health include: (i) Substances that microbes produce naturally which possess anti-inflammatory or cortisonelike properties, (ii) metabolites that have anti-cancer potentialities, and (iii) compounds that reduce hypertension or cure peptic ulcers - at least in experimental animals.

MICROORGANISMS AND ANIMAL AND HUMAN NUTRITION

In animal and human nutrition, there is great need to improve the quality and increase production of protein feeds and foods, essential amino acids, and other food supplements.

Traditional protein resources can be expanded by converting carbonaceous substances such as alcohols, petroleum fractions, or excess carbohydrate materials to microbial proteins. Calculations by

Table 2.1. The World's 4,300 Million People

Condition	Million
Living in Absolute Poverty	750
Malnourished or Undernourished	600 to 1,400
Lacking Potable Water	2,000
Inadequate Sewage Disposal	3,000
No Access to Effective Medical Care	1,500
Life Expectancy Below 60 Years	1,700
Infant Mortality/1,000	128
Suffering from 6 Tropical Diseases	700
Adults Illiterate	800
Children Not in School	250
Inadequate Housing	1,030
Income Less than $90 per Year	1,300

Source: McNamara, 1976; McHale and McHale, 1978.

Lewis (1976) and others indicate the applicability of so-called single cell microbial proteins (SCP) to Third World food problems seems limited because of their high-energy requirements for production. But Senez (1976) believes sooner or later the production of SCP on a large scale will become an absolute necessity for Europe and other industrialized countries, as well as an important means of relieving the world protein shortage.

Senez gives the following logical reasons for this belief that microbial protein can and must be substituted for these purposes:

1) Microorganisms grow at rates 100 to 1,000 times faster than animals and plants and they are more efficient in their food conversions.

2) Genetic strains of microbes are available that contain 50 to 60 percent protein on a dry weight basis.

3) Microorganisms can utilize extremely diverse substrates as a source of carbon, ranging from CO_2 for photosynthetic algae and certain bacteria to more complex substances, such as alcohols, carbohydrates, and hydrocarbons for bacteria, yeasts, and higher fungi. Simple nitrogen sources such as ammonia or nitrate, and inorganic salts are the only other nutritional requirements.

4) Microorganisms can be cultivated in large quantities in relatively small areas in any region of the world, and they are not dependent on soil or climatic conditions.

Selected genetic strains of microorganisms are now being studied in fifteen to twenty countries as possible sources of protein, although actual commercial production beyond the pilot-range stage occurs in only a few nations. For example, several hundred thousand tons of yeast used for baking, feed, and food supplements have been manufactured annually in several countries for many years, and the demand is growing. And, a new, continuous, closed-system plant has recently been put into operation to produce yeast (*Candida utilis*) from surplus cheese whey, which can manufacture 7,500 tons per year.

A protein product called *Pruteen* is being manufactured from methanol by bacteria on a trial basis in England (fig. 2.1); over ten years of research and $100 million have been spent to perfect this process. Multimillion dollar facilities have been built in Italy (Sardinia) to produce up to 100,000 tons per year of a protein product named *Toprena*. In early 1978, a pilot-plant in Frankfurt, West Germany, started producing a bacterial product, *Probion*, as an animal feed supplement; it contains 70 percent protein, 10 percent nucleic acids, 8 percent fats, and 7 percent minerals. Plans are underway to use a novel purification technique to remove the nucleic acids from the product so it can be used in such food products as bakery goods, soups, and prepared meat pastes.

Another promising microbial process for producing high-protein

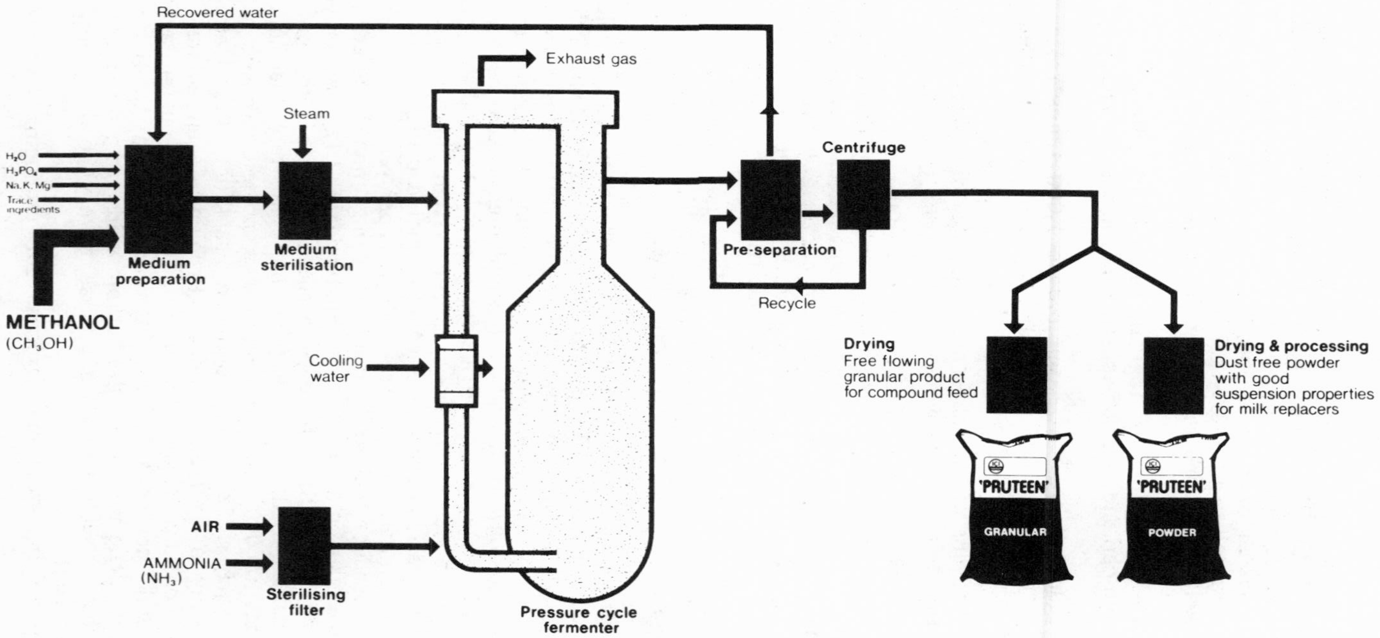

Fig. 2.1. Schematic process for commercial production of bacterial single cell protein in a pressure cycle fermenter.

Source: Courtesy Imperial Chemicals Industries, Ltd.

biomass and other useful products is algal culture. Although the technology may be beset with certain problems, the product is not harassed by the unfortunate and unjustified situation that has occurred with microbial protein manufactured from n-paraffins. Figure 2.2 from a recent paper by Colombo (1978) shows the broad spectrum of development possibilities, and different sectors of application, of the algal biomass.

PHOTOSYNTHETIC REACTION:

$$CO_2 + NO_3^- + PO_4^{--} + H_2O \xrightarrow[\text{energy}]{\text{solar}} \underset{\text{algal biomass}}{[CH_2ONP]} + O_2$$

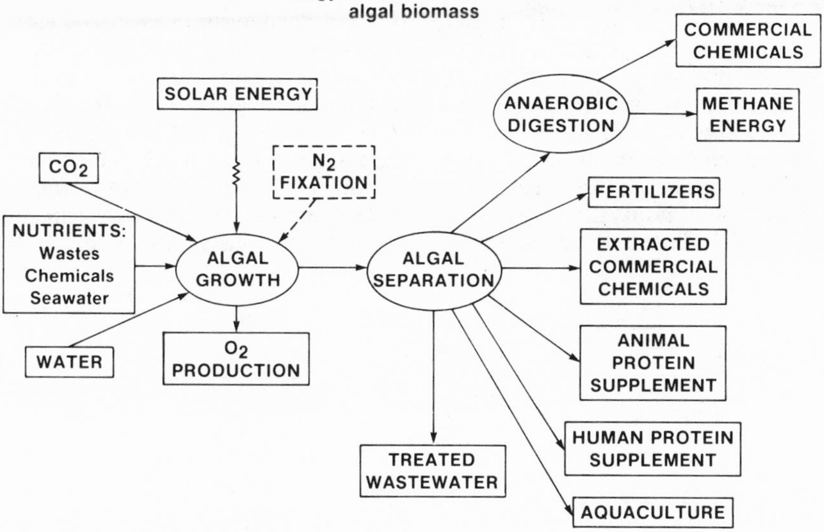

Fig. 2.2. Photosynthetic growth reaction and possible applications of algal biomass.

Source: Colombo 1978.

The unique innovative approach taken by Colombo and associates, at Montedison, in Milan, and the University of Florence, is the cultivation of algae (Spirulina, sp.) inside thin-walled transparent plastic tubes. Such tubes can be placed on nonfertile land, are not subject to external contamination, and conserve water in arid or semiarid climates. Experiments so far indicate high yields of algal-protein biomass can be produced; in fact, 32 tons/hectare/year, which is several times more than can be obtained by growing feed grain crops on poor soils. Furthermore, the technology represents one of low-capital, low-labor cost that could be easily adapted to rural areas.

All the microbial proteins so far manufactured have been shown to have a composition comparable to fish meal and soybean proteins. Experimental feeding studies using rats, poultry, cattle, and pigs show the SCP is utilized extremely well as a feed supplement. Studies using human beings have also been conducted.

Several tons per month of various L-amino acids are being produced for the feed and food industries by treating DL-acylamino acids with a special microbial enzyme L-amino oxidase. Estimates are that monosodium glutamate is now being so manufactured in amounts of about 200,000 metric tons annually, and over 20,000 tons of lysine are produced to supplement foods deficient in this amino acid.

Besides contributing to nitrogenous foods and feeds, microorganisms are also having a great impact on the manufacture of vitamins and carbohydrate products; in fact, microbes are helping alter the entire sugar industry.

The first commercial fructose sweetened corn syrup was introduced in 1967 using the microbial enzyme, amylase, to help convert soluble corn starch to glucose, and then microbial (streptomyces) glucose isomerase to transform part (42 percent) of the glucose to fructose, which is about twice as sweet as common sugar. By 1972, the process known as enzyme immobilization was applied to these transformations; in this process enzymes are attached to an insoluble substrate without altering their catalytic properties, and the immobilized enzyme can be recovered and used again, or employed in a continuous system (fig. 2.3).

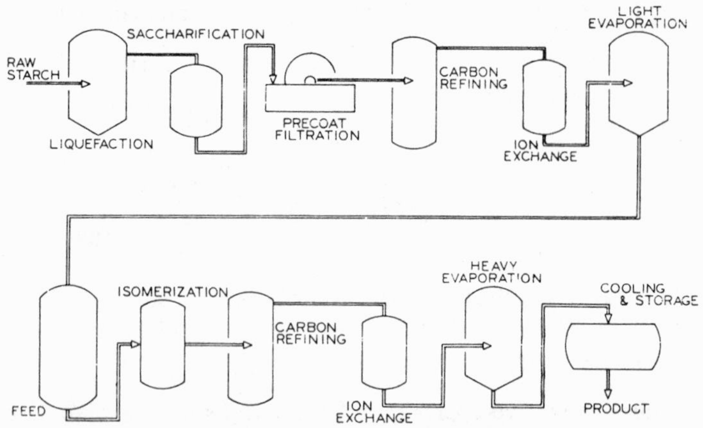

Fig. 2.3. Flow chart for converting starch to high-fructose sweetener by batch, semicontinuous, and continuous operations using microbial enzymes for saccharification and isomerization.

Source: Mermelstein 1975.

An added advantage of the continuous system over older processes is that the required contact time for the enzyme with its substrate is reduced from about two days to hours or even minutes. Using this continuous process over 2 million tons of high-fructose corn syrup were manufactured in the United States in 1977; about 1,000 tons of microbial amylases and glucose isomerase were employed for the process.

Estimates are that by 1980 high-fructose corn syrup will replace up to 30 to 50 percent of the market now supplied by sucrose, since it is being successfully used to sweeten carbonated beverages, confections, pie fillings, ice cream and other frozen specialties, and in yeast raised baked goods.

The use of microbial processes to produce food additives is now expanding rapidly in other areas, notably to the production of microbial polysaccharides (also called gums, hydrocolloids, and polymers), and especially a bacterial polysaccharide called xanthan from Xanthomonas campestris (Sanford and Laskin 1977). The annual production of xanthan from low-grade sugar is estimated to be between 10,000 and 20,000 tons, with a growth rate of 8 to 10 percent per annum. About 60 percent of the production of this substance is used as a stabilizing, thickening, or water retaining agent in such prepared foods as salad dressings, processed cheese spreads, instant pudding mixes, frozen desserts, gravy type pet foods, and as a substitute for gluten in bread. But it is also finding wide usage in detergents and laundry products, in adhesives, in toothpaste, and in the petroleum, textile, paper, paint, and numerous other industrial processes.

Two issues might be raised concerning the examples mentioned above. One, they will require more high technology and much more capital for development than lower levels of technology. And two, technologies alone, whatever their scale, cannot eliminate inequities or the need for sociopolitical changes. In contrast, some of these processes have been utilized in the homes and villages of countries where people have prepared fermented foods for centuries. A partial solution to the problem of protein nutrition may be to improve and expand what is already being done in these countries. This may reinforce home and village industries. Also, it should now be possible at the village level to make sugars (glucose, fructose) from cooked starchy materials, using simple equipment containing the microbial enzymes mentioned above.

MICROORGANISMS IN THE PREVENTION OF CROPLAND DEGRADATION

A survey of sixty-nine countries by Bente (1976) shows widespread overcropping, overgrazing, deforestation, and such water problems as lowering water tables, salinization, and waterlogging. As a result, soil is lost by erosion, essential crop nutrients are depleted, and biological activity is decreased.

Under normal agricultural practices, it is estimated that it takes nearly 100 years to form 2.5 centimeters (1 inch) of fertile topsoil. To replace biomass and nutrients in deforested ecosystems, it may require 60 to 80 years (Likees, Bormann, Pierce, and Reiners 1978). But under current practices, in some countries topsoil is being lost at a rate of about 2.5 centimeters every 10 to 11 years.

Since 1974, partial restoration of some nutrients in soil has resulted from the Food and Agricultural Organization (FAO) providing forty-six less fortunate countries with fertilizer, trace elements, and pesticides. But Eckholm (1976), Brink, Densmore, and Hill (1977), and Pimentel et al. (1978), have pointed out this is not sufficient to maintain high fertility of croplands without additional conservation measures being practiced.

The millions of microorganisms in each gram of fertile soil are largely responsible for the production of humus from crop residues, and they also play a part in cycling the essential elements for plant growth. In addition, some 25 genera of bacteria and blue green algae are known to fix various amounts of atmospheric nitrogen in the soil. The genus Rhizobium itself, living in the nodules of leguminous plants, is estimated to fix 150 to175 million metric tons of nitrogen annually, which is several times more than all the commercial nitrogen fertilizer manufactured from expensive fossil fuel.

With fossil fuels becoming more expensive and eventually scarce, we should begin to give greater attention to natural processes for maintaining the fertility of our soil. Microbiology has a prime role to play in such processes.

Interesting and important research is now being pursued in the soil sciences, including microbiology, but more is necessary to increase food and feed production, and conserve valuable cropland. The recent announcement by Valentine and colleagues, and by Maier and Brill (1978), that microbial genetic engineering using rhizobial strains may soon result in a mutant that will form nodules on all legumes and increase N_2 fixation could have far reaching practical significance. And the possibility that the N_2-fixing gene of bacteria may be transferred directly to plants could be one of the great scientific breakthroughs of the century.

The concentration of phosphates and other essential elements by certain fungi in the region of roots (rhizosphere) must be considered highly important for future developments in agriculture and forestry.

MICROORGANISMS IN THE PRODUCTION OF ENERGY AND NEW PRODUCTS

Because of the complex and controversial problems associated with the world energy dilemma, it is difficult to assess their impact on future developments. But everyone should heed the statement made recently in Toronto by Irving S. Shapiro (1978), Chairman of E.I. Dupont Company. He was appearing on IUPAC's program dealing with Chemical Research Applied to World Needs (CHEMRAWN) when he said: "We face an immense task - nothing less than the conversion, over a period of decades, to a post-petroleum economy. If we need dramatic new technologies to meet...energy needs the fundamental scientific work should be underway now." In this same area, Philip Abelson (1977) stated the following in a lecture last year before the American Society for Microbiology:

> The long-term shape of activities around the world is going to be in large measure determined by energy choices that become available during the next decades. Microbiology can have an important role in creating attractive alternatives.

It is the responsibility of each of us to give imaginative thought to how the world might adjust to a postpetroleum economy.

In some countries, ethanol production by microbial fermentation and biogas generation at the home and village levels are currently helping certain people adjust to lack of expensive fossil fuels. These alternate sources of energy generated by microbial activities need to be given more consideration but there are certain economic and scientific problems to be solved. Let me discuss briefly two of these microbial processes; namely, ethanol fermentation and biogas production.

Ethanol As A Source of Energy

The use of corn, sorghum, potato, cassava, sugarcane, and other fermentable substances to produce ethanol for fuel has been studied since the early 1930s. Gasoline/ethanol mixtures were widely used in Europe after World War I, and by 1934 consumption was more than 700 million gallons (2,650 Ml) annually. The first commercial product in the United States, called Agrol, was manufactured in 1935 to help reduce large farm surpluses and unemployment. Currently, there is renewed interest in using a mixture of anhydrous ethanol and gasoline (called gasohol) as a source of fuel for transportation.

When grains, tubers, or sugarcane are suggested as a substrate for providing alcohol as a fuel, two opposing arguments of scientific, nutritional, and economic nature must be considered. There is no question that ethanol can be produced from a variety of biomass substrates by fermentation, and it works well as a gasoline supplement. But there are also convincing data that support the positions: (i) should high quality grains be converted to fuel with a pending world food shortage? and (ii) is the process economical and practical?

The need for feed and food grains will unquestionably increase in the future, and some data indicate that the production of ethanol from grain for fuel may result in a net loss of energy. Cloud L. Cray (1977), of Mid-West Solvents, has made careful study of this point and presents results to show it requires 139,000 Btus. to manufacture one gallon (3.78 liter) of anhydrous alcohol, which has a heat value of only 90,000 Btus. per gallon. Also, the current price of grain alcohol is two or three times the wholesale cost of gasoline in the United States. Cray points out, however, that ethanol made by fermentation can easily compete as a basic chemical for pharmaceutical and other industrial purposes.

On the other hand, several persons describe the favorable possibilities of ethanol production by fermentation as a source of fuel. Lipinsky (1978), for instance, believes it is possible to reorganize the present corn biomass system in the United States to permit economic production of 10 to 18 billion liters of ethanol for use as a 10 percent blend with gasoline.

Major breakthroughs are occurring in the treatment of corn stover and sugarcane bagasse with microbial enzymes to convert the cellulose to fermentable sugars, which in turn can be employed to produce ethanol and a nutritious residue for use as an animal feed supplement. Thus, the manufacture of alcohol by fermentation may become more feasible in the United States.

In certain countries, such as Brazil, ethanol from sugarcane, manioc, and other tropical plants has become a major project of the government. Of 170 distilleries proposed, several are in operation. The plan calls for increasing alcohol production to over 3.8 billion liters by 1982 to reduce the importation of $4 billion worth of petroleum. Figure 2.4, from a recent report by Altenpohl (1978), illustrates the appropriate Brazilian technology for the production from biomass of alcohol and other useful organic chemicals, and the returning of humus to the soil after composting the waste of the process.

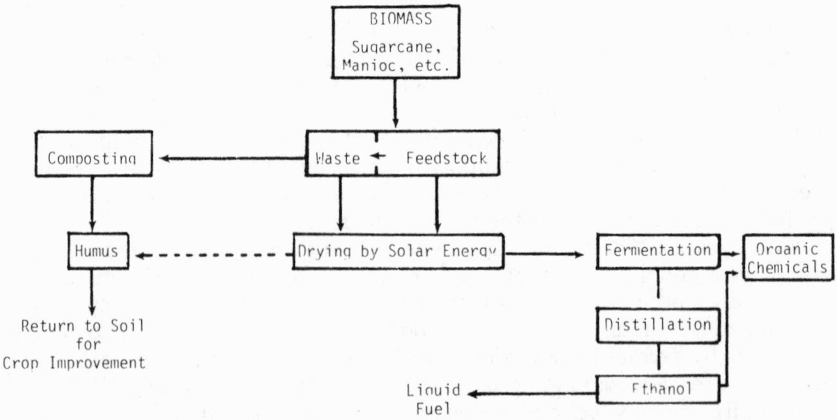

Fig. 2.4. Production of ethanol and other useful substances by fermentation from biomass.

Source: Altenpohl 1978.

So many economic and technical factors currently exist that it is difficult to say whether the production of fuel by microbial fermentation of grains will become practical in most countries (Anderson 1978). On the other hand, the microbial conversion of agricultural, forestry, industrial, and household wastes or residues may become an important source of fuel. One estimate is that 1.7×10^{11} tons of biomass are produced annually, and that 98 percent of this amount is not used in an economically sound manner.

Biogas As A Fuel

When organic matter undergoes anaerobic fermentation, the principal off-gases formed by microorganisms are methane (50-70 percent), and carbon dioxide (30-50 percent), with traces of hydrogen sulfide. This natural process has been known for many years. In fact, gas from a septic tank was used for street lighting in Exeter, England as early as 1895.

By 1938-1939, scientists at the Indian Agricultural Research Institute began studies on the anaerobic digestion of cattle dung, and waste barnyard and household materials, with the objectives of producing methane as a source of fuel and of retaining or improving the qualities of the residual substances as fertilizer. After considerable research and technical work, biogas plants were designed for family and village use which were functional and acceptable for cooking, lighting, and even mechanical power. This technology has now expanded rapidly in other developing countries (table 2.2). In fact, in Southeast Asia integrated biogas farming systems of various sizes are developing (fig. 2.5). Such systems not only provide a source of fuel and a hygienic method for disposing of wastes, but they decrease the incidence of water and insect-borne diseases, provide edible fish, and are a good source of fertilizer for crops (Srinivasan 1977).

Methane from sludge digesters at municipal sewage plants has been used for many years in several countries. But until recently little attention has been given in the more industrialized countries to this source of fuel and fertilizer from residues and wastes. Klass (1976), and more recently Pimentel and associates (1978) (table 2.3) have presented estimates of the biomass in the United States that has a potential energy value. More needs to be done to recover the solid and liquid residues from all these forms of biomass, especially those from cattle feedlots, where the off gases from the anaerobic fermentation of wastes can be used for fuel, and water, soil, and air pollution can be avoided.

Several research and commercial projects are currently underway in various countries to develop biogas as a large-scale operation. For example, an experimental plant being developed by United Standard in Florida (fig. 2.6) is designed to utilize about 230 tons of feedlot wastes a day, from which 5,810 m^3 (207,500 ft^3) of biogas and 48 tons of worthwhile solids may be recovered. A commercial plant in Oklahoma has access to manure from feedlots exceeding 100,000 head of cattle. Enough methane gas is produced from this manure to meet annual heating requirements of 3,500 homes, to provide residue for cattle feedstuff, and to yield a dilute liquid fertilizer for farmland near the facility.

Table 2.2. Research and Developments Related to Biogas in Various Countries

COUNTRY	NUMBER OF BIOGAS PLANTS	USES OF RESIDUAL MATERIAL AND GENERAL REMARKS
Bangladesh	20 (under construction)	Fértilizer
People's Republic of China	2,000,000	Fertilizer Family-size plants
Cook Islands	1	Integrated cattle and pig farm, with algal and fish ponds for protein
Fiji Islands	10	Integrated farming with algal and fish ponds for protein and fertilizer
India	30,000 (Target 100,000 units)	Fertilizer. Biogas used for households and power for engines
Indonesia	4	Experimental and training
Iran	1	Public health of communities
Japan	Proposed	Pollution control
Korea	29,450 (Target 55,000)	Feed and fertilizer
Malaysia	Proposed	Develop biogas technology
Nepal	10 (Target 200)	--
Pakistan	40 (Target 100)	Fertilizer on barren lands
Papua, New Guinea	25	Fertilizer
Philippines	14	Algal ponds; fertilizer
Singapore	2	Experimental and training
Sri Lanka	1	Basic needs of villages of 50-200 families
Thailand	50 planned	--

Sources: Smil, 1977; DaSilva, Olembo, and Burgers 1978.

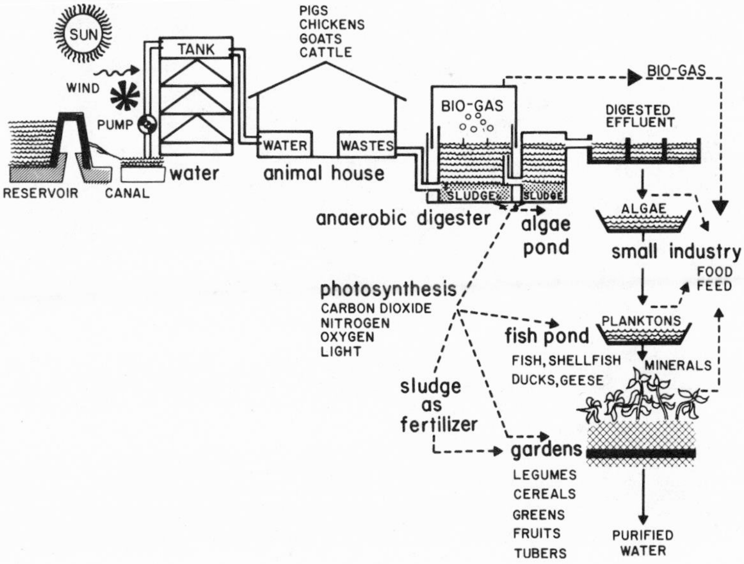

Fig. 2.5. Schematic flow diagram for an integrated biogas system using livestock wastes, an algal pond, fish pond, and fertilizer for crops.

Source: Courtesy ESCAP Workshop, Manila, 1975.

To promote the use of animal manure as a source of biogas a mobile waste-digestion system (fig. 2.7) has been built by BioGas, of Colorado, and demonstrated in six states.

Biogas production may be an important source of energy in some areas, and every effort should be made to use agricultural residues, and municipal and industrial wastes. But until large-scale operations using biomass can be made more efficient, one must appreciate the limitations. For example, Pimentel and associates (1978) have made careful calculations that lead one to the following conclusions:

1) Utilization of the readily available 372 million tons of the various waste or refuse biomasses (table 2.3) would yield energy of approximately 342 x 10^{12} kcal; this is only about 1.9 percent of the current fossil energy consumption in the United States.

2) Expectations of large increases in energy from so-called biomass farming are somewhat unrealistic because of limited availability of good land and constraints on water resources.

3) Most crop residues should not be used for energy conversion because of environmental factors, such as their providing humus in the soil, preventing erosion, and removing important nutrients that need to be recycled for plant growth.

Table 2.3. Sources of Biomass Available Annually in the United States for Energy Conversion

Source	Available: Hypothetical Mt, dry	Available: Ready Mt, dry	Energy Conversion kcal x 10^{12}
Livestock manure	255	128	27
Crop remains	430	0	0
Food-processing wastes (20-70% moisture)	4	4	18
Food-processing wastes (70-90% moisture)	14	14	10
Forestry remains	340	44	50
Forestry-processing wastes	81	20	85
Fuel wood production	10	10	40
Fuel wood plantations	60	60	52
Hydrocarbon plantations	16	16	13
Aquatic plants	17	3	0.6
Urban refuse	123	66	41
Industrial wastes	40	5	4
Municipal sewage	13	2	1.3
Total	1,403	372	341.9

Source: Pimentel et al. 1978.

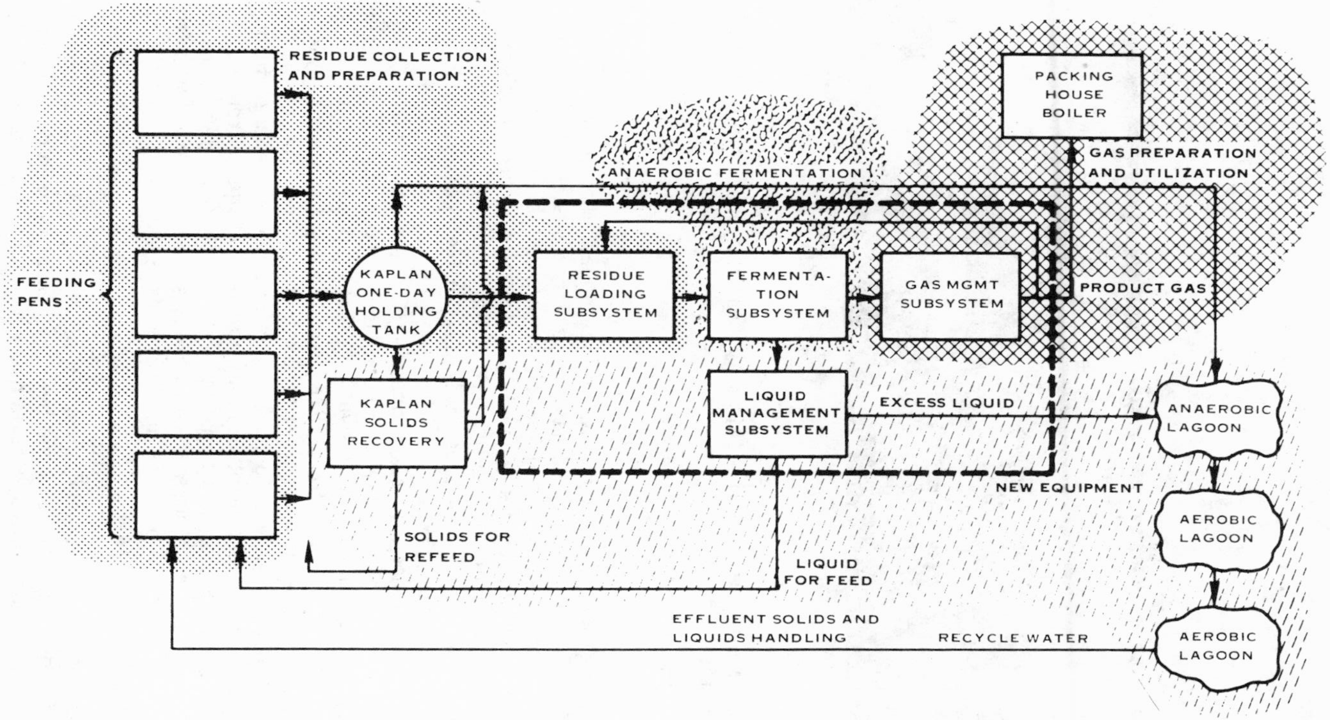

Fig. 2.6. An advanced-system experiment utilizing feedlot residue and fermentation to produce biogas and solids for refeeding, and to protect the environment.

Source: Courtesy Hamilton Standard, Division of United Technologies 1977.

Fig. 2.7. Mobile waste-digestion system for producing biogas and fertilizer.

Source: Bio-Gas of Colorado.

Even though the above conclusions may appear discouraging for the future use of high quality biomass on a large scale as a source of energy, further research and developments in bioengineering and biotechnology will undoubtedly make the processes more efficient and practical. In fact, much excellent research is being accomplished in this area as one can learn from reading the Newsletter, Fuels from Biomass Fermentation.

Because of the need to start planning for the post-petroleum era research programs involving what Heden (1977) refers to as equilibrium technology, or Golueke and Oswald (1973) call self-sufficient life support units, or Calvin (1976, 1978) speaks of as synthetic systems should receive more attention. For example, it may be possible to provide partial alternatives to fossil fuels and nuclear energy through photosynthesis using certain plants and microorganisms. From current knowledge of the natural quantum conversion in photosynthesis, several photoelectron transfer processes can be envisaged. Some steps in this sequence have already been demonstrated in synthetic systems using microorganisms as follows:

1) Biophotolysis, the decomposition of water by use of chlorophyll and hydrogenase to produce hydrogen gas, has been demonstrated with algae and photosynthetic bacteria in the laboratory.

2) Bacteriorhodopsin, the purple protein produced by the bacterium Halobacterium halobium. This purple pigment functions as a light-driven proton pump. Since the protons are electrically charged, this purple bacterium in effect converts solar energy into electrical energy (Stoeckenius 1978).

Energy production by one of these methods would probably have little impact on the enormous energy consumption by highly industrialized countries. But such bioconversions might be important in rural areas of less industrialized countries, since such technology would require little or no investment in scarce raw materials or expensive and complex hardware.

Other Useful Products

In addition to the role microorganisms may play in regard to energy production, they can also be employed to produce many useful substances. Mention has already been made briefly to the production of certain health products, of various foods and feed supplements, and to the manufacture of industrial alcohol and other pure chemicals. A recent review shows that nearly 5,000 metabolic products have been identified from microorganisms; these include not only alcohols, organic acids, and carbohydrates, but also antibiotics, complex hetero-cyclic compounds, enzymes, bioinsecticides and certain other unique substances. Some of these are important and are produced commercially in large quantities. For example, over 90 antibiotics are manufactured; in quantity, penicillin leads with over 50,000 tons annually. But many of the compounds and enzymes represent microbial processes that should be given greater consideration by bioengineers as potential biotechnologies for future development. Currently, for example, it is estimated that the commercial production of enzymes from microorganisms is a $100 million business, and the market is expanding owing to the potentials of enzyme engineering, the use of immobilized enzymes, etc.

MICROORGANISMS AND PROTECTION OF THE ENVIRONMENT

Unfortunately until recently, mankind has assumed the atmosphere, the natural water, and the soil have unlimited ability to cleanse and repair themselves rather than being integral components in delicate balance in our complex ecosystem. We have now reached a stage in civilization where we must anticipate or appreciate the consequences of the potential hazards that are being inflicted on the environment. Many seemingly innocuous activities may set off reactions which in time become serious problems for mankind as well as the microbial world.

With our present knowledge of microbiology and sanitation, the spread of air-borne and water-borne diseases should no longer be a problem. But these means of transmitting diseases, together with insect-transmissions still exist. At a recent World Health Organization (WHO) Assembly, for example, one delegate stated that poor quality water accounted for 60 percent of all illness and 40 percent of all deaths in his country. He said 90 percent of the rural population was drinking potentially hazardous water. Estimates are that 3,000 million people live in areas where sewage disposal is inadequate, and over 1,500 million tons of pesticides and other complex synthetic substances find their way into the soil and water each year. Much work still lies ahead if harmful microorganisms are to be eliminated from drinking water, if human wastes are to be properly treated, and if questionable biodegradable substances are to be eliminated from the environment. Continued microbial surveillance of the environment is essential.

Microorganisms are a significant and important part of our biosphere, and they are closely related to the most basic human needs, namely, health, water, food, and air. They possess great synthetic abilities under varied environmental conditions. Proper control of the harmful types, and more extensive use of the beneficial ones may be a great help in future developments.

REFERENCES

Abelson, P. 1977. The future role of microbiology in world energy. Lecture presented at the 77th Annual Meeting of the American Society for Microbiology, May 11, in New Orleans.

Altenpohl, D. 1978. Assessment of appropriate technology (AT) for emerging nations. p. 19. Paper presented at Asian Regional Seminar on the Contributions of Science and Technology to National Development, October 4-6 in New Delhi.

Anderson, E.V. 1978. Gasohol: Energy mountain or molehill? Chem. Eng. News, July 15, 31, p. 812.

Bente, P.F., Jr. 1977. The food-people problem: Can the land's capacity to produce food be sustained? 25 pp. Paper presented to the 1977 U.N. Conference on Water and Desertification. Council on Environmental Quality. Washington, DC.

Brink, R.A.; Densmore, J.W.; and Hill, G.A. 1977. Soil deterioration and the growing world demand for food. Science 197:625-630.

Calvin, M. 1976. Hydrocarbons via photosynthesis. Rept. 1976, LBL-5387, 62 pp.

Calvin, M. 1978. Green factories. Priestley Medal Address. Chem. Eng. News 56(12):30-36.

Colombo, U. 1978. A contribution towards solving the protein deficient problem in deficient countries. p. 9. Paper presented at Asian Regional Seminar on the Contributions of Science and Technology National Development, October 4-6, New Delhi.

Cray, C.L., Jr. 1977. Gasohol seminar, September 26, Rio de Janeiro, Brazil.

DaSilva, E.J.; Olembo, R.; and Burgers, A. 1978. Integrated microbial technology for developing countries: Springboard for economic progress. Impact Sci. Soc. 28:159-182.

Eckholm, E.P. 1976. Losing ground: Environmental stress and world food prospects. New York: W.W. Norton & Co.

Economic and Social Commission for Asia and the Pacific (ESCAP). 1975. Workshop on bio-gas technology and utilization, October 13-18, Manila (RAS/74/041/A/01/01).

Golueke, C.G., and Oswald, W.J. 1973. An algal regenerative system for single-family farms and villages. Compost Sci., p. 12.

Hamilton Standard, Division of United Technologies. 1977. Experimental facility for producing fuel gas from cattle feed residue. HSPC 77T09, vol. II., Windsor Locks, Conn.

Heden, C.G. 1977. Enzyme engineering and the anatomy of equilibrium technology. Quart. Rev. Biophys. 10:113-135.

Imperial Chemical Industries, Ltd., Agricultural Division 1977. Billingham, U.K.

Klass, D.L. 1976. Wastes and biomass as energy resources: An overview. Paper presented at symposium on clean fuels from biomass wastes. Orlando, Florida. Institute of Gas Technology, Chicago, Illinois.

Lewis, C.W. 1976. Energy requirements for single-cell protein production. J. Appl. Chem. Biotechnol. 26:568-575.

Likeus, G.E.; Bormann, F.H.; Pierce, R.S.; and Reiners, W.A. 1978. Recovery of a deforested ecosystem. Science 199:492-496.

Lipinsky, E.S. 1978. Fuel from biomass: Integration with food and materials systems. Science 199:644-651.

Maier, R.J., and Brill, W.J. 1978. Mutant strains of Rhizobium japonicum with increased ability to fix nitrogen for soybeans. Science 201:448-450.

McHale, J., and McHale, M.C. 1978. Basic human needs: A framework for action. 249 pp. New Brunswick, N.J.: Transaction Books.

McNamara, R.S. 1976. Address to the Board of Governors. 40 pp. Washington, D.C.: World Bank.

Pimentel, D.; Nafus, D.; Vergara, W.; Papaj, D.; Jaconetta, L.; Wulfe, M.; Olsvig, L.; Frech, K.; Loye, M.; and Mendoza, E. 1978.

Biological solar energy conversion and U.S. energy policy. BioScience 28:376-382.

Sanford, P.A., and Laskin, A., eds. 1977. Extracellular microbial polysaccharides. Amer. Chem. Soc. Symposium Ser. Washington, D.C. 45:326.

Senez, J.C. 1976. The role of SCPs grown on hydrocarbons. PAG Bull. 4:8-14.

Shapiro, I.S. 1978. Future sources of organic raw materials. Science 202:287-289.

Smil, V. 1977. Intermediate energy technology in China. Bull. Atomic Sci. 33(2):25-31.

Srinivasan, H.R. 1977. Bio-gas (gobar gas) and manure from the waste of farm animals. Paper presented at UNEP/FAO Seminar on Residues: Utilization-Management of Agricultural and Agro-Industrial Wastes, January 18-21, Rome.

Stoeckenius, W. 1978. A model for the function of bacteriorhodopsin. Soc. Gen. Physiol., Ser. 33 (in press).

3 Native Plants for the Improvement of Life in Arid Environments

W.G. McGinnies
J.D. Johnson

Many plants that have been developed by man to thrive in humid conditions originated in dry climates. However, by selection, they became dependent on more favorable growing conditions, and their progeny were not able to survive in the more arid climates. This has resulted in a scarcity of crop plants that could be grown in arid regions.

In the selection process, plants that did not meet immediate needs or were not easily domesticated were not used. Some of the underused plants deserve a second look as they may serve modern world needs.

POTENTIALS FOR NATIVE PLANT USE

Potentially economic native plants may be divided into five general categories: 1) food for man and livestock; 2) wood products for fuel, construction, and manufacturing materials; 3) fiber; 4) extracts for gums, waxes, rubber, and pharmaceuticals; and 5) energy.

Food

In this age of modern technology and agribusiness, there are men who still gather seeds and wild plants for sustenance. From these men we can obtain clues leading us to plants with the potential of domestication for food production.

Indians of South America collect *Chenopodium* seeds, and the product known as *guinoa* is a dietary mainstay. North American Indians collect the seeds of the grasses *Sporobolus* and *Oryzopsis*; the Seri Indians living near the Sea of Cortez (Gulf of California) harvest underwater eel grass (*Zostera marina*). Roots and tubers are important dietary contributions to people who gather vegetation for survival and economic benefit.

When considered for propagation and economic harvest, native plants present special problems. Yet, these problems probably are not more difficult to solve than those faced during the development and domestication of present day crops (e.g., the early cereals shattered, causing much of the seed to be lost.) Knowing that man has genetically manipulated all domesticated crops should encourage, rather than discourage the development of some potentially economic native plants.

Wood

Man has cultivated relatively few woody plants. Today, our forests are managed as natural enterprises rather than cultivated crops. Forests, in the true sense of the word, have never occurred in arid habitats; however, stands of trees do. These trees are dependent on moisture in locations along streams or dry watercourses. In arid environments, the scarcity of woody plants is a handicap to human life.

Mesquite (Prosopis juliflora) is a food- and wood-producing plant. Very much at home in the desert, mesquite is usually found along drainage systems which supply extra moisture. Its roots may extend as far as 175 feet downward, if moisture can be found at that depth, or 100 feet or more laterally near the surface. It produces a multitude of edible flowers and as much as 1,000 kilograms of seed pods per hectare. The pods, including seeds, contain 17 percent sugar; the pods alone contain 21 percent. Seeds have more than 50 percent protein content, and the leaves have approximately the same composition as alfalfa. The wood is heavy and dense, making good firewood. It also has a high tensile strength, important in certain types of construction.

The native populations of North and South America have long esteemed the mesquite as a source of food; but in modern societies it has been relegated to a source of fuel and forage for livestock. Livestock do not digest the seed; the undigested seeds germinate readily, forming thickets where little or no vegetation can survive. The North American Prosopis species has been planted in Africa and Asia with mixed results, but little attention has been given to the thirty-five South American species.

Fiber

Many fiber-producing plants have always been present in arid habitats. Cotton, an important member of this group, developed with additional moisture from various outside or underground sources. Today, cotton is the world's most important fiber plant.

Other fiber plants such as the yucca, agave, and hemp are used largely through the harvest of native stands. Harvesting and marketing are primarily cottage industries in low annual income regions. In many instances, the fiber industry alone is not an economic enterprise, and some plants, particularly yucca fruits and agave hearts will be harvested as additional sources of food and alcohol.

Henequen, a fiber obtained from the leaves of Agave fourcroydes is produced primarily in the Yucatan Peninsula, Mexico,where the average annual fiber production is about 1,000 kilograms per hectare. The juice and bagasse remaining after fiber extraction are used for fertilizer. Much effort has been expended developing products from other waste constituents with little success. Some chemical and medicinal uses have been found, however, and with continued research more uses undoubtedly will be discovered.

Excluding cotton the largest and most advanced desert plant industries are henequen and sisal. The United States, for instance, imports a total of 175,000 to 300,000 tons of fiber per year.

More than 20 arid-zone plants of the genera Agave, Furcraea Bromelia, and Attalea are grown in various countries, producing small amounts of hard fibers, generally supplying local needs. Agave lechuguilla is common in areas averaging 150 to 200 millimeters of rainfall in northern Mexico and western Texas, United States. Mexican production amounts to 10,000 tons of fiber annually, a $3,000,000 value. The most important uses of desert fiber-producing plants have been for rope, upholstery, and inexpensive brushes.

Extracts

Arid-lands plants are often blessed with a variety of substances potentially important in the world economy. Guayule (Parthenium argentatum) is a known producer of rubber. Jojoba (Simmondsia chinensis) produces an oil used as a high speed, high temperature lubricant, and as a component of various cosmetics. Candelilla, (Euphorbia antisyphiletica) supplies wax and fiber and is a source of useful, low molecular weight hydrocarbons. Other Euphorbia species are now being examined for their hydrocarbon-producing potential.

KNOWN NATIVE PLANT USES

The native plants discussed here are only some of those that are known to have economic potential: they are jojoba (Simmondsia chinensis); guayule (Parthenium argentatum); buffalo gourd (Cucurbita foetidissima); and Euphorbia (Euphorbiaceae).

Jojoba

Jojoba (Simmondsia chinensis) is a shrub that grows naturally in the Sonoran Desert of the United States (California and Arizona), and in Mexico (Sonora and Baja California). The seed from this thick-foliaged shrub is about 43 percent liquid wax with chemical properties in most respects identical to the oil of the endangered sperm whale. Activities aimed at domesticating and cultivating jojoba are being actively pursued in Israel, Arizona and California in the United States, and Baja California in Mexico. Attempts to cultivate jojoba are underway in Saudi Arabia, Ghana, Iran, Egypt, and many other countries.

The jojoba seed yields an oil which requires little or no refining for use as a lubricant. The oil content of the seed does not decrease with long-term storage and is resistant to bacterial degradation. Where rancidity is a problem, jojoba oil might replace ordinary vegetable oils in food, cosmetics, and hair oil. The oil is also a source of long-chain alcohols, useful in preparing detergents and lubricating precision high-temperature machinery.

Hydrogenated jojoba oil is a hard, white, crystalline wax reportedly almost as hard as carnauba, for which it may become a substitute. It also has potential in the preparation of waxes for floors and automobiles, waxing of fruit, impregnation of paper containers, manufacture of carbon paper, candles and many other products.

Tables 3.1 through 3.3, adapted from Products from jojoba: A promising new crop for arid lands (National Academy of Sciences 1975), delineate the physical and chemical properties of jojoba oil and hydrogenated wax.

While the jojoba plant has appeared in botanical literature since 1821, the earliest example appears in 1716 when the Spanish Jesuit Luis Velarde described jojoba's medicinal value (Sherbrooke 1978).

Since the 1930s, it has been known that the liquid oil expressed from jojoba seeds has physical and chemical properties resembling sperm whale oil. There was some research done on jojoba during and immediately following World War II, but the postwar boom in sperm whale fishing, and the increased use of synthetics removed jojoba from further serious consideration until the early 1970s. Increased interest resulted primarily from placement of the sperm whale on the endangered species list, and the subsequent ban on importation of sperm whale oil into the United States. A further incentive for research on jojoba was found when it was realized that much of the natural jojoba crop exists on American Indian reservations in the southwestern United States. A major development occurred in 1972 when the United States government contracted with the Universities of Arizona (Tucson) and California (Riverside) to harvest seed from the natural stands on Indian reservations, to express oil, and to distribute the oil, wax, and meal for industrial testing. Approximately 44 tons of seed were harvested during the summer of 1972. Since that time the oil and hydrogenated wax have been tested by private industry for possible commercial applications.

Currently oil is selling for as much as $8 per pound for use in shampoos and hair oil. Projections forecast a per-acre yield from mature jojoba plants (seven years old) of 1,760 pounds of seeds which, in turn, yield about 750 pounds of oil.

Table 3.1. Properties of Jojoba Oil [a]

Freezing point	10.6-7.0 C
Melting point	6.8-7.0 C
Boiling point at 757 mm under N_2	398 C
Smoke point (AOCS Cc 9a-48) [b]	195 C
Flash point (AOCS Cc 9a-48) [b]	295 C
Fire point (COC)	338 C
Heat of fusion by differential scanning calorimetry	21 cal/g
Refractive index at 25 C	1.4650
Specific gravity, 25/25 C	0.863
Viscosity	
Rotovisco (25 C)	
MV-J rotor in MV cup	35 cp
Plate and cone with Pk-1	33 cp
Brookfield, spindle #1, 25 C	37 cp
Cannon-Fenske, 25 C	50 cp
Cannon-Fenske, 100 C	27 centistokes
Saybolt, 100 F	127 SUS [c]
Saybolt, 210 C	48 SUS [c]
Iodine value	82
Saponification value	92
Acid value	2
Acetyl value	2
Unsaponifiable matter	51%
Total acids	52%
Iodine value of alcohols	77
Iodine value of acids	76
Average molecular weight of wax esters	606

[a] Oil from expeller-pressed jojoba seeds starts to freeze at 10.6 C (51 F). It solidifies into a thick paste at 7 C. Frozen oil, allowed to warm up, melts at 7 C (45 F).

[b] Smoke and flash points determined according to the official method, Cc 9a-48, of the American Oil Chemists' Society.

[c] Saybolt Universal seconds.

Source: D.M. Yermanos, in Products from Jajoba: A Promising New Crop for Arid Lands, National Academy of Sciences/National Research Council, Office of Chemistry and Chemical Technology, 1975, p. 13.

Table 3.2. Characteristics of Sulfurized Jojoba and Sperm Oils

Test	Sulfurized Jojoba Oil	Sulfurized Sperm Oil
Sulfur, percent	9.88	9.98
Viscosity, at 37.8 C	3,518 SUS [a]	1,961 SUS [a]
Viscosity, at 99 C	491 SUS [a]	201 SUS [a]
Specific gravity at 15.6 C	0.9476	0.9613
API at 15.6 C	17.82	15.71
Flash point	250 C	243 C
Fire point	282 C	280 C
Free fatty acids (Olic)	1.55	2.35
Saponification no.	162	195
Pour point	16.1 C	15.6 C
Corrosion, 90/10, 3 h at 100 C	2A	2A
Colon, API, 10% in 1-3/4 color oil	4-3/4	8+

[a] Saybolt Universal seconds

Source: H. Gisser, ibid., p. 17.

Table 3.3. Hardness of Hydrogenated Jojoba Wax and Several Other Vegetable Waxes

Wax	Hardness [a]
Hydrogenated jojoba oil	1.9
Carnauba wax	2.6
Cane wax	2.1
Beeswax	0.38
Paraffin	0.24

[a] Bmnel Hardness Number at 35 C, 4.3 kg load for 60 sec. on 10.0 mm diameter steel ball.

Source: T.K. Miwa, ibid., p. 22.

Guayule

Guayule (Parthenium argentatum) is a rubber-producing shrub native to the Chihuahuan Desert in the southwestern United States (Texas) and northern Mexico, and it was a commercial source of rubber in the early 1900s. During World War II, the U.S. Emergency Rubber Project planted 32,000 acres of guayule; congressional plans projected placing 500,000 acres under production. Of 32 million acres of land surveyed in the western, southwestern, and midwestern United States, 5 million acres in California, Texas, New Mexico, and Arizona were declared suitable for guayule cultivation. However, development of synthetic rubber and the easing of World War II emergency conditions led to cancellation of the guayule program (McGinnies and Haase 1975a).

It has been established that guayule can be grown in warm climates (minimum temperatures above 15°F.) with 15 inches of precipitation. With 18 inches of irrigation, greater growth and rubber production is assured. Guayule is relatively disease-resistant and insect-free but requires a well-drained soil with a pH between 6.0 and 8.5.

Tests indicate that guayule rubber has chemical and physical properties essentially identical to that produced by the Malaysian rubber tree (Hevea brasiliensis). The principal barrier to economic viability is the cost of production. If guayule can produce favorably under large-scale cultivation, it can become a major contributor to an arid-region economy because of the worldwide demand for rubber. This is true whether that guayule rubber-producing region includes the Americas, Africa, Asia, Australia or the Middle East.

The Comision Nacional de las Zonas Aridas (CONAZA) has a rubber research production program and a pilot extraction processing plant at Saltillo, Coahuila, Mexico, the scene of a recent (August 1977) International Guayule Conference. CONAZA estimates that it can produce 30,000 tons annually from wild guayule alone (Comision Nacional de las Zonas Aridas, 1976).

Guayule yield figures (about 680 pounds per acre) were estimated from plantings in the Salinas Valley, California. Between 1931 to 1941, 4,400 acres were harvested, yielding more than 3,000,000 pounds of guayule rubber. This was dryland shrub and not representative of production under irrigation where yields up to 500 to 1,000 pounds of rubber per acre have been obtained (McGinnies and Haase 1975a). Kelly (1975) showed higher yields from one special test plot producing 1,336 pounds per acre over a 21-month period, or about 700 pounds per acre per year.

Buffalo Gourd

Buffalo gourd (Cucurbita foetidissima) has exceptional potential as a food plant because: 1) the plants are perennial; 2) they grow on wastelands in regions of low rainfall; 3) they can produce an abundant crop of fruit containing seed rich in oil and protein; and 4) the fruit lends itself to mechanical harvesting (Bemis et al. 1978).

A drought-resistant native of the drylands of North America, buffalo gourd grows under very low rainfall conditions and is intolerant of wet, poorly-drained soils. It is a perennial but the frost-sensitive vines are killed by temperatures below $0^{\circ}F$. although the roots may survive air temperatures as low as $-25^{\circ}F$.

The seeds, which are produced in large numbers, can be used to make drying oils, high protein flour, and a protein concentrate. A single plant is capable of producing 200 spherical fruits with diameters of 5 to 7 centimeters. Each fruit contains 200 to 300 small seeds, with an average weight of 4 grams per 100 seeds. Seeds contain 30 to 40 percent edible oil and 30 to 35 percent protein.

It is a buff-colored flour, and 54 to 60 percent protein has been produced from defatted seed meal by a simple process. Additional processing has produced a protein concentrate suitable for inclusion in such products as water paints, paper coatings, adhesives, and textile sizes.

The roots of a single plant may reach a weight of 50 kilograms in three or four seasons. They contain about 15 percent starch which can be removed by conventional methods. The starch can be hydrolyzed to glucose (dextrose), which in turn may provide the raw materials for fermentation.

The vines, which are not climbers, have been known to reach a total length of 220 meters in a five-month growing season. This extensive growth represents a potential food resource for herbivorous animals. It has a protein content of 10 to 15 percent, and a digestibility near 60 percent.

Based on experiments at the University of Arizona, W.P. Bemis (Bemis et al. 1978) proposes the following cropping system.

> A field or plantation would be established by direct seeding, using hybrid seed, to a plant population of about 3,000 plants per hectare. At the end of the first growing season a destructive vine harvest would be made using some type of vine seed thrasher to recover the seed. The perennial roots would be 7 to 10 centimeters below the soil surface and protected from mechanization of seed extractions from the fruits. The second season the plant stand would be increased by adventitious rooting by a factor of five to 10, depending on the amount of previous vine growth. At the end of the second season another destructive vine harvest would be made to recover seed for its oil and protein. During its dormant season, alternate one-meter swaths would be mechanically dug for roots. This would accomplish two purposes: 1) the harvesting of roots for starch, and 2) the thinning of plants to keep them from overcrowding. During the third season the alternate swaths would be dug for roots while the plants would be regenerating roots in the previously dug areas. Following this method of harvesting, a fruit yield, a root yield, and a possible forage yield could be obtained each year the plants remain productive.

Euphorbia

There are many species of Euphorbia with latex-containing hydrocarbons of low molecular weight. These are potential producers of petrochemical feedstocks and energy source. One of these, Euphorbia lathyris, has been studied by Melvin Calvin, Nobel prize-winning chemist, at the University of California.

There are more than 1,600 species of Euphorbia. Many of them are large succulents found primarily in South Africa; some are treelike, many are shrubs and herbs. All of them produce hydrocarbons, in greater or lesser amounts, hence they are potential energy-producing plants. The family Euphorbiaceae extends the number of latex-producing plants, including cassavae (Manihot utilissima). Outside of the Euphorbiaceae, there are many other latex-producing plants, notably in the milkweed family Asclepiadaceae and the dogbane family Apocynaceae.

Several institutions, including the University of Arizona, are undertaking studies to determine which species of Euphorbia have the greatest promise for cultivation from the standpoint of production and adaptability. Later, cultivation, harvesting, milling, and marketability studies will be undertaken.

TECHNIQUES TO CONCENTRATE WATER FOR ARID LAND CROPS

When selecting plants for the desert environment, it should be kept in mind that not all parts of the landscape receive equal amounts of moisture. Runoff removes moisture from some areas and increases moisture in others (e.g., basins and stream channels). It is possible to take advantage of these inequalities, concentrating moisture to support vegetation in selected areas of low precipitation. For example, rock dams in wadis and arroyos may produce terraces that will restrain runoff, increase soil moisture, and thus support vegetation which would otherwise have insufficient moisture. Small drainage basins may be treated to decrease infiltration, increasing watershed runoff, which can be collected for use at the lower part of the drainage basin. In larger drainage basins, diversion dams may be used to spread water over wide areas, providing moisture for trees, grasses and other food-producing plants. In some instances, particularly for trees, small basins can be constructed to catch and hold precipitation. Water-harvesting methods and irrigation devices (e.g., trickle irrigation) can be used to produce food, fuel, and fiber in desert areas. The use of native plants may be of greatest value in situations of natural or enhanced moisture.

CONCLUSION

A worldwide assessment of natural products needed in arid climates should be made. The study should consider food, wood, fiber, extracts, and energy. A second step would be to make an appraisal of the environments involved, including the possibility of moisture-enhancement by control of runoff, and the use of imported and underground water sources. Consideration should be given to food, energy, and building needs of indigenous people. Finally, potential producers should be selected for an intensive and exhaustive study. In undertaking this last step, the magnitude of the task should not stand in the way of development. It should be remembered that a great amount of work over a long period of time has gone into the development of cultivated plants. Also, in the rigorous desert climate, the difficulties of production are greater than in more benign climates.

REFERENCES

Bemis, W.P.; Berry, J.W.; and Weber, C.W. 1978. The buffalo gourd, a potential crop for arid lands. Arid Lands Newsletter 8:1-7.

Calvin, M. 1974. Solar energy by photosynthesis. Science 184(4134): 375-381.

Centro de Investigacion en Quimica Aplicada. 1978. Guayule: Reencuentro en el desierto. 436 pp. Second International Conference on Guayule, August 1-5, 1977, Saltillo, Coahuila, Mexico.

Johnson, J.D. 1977. Plants as potential economic resources in arid lands. Arid Lands Newsletter 6:1-9.

Kelly, O.J. 1975. Soil-plant relationships--guayule. In W.G. McGinnies and E.F. Hasse, eds. An International Conference on the Utilization of Guayule, November 1975, pp. 83-93. University of Arizona, Office of Arid Lands Studies, Tucson.

McGinnies, W.G. 1978. The potential of native plants for food, fiber and fuel in arid lands. Bioscience (in press).

McGinnies, W.G., and Haase, E.F., eds. 1975a. Guayule: A rubber-producing shrub for arid and semiarid regions. Historical review and bibliography. 267 pp. Arid Lands Resource Information Paper No. 7. University of Arizona, Office of Arid Lands Studies, Tucson.

__________. 1975b. An International Conference on the Utilization of Guayule, November 1975. 176 pp. University of Arizona, Office of Arid Lands Studies, Tucson.

National Academy of Sciences. 1975. Products from jojoba: A promising new crop for arid lands. 30 pp. National Academy of

Sciences, Washington, D.C., National Research Council, Assembly of Mathematical and Physical Sciences, Office of Chemistry and Chemical Technology, Committee on Jojoba Utilization.

__________. 1977a. Guayule: An alternative source of natural rubber. 80 pp. Board on Agriculture and Renewable Resources, Commission on Natural Resources, Advisory Committee on Technology Innovation, Board on Science and Technology for International Development, Commission on International Relations, National Academy of Sciences, Washington, D.C.

__________. 1977b. Jojoba. Feasibility for cultivation on Indian reservations in the Sonoran Desert region. 64 pp. National Research Council, Commission on Natural Resources, Board on Agriculture and Renewable Resources, Committee on Jojoba Production Systems Potential. National Academy of Sciences, Washington, D.C.

Sherbrooke, W.C. 1978. Jojoba: An annotated bibliographic update. Supplement to Arid Lands Resource Information Paper No. 5. 80 pp. University of Arizona, Office of Arid Lands Studies, Tucson.

4 Renewable Resources: Implications for Industry and Education

Ingemar Falkehag

Industry can be viewed as organization to produce goods and services to meet human needs and wants. Such organizations, however, are being increasingly called to account for ecological considerations in the use of land, water, and nutrients, because large-scale conversion of natural ecosystems might cause major ecological drawbacks.

We already have indications of a disequilibrium in the biosphere through the increase in atmospheric carbon dioxide concentration that can only be partly explained by the burning of fossil carbon. This indicates that the ratio between photosynthesis and biodegradation has decreased, a very serious signal that the biosphere is disturbed, and that we have to exercise caution in how we manage biosystems.

If we are reaching limits, the next step should be to make sure that the exploitation of the photosynthetic process is directed towards the most meaningful ends and accomplished in the soundest ecological manner.

There are hardly any products made from, or services performed by fossil carbon sources in which biomass and renewable resources could not be a substitute. This is not to say, however, that the highly industrial societies could be sustained at anywhere near their present intensity of production-consumption by the sole use of biomass.

For many less developed countries, the biomass potential would be more than adequate for a several-fold increase in development, but because of the great variations in bioproductivity and ecological resilience in different parts of the world, one has to be cautious with generalizations. We need scenarios of self-renewing, self-sustaining communities and societies that consider the unique potentials and limitations of various geographic regions and their capability of supporting a certain number of people at an adequate living standard, with or without a minimal reliance on depletable resources. This will inevitably suggest a variety of industries and types of developments that are related to ideas of decentralization, or rather recentralization

Table 4.2. Demand for Wood in Conventional Uses, U.S.A., 1970, 1985, 2000

Commodity	Wood Requirement					
	1970		1985		2000	
	MM O.D. tons		MM O.D. tons		MM O.D. tons	
	From Roundwood	From By-Product	From Roundwood	From By-Product	From Roundwood	From By-Product
Structural						
1. Softwood lumber	73.41	2.6	80.4	3.5	64.6	4.0
2. Softwood plywood	15.08	-	17.7	-	14.6	-
3. Hardwood lumber	24.51	-	34.5	1.4	42.2	1.4
4. Hardwood plywood	2.28	-	3.1	-	3.1	-
5. Particleboard	-	2.4	-	5.3	-	8.5
6. Med. density fiberboard	.18	.2	0.4	0.4	0.6	0.6
7. Insulation board	-	1.2	-	1.9	-	2.2
8. Wet-formed hardboard	-	1.1	-	1.9	-	2.9
9. Structural flakeboard No. 1	-	-	3.0[1]	-	5.1[1]	-
10. Structural flakeboard No. 2 (RCW)	-	-	3.0	-	5.1	-
11. Laminated-veneer lumber	-	-	2.3[2]	-	4.4[3]	-
Fibrous						
12. Paper and paperboard	61.30	24.5	104.2	38.2	154.9	45.1
13. Miscellaneous-industrial and fuelwood	16.62	-	11.3	-	12.2	-
Total	193.38	31.9	259.9	52.6	306.8	64.7

materials from wood, paper from wood fibers, and shirts from cotton. Technical advances are needed, however, before we can economically produce filmforming plastics, such as polyethylene from cellulose via glucose - ethanol - ethylene.

Plant produced specialty chemicals, such as rubber, will be increasingly competitive in synthetic products, and research in these areas is likely to be highly rewarding. Better understanding of how plants can optimize production of photosynthate, and how biosynthetic pathways can be opened up to the most desirable products will lead to greatly expanded opportunities for plant produced chemicals. The coupling of plant genetics, biochemistry, and separation technology can prove to be a fertile ground for new discoveries.

In principle, substitutions can involve:

1. Shift in raw material or feedstock base.
2. Replacement of a macromolecular material or composite, i.e., substitution of cotton for polyester in a shirt, paper for polyethylene in a milk container, etc.
3. Shift in system of need satisfaction, i.e., walking or bicycling rather than automobile transportation.

We can judge the relevance of a particular substitution according to various value systems:

1. Economic criteria using free market demand-supply models.
2. Regulated economic conditions based on e.g., the desire to reduce oil import by giving incentives for domestic materials.
3. Thermodynamic criteria, judging what is right from an energetic point of view and considering not only heat values but also order in the system (energy concept).
4. With a futures accounting, considering the entropic loss of depletable resources and the value of renewability of photosynthesized materials.
5. Ecological and moral value judgments, ultimately as related to what is right for the biosphere and the well-being of its organisms.

It is not possible to generalize from one country to another, or even one region to another, in terms of the aptness of a substitution of renewable resources for fossil resources. It depends on the local situation as well as the relative attention given to the value systems listed above. We have, in fact, not one world, one ecosystem, or one industrial system, but rather a diversity of such systems. We can view it as an ecology of industries. In the future we might be less concerned with efficiency and economics of scale and more concerned with resilience and adaptability to new stresses. This could mean a shift to renewable resources but, under certain circumstances, could as well justify the continued use of fossil carbon sources. An example of the complexity in making these judgments is that of nitrogen fixation. Biological fixation should be desirable in terms of its reliance on solar energy and its ecological compatability, but it appears to be thermodynamically much less efficient than the thermal fixation processes.

Thus, substitution analysis, a science in its infancy, must start with a clarification of values, and a description of what might be right or best for a particular society. We can benefit from looking at industry from a biological or ecological point of view and not only a mechanistic one.

INDICATORS OF CHANGE

The outlook concerning the feasibility of natural products competing with petrochemicals is changing. This is the time to initiate research efforts on new alternative uses of plants. The strongest initiatives are likely to come not so much from the traditional actors in the system, such as the paper industry or agricultural firms, but from the outside. New structures are emerging, the Department of Energy being one of them.

This conference with at least two other events during 1978 are signs of the change in attitudes about organic resources and the factors affecting them. The Gordon Conference on Renewable Resources replaced an earlier conference on Chemistry and Physics of Paper. An attempt was made to bring together diverse groups and to discuss principles of renewal - from photosynthesis and biosynthetic pathways to renewing and symbiotic relationships.

The World Conference on Future Sources of Organic Raw Materials, referred to as CHEMRAWN I, attracted eight hundred persons from all over the world to a unique discussion of directions research in organic resources will take. Half of the technical program dealt with bioresources, and a serious effort to communicate its conclusions and recommendations to decision-makers in different countries is underway. It is clearly important to communicate the results concerning the shift in resource systems and required research of such discussions.

The problems raised by such a conference should be dealt with in a systemic manner, with consideration to interdependencies and the value of diversity. It should be possible to deal with these problems with foresight and not just as a matter of crisis management. A number of experiences were discussed. One example in regard to biomass production and utilization dealt with the emerging patterns arising from the increased competitiveness over natural rubber, and a trend towards small holdings in Malaysia and Mexico.

The diversity in biomass production and conversion systems means that one cannot make a direct comparison between the petrochemicals and biochemicals industries, or between different geographical regions or countries. We need an ecology of approaches. Biomass conversions are conducive to smaller scale and, appropriately, a less capital intensive technology. It is quite possible that we will see more of a two-way technology transfer process in the development of bioresources. The less developed countries can assume a responsibility in teaching the overdeveloped countries how to develop a harmonious relationship between industry and a renewable resource base on a smaller scale.

SELF-RENEWING PROCESSES

The circumstances might not in many areas be suitable for a shift to renewable resources, but the benefits from an intensive research effort on renewing, evolutionary processes can raise an awareness about the uniqueness of living systems at all levels and help to generate enthusiasm about this subject. The new effort will, however, require a broader commitment than possible by only an individual company or nation. It is the kind of challenge that can instill a sense of purpose in various scientific disciplines and an attitude of cooperation, preparing the way for a new order.

5 Bioresources for Development*

Bertrand Chatel

Resources have been traditionally drawn by men from biological systems for the purpose of food supply, a matter of vital importance to developing countries:

> The solution to world food problems lies primarily in increasing rapidly food production in the developing countries. Developing countries should accord high priority to agricultural and fisheries development. It is a responsibility of each state concerned to promote interaction between expansion of food production and socio-economic reforms with a view to achieving an integrated rural development.

This view was stressed by the General Assembly on September 19, 1975 as one of the bases for the establishment of the New International Economic Order (CA resolution 3362 [S-VII]).

But we are now becoming more and more aware that biological systems may be utilized for many new purposes in addition to food production, for instance: to generate energy by harnessing solar or microbial energy, to produce non-food agricultural material, to recycle biowastes, to maximize marine bioresources, and to improve the products from life by genetic engineering.

As we gain a better understanding of the scientific phenomena underlying the operation of living systems, we are now better equipped to provide the appropriate conditions whereby we can utilize bioresources for our benefit, while expanding and optimizing the lives of

---

* The opinions expressed by the author are his own and do not necessarily reflect those of the United Nations.

the species instead of destroying them as it has been done for so many centuries in the past.

Developing countries have for long been considered as underprivileged in many respects, but in fact many of them are characterized by favorable meteorological conditions for the blossoming of life. The abundance of sunshine and the rain-regime in certain areas make possible the remarkable growth of tropical forests and multiple crops in agriculture which are not feasible in temperate or cold climates. The same freshwater pond when located in Dortmund, FRG, produces 25 tons of algae in dry matter per hectare and per year, and produces 55 tons when located in Bangkok, Thailand (1).

SOLAR ENERGY

Solar energy can be harnessed for the development of arid lands, for example, by providing small-scale, decentralized sources of electric power for a population scattered over vast areas at low density. Photovoltaic solar cells or thermal solar electric generators, when their prices decrease to competitive levels, may provide power to activate the pumping of underground water. This scheme will enable the development of bioresources in arid areas, such as the Sahel region in the south of the Sahara, where at present drought-stricken countries can hardly survive, although water is available sometimes at depths of 30, 50, or 100 meters.

Solar cooking may provide an alternative to wood burning and decrease the present disastrous rates of deforestation. Solar drying of crops may be utilized to conserve food for mere survival, or to alleviate considerable food losses due to lack of appropriate storage facilities. (2)

MICROBIAL ENERGY

Microbes and bacteria, when they were identified under our microscopes, were quickly condemned as disease-generators, and were singled out as causes for global genocide. Today, a better understanding of the diversity of the species of microorganisms has led to a new attitude aimed at applying some types of microbes for our benefit.

- For instance, bacteria can biologically fix nitrogen and consequently be used as biofertilizers to replace chemical fertilizers as the detrimental side effects of the latter become better known. Nitrogen-fixing bacteria can be utilized for increasing the growth of crops or forest plantations, and stimulate the production of biomass to be used for food, fibers, or energy.
- Some species of bacteria can produce methane (CH_4), an

essential component of natural gas. This process - methanogenesis - occurs when these bacteria are placed in vegetal or animal wastes under anaerobic conditions, i.e., without contact with air. Biogas has already been experimented with on many farms in Asia (China, India, Indonesia, Pakistan), and may also be particularly relevant to the needs for recycling the urban wastes of many cities in developing countries.

- Other types of bacteria may generate hydrogen by using enzyme systems. The production of hydrogen represents an important potentiality for alternative sources of energy as hydrogen can be supplied to a fuel cell together with oxygen - easily available from the atmosphere - to provide electricity. Fuel cells are being used extensively on spacecraft to generate electricity. At present, Research and Development activities have intensified to produce fuel cells of 10 or 20 kilowatts for earth applications.

Algae can also produce hydrogen. When sunlight shines upon chloroplasts placed in water, oxygen is liberated, and an electron carrier reacts upon enzymes (hydrogenase) to produce hydrogen. This process has been exemplified by Gudin in France. The equipment is composed of transparent tubes of which the lower half is filled with water and bacteria, and the upper half with air and algae. The energy from sunlight is converted by photosynthesis by the algae and the phytoplankton which produces hydrogen.

These biological processes have been demonstrated at the laboratory level. It is anticipated that they will not be available on an industrial level before 1990.

- Bacteria can be harnessed to produce or recover hydrocarbons (oil). The potential from this research would be of great importance to nonoil producing developing countries which spend scarce capital on oil imports.

The present trends in research consist of selecting the microorganisms which could generate hydrocarbons and improve their production potentials. Other programs are devoted to using microbes to improve the oil recovery in wells, where half of the oil reserves still cannot be extracted due to a lack of adequate technology. Bacteria may be injected into the water sheet below the oil well to produce hydrogen, which pressurizes the oil for recovery. Bacteria may also be injected into the well to reduce the viscosity of oil and enhance its recovery. Some types of bacteria, which digest the rocks of dolomites and calcites, may be used for the recovery of oil shale rather than extracting and mechanically handling the rocks.

- Bacteria can also be used in mines to leach ores and produce metals, such as iron, copper, or uranium by biological processes.

Microbial energy conversion appears as a promising field for research and development programs which aim to benefit developing countries in the production of biomass, methane, hydrogen, the recycling of agricultural and urban waste, as well as for hydrocarbon or metal reclamation.

It is significant to note that this area has been long neglected in R and D programming, and only a few hundred scientists and engineers are involved in pioneering efforts, such as the Conference on Microbiological Energy, in Gottingen, sponsored by UNITAR and the Federal Republic of Germany in October 1976. (1)

FOOD

Some trends in science and technology activities for food production would be of particular relevance to the needs of the developing countries.

- The manipulation of the genetic structure of crop plants for improving food production, notably by somatic hybridization and direct insertion of genes into the DNA of plant cells.
- Biological fertilizers.
- Growing plants without soil.
- Conservation process.
- Irrigation techniques.
- Agriculture for arid lands.
- Multiple cropping.
- Aquaculture.

More details on the two latter topics follow.

Multiple Cropping

The production of several crops per year on the same land provides an important way to increase agricultural production in developing countries when climatic conditions are favorable. The most intensive forms of intercropping occur in areas where temperature and moisture do not limit growth during most of the year. As temperature and moisture become more limited with increasing latitude or decreasing rainfall, multiple cropping patterns shift to sequential cropping. (3)

Multiple cropping is also more intense when power sources are largely human or animal, as in the small farms in the tropics. The most complex forms of intercropping are practiced on farms ranging from 5 to 7 hectares of arable land. The bulk of food consumed in tropical

Asia, Latin America, and Africa is produced on these small farms. The importance and efficiency of these small farming systems have been generally considered primitive and, until recently, virtually ignored by researchers and policy makers.

Now there are a number of active research programs in several tropical areas, inspired by the pioneering research of R. Bradfield, in the Philippines. The potential for intensifying food production via multiple cropping is not limited to tropical climates.

Studies are needed on the techniques developed in the tropics to improve them at their places of origin, and to adapt them to different physical, social, and economic environments in other regions. Additional research is required to fill serious gaps in our present knowledge of multiple cropping techniques.

Aquaculture

A worldwide program on Aquaculture, which includes interregional and national projects, has been set up by the United Nations Development Programme (UNDP). The scope of the program is to increase the capacity of developing countries in aquaculture technology and training, and the adaptation of species of fish to their particular environment. Regional Centers for Aquaculture Development are being set up in Africa, Latin America, Asia, and the Pacific.

Research is particularly needed in the areas of: (a) genetic investigation; (b) fish fly production and fish breeding; (c) nutritional requirements and foodstuffs; (d) the integration of agriculture and aquaculture; (e) the use of windpower for ponds.

NON-FOOD AGRICULTURAL MATERIALS

The materials derived from agricultural production and not utilized for food embrace a vast range of products, which include a large variety of little known or underexploited bioresources.

Such materials which may be used for non-food industries include: vegetal fibers, nonedible oils and fat, latex, gum, wax, resins, dyes and colorants, phytopharmaceutics and biocides, pharmaceutics, drugs, perfumes, cosmetics, fuel wood, charcoal, wood alcohol, pulp, paper, forest products, plants, wool, silk and other products derived from animals such as hides, skins, leather.

The concept of the extensive use of bioresources is exemplified by the evolution in forest management. Initially forests were exploited mainly for tree trunks; now the global biomass of the forest is considered for its utilization in the form of wood, fibers, energy, and food. The goal is to maximize the harvest of biomass. A natural forest of pines produces 35 tons/hectares/year; with forestry practice it can grow to 100 tons/hectares/year; with recent techniques, it may increase to 160 tons/hectares/year. These techniques reflect a forest plantation considered as a culture, to be harvested every 2 or 4 years rather than waiting 30, 50, or 100 years.

Research programs may be oriented towards the assessment of the industrial, economic, social, and ecological value of these materials, the optimization of the biological development of animals and plants, and the identification of the levels of exploitation compatible with biological growth. Particular attention should be given to the competition between natural and synthetic products and the evaluation of their respective economic, social, and environmental merits. The main bodies involved in the UN system are the UN Office for Science and Technology which is conducting a survey in this area, the UN Centre for Natural Resources, Energy and Transport, the Food and Agriculture Organization, United Nations Industrial Development Organization, and the United Nations Conference on Trade and Development.

BIOWASTE RECYCLING

While many studies have been made on industrial and municipal waste recycling, research is needed on the economic and technological aspects of recycling biological wastes. This is due to the fact that the biowastes are generally biodegradable, and are not damaging our environment. Their recycling is therefore mainly based on the economic aspects of their reclamation. When the economic profitability of recycling biowaste has been ascertained, technologies will have to be developed to collect and process them, preferably on a small scale at the farm level.

MARINE BIORESOURCES

The concept of ocean farming is currently under consideration through several important research programs in the world. One of the main aims is to cultivate seaweed artificially over large areas of the sea, and to breed appropriate animal communities. The seaweed would utilize the carbon dioxide and water of the surface; the nutrients necessary for growth would be provided by bringing up cool, nutrient-rich water from 200 to 300 meters below the surface, and also by recycling waste from harvested seaweeds. The seaweed, called Giant Kelp, has been selected for the initial feasibility studies of ocean farms off the West Coast of the United States.

The seaweed and associated animal communities would be harvested periodically at coastal facilities for human food, feed supplements, fibers, fertilizers, and energy fuels such as methane production. Although several studies have been made on the conversion of ocean farm kelp to methane and other products (4), many scientific and technological aspects have yet to be investigated. Research is particularly needed on the production and cultivation of biomass from ocean farms in developing countries with a view to preparing feasibility studies, practical experimentation, and demonstration projects on selected coastal areas.

GENETIC ENGINEERING

Recombinant DNA techniques developed in the last five years have made it possible to splice together genetic materials from diverse species - genes of plants, animals, and bacteria for example - so that individual genes of higher organisms can be grown in bacterial cultures in large quantities.

Other techniques include the improvement of the genes of a species by selection, cross-fertilization, hybridization, and insertion of genes into DNA of plant cells. Genetic engineering has been successfully applied to produce high-yielding varieties of staple foods, disease-resistant or protein-enriched plants.

International institutes for agricultural research in Mexico, Guatemala, and the Philippines are active in the improvement of wheat, rice, and vegetables; more research is needed to optimize the characteristics of cattle for meat or milk production in tropical conditions. Research concerning the possible application of genetic engineering is still a matter of controversy.

SOME ACTIVITIES IN THE UNITED NATIONS SYSTEM

The preparation of a program on bioresources for development in the United Nations would be the concern of several bodies such as:

- The Department of International Economic and Social Affairs, the United Nations Office for Science and Technology (OST), the Ocean Economics and Technology Office, the Centre for Social Development and Humanitarian Affairs, the Population Division;
- the Department for Technical Co-operation, the Centre for Natural Resources, Energy and Transport (CNRET), and the branches responsible for operational projects in each region.

In addition, two conferences will have appropriate forums to explore the importance of the subject of bioresources for development: (a) The United Nations Conference on Science and Technology for Development held in Vienna in September 1979; (b) the United Nations Conference on New and Renewable Sources of Energy to be held in 1981.

- The United Nations Regional Economic Commissions could be consulted to propose regional programs on Bioresources for Development in Africa (ECA, Addis Ababa), Asia and the Pacific (ESCAP, in Bangkok), in Latin America (ECLA, Santiago), and in the Western Asia (ECWA, Beirut).
- The Economic and Social Commission for Asia and the Pacific (ESCAP) is, among its other activities, taking an active part in the field of biogas.

The Commission formulated a project (No. RAS/74/041/01/01) entitled, "Workshop on Biogas Technology and Utilization". The objective of this project was to develop nonconventional sources of energy (biogas) and improve the quality of organic fertilizers (biomass) from renewable waste materials particularly in rural areas, and also to provide opportunities to exchange information on biogas technology and its utilization and the use of effluent from a biogas plant as fertilizer in an integrated farming system. The project's report foresees that if the biogas units are properly developed, the rural areas in most of the countries in the ESCAP region would not only become self-sufficient in their requirements of energy for cooking and lighting, but also meet the needs of agricultural machinery and small-scale industrial units.

Under the auspices of ESCAP itself, four Roving Seminars on Rural Energy Development were held at: Bangkok, Thailand; Manila, the Philippines; Teheran, Iran; and Jakarta, Indonesia between July 18 and October 21, 1977. Many subjects, such as firewood and energy plantation, biogas and integrated farming system, solar and wind energy, rural electrification, minihydroelectricity, etc., were discussed.

Also, taking into account the important role of agriculture for the achievement of economic and social development, the Commission has directed its strategies towards increasing food production and reducing hunger and malnutrition. The Commission is working in close cooperation and coordination with òther United Nations agencies, especially Food and Agriculture (FAO), in order to achieve maximum efficiency and avoid any duplication.

The Economic Commission for Latin America has completed a study on the fertilizer industry in Latin America, and is making an analysis on the possibilities of increasing the production capacity of fertilizers in Central America. Studies are also being undertaken on the prospects for using nonconventional sources of energy in Latin America, the review of technological progress in this area, and the possibilities of competing economically. In the field of rural development, ECLA has conducted research on agricultural modernization, rural changes, peasant movements, agroindustrialization and rural social conditions.

The Economic Commission for Western Asia (ECWA), in cooperation with other related UN agencies, is carrying out different projects in the fields of food, agriculture, energy, and petrochemicals in the regions under its jurisdiction. With the help of consultants, the Commission has prepared two studies entitled, "Techno-economic study for the development of fertilizer industry in the Arab" world and "Feasibility study for the development of olefin and aromatic industries for international and national markets in the Arab States." The Commission has also initiated a study to investigate, analyze, and formulate an optimal production and investment strategy for petrochemical industry in the Arab world.

The Food and Agriculture Organization (FAO) is playing an important role in the developmental process of the developing countries in the field of food production, nutrition, agrarian reforms, and rural development. One example is the 1979 World Conference on Agrarian Reform and Rural Development. FAO organizes missions in the field of agricultural planning and policy analysis. Regarding forestry, in 1977 FAO deputed 270 experts, consultants and volunteers to assist in the implementation of 135 field projects in 63 countries. The Organization also sponsors programs jointly with the International Atomic Energy Agency (IAEA) with the objective of using nuclear techniques to improve agriculture, and to reduce health hazards in food.

UNESCO has many programs related to bioresources, for instance, the Programme on Man and the Biosphere (MAB), which represents a comprehensive approach to the subject matter at the global, regional, and national levels. National committees have been created and regional meetings organized, such as the MAB Mediterranean Scientific Conference, Montpelier, September 1976. Other programs include international research on the environment, natural resources, water, and the sea.

The World Meteorological Organization (WMO), the United Nations Environment Programme (UNEP), the World Health Organization (WHO), the United Nations Children's Fund (UNICEF) are involved in many activities related to bioresources for development.

In the framework of its activities for the industrialization of developing countries, the UN Industrial Development Organization is conducting studies and technical assistance programs notably in the field of agroindustries and fertilizers. For instance, UNIDO has published a worldwide study on the Fertilizer Industry (1975-2000) and a report on "Technology for Solar Energy Utilization." (5)

The United Nations University undertakes research studies in cooperation with a network of universities and institutions. It is presently carrying out three programs, namely, World Hunger Programme, Human and Social Development Programme, and Programme on the Use and Management of Natural Resources. Within the World Hunger Programme, the University is specifically concerned with projects concerned with human nutritional needs and their fulfillment, post-harvest conservations of food and food and nutrition objectives in the national planning and development.

The United Nations Institute for Training and Research (UNITAR) also conducts research and studies on selected subjects.

The United Nations Development Programme (UNDP) and the World Bank (IBRD) are supporting programs which may contribute to the development of bioresources. For instance, the UNDP has undertaken an important program on aquaculture. The World Bank has recently approved a $10 million project on forestry in Guyana, $4.5 million for irrigation on Mali, and $14 million in Nepal to improve indigenous agriculture practices and increase production and employment opportunities for 216,000 persons.

CONCLUSIONS

The biological sciences, which have already achieved remarkable progress in recent years, are expected to provide important potentialities for development in the second half of the twentieth century which may be compared with the breakthrough in electronics between 1950 and 1970.

International cooperation - between developed and developing countries or among developing countries - may benefit this progress for the developing countries. Toward this end, it would be useful to prepare an evaluation of the potentials for bioresources development in each country. Such an inventory, which could be called the "Biological Assessment" at the national level, would provide a basis for estimating the resources as well as the promises and preparing national and international programs for bioresources development.

REFERENCES

(1) UNITAR and the Federal Republic of Germany. 1976. Microbial Energy Seminar. Gottingen, October 4-8, 1976.

(2) Chatel, Bertrand. 1977. Potentialities of solar and wind energy for deserts development. Alternative strategies for deserts development. UNITAR. May 31-June 10, 1977, Sacramento, CA.

(3) Sanchez, P.A. 1976. Multiple cropping - An appraisal of present knowledge and future needs. In Symposium on Multiple Cropping, American Society of Agronomy.

(4) Leene, T.M. 1976. The conversion of ocean farm kelp to methane and other products. Conference on Bio-Mass Conversion, Orlando, Florida (January, 1976).

(5) United Nations Industrial Development Organization (UNIDO). 1978. Second world wide study on the fertilizer industry - 1975-2000. In Technology for Solar Energy Utilization, Series No. 5. UNIDO/ICIS. 81-11, September, 1978.

II

Social and Economic Impacts

Introduction to Part II

In the opening paper of the second group, Richard Meier analyzes the problems of urban planning and city management from a resource-conservation angle, with special reference to the problems which will arise through the expected rapid growth of cities in the more rapidly modernizing countries of the Third World. His discussion, for example, of the provision of water and of urban transportation is in an economic perspective and leads to a description of the assumptions which must underlie new planning processes.

Clive Simmonds develops the theme of ecology of change mainly in relation to bioresource development, envisaging a situation in which goals will be more varied and less clearly defined than they have been in the age of growth (e.g., efficiency balanced with equity and the potentiality for survival, resilience more prized than stability, and heterogeneity accepted as normal and necessary). He makes a plea for the development of a dynamic, holistic economic theory, and stresses the need for cultural diversity.

The paper by Malcolm Slessor focuses on the economics of bioresource technology, particularly the energy aspects. The paper by Armand Pereira and Seymour Warkov is also concerned with the economics of energy. It presents a balanced and detailed account of a variety of developments aimed at providing energy for rural development in the semiarid areas of northeastern Brazil.

6 Creating Resource-Conserving Communities for the 1980s and Beyond

Richard L. Meier

Rapidly changing world conditions are challenging the processes of physical planning. Well-established procedures must be questioned because the future price structure and social conditions will be very different from those in the past. Until now, a successful community has been judged by the amount of resources it could usefully consume; in the future it will succeed only if it manages to conserve resources without loss in quality-of-life. Most institutions recognize that they are employing techniques of planning that are now obsolescent, but as yet, very few of the new approaches have been formulated for general practice.

A comprehensive planning approach, using the principles of ecology for integration of the diverse requirements, has been examined in my Planning for an Urban World - Design of Resource-Conserving Cities (1974). A few new concepts are here added, but what follows is principally an attempt to lay out a path for the provision of housing and infrastructure in societies like Korea, Malaysia, the Philippines, Brazil, Mexico, Nigeria, Morocco, and other rapidly modernizing countries. Examples are usually drawn from Korea, because major commitments must be made there very soon.

The changing situation is best put in the form of expectations regarding future costs. These societies will be subject to periodic regional and world shortages, causing sharp price rises and failures in supply, as well as secular trends. The outlook for the future in these parts of the world is summarized in fig. 6.1. The problems with respect to materials (mainly nonferrous metals, wood, and cotton) are too complex to be represented graphically, but the need to draw upon much lower grade resources will result in substantial increases in cost, which can be only somewhat diminished by the use of substitutes and better-fitting product design.

During this same period the increasing contact between metropolises, and the enhanced flow of enterprise, high-grade human

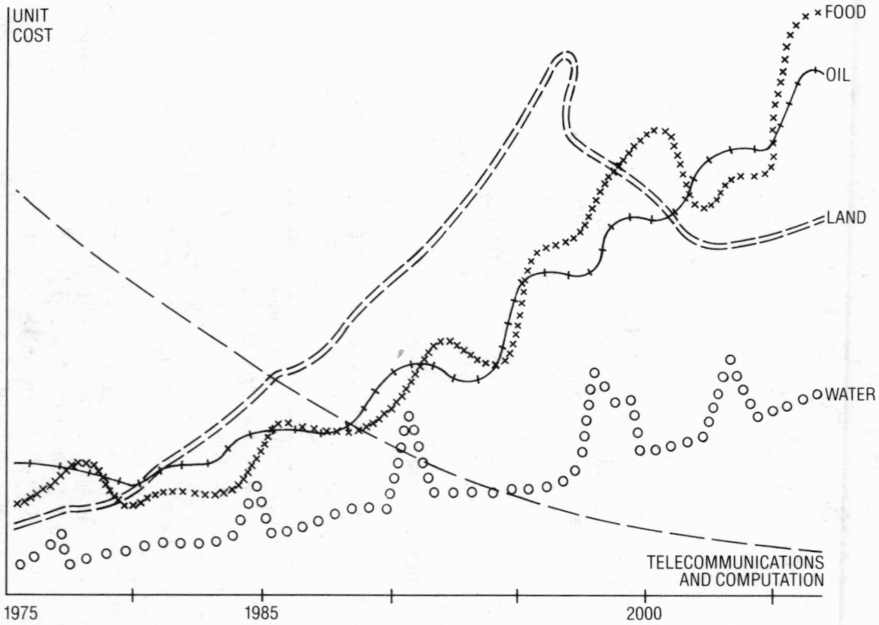

Fig. 6.1. Expectations for Third World Metropolises: Crises. The crises in inputs, indicated by discontinuities in trends, tend to paralyze many of the functions of a city. The impact of shortages, or escalations in costs, is more serious when they affect government and other regulatory and distributive institutions in a society. The best community design buffers the social system from such perturbations, most often with instruments employing telecommunications and computation.

resources, and capital between them make it imperative that each metropolitan region maintain a competitive quality-of-life. If the quality-of-life in one slips with respect to the others, the supply of mobile capital dries up, the technological expertise drifts away in search of better living conditions, and a shrinkage occurs in the operations of the multinational organizations represented there. (Beirut and, to a lesser extent, Lima offer recent examples of such losses.)

If it is in the national interest that a metropolitan community should expand, then it follows that such a community must offer a visibly superior quality of life - at least for the social class containing the specialists required for its contributions to the nation. The components found to be highly significant when measuring quality-of-life in the United States and Japan are illustrated in fig. 6.2. The survey research instruments for identifying the domains of activity contributing to quality were devised in the Institute for Social Research, University of Michigan, (Angus Campbell et al. 1975). A somewhat different approach, based in part upon levels of community service, was developed by the Research Institute for Telecommunications and Economics in Tokyo (1976). Both depend upon personal reports regarding overall satisfaction with the life the respondent is able to live. Other models for the concept are still appearing.

Finally, it is now accepted that the new urban settlement must be built up in a fashion that is ecologically sound. An internal stability, free of degradation and threats of imminent collapse should evolve. People expect cities to be robust, diverse, responsive, and adaptive - properties introducing the subtlety of resource conservation. The principles of community ecology, broadly conceived, should guide the development of new human settlements. There is a threat, however, arising from an uncritical borrowing of American environmental standards, since the quality standards were set far more strictly than the measured impairment of health and safety. A very important new work, significant for planners in developing countries as well as developed, is that of W.D. Rowe, in An Anatomy of Risk (1977). If one accepts pollution to be a risk to the health of man and other living populations, (enthusiastic environmentalists regard a violation of esthetic norms as equally important to health risks,) then Rowe's generalizations apply comprehensively. For example, in Manila in the summer of 1978, a meeting on the next planning period was held. Eighty-nine million dollars was needed to cope with growth at the present levels of service; \$200 million was estimated to meet basic health requirements; and at least \$2 billion was needed to reach esthetic standards similar to the United States. At present the United States standards require escalating expenditures to control pollutants (fig. 6.3).

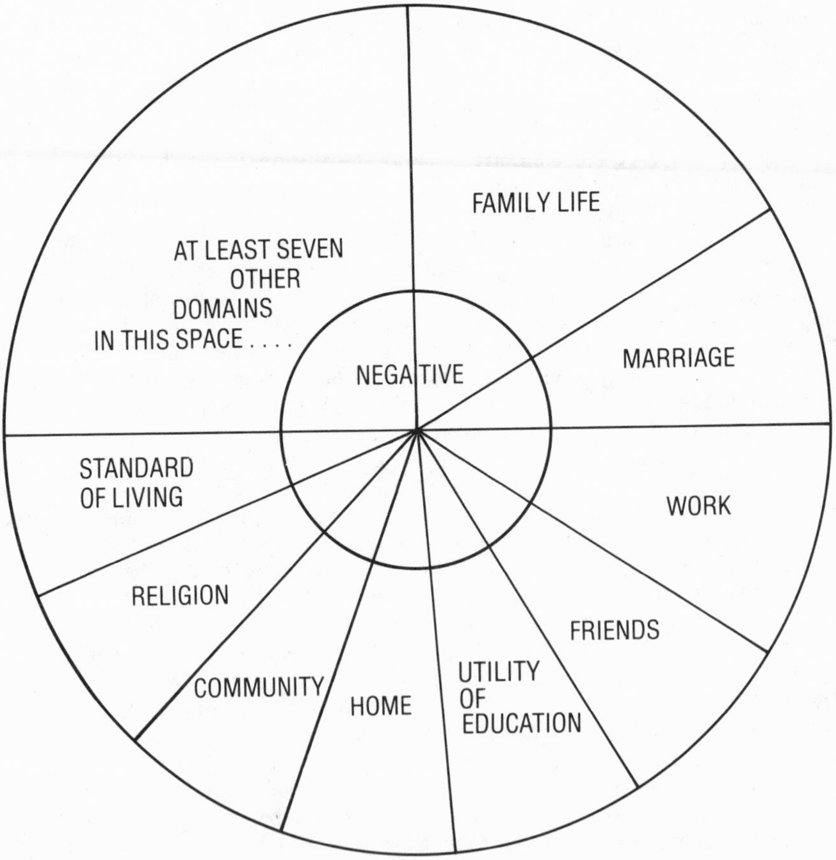

Fig. 6.2. Quality of Life: Domains of Satisfaction. When people submit to carefully structured interview intended to explore the sources of general satisfaction with life, the domains of experience which contribute can be weighed for the overall population. A community should support many niches which require different allocations of attention and resources on the part of individuals, but the means for urbanized communities are expected to resemble the distribution shown above.

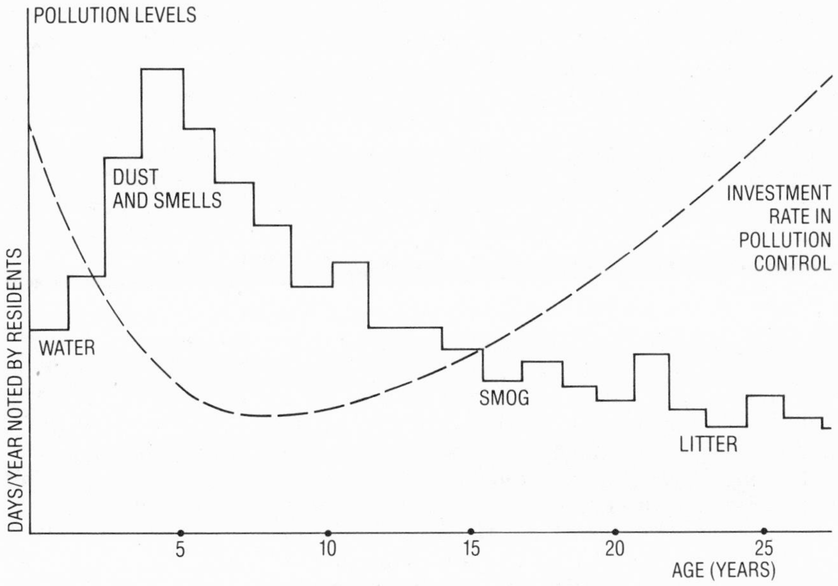

Fig. 6.3. Control of pollutants in new communities. Some of the pollution control is incorporated in the homesites and vehicles at the time of construction and settlement. Later, further installations are made, once the monitoring of the environment has established deviations from legislated standards. The levels of investment needed to mitigate air, water, and land pollution in the maturing community may well be debated in the future, but in Europe and America at present they are rarely questioned, and a significant share of the available capital is being committed.

WATER CONSERVATION AND SANITATION

New ways of planning water and sanitation have not yet reached a consensus of opinion; many battles remain to be fought in the World Health Organization and professional bodies over the next decade or so as the implications of the new information are digested.

The best strategy, perhaps, is to guarantee rock bottom minimum standards according to experience, and to set up daily operations in a manner that allows for the conservation of scarce resources. This is the same as arguing that the survival of the city has top priority (a city can die from lack of water more quickly than it can from disease or starvation or failure of transport systems).

Cities can withstand shortages better than most engineers and planners imagine. Two multimillion metropolises, Bombay and Kong Kong, have been reduced to providing water in the mains for two two-hour periods per week. (The strategy was to provide water for restricted periods during the day so as to reduce the waste through leakage, but later supplies became so short some days had to be skipped, until finally at the most critical period most days passed without a pressurizing of the grid.) After the rains came the metropolis bounced back to normal, except for a flurry of dysentery, within a month. An estimated 10 liters of water per capita per day were provided for direct consumption during the critical period; the real level of consumption can never be known because the statistical foundations break down under these circumstances.

Neither Bombay nor Hong Kong were capital cities with large populations dependent upon continuation of central guidance. If Delhi, Bangkok, or Manila could not respond quickly to some regional catastrophe, the loss due to extreme water shortage could be multiplied many times. Therefore, for capital cities the planning should aim at delivering an absolute minimum of 20-30 liters per capita per day. This guarantee can be achieved through redundancy (several reservoirs and independent watersheds) and transport with tankers, barges, emergency pipelines, and tank trucks mobilized on short notice. Desalination is not the answer to such crises, unless it is economic over the long run as well, due to the high capital cost. The Greek dragone, a plastic bag resembling a huge sea serpent, which is filled up in the nearest free-running river delta or other raw water supply and is pulled by tug to a point from which fresh water can be pumped into the grid, will almost always be more economical than desalination. (Hong Kong was heard to regret its new computer-operated desalination plant, due to the high energy cost, but was grateful at the peak of the last critical drought that it could work to capacity.)

For routine operations, which overcome the effects of seasonality of rainfall, moderate droughts and occasional floods, the institution of a quasi-market appears to be the best policy. This means that prices rise automatically during times of shortage and will otherwise be kept at a level that will pay for all expenses, including external costs. Provision may even be made to allow for long-term contracts for future delivery. The nearest approach at the moment to the balancing of supply and demand by market prices is to be found in Israel. There, as in the world elsewhere, a number of compromises needed to be reached with vociferous special interest groups.

Imagine a quasi-market for water with three or four qualities, or commodities. Each of the lower qualities can be upgraded through the expenditure of known quantities of capital and energy so the ceiling price for the top two grades can be known in advance and should be quite stable. The installations can be intermediate scale technology. Drinking water of top quality would be packaged and distributed at a fair price. (For the poor, it might be subsidized like rice or bread.) The second commodity would be filtered, raw water, and would be distributed to points where bathing, laundry, food preparation, and small-scale manufacturing occur. The cleaner water waste water can be filtered and recycled back for reuse, sometimes for the same purpose, but usually for laundry and industry. Within urban districts, the resulting gray water can become a commodity transferred from one enterprise to another. It is the third commodity (see fig. 6.4).

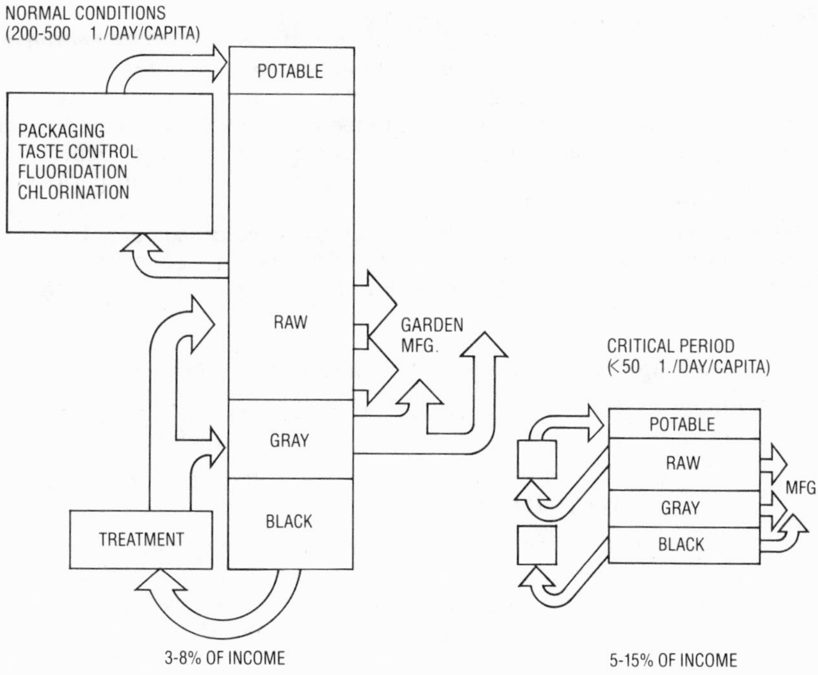

Fig. 6.4. Water commodity production. The water and sanitation industry in resource-conserving urban settlement should be concerned with the production of four different commodities in most sites. Note that when water becomes truly scarce the gardens dry up, and light manufacturing depends much more on gray water. Potable water consumptions remain virtually unchanged. Gray water, sometimes even sewage, can be used for productive cooling purposes in an emergency, so outflow as sewage shrinks to a small fraction of raw water input.

Finally, the water can be used for intensive gardening, or for flushing away waste. By then it becomes a fourth commodity, one with a negative value, because people must pay to get rid of it. Concentrated sewage can be converted in part to biogas and fish, while the water can be used for gardening, thereby significantly reducing the charge for removal. When rainfall is sufficient or much too plentiful, the city's storm drains must carry away the surplus. The sanitation treatment system must be kept separate, because dilution adds to costs.

The water market concept saves energy when it is applied, because only 5-10 percent of the volume is chlorinated and fluoridated. Recycling is begun whenever the market price indicates that it is worthwhile; except in large industrial installations, it is expected to require intermediate technology installed as needed. Recycling uses energy for pumping and materials to produce whatever grade of water is scarce. The water market can be extended to a whole watershed, or an even larger region, depending upon the possibilities of water export and import, but it is likely to be considered worthwhile only in periods of critical water shortage.

The market concept is readily understood by consumers, but as a practical matter a number of adjustments need to be made in city design to allow the system to function as intended. The changes include:

1. Installation of water meters and spring loaded faucets.
2. Linking together the locations of activities such as bathhouses, laundries and toilets, food processing and local markets, etc.
3. Provision of space for kitchen gardens, hothouses, and hydroponic uses wherever land rents justify.
4. High concentration sewage collection systems, varied according to the convenience that can be afforded. (Luxury elevator apartments in Athens and Tokyo store human wastes in a tank with two to three days capacity for removal by tank truck at night, while squatter settlements may have public latrines delivering directly to a main sewer line.)
5. Provisions for readily modifiable piping, either flexible, plastic, or rigid polyvinyl, rather than metal.
6. Most fundamental is an educational program intended to instruct people to change water-using habits to fit the resource-conserving style of living for that locale.

The principal saving takes the form of security against loss of urban function and against illness. Packaged water, prepared under technical supervision and analyzed continuously, assures that waterborne disease will be minimized. The next saving is in the form of capital. The present water and sanitation standards are likely to cost 15-25 percent of the total cost for low income housing, a figure which can be cut substantially by fitting living patterns more closely to water supply conditions. An important saving may show up in the reduction of time required to convert raw land into habitable settlement. The energy economies become significant much later - after energy prices have risen further - and are primarily important for providing insurance against early obsolescence of the infrastructure.

The overall domestic consumption of water can then be planned at around 200 liters per capita per day. At that flow, the reuse of water is quite limited. But if supplies should be restricted, these planning and management provisions make it possible to keep the city functioning at a level of efficiency that to an outsider would seem unimpaired. The industries and gardens cutback on consumption according to the changes in price. (In the last drought in California, these price charges for water use beyond a quota ran as high as ten times the normal rates when reservoirs stood at 10-20 percent of normal.)

The treatment of the sewage, leading to the production of industrial quality water and by-product energy, is also opening new possibilities. Rapidly developing cities have exceedingly high land rents, which greatly add to the cost of conventional treatment facilities, and even more to the high rate oxidation ponds, which are capable of harvesting the nitrogenous and phosphatic components in wastewater for recycling back into the urban ecosystem in the form of fish and chickens or eggs (fig. 6.5). The complete recycling loop was very recently closed in Israel at the semiplant scale.

The new procedures under development use well drilling technology for the provision of space for waste treatment, thus minimizing the use of land surface, and reducing energy costs in the cold season. The pond can be postponed until the value of output can pay the land rent. Very marginal surfaces are suitable.

The aerobic treatment involves mixing air with sewage and pumping it down the pipe 100-300 millimeters. Oxygen dissolves much more efficiently under those pressures, the oxidation requiring minutes instead of hours. When the liquid rises, bubbles form, producing an additional lift, and greatly reducing the pumping cost. The process was developed by I.C.I. Ltd. as a byproduct of their single cell protein technology, and is being installed on a commercial basis in Canada.

The new continuous flow anaerobic unit employs a bed of clay rings, upon which a culture of filamentous bacteria build up. The best conditions appear to be mesophilic, i.e., intermediate or warm temperatures. About 50-70 percent of the organic material can be converted to standard biogas. Process development has been assigned top priority by the U.S. Department of Energy and the work is being carried out at the Oak Ridge National Laboratories, in Tennessee.

Progress on both of these techniques was reviewed at a conference sponsored by the Department of Energy, in Forth Worth, Texas, May 1978, to be published in 1979. These technologies are complementary when water is scarce, and are fitted to climatic conditions similar to those present in Korea. One big advantage is that it appears likely that facilities at intermediate scale will be competitive, so the complete sewerage grid does not need to be planned in advance. The facilities

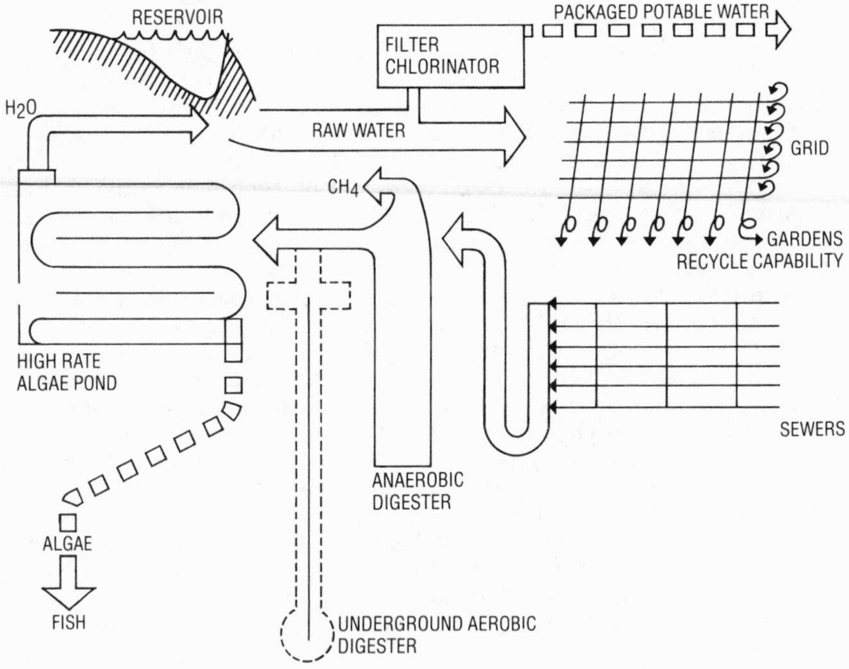

Fig. 6.5. A water and sanitation system to cope with scarcity. Attempts to conserve water, energy, biomass and capital for a city to be founded in the near future depicts the above sequence of technologies. Each one of them has already been linked into partial sequences, but the total sequence is unprecedented. It should evolve over time as the byproducts and output promise to be economic. It is important that the short-term solutions should not prevent the further elaboration of this scheme; otherwise, over the long run, the city's ability to compete internationally will be constrained.

could be installed in the basements of large buildings, or in the small industry sector of an urban neighborhood.

TRANSPORTATION AND COMMUNICATION

The movement of people and goods in cities of the future must be quite different from what we know at present. The demand for liquid fuel by Third World cities is expected to rise beyond that of the already developed metropolises in a time span that is less than a human generation. This overtaking is expected to occur even though the per capita consumption in Third World metropolises remains low (a half to a fifth that of the increasingly conservation-conscious developed cities). It is the heavy pressure for urbanization noted everywhere in the less developed countries - the multiplication in numbers of the urban settlers - that pushes the Third World into the role of dominant consumer.

The prospects for hydrocarbon fuel scarcity are so imminent that one must design settlement patterns that will work smoothly, using a third or less of the liquid fuel presently considered to be necessary for modern functions. If this is not accomplished, the last half or three-quarters of the life cycle of buildings constructed in the 1980s will be lost, and the overall ability of the metropolis to compete effectively on the world scene will be greatly diminished.

The most recent ideas and strategies suited to Third World metropolises were assembled not long ago by a team led by myself for the Department of Energy. (Meier, Berman, Dowall et al. 1978). This was, of necessity, directed primarily at tropical and subtropical environments, since most of the new urbanization will occur there. It is useful to consider also an appropriate set for new urbanization in the temperate climate - new settlement that can demonstrate how existing plans for older cities and towns can be revised.

The cheapest and most flexible means of urban mass transport, expressed in energy as well as overall cost, remains that of the bus. Its all-weather characteristics are especially appreciated. The cost of subways, better suited to long trips, becomes comparable only when the value of human time saved from waiting is taken into account; the value of time becomes particularly significant for middle to higher income passengers moving longer distances. The latter may alternately be collected by radio-controlled minibus-jitneys for the trip to work or school, which is usually more efficient (see table 6.1).

A very strong demand for a private vehicle is expected to continue regardless of the energy shortage. The bicycle is highly economical (equivalent to that of the bus, because the energy source is food, which will still remain more valuable than liquid fuel,) but except on the periphery of China its social status is low. Totally different bicycle designs and images are possible, and a few are beginning to be produced. A variety of stylish bicycles may be used in the future for fair-weather transport; examples are appearing in America and Europe.

Table 6.1. Relative Costs of Alternative Modes of Passenger Movement for 1980s

Modes	Energy Cost (Cal/ pass.-km.)	Capital Cost (1980 won/daily passenger)	Operating Cost per pass.-km.)	Time Cost (minutes/ km.)	Value of Pass. Time (won/hr)	Total Cost (won/km)
Walking	60 (food)	20,000	13	18.0	500	180
Bicycle	15 (food)	100,000	18	4.0	1,000	140
Mo-ped (1.2 pass.)	60	200,000	17	3.0	1,500	200
Electric Car (1.2 pass.)	500	1,600,000	35	2.5	2,000	1,000
Bus	60	150,000	15	3.0	1,000	80
Rail Rapid Transit	60	5,000,000	15	2.0	1,500	2,800
Jitney (5 pass.)	160	750,000	27	2.5	1,500	490
Taxi (1.5 pass)	500	2,000,000	55	1.5	2,000	1,200

The assumptions in the crude calculations of expected comparative costs were as follows:

1. The exchange rate will stabilize at 500 won to the dollar.
2. The value of liquid fuel will rise 50-100% over 1978 prices.
3. The cost of electric power will rise another 30-50%.
4. The interest paid on capital will decline, so 20% of existing value is expected to pay for both amortization and interest.
5. Rail rapid transit has not been granted any credits for central city decongestion - the prime reason for installation in Third World metropolises.

A descendant of the bicycle, the moped or velo, is starting to become popular again in developed countries as a substitute for the second car in the household. If gasoline rationing should occur, the 30-50 kilometer/liter consumption should make it very popular indeed in medium to low density settlements. Again, however, it is primarily a fair-weather vehicle.

Electric neighborhood cars are feasible for those who can afford them (at $3,000-5,000 apiece). They are particularly appropriate if nuclear reactors are producing most of the power for operating the city and its hinterland. Most dwellings and some shops can then front on slow-ways, which combine pedestrian, bicycle, moped, and battery-powered vehicle movement on a route six to ten meters wide. These dimensions fit the Asian neighborhoods very comfortably. At present in America, the newly adopted standards call for an independent network of bikeways, but still more recent observations suggest that the traffic, ranging from bicycles to electric cars, will mix very safely with road traffic comprised of automobiles (taxis), buses, and trucks (William Garrison et al. 1977). Combining intermediate transport vehicles with the full-scale road transport will save some land (perhaps about 2-3 percent of the total area), but it also simplifies planning and urban management, and eliminates the need for many expensive overpasses and tunnels.

These intermediate technology vehicles are simple enough to manufacture, therefore most Third World countries can quickly incorporate the production within their own economies. Korea, the Philippine Republic, Taiwan, Thailand, and India could easily institute this production, and others could follow within a few years. Therefore, the export market in intermediate vehicles and associated equipment is expected to be of short duration.

Telecommunications to some degree can substitute for urban transportation and should be encouraged whenever possible, because the savings in energy and time are considerable. Therefore, the telephone service should be planned as early as the water supply, the street grid, and the vehicular modes, and electronic data processing will link up the offices of the new urbanization with other urban centers around the world.

A communications satellite, microwave relays, and fiber optics will combine to eliminate most of the complex underground network presently required for comprehensive telephone service. In the past, the telephone has almost always followed electrification; by the end of the 1980s it should be possible to purchase a line (the quasi-market approach is advisable here, as in water and transport service) in hastily settled parts of a metropolis before the electrical grid has been expanded into the district. Portable telephones would also be feasible (although the military regimes in charge of many of these countries have prohibited the introduction of citizens' broadcast band sender-receivers, which are progenitors of the more flexible systems to come). These communications advances offer strikingly novel forms of human organization in cities, capable of meeting human needs more promptly and precisely, with less effort. Growing cities have the opportunity of installing this advantageous new technology before established state metropolises.

The land use assignments available in the near future that follow from this range of accessibilities remain to be calculated from alternate quantitative models. It is expected that households taking advantage of intermediate transport and communications technology can be rather tightly packed and still leave a latitude for self-determination of style, amount of living space, an openness to kinfolk and neighbors, and the incorporation of special interests such as gardens, pets, the plastic arts, books, etc., because parking space can be largely eliminated, while convenience retained or slightly enhanced, compared to automobile ownership (fig. 6.6).

HOUSE AND NEIGHBORHOOD

Between 20 and 60 percent of the cost of a dwelling unit in a developing metropolis will depend upon land price or its equivalent in infrastructure investments. The free market in land tends to anticipate future savings in time and convenience, and incorporates them into the selling price at the time of construction. Therefore, a transport system which increases the accessibility of land in various categories will also increase the supply, so the price should stay relatively economical. Extension of efficient transport networks into fringe areas of a metropolis should keep buildable land cost at the bottom end of this range. The principal factors leading to satisfaction with low cost housing are well-balanced transport and communications networks. This is an argument understood by land economists, but it is rarely understood by others.

The next factor in importance is space economy. Too often people are moved into a mass-produced unit with little opportunity to fit it to their own needs. Some space remains unused (e.g., the balcony that remains no more than an expensive decoration of the facade, or the sterile rooftop), while at the same time other needs (e.g., the storage of clothes, toys, and plants, or provisions for babies) remain unfilled due to a lack of appropriate space. Houses put on the market are designed to meet the needs of average people; that leaves about a half, who differ in significant ways from the mean, as misfits. These costs are only partly reflected in the marketplace, but they show up strongly in the measures of satisfaction that underlie the quality of life.

Some people wish to socialize with their immediate neighbors, setting up friendly cooperative relationships. Others find their friends among colleagues and habitues of hangouts, and wish to minimize contacts with neighbors. (These are members of non-place communities.) The metropolis should accommodate both extremes, and many of the compromises existing in between. Organizing the occasions where people do things together, even if it is only talking and eating, is a great source of satisfaction for many people. In many developing

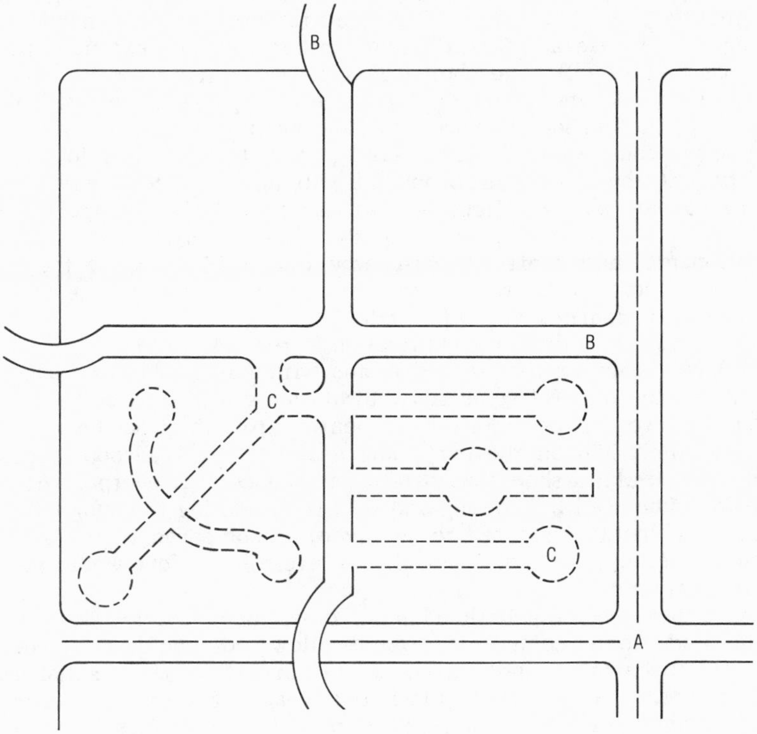

Fig. 6.6. Potentials for intermediate transport. The possible combinations of intermediate transport technology with the existing network are quite numerous. In the above arrangement the A channels carry buses, trucks, taxis, and other automotive transport. B might introduce jitneys and vans into the interior of the superblock, while C routes might be treelined slow-ways for pedestrians, bicycles, mopeds, and handcarts. The merging of traffic is gradual, fitting what has recently been reported about the design of environments safe from accidents.

countries, family ties are so strong there is a need for clustering kinfolk together in a neighborhood. (This need for propinquity is particularly strong for Chinese and South Asian families once the extended family unit has broken up.) The choice of appropriate locations for dwelling within a city depends upon the willingness of prospective residents to form and maintain social bonds with other people.

Energy conservation, water saving, and the preservation of the qualities of the natural environment will have a strong effect upon future housing policy. Housing that can be relatively impervious to periodic crises in supply, and keep the risks of fire, flood, accident, street crime, and theft at reasonably low levels is what the great majority of urban dwellers hope to achieve. Often the prerequisites for risk reduction conflict with other values.

We can be explicit for conditions in Korea. A traditional house for the 1980s might consist of two rooms with 40-60 m^2 floorspace for regular use by four to five persons. Insulation should be added under the ondol (a stove that provides radiant heating from the floor level), under the roof tiles, and on the north and east walls. A carbon monoxide detector and alarm should be installed to reduce that everpresent fear. Fans would be used for cooling and ventilation during the summer. The amount of energy expected to be saved, as compared to the present, would be perhaps a third, although the level of comfort would still be significantly improved.

A cooperative neighborhood plan, based upon energy flow instruments and small computers, would allow householders to detect wasteful behaviors, and introduce or invent equally satisfactory alternatives. That strategy after two years of learning, season by season, might save as much as 50 percent over what is presently assumed to be adequate. A program of public education would need to be established to make such cooperation effective.

A third approach could provide the same levels of comfort and convenience, and would save 70-90 percent of the energy, but it is too radical to be accepted readily. It would employ south-facing hillsides, including man-made hills, to install earth sheltered dwelling units. One to three meters of soil would be placed on the roof, thus buffering the house against heat and cold. Cooking would have to be electrical, and the ondol would disappear. Since the economical ceiling is a dome, extra sleeping and storage space would be on the second level. Windows would open to the south and west, doors would connect with a private yard and vehicle storage area, and the gate would connect to a lane (or slow-way). The top would be a hilly mound with grass or shrubs, a vegetable garden, or a sun deck. The density of single family dwellings with associated circulation space, schools, and shops could be as high as 100 units per hectare. The introduction of local markets, small scale industries, public baths, and other specialized public spaces (churches, parks, etc.) would reduce this somewhat (fig. 6.7).

This most efficient housing solution is likely to be accepted first by intellectuals, who would add many unique features, and would build in small tracts or even individually, so the density of settlement might run

Fig. 6.7. Earth Sheltered dwelling units. In continental climates earth-covered shells, with openings to catch the winter's sun and sealed against moisture, offer many opportunities for variation of form. Virtually all the heating and airconditioning energy normally required to operate a home or family business can be saved. Daylight can be beamed to the top and back by a light transmitter positioned at the top of the mound; it is operated with the aid of clockwork. The lane is designed primarily for pedestrians and intermediate transport modes, possibly 6 meters wide. Landscaping opportunities are strikingly novel.

20-50 to the hectare. When viewed from the top, houses would probably resemble ancient Silla tombs for noblemen and warriors, but other shapes for the earth mantle no doubt will be adapted. (Sand dunes covered with ice plant vines and north-facing ceiling level openings were chosen for middle class Mexican tourists at a site where desert and ocean meet.)

A NEW PLANNING PROCESS

To repeat, the aim of the recommended changes is to enhance quality of life, even as the supply of resources declines. The solutions should not be postponed; the outlook for improvement should be continuously positive for anyone willing to put in the effort to help himself. Some assumptions must be made regarding processes that produce satisfaction with life. They are assumptions because studies were undertaken primarily with North American cultures, a few related European, and the Japanese, but not in the urbanizing Third World. Small-scale inquiries suggest that findings based upon social science techniques are generally replicated in modernizing urban settlement, while indigenous tribal cultures studied by anthropologists respond less predictably. The partially supported assumptions may be stated as follows:

I. People are satisfied if they are allowed to participate in face-to-face neighborhood, workplace, and community decisions even if their arguments do not result in action, often even if they have not spoken up at all.

II. People are satisfied if the variety of available choices in some important features of life are increasing in number and diversity (psychic income).

III. People are satisfied if they can preserve important achievements and experiences, even if only symbolically.

IV. People are satisfied if they are allowed and enabled to structure their immediate environment.

V. Many people are satisfied if they feel that their social status, which usually depends upon property and education but may involve pilgrimages and other achievements, is improving or can be improved through personal effort.

All the above propositions occur with a high frequency, but are not uniformly true. There are other foundations for satisfaction which apply to smaller proportions of the population. The most important of these ways to promote quality of life that are accepted by potential settlers should be discovered before settlement begins.

Assessment of the sources of satisfaction among the barely literate population can be carried out by means of consultation with the wisest of the social workers, followed by a survey using brief, structured interviews. For the better educated portion of the new settlers the initial survey should be followed by simple self-administered followup.

These social survey instruments might well be of the type devised by planners which identify comparative preferences for features of a home, qualities of neighborhood, services provided by community, and aspects of employment, including the manner by which they can be fitted into the confines of a realistic budget. In societies where gambling is important, it is also necessary to discover how people would spend their gains when they are lucky in acquiring income. The choices indicated when aware of the full spectrum of options are most informative when planning for satisfaction over the long run. (A game which offers a catalog of possible features of a dwelling in a new settlement can even be played over television for public education purposes. It might offer a prize of, say, $2,000 to $5,000, but only in the form of the best house for the winner. A dozen features might conceivably be entered in a catalog at three quality levels, each of them priced. Time pressure causes people to forget costs of choices, so when they are added up the total almost always exceeds the original million by a considerable sum. The comparison of disparate items to cut back is very revealing, particularly in a family context. A jackpot sum of half the original sum, representing an unexpected windfall, will almost always be allocated differently. A similar phenomenon is seen in the responses to the Asian company custom of a variable bonus based upon profits.)

Catalogs based upon real possibilities for commercially constructed dwellings can be provided to prospective urban settlers. They may range from contemporary developer-designed units to prefabricated alternatives, through core assemblies to be completed by oneself with the aid of artisans, all the way to bare site-and-services, which allows one to build in his own fashion, using available subassemblies on the market such as wall panels, windows, doors, and closets. By this means the market can be estimated and planned by standard procedures, yet, the quality-of-life approach must go much further.

The next overlapping stage is self-organization. In Korea, for example, churches are very important. In Song Nam New City they were built simultaneously with the houses, apparently stimulating much of the neighborhood cooperation. There are various Protestant denominations, Roman Catholic, a strong syncretic Buddhist-Christian synod, and the traditional forms of Buddhist and Confucian groups. For many of them, singing together is rewarding, and this is symbolic of other modes of cooperation.

Also to be organized are businesses, health association, sports teams, Boy Scouts, garden clubs, and other voluntary groups. Self-organization is so important for satisfaction, the process should be subsidized out of taxes. Thus, building churches should be encouraged (they usually are), along with various forms of cooperatives and shared neighborhood facilities. Telephone service speeds up self-organization, so it should be given an early and very high priority.

Another feature is the choice of neighbors. This is not quite as sensitive an affair as arranging a marriage, but compatibility with neighbors having closest contact, allowing arrangements about common walls, trees, vehicle parking, and cleanup responsibilities to be negotiated have quite similar properties. Prior negotiations about neighboring have allowed greatly differing social classes, religious communities, and ethnic groups to live together peaceably even during public disturbances. Special arrangements for the use of the postal system would have to be made to reinforce face-to-face meetings and the use of the telephone.

What this policy implements is the rapid expansion of social networks, despite the extra effort of setting up housekeeping in a new place. Many personal networks crystallize into businesses and non-market social organizations. The social structure of the community can determine the further growth of services. The degree of subsidy would depend upon consensus. If, say, two-thirds agree and it is constitutionally feasible, then the start-up cost for a new facility should be taken out of taxes; while if half consent, then the community could help promote the new activity through extension of credit or other devices. Promotion of self-organization and cooperation builds up a variety of leaders in the community, who can get together to manage the next stages in its development and maturation. It also reduces the detail required in the planning, since the planting of trees and shrubs, for example, could be undertaken by the residents with the help of horticultural and landscape consultants, the parking of intermediate transport and many similar features could also be planned.

Most new communities are made up of two kinds of people: the members and clients of bureaucracies, firms and agencies, who know they will be assigned to the new site; and the opportunistic members of the urban poor, who do most of the maintenance and service work together with surplus labor force from the countryside, many of whom will not stay. Dissatisfactions appear soonest among the educated people, and later their children. When complaints are voiced, and formal protests produced, portions of the less educated population will find themselves in agreement. This normal process can interfere with the efficiency of the agencies (fig. 6.8).

In Korea, for example, the extraordinary value placed upon education and the reputation of schools suggests that the institutionally employed population would focus their complaint upon the schools, joined by the ambitious families from among the poor. This means that educational planning in particular must be designed to produce satisfaction on the part of parents.

One approach that suggests itself is to tap the opinions of educators and the elite about which specific secondary schools offer the best preparation for the university. A few special elementary schools should be added to the list. In addition, a Ministry of Education could review the features of curriculum and selection of teachers in schools that would provide better preparation for the postindustrial period. Both the public and private institutions would be asked to undergo fission by setting up a twin school in the newly established community with a large share of the original faculty. The reputation of the school's faculty and alumni would help to establish it. The building itself should be designed in conjunction with the teachers and administrators, for then should some aspects of it fail, they would have themselves to blame and not the government, as well as the incentive to overcome the difficulty.

This example is intended to illustrate the style of planning that seems to be required, without specifying the final solution. Recent

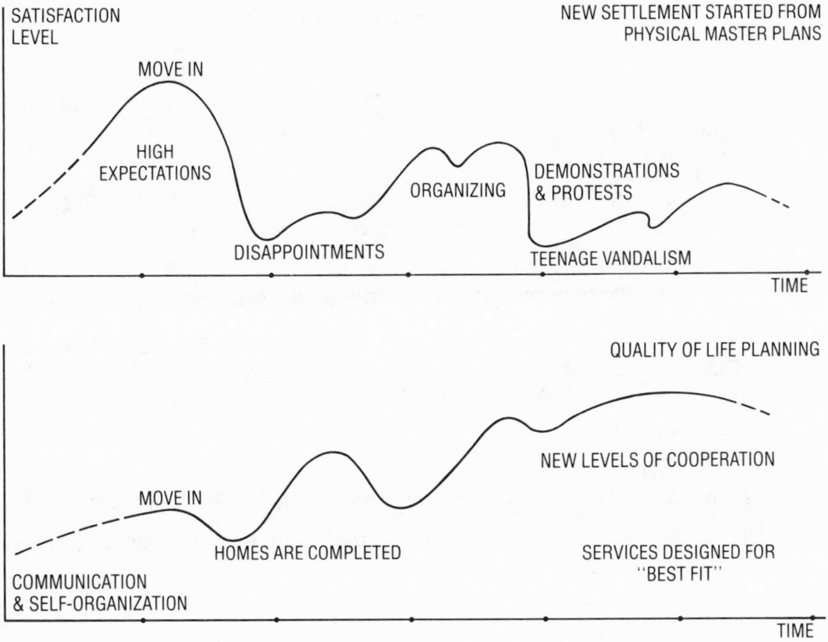

Fig. 6.8. Expectations regarding alternative approaches to planning. Aiming to maintain levels of satisfaction adds to the competitive capacity of new communities. A reduced amount of central planning allows earlier start. Subsidies for cooperation and self-organization will uncover a cadre of local leaders, and a capacity to solve mutual problems. The resulting social and cultural services should overcome the kinds of deficiencies that generate teenage vandalism, new town blues, similar conditions arising from constrained social networks, and feelings of isolation.

American experience (Smith 1978), reinforced by Indian experience (Olivola 1979) suggests that the architect capable of making alternative sketches in the presence of a group of interested people is most likely to approximate a design that will be satisfactory to its members. Equivalent skills are needed in education and transport consultations.

The overall process implies that the physical input of materials provides a setting for the development of human resources, while the water and energy sustain the community, and the transport and communications services allow the urban system to yield satisfactions. The organizations - public, private, and voluntary - enhance the quality, the goodness of fit. The effective resource-conserving community must accomplish all of these tasks.

REFERENCES

Campbell, Angus et al. 1975 The Quality of Human Life. Institute of Social Research, University of Michigan, Ann Arbor. New York: Twentieth Century Fund.

Garrison, William et al. 1977. Series of reports from the Program of Interdisciplinary Studies, University of California, Berkeley.

Meier, Richard L. 1974. Planning for an Urban World - Design of Resource-Conserving Cities. Cambridge: MIT Press.

Meier, Berman, Dowall et al. March 1978. Urbanism and Energy in Developing Regions. Center for Planning and Development Research, University of California, Berkeley.

Olivola, Kenneth. 1979. M. Arch. Thesis, University of California, Berkeley.

Rowe, W.D. 1977. An Anatomy of Risk. New York: Interscience-Wiley.

Smith, Richard. 1978. Ph.D. Dissertation in Architecture. University of California, Berkeley.

7 New Directions for Economic and Social Growth: The Ecology of Change

W.H.C. Simmonds

The socio-economic impact of successful bioresource development is likely to prove profound. We have lived through a period characterized by one major goal - economic growth - fueled increasingly by one source or energy - petroleum hydrocarbons - based on two major emphases - sameness and efficiency - with materialism as king and consumers as his loyal subjects! A new world based on bioresource development is likely to prove very different: multiple goals in place of one goal; utilization of several sources of energy rather than reliance on one; acceptance of heterogeneity as normal rather than a forced homogeneity; efficiency balanced against equity and survival; a goal of greater overall well-being rather than just more money or possessions. In other words, we will have enlarged our point of view and probabilistic points of view. Hence, this paper is subtitled The Ecology of Change to underscore a widening of viewpoint even in regard to change itself.

ORGANIZING PRINCIPLES

In dealing with complex problems, it is helpful to identify certain organizing principles to penetrate and sort out complexity. The three basic organizing principles and their main effects are shown in table 7.1.

In this context, wealth does not mean just money, but also how each society uses that money, thereby including the influence of culture.

The importance of bioresource development lies in its ability to help ensure survival, and through the social consequences of bioresource technologies for its effects on equity. Efficiency, in its technical and economic sense, clearly continues to be desirable, but placed in balance with equity and survival.

Assuming that successful bioresource development will extend

Table 7.1. Three Basic Organizing Principles and Their Effects

Organizing Principle	Main Effect
Efficiency	Generation of wealth
Equity	Distribution of wealth
Survival	Continuation of wealth

ecological viewpoints, and that ecological viewpoints will influence the three organizing principles described above, we can now examine some of the ramifications of this influence.

THE ECOLOGY OF PEOPLE

In the past, it was sufficient to describe a society in quantitative terms, such as the rate of growth of its population, its age and sex distribution, and its employment statistics. Today and tomorrow such descriptions are requiring more and more qualifications. Part of the world is aging, most is growing younger. Cohort sizes vary considerably from country to country, but not uniformly. These variations are directly linked to questions of and changes in work and employment, with educational background, ethnicity, and culture close behind. Thus, human beings are becoming increasingly differentiated into groups in much the same way that the animal kingdom is divided into genera and species. To the extent that this occurs, an ecological viewpoint of people becomes increasingly relevant.

HOLISTIC ECONOMICS

Similar changes are occurring in economics. The old approach with its emphasis on efficiency, production and consumption, and economic growth as the major goal no longer seems able to cover the problems of today. The reason is also clear; yesterday's problems were those of know-how, how to achieve economic growth. Today and tomorrow's problems are those of know-why, one system level higher (see fig. 7.1). Why grow? What kind of growth? Why consume energy? How much

SYSTEM LEVEL	HUMAN LEVEL	TYPE OF QUESTIONS	METHOD OF APPROACH	TYPE OF ECONOMICS	FUTURES METHODOLOGIES
LEVEL I Planetary	Evolutionary	Know where-to	Intuitive, Insightful	Planetary worldwide economics ↕	↓
LEVEL II National	Subjective	Know why	Synthesis-holistic, interactive, option-increasing, synthesizing, safe-fail, qualitative: whole $> \sum$ parts	Holistic economics ←---→ ↓ Flow-economics	New futures methodologies ↑ Means-ends chains ↓
LEVEL III Institutional, organizational	Objective	Know how	Analysis - linear, sequential causal, rational reductionist, fail-safe, quantitative: whole $= \sum$ parts	Equilibrium-neoclassical economics ⇄	Current futures methodologies

Fig. 7.1. Relationship between type of economics and nature of questions to be answered.

energy per capita? etc. Such questions cannot be answered except in terms which include the economic consequences of society's noneconomic assumptions and beliefs. The branch of economics which deals with this situation is called holistic or institutional economics, and dates from Adam Smith through Thorstein Veblen to Gunnar Myrdal and J.K. Galbraith today. What is now required is a development of the mathematics of the dynamic economics shown in figure 7.2.

Eco-System

Inputs Net waste

Economy

	Year 1	Year 2
	transactions	
Stocks:	Producers' $goods_1$	Producers' $goods_2$
	Consumers' $goods_1$	Consumers' $goods_2$
	Human $beings_1$	Human $beings_2$

Fig. 7.2. Basic flow-economics

Source: Herman Daly's "Steady-State Economics," 1977.

Daly's approach sets out clearly the relationship of the economy to the ecosystem and is, thus, the kind necessary for evaluating the bioresource alternative and its ability to satisfy basic human needs as well as wants. It also accommodates Georgescu-Roegen's emphasis on the second law of thermodynamics and the need for energy to give rise to economic activity. Only a fraction of the primary energy required for living and for production can be usefully used; the balance always appears as waste heat. Economic growth thus entails the degradation of energy and this cannot be counted as part of growth as it is currently represented in GNP (gross national product). A dynamic economics thus requires the costs of growth arising from short-term production efficiency to be traded off against long-term survival and the day-to-day equity required to make such tradeoffs acceptable.

Equilibrium economics deals with the conditions for equilibriums, for which it is not necessary to know what goes on in the black box. The approach shown in figure 7.2 is dynamic, nonequilibrium, and must therefore take into account and explain the mechanisms of change explicitly. Can we proceed today without such an extension in economic theory, and can such a theory not be ecologic in its viewpoint?

THE NEW ECOLOGICAL PERSPECTIVE

Table 7.2 summarizes C.S. Holling's views of the new ecological perspective:

Table 7.2. The New Ecological Perspective

Resilience	vs.	Stability
Variability	vs.	Uniformity
Multiple objectives	vs.	Single objective
Spatial heterogeneity	vs.	Spatial homogeneity

The environmental and the social elements must be approached integrally with the technical, the economic, and the financial aspects of any investment, project, program, or policy, and this can only be done by applying the ecological principles of resilience and multiple objectives.

There are profound implications for management in this restatement of organizational objectives (Emery and Trist 1975).

For the first time, these principles may open the way for nontraumatic institutional change. Single-objective institutions automatically resist change as a threat to their continuing existence; genuinely multiple-objective institutions can adapt by shifting relative priorities.

There appear to be significant implications here for managing the introduction of bioresource development.

The above remarks clearly fit into and reinforce Maurice Strong's coinage of the term eco-development at Stockholm in 1972.

THE ECOLOGY OF KNOWLEDGE

Professor Jerzy Wojciechowski has presented the case for an ecology of knowledge, which arises logically for any extension of ecological thinking beyond ecology itself.

We live in a time of rapidly expanding knowledge, for which we need still more knowledge simply to understand the new knowledge. This is an unstable situation. We must, therefore, know more about knowledge itself, but we are unlikely to be successful in this endeavor if we approach it in the Baconian manner of man over nature. We seem far more likely to achieve greater insights if we adopt the ecological approach - man and nature as complementary parts of a bigger whole. This requires us to enlarge our frame of reference (see Holling above) and transcend previous beliefs and limitations in our thinking. In the writer's terminology, it means accepting Eric Jantsch's challenge to begin to think at the next higher or world level, in terms of the planet as a whole. Only then can we begin to transcend our past limits of knowledge as a private source of gain or national source of power, and create the larger framework necessary for the resolution of problems at the world level. Concurrent with this, we can add John Platt's proposal for an ecological ethics.

These developments should in a very real way be supportive of the bioresource approach to world problems.

CONDITIONS OF CHANGE

Acceptance of an ecological view of change - an ecology of change - becomes virtually automatic once problems are posed in these terms. We gain a viewpoint within which to accommodate for example, Aurelio Peccei's six missions for mankind, the McHales' work on basic human needs, the Aspen studies on interdependence, the eco-development self-reliance movements, and the numerous studies on energy and conservation. But at the same time, the mechanisms of change begin to assert their importance in the scheme of things, for example, the value of cultural diversity or the need for minimum disturbance, in addition to the new holistic economics.

CULTURAL DIVERSITY

Sir Geoffrey Vickers has convincingly outlined the need for diversity of culture as just as pressing as that for biological/genetic diversity. We do not know the best cultural form or forms for the future; we do know that current forms are less than adequate. Hence, we should keep our options open, no matter what.

Bioresource development is unlikely to succeed unless it is actively integrated into the cultures of its proponents.

MINIMUM DISTURBANCE CHANGE

The writer has posited the conditions for maximizing confidence during prolonged techno-economic changes, such as those occurring in energy or food. The conditions for minimum disturbance change can be established; the further we depart from them, the more difficult change becomes. The future in a know-why type world requires a light governmental touch since the outcomes are not known now nor are they knowable in advance; it also requires an active Gregory Bateson two-way learning process between different sectors of society and the general public to allow people to adjust, faster or slower as occasion demands.

Bioresource development stands to gain to the extent that active learning takes place in a society, and the upsets of change can be minimized.

CONCLUSIONS

We are now reaching the point where the universality of the ecological point of view can be explicitly recognized and acted upon. Bioresource development, which constitutes a major ingredient in this recognition, will advance in a major way as the ecology of change is in turn accepted.

REFERENCES

Bateson, Gregory. 1972. Steps to an Ecology of Mind. N.Y.: Ballantine.

Cleveland, Harlan and Wilson, T.W. 1978. Humangrowth, Aspen Inst. for Humanistic Studies.

Daly, Herman E. 1977. Steady-State Economics. W.H. Freeman, San Francisco: Common Misunderstandings Concerning a Steady-State

Economy. Paper presented to the World Council of Churches, June 5-10, 1978. Zurich.

Emery, F.E. and Trist, E.L. 1975. Towards a Social Ecology. N.Y.: Plenum.

Georgescu-Roegen, N. 1971. The Entropy Law and the Economic Process. Cambridge: Harvard Univ. Press.

Gruchy, A.G. 1947. Modern Economic Thought: The American Contribution. Augustus M. Kelley reprint 1967. Contemporary Economic Thought - The Contribution of Neo-Institutional Economics.1972. N.Y.: Macmillan. (History of holistic/institutional economics.)

Harman, Willis. 1976. An Incomplete Guide to the Future. San Francisco: S.F. Book Co. (The ecological ethic.)

Holling, C.S. et al. 1978. Adaptive Environmental Assessment and Management. N.Y.: John Wiley.

Jantsch, E. and Waddington, C.D., eds. 1976. Evolution and Consciousness. Reading, Mass.: Addison-Wesley.

Jeanneret, C. and Fletcher, H.F. Reports on Eco-Development Workshops organized by the Canadian International Development Agency and Environment Canada, with papers by Johan Galtung, Ignacy Sachs, Michel Chevalier and Tom Burns, George Francis, Tibor Mende.

Kapp, K.W. 1976. The Nature and Significance of Institutional Economics. Kyklos, Vol. 29-1976-Fasc. 2, 209-232.

McHale, J. and McHale, M.C. 1975. Human Requirements, Supply Levels and Outer Bounds. Center for Integrative Studies. and Basic Human Needs: A Framework for Action. 1978. Transaction Press.

Ophuls, W. 1977. The Politics of the Sustainable Society, in Pirages, D.C., ed., The Sustainable Society. N.Y.: Praeger. (Ecological scarcity.)

Page, Talbot. 1977. Conservation and Economic Efficiency. Resources for the Future. Baltimore: Johns Hopkins.

Peccei, Aurelio. 1977. The Human Quality. N.Y.: Pergamon.

Platt, John. 1974. World Transformation: Changes in Belief Systems. The Futurist, 8, #3, June, 1974, pp. 124-5. (Ecological ethics.)

Simmonds, W.H.C. 1978. Minimum Disturbance Social Change. Futures Canada, 2, #3 6-9; and Flow-Economics: A Statement. Sept., 1978. National Research Council of Canada, Ottawa.

Vickers, Sir Geoffrey. The Future of Culture, in Linstone, H. and Simmonds, W.H.C., 1977. Futures Research, New Directions. Reading, Mass.: Addison Wesley. Value Systems and Social Process.

1968. London: Pelican. (Ecology of ideas, science of human ecology.); Equality of responsibility: cultural conditions for western survival. 1979. Futures, Feb., pp. 16-31.

Wojciechowski, J.A., 1975. The Ecology of Knowledge, in Science and Society, Past, Present and Future, Steneck, N.H., ed., Ann Arbor: The Univ. of Michigan Press.

8 The Economic Conditions for Success in Bioenergy Technology

Malcolm Slesser

There are very few solar energy systems, whether physical or biological, that are economic at today's prices. Yet there are an enormous number of propositions of one kind and another. Very often the argument in their favor goes like this: some particular solar energy source may not be economic today, but it certainly will be by the time oil and gas and other fossil fuels have risen in price. This paper seeks to show that such an argument is incorrect, and that for solar energy technologies to succeed we need two other considerations.

The energy price rise argument is also often applied to nuclear energy, to the exploitation of tar sands and oil shales. But it fails to take account of the insidious nature of the role of energy in the economy. In fact, we must cost these new energy sources not against existing energy sources, but through them. This is because, though the energy cost in the manufacture of industrial goods averages about 6-8 percent of total costs, it has a gearing effect so that system costs enter the rough energy costs. The evidence for this is apparent in the prices of goods and services following the steep change in oil price in 1973 (1). Moreover, the rate of change of prices is found to be related to the energy intensity of the good or service provided. Energy intensive commodities like electricity, fertilizer, or cement rise rapidly in cost, while lower energy intensive services, such as hospital beds or cigarettes, rise more slowly.

This perception of the role energy plays in prices is by no means universally accepted. Indeed, the first economist to acknowledge it was probably Brookes (2) in a very recent paper, in which he refers to it as the energy price fallacy. It has been identified in earlier analysis texts (1,3). Using energy analysis techniques, it is comparatively simple to demonstrate the strong causal relationship between energy content and price. For example, there is a fascinating study by Edwards and Phillips (4) showing that one could virtually predict the price of metals in a London metal exchange by knowing the free energy required to reduce their ores to metal. It explains why, for example, Colorado oil shale remains unviable with the price of traditional ground-oil at $14 the barrel, even though the U.S. Petroleum Council was predicting that it would have become economic if and when traditional ground oil rose to $6 the barrel. The price forecast for viability of Colorado shales has now risen to something like $22. It seems that within the Department of Energy in Washington there is now some dismay at the inability of traditional economic methods to forecast future energy prices.

All this, if correct, suggests that it is foolish for us to hope for viability in solar energy systems, whether physical or biomass, in terms of the rising price of fossil or traditional energy sources. However, this is where the first condition mentioned in the opening paragraph plays its part. When (and if) we get to a stage in which solar energy dominates the energy supply market, we shall begin costing solar energy through solar energy - then we can begin to think in terms of solar breeders (5). Now that situation is a very long way off, our immediate concern should be to consider how we can penetrate the energy market that exists today with solar energy sources at the very low level to a significant penetration level some time in the next thirty years. Expressed bluntly, our solar energy systems must simply become technologically more effective than they are at present, and this must be the primary objective.

SYSTEMS ANALYSIS IN TERMS OF NON-RENEWABLE RESOURCE

The world has only two nonrenewable resources: time and negentropy. Negentropy can be expressed somewhat inaccurately through the surrogate word energy. All other resources remain unconsumed. Thus, the lump of iron ore which is turned into iron and then into a washing machine ends up as scrap iron or rusting metal. There are as many molecules of iron at the end of that process as at the beginning. This suggests that our resource situation should be looked at in terms of how best to use these two nonrenewable elements. Economists have always recognized the unique property of time and have introduced the concept of discounting and net present value.

To demonstrate that a positive net present value is not a sufficient condition of economic viability: an energy plantation might be set up requiring a capital of $1 million and producing 10,000 t per year of wood. By anaerobic digestion this is then converted to methane, which is sold on the market. The annual energy output of the system will be about 2×10^5 GJ/year in the form of methane. Since these figures apply to 1974, the 1974 value for natural gas should be taken, which was about $1.7 per GJ. The financial value of the system was therefore $3.4x10^5/year. Estimated inputs were $2.4x10^5, which for a plant life of twenty years would give an internal rate of return of 7 percent investment, which is not very attractive (6). If, however, there is a

Table 8.1. Economic Costs of Photobiological Fuels and Prices of Fossil Fuels (1975 figs.)

Fuel	Raw material	Process	Saleable by-products As Fuel	Saleable by-products Other	Cost ($/t)	Cost ($/GJ)	Net Energy (GJ/ha)
Alcohol	Cassava tops & tubers	Enzyme hydrolysis, Batch fermentation	-	Fiber (animan feed); fusel oils	250	8.4	17
Alcohol	*Eucalyptus*	Acid Hydrolysis, Batch fermentation	-	-	400	13.4	-180
Alcohol	*Eycalyptus*	Enzyme Hydrolysis, Batch fermentation	-	-	600	20.1	negligible
Methane	Cereal straw	Anaerobic digestion	-	Biomass slurry	235	4.2	34
Methane	*Eycalyptus*	Anaerobic digestion	-	Biomass slurry	310	5.5	34
Pyrolytic oil	Cereal straw	Flash pyrolysis	Char	-	75	3.3	52
Pyrolytic oil	*Eucalyptus*	Flash pyrolysis	Char	-	100	4.3	52
Alcohol		Non-biological Chemical synthesis	-	-	275	9.3	?

regular rise in the price of natural gas, say 5 percent a year, then the viability improves dramatically. Under these circumstances the rate of return rises to 13 percent (7); high enough, one might hope, to justify going ahead. There are two problems, however. The first is complete inability to forecast energy prices. The second is that costs will rise as energy prices rise.

Let us know look at it from a net energy point of view, i.e., by assessing the energy content of the output minus the energy content of the input. One study has shown that from an energy input of 30 GJ/ha, 64 GH/ha of methane could be produced, that is, a net energy of 34 GJ/ha. In other words, the system will produce from one hectare of land 34 GJ, after taking into account all energy needed, including capital equipment. In the year of the study the net energy was worth 34x1.7 = $58. Can land be rented for $58/ha? That is the minimum breakeven figure. We see that what is important is not system energy output, but net output.

RUNNING THE NATIONAL SYSTEM ON BIOENERGY RESOURCE

In addition to the questions of land value, it is useful to consider the overall potential of solar energy for satisfying energy needs. We do this by considering the net energy productivity per hectare, and the national energy density (useful energy)/ha of national territory. Table 8.2 illustrates the situation with some approximate numbers for three countries. The 30 GJ/ha column is the sort of net energy productivity of many bioenergy processes for producing liquid and gaseous fuels, the 65 GJ/ha for more advanced systems and the 100 GJ/ha for biomass and physical solar energy systems.

Table 8.2. Land Area Needed for Energy Autonomy in Rhodesia, Austria, and Belgium

	Land area km^2	1973 estimated useful energy use in GJ	1973 energy density GJ/ha	% of land area needed for energy autonomy given systems of net energy		
				30 GJ/ha	65 GJ/ha	100 GJ/ha
Rhodesia	375,000	10×10^7	2.6	8.7%	4%	2.4%
Austria	81,800	32×10^7	38.5	130.0%	60%	36.0%
Belgium	29,400	110×10^7	38.0	1260.0%	580%	350.0%

REFERENCES

(1) Slesser, M. 1978. *Energy in the Economy*. London and New York: Macmillan.

(2) Brookes, L.G. 1978. The energy price fallacy, *Energy Policy*, June 1978, pp. 94-106.

(3) Int. Inst. for Applied Systems Analysis. 1978. *Energy Analysis: Uses and limits*. Research Memorandum. Laxenburg, Austria.

(4) Edwards, D.P. and Phillips, W.G. 1967. *Metal prices as functions of ore grade*. p. 167. Resource Policy *1*.

(5) Hounam, I. and Slesser, M. 1976. Solar Energy Breeders. *Nature* (262), July 1976, pp. 244-245.

(6) The net present value (NPV) of an activity, discounted at the rate I percent, is given by

$$\text{NPV} = \text{Initial capital} - \left| \begin{matrix} \text{annual} \\ \text{income} \\ \text{or} \\ \text{saving} \end{matrix} \right| \left\{ \frac{(1 + I)^n}{I(1 + I)^n} \right\}$$

(7) For the case where a cost factor (e.g., energy) rises monotonically as R percent per annum,

$$\text{NPV} = \text{Initial capital} - \left| \begin{matrix} \text{initial} \\ \text{annual} \\ \text{income} \\ \text{or} \\ \text{saving} \end{matrix} \right| \left\{ \left(\frac{1 + R}{1 - R} \right) \left| 1 - \frac{1 + R^n}{1 + I} \right| \right\}$$

9 Energy for Rural Development in Semiarid Areas of Northeastern Brazil*

Armand F. Pereira
Seymour Warkov

An international literature on alternative energy sources of substantial proportions has emerged in response to the 1973 energy crisis. Our contribution to this literature is a paper reporting the prospects for alternative energy systems, especially solar and biomass, and the interrelationship of energy and rural development in the semi-arid areas of North-East Brazil. The data are derived from exploratory field work (primarily in the State of Paraiba), interviews with energy specialists and government officials, technical reports, and other published sources of information. The approach is interdisciplinary and raises questions about economic and social costs and benefits.

Nonconventional energy sources for Brazil firstly are nuclear power, shale oil, and direct conversion of biomass to alcohol, and secondly, such indirect sources of solar energy as wind, and biomass for production of electricity. The first 20 kilowatt complex of wind powered turbines has already been installed, and plans have been made for a second unit, both under the direction of state enterprise with the technical cooperation of Centro Aeroespacial of Sao Jose dos Campos, S.P. (CTA). Also, a 55 kilowatt experimental project has been developed in Cacoes, Bahia, generating electricity based on an integrated biomass system, and producing alcohol to replace gasoline. Gas and fertilizer are by-products of this biomass conversion system.

Thirdly, a group of energy sources includes microhydroelectric plants, and the utilization of waves and tidal power. In both cases, Eletrobras is already conducting experiments at a pilot level. (1) Direct application of solar energy has received less consideration despite the

---

* The original, full length version of this paper was published as "Energy for Development in Semi-Arid Areas of Northeastern Brazil," Intersciencia 4, no. 5 (Sept.-Oct. 1979): 272-281.

emphasis given to its potential in the Second National Development Plan (II PND). (2)

ENERGY AND RURAL DEVELOPMENT

It was not until the quadrupling of world petroleum prices in 1973 that lesser developed countries, such as Brazil, started to pay attention to the energy factor in formulating strategies for rural development. The links between wood burning, deforestation, irrigation, soil fertilization, migration, and rural development are now recognized in government planning.

Fire wood today remains the major energy source for Brazil's agricultural sector (see table 9.1). However, only in recent years has the Forestry Development Institute (IBDF) devoted special attention to reforestation in the context of ecology, energy, and rural development. (3) When the Brazilian Reforestation policy was first launched in 1966, it was designed solely to assist the National Program of Paper and Cellulose. (4) "Poor forest management meant that by 1975 the national forest had been reduced to 41.3 percent of their original area and that the Amazonic region had lost 24 percent of its total forest reserves." (5)

Some forms of household energy consumption are well fitted to reforestation programs, (6) e.g., the use of solar cookers and methane in semiarid areas. Considerable emphasis is presently being given to gas via biomass, but not in ways that benefit low income producers. The research that is being conducted in universities and research institutes is still in an early stage, and has very little emphasis on rural applications. Eletrobras is concerned with biomass, but its prime focus is on production of electricity.

From a technical point of view, solar cookers are suitable for those in semiarid areas who currently use fire wood. However, cultural and economic factors work against their acceptance. (7) According to the technicians at the Solar Energy Lab of the University of Paraiba, they could be produced cheaply (US$ 17-34), although they would never be as economically attractive as wood, which is mostly free.

The National Department of Public Works Against Droughts estimates that the average cost of irrigating one hectare a year by conventional methods now in use averages Cr$ 20,000/hectare/year - about twice the figures for Morocco and Australia. (8) However, many of the canals and reservoirs are already unusable for agricultural purposes, due to salinization of the water and soils, (9) and the fuel which runs their pumps, petroleum or electricity, faces unanticipated rises in costs. There are opportunities here for examining possible use of wind power and solar energy for both pumping and electricity generation.

About 60 percent of fertilizers used in Brazil are imported (see table 9.2), and the absolute figures continue to rise. Domestically produced fertilizers, produced mostly by multinationals in the urban areas, use

Table 9.1. Energy Consumption in Agribusiness Activities - Brazil and Paraiba (State), 1970

	Total Value (million $crs.)		Quantity		Proportion of Total Value used by: Proprietors (%)		renters/occupants/ partners (%)	
	Brazil	Paraiba	Brazil	Paraiba	Brazil	Paraiba	Brazil	Paraiba
Firewood	382	9	96 mil. m^3	2.38 mil. m^3	71	69	29	31
Gasoline	222	1.2	453 mil. liters	2.5 mil. liters	89	68	11	32
Diesel Oil	201	1.5	474 mil. liters	3.2 mil. liters	80	86	20	14
Kerosene	111	3.5	192 mil. liters	6.5 mil. liters	65	68	35	32
Electricity	89	0.5	440 mil. KWH	2 mil. KWH	93	92	7	8
Liquified Gas	22	0.2	27,000 tons	2 tons	82	75	18	25
Coal	9	0.5	89,000 tons	6,000 tons	55	83	45	17
Bagasse	2	0.05	175,000 tons	6,000 tons	77	66	23	34

Source: Censo Agropecuario de 1970 (dados eleborados).

Table 9.2. Imports and National Production of Fertilizers, Brazil, 1970 - 1977 (in thousands of tons of nutrients)

YEAR	N		P_2O_5		K_2O
	NATIONAL	IMPORTED	NATIONAL	IMPORTED	IMPORTED
1970	20	255	169	226	306
1971	69	222	243	242	347
1972	88	274	289	432	361
1973	114	293	332	615	623
1974	150	185	387	515	538
1975	160	249	545	502	587
1976	201	276	846	354	696
1977*	220	418	1,070	329	783

*SUPLAN estimate.
Source: SIACESP and IEA.

capital intensive technologies, and show prices up to 50 percent higher than their imported counterparts. (10)

The capital intensive technologies that manufacture fertilizers and other agricultural products (e.g., insecticides, pesticides, etc.) use petroleum or coal as the basic raw material. The poorer the agricultural producers the less capable they are of purchasing fertilizers. The Northeast (the poorest region in terms of per capita) has a fertilizer consumption rate six and one-half times lower than that of the Rio/Sao Paulo region (see table 9.3).

There are opportunities here for the production of fertilizers in situ through relatively simple and labor intensive bioconversion technologies based on the fermentation of anaerobic materials or agricultural residues. Integrated systems based on manioc, sugar cane, or other products could yield alcohol, which in turn could produce electricity, gas, and fertilizer. Brazil already has the technical infrastructure for the development of such alternatives, and it might even learn from the Indian example, in which the government initiated a domestic plan in

Table 9.3. Brazil and Region: Real Fertilizer Consumption Estimates - 1977

REGION	KG/HA			
	N	P_2O_5	K_2O	TOTAL
North	11.3	10.9	11.1	33.3
Northeast	4.9	5.3	5.3	15.5
Southeast	21.2	46.2	29.7	97.1
South	10.8	37.3	17.5	65.0
Center-West	6.3	17.6	10.3	34.2
BRAZIL	11.1	28.8	16.3	56.2

Source: Sistema Nacional de Planejamento Agricola.

1976 to produce 230,000 tons of nitrogen per year. The alternatives were either to build a huge capital intensive factory in a large city, or to develop small bioconversion production centers in 26,150 villages. The urban option would create 5,000 jobs, and would entail additional costs of shipping and adapting the fertilizer for local use. The rural option would create up to 130,750 jobs in rural areas through local production, eliminate transportation costs, and significantly reduce costs associated with commercialization. Furthermore, the local centers could start production rapidly. (11)

THE SEMIARID AREAS OF NORTHEASTERN BRAZIL

Northeast Brazil is one of five national regions. Its inhabitants comprise 30 percent of the country's population, some 35 million people with a per capita income about one-half the national average. The rural Northeast, furthermore, has a per capita income only about one-quarter the national average. Almost 70 percent of the agricultural producers live and work in land units of less than 10 hectares, and nearly 90 percent in units under 50 hectares (see table 9.4). (12) The numbers of small producers are growing and so are their problems. (13)

The semiarid areas are situated in the interior of the Northeastern

Table 9.4. Land Distribution by Groups of Area - Brazil and Paraiba, 1970

Size of Land Units	% of total number of establishments		% of total area of proprietors		% of total area of non-proprietors	
	Br.	Pb.	Br.	Pb.	Br.	Pb.
Less than 1	9	6	25	31	75	69
1-<2	10	17	32	37	68	63
2-<5	18	29	47	57	53	43
5-<10	14	16	62	75	38	25
Less than 10	51	68	53	64	47	36
10-<20	15.5	12	77	81	23	19
20-<50	16.5	10	84	87	16	13
50-<100	7	4	85	89	15	11
10 to less than 100	39	27	83	87	17	13
100 to less than 1,000	8	4	83	90	17	10
1,000 to less than 10,000	0.7	0.3	90	94	10	6
Above 10,000	1.3	0.7	-	-	-	-
Total	100	100				

Source: Elaborated from the Censo Agropecuario de 1970.

region. They cover 52 percent of the area, and hold 42 percent of the regional population. Nearly 70 percent of this population is considered rural, although even those living in the towns are largely rural in their style of living. Official publications characterize this drought area as follows:

- Predominance of small land units, which tend to be the poorest lands.
- Scarcity of surface water.
- Predominance of subsistance agriculture.
- Predominance of underdeveloped rudimentary technologies.
- Predominance of family-intensive labor with little incentive for population control.
- Extremely low capital formation.
- Minimal access to institutional credit.
- Minimal access to markets because of isolation and deficiencies in transportation.
- Little contact with social change agents at public and private institutional levels.
- Great sociocultural resistance to change in general, e.g., through institutional programs of technical assistance; production surpluses are usually sold to merchants rather than to cooperatives.
- Little propensity to invest because of fear and little or no savings.
- Little use of anaerobic material; general scarcity of animal traction in agricultural activities.
- Great reliance on fire wood and kerosene.
- Great propensity to migrate first to the nearest urbanized centers within the region, then primarily to the largest coastal cities.

The cyclical droughts have historically been a key obstacle to the development of these extensive areas. For example, during the drought of 1970 (not the latest) the production of beans and corn decreased by 78 percent and 68 percent respectively in one year, while cotton and manioc - the two other most important crops of the subregion - decreased by 87 percent and 61 percent from 1969 levels. (14)

The Northern part of the drought area has only 6 percent of its soil with good agricultural characteristics; 22 percent with moderate restrictions, and the remaining 72 percent with strong restrictions or unsuitable. (15) The geological character of the soils and climatic conditions suggest two basic strategies for coping with drought. The first calls for the introduction of cultures that do not need much water. (16,17) The other strategy emphasizes water for irrigation.

However, the technological means to make this work are insufficient, in part because of inadequacies in land tenure, transportation, commercialization, minimum prices, and credit, all of which indirectly affect the success of irrigation projects.

CURRENT DEVELOPMENT PROJECTS IN THE SUBREGION

There are at present several programs and projects aimed at achieving improved rural development. They include programs to:

- Create conditions which deter urban-bound migration.
- Deal with land redistribution, foster agricultural development, and stimulate a rational land-use policy.
- Aid in the development of cooperatives.

In none of these programs is energy considered a key factor, which is a fair indication of how little public policy and planning emphasis is placed on energy. Our interviews with officials showed that any consideration that is given to energy is limited to conventional rural electrification, and no consideration has been given to other alternatives. The ecological, social, and economic condition in parts of this area, however, are such that a comparative analysis of alternate energy sources and applications would be useful and appropriate.

ENERGY AND WATER

Many of the semiarid areas have underground water of variable quality. In some, the water is good enough for irrigation and even domestic consumption, although it is mostly brackish and requires upgrading via distillation. (18)

Notwithstanding the paucity of data on the costs of solar and wind powered pumping schemes, a preliminary analysis of costs and benefits of various alternatives should take into account the following:

1. Oil-operated pumps require:
   (a) scarce high cost resources;
   (b) transportation of such fuels to field sites; and
   (c) fairly sophisticated machinery requiring periodic expert maintenance.
2. Oil-operated pumps are more expensive and less efficient than electrical pumping.

3. While oil-operated pumps are portable, this feature may not be very important due to the more or less fixed location of underground water deposits.
4. Electric pumps are obviously suitable only in places where there is electricity, a crucial obstacle in many areas.
5. Wind mills have the advantage of:
   (a) technical simplicity;
   (b) cost-free energy readily available in the North-East;
   (c) virtually maintenance-free operation; and
   (d) grain-grinding and electricity generating capability.
6. Wind mills have very limited portability.
7. Solar pumps
   (a) use cost-free energy: the North east is a zone of high insolation;
   (b) are operationally simple and practically maintenance-free; and
   (c) can be eventually used in the generation of electricity.

A simple technology for distilling water in a way that is appropriate to the semiarid areas in the North east has been developed by the Solar Energy Laboratory of the University of Paraiba. (19) The distilling units are parallel pipe-shaped water reservoirs made of cement or galvanized metal with triangular-shaped vaporization/condensation zones made of glass or plastic. The salty, brackish water enters the distillers through a locally developed sand filter and fills the parallel pipe-shaped reservoir. The bottom of the reservoir is covered with a black plastic material and granite pebbles. (20) The distiller can produce about five liters/m^2/day, with a projected cost of Cr$ 1.54 per 18 liters. (21) This local cost estimate is from 2.9 to 5.8 times higher than costs in the United States, which vary from US $3 to US $6 per 1,000 gallons. (22) Domestically produced glass is more expensive in Brazil, and there is an absence of a resistant plastic. If such a product were commercially available, it "could reduce the distillation cost by 30-40 percent." (23)

Institutional support could play an important role in encouraging the production and use of solar distillers. The first such incentive was a law passed in July 1978 exempting all solar heating materials from the Tax on Industrialized Goods.

The portable units of 1 m^2-base currently under development use plastic imported via a technical exchange program with a Canadian university. These simple units weigh 40 kilograms and are designed for rural domestic consumption. Using Brazilian glass rather than the preferred but normally unavailable plastic, the cost per unit could be about Cr$ 700 (US$ 37). Such a solar still, combined with solar or wind pumping, would improve the agronomic and health levels of semiarid areas, contribute to drought resistance, and possibly enhance the economic status of relatively poor users.

The social and economic benefits need further study through a micro approach aimed at:

(a) calculating the economic benefits of portable versus stationary units;

(b) assessing their benefits for different categories of producers, proprietors and nonproprietors (renters, partners, and legal occupants);

(c) estimating the social and economic effects of increased water for specific areas; and

(d) evaluating their possible implications for the organization of agroindustrial and other institutional relationships.

ELECTRICITY

Despite the emphasis on rural electrification in regional development programs, some areas in the semiarid sub-region (especially those located at a distance from the major towns) stand very little chance of acquiring electricity in the short run. In 1974, only 2.2 percent of the rural population of the Northeast consumed electricity. (24) For small, relatively isolated communities at a distance from electric distribution lines, it is increasingly necessary to examine alternatives to conventional electrical expansion, such as microhydroelectric plants, windpower, solar and bioconversion systems. About 45 percent of the Northeast is considered urban, but only 54.7 percent of that urban population consumed electricity in 1974. (25) Solar energy, therefore, (in its direct or indirect forms, including bioconversion), not only makes sense in small villages but also in some of the so-called urban locations that are relatively isolated from central electricity networks.

In the long run, however, with population growth, the small, decentralized, nonconventional systems might become obsolete. What is required, then, is to identify the best short run, viable alternatives to conventional electrical energy systems before such systems can become viable.

WINDPOWERED GENERATION OF ELECTRICITY

Windpower applications in agriculture are well established. Prior to the 1960s, (which witnessed a drop in the price of petroleum,) several European countries produced electricity via such systems. For example, Denmark had as many as 88 installations of various sizes, the largest a 70 kilowatt generator. In seven years, nearly 18 million kilowatts were generated. (26) Windpower generation of electricity not only has potential for small development projects in isolated areas, but has the advantage of being useful for a number of extra functions in rural settings, e.g., waterpumping and graingrinding.

According to Eletrobras, small windmills of up to 6 kilowatts could serve one or perhaps a few rural families. Medium-size units of 6-70 kilowatts would satisfy the needs of a large farm, several families, or even small, low income communities with relatively low energy consumption per capita.

Windpower generation of electricity and pumping is a promising alternative worth considering for rural development in semiarid areas, since: (a) wind frequency in the region is the highest in the country; (b) both energy and water are fundamental resources needed in these areas, and (c) much of the technology is simple.

SOLAR GENERATION OF ELECTRICITY

Direct applications of solar energy in the development of semiarid areas are similar to those of windpowered energy, i.e., generation of electricity and pumping of water. It may eventually become the most economically feasible of all alternatives in semiarid areas for the following reasons:

- It eliminates the problems associated with transmission of electricity.
- The cost per kilowatt does not depend on the size of the installation, which means that they are appropriate for isolated areas.
- As the research on solar generation increases, the present high cost will drop and the models undergoing development will be relatively maintenance-free.
- Direct solar thermodynamic applications could replace electricity in heat production thus contributing to a more rational utilization of energy. (27)

According to the technical staff of the Paraiba Laboratory, the potential users of solar systems are the isolated communities located about 10 kilometers away from electricity distribution lines. The staff concluded that a 1 kilowatt solar generator would be most appropriate for the region on the basis of rural patterns of energy consumption. (28) Electricity via solar for poor isolated areas of Northeast Brazil is unlikely as long as the cost per kilowatt remains considerably higher than that of other nonconventional alternatives, including windpower and bioconversion systems.

ELECTRICITY, GAS, AND FERTILIZER VIA BIOMASS CONVERSION

Two basic biomass conversion alternatives - agricultural products (primarily sugar cane and manioc), and urban/rural waste - have been considered for research and development in Brazil. Eletrobras, jointly with CTA, has initiated a two-stage pilot project: the first stage designed for generation of electricity via alcohol to meet the needs of isolated communities (1978), and second, using larger units with a potential of up to 3,000 kilowatts (1979-80). If these phases of the project meet technical and economic goals, a third stage, yet to be initiated and dependent on financial commitments, will explore the feasibility of a system with gas run turbines of up to 30 megawatts (1982-85). (29)

The basic system producing electricity, methane gas, and fertilizer in an integrated operation, is illustrated in figure 9.1. Based on sugar cane, or manioc - the most suitable raw materials in the region (30) - this technology represents an important energy alternative for the Northeast.

In a production system based on sugar each ton of sugar cane produces an average of 95Kg of sugar and 12 liters of alcohol. If alcohol is the principal product, 70 liters can be obtained from one ton of raw material. (31) Sugar cane productivity in Brazil averages about 50 tons/hectare/year (32) compared with the world's highest rate of 150 tons/hectare/year in Hawaii. (33) The productivity for manioc averages 15 tons/hectare/year, although it could reach 40 tons. Up to 200 liters of alcohol per ton could be produced, but not in semiarid areas.

An integrated system that could provide water, fertilizer, and energy on the basis of a raw material cultivated in the semiarid soils of the subregion could indeed be an attractive alternative to current practices.

Water could be pumped via windmills, solar pumps, or electric motors (with energy provided by the bioconversion system); the water supply could be augmented by solar distillers; and manioc and other food products could be cultivated for conversion by a system producing electricity, fertilizer, and gas.

Sugarcane is not appropriate for cultivation in the semiarid areas. Most sugarcane plantations in the Northeast are located near the coastal urban areas, in the hands of medium and large landowners, who have traditionally exported molasses and not used their sugar mills to produce alcohol. Alcohol production, however, is starting up in the region, and new sugar distilleries are planned to be built.

Manioc plant alcohol produced in the semiarid regions is much more plausible, despite the absence of entrepreneurial experience with this plant. (34) It can be grown on soil of poor quality, requires little fertilizer, and can be grown year-round. In contrast, sugar cane requires good soil, heavy fertilization, and is a seasonal crop. Sugarcane mills operate only half the year, while manioc distilleries would never stand idle. The declining demand for manioc for food,

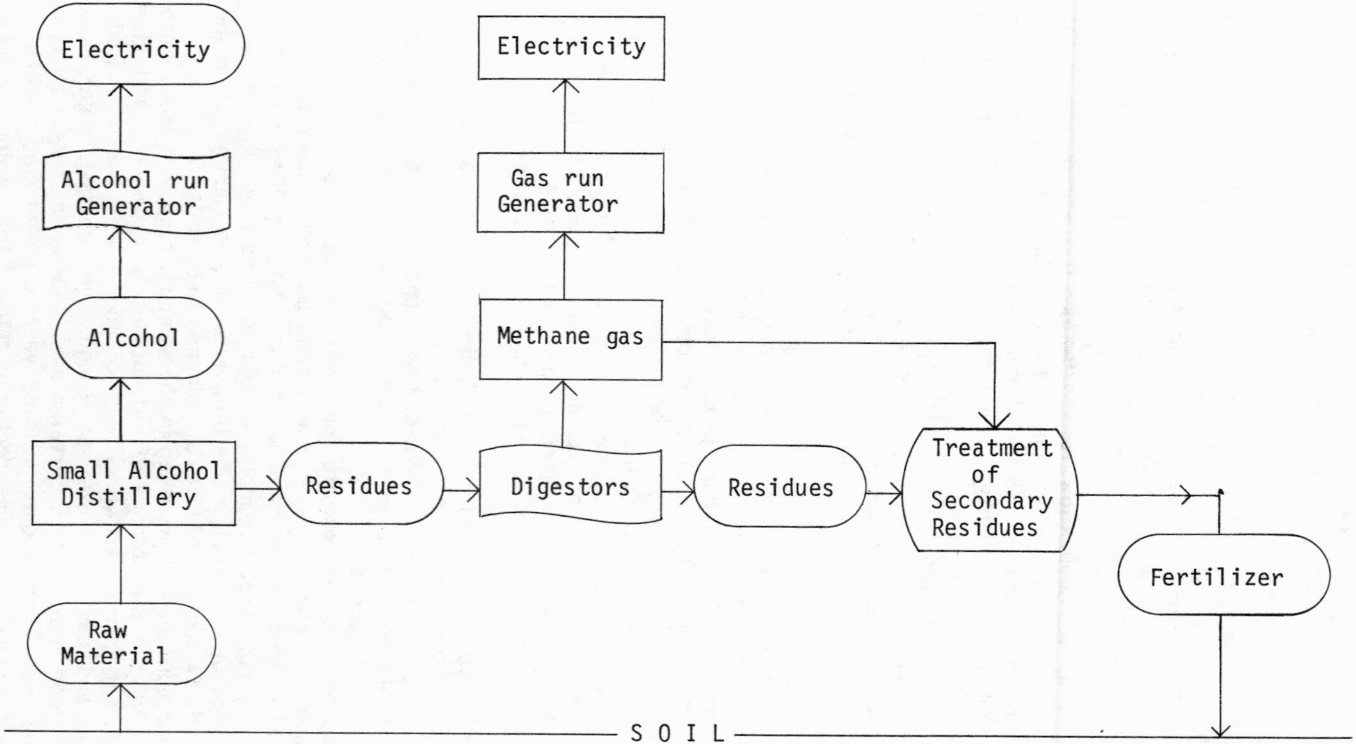

Fig. 9.1. Usina de Cacoes - a bio-conversion experimental project.

Source: ELETROBRAS. <u>A Usina de Cacoes</u>. Rio de Janeiro, fevereiro 1977.

because of migration from rural areas to the cities, coupled with changing consumer food preferences will make larger supplies available for alcohol production. The Paraiba Solar Energy Laboratory's work on industrial applications of solar energy raises the possibility that this source of energy can eventually provide the fuel for mills converting manioc to alcohol.

CONCLUSIONS: INSTITUTIONAL AND SOCIOECONOMIC FACTORS

Conventional wisdom suggests that the underlying cause of underdevelopment in and migration from the semiarid zones of the Northeast is uneven rainfall, and erratic prolonged periods of drought. Irrigation strategies designed by various government agencies, nonetheless, have been criticized for bringing benefits to the privileged and for ignoring the most vulnerable, economically marginal, rural low income population. In short, irrigation schemes do not challenge the prevailing power arrangement by proposing land redistribution, small farmer credit, and the like. (35)

The conventional economic cost-benefit analysis, governed by the criterion of economic success, operates to the detriment of those most in need. If the diffusion of nonconventional energy systems is placed in the hands of large producers, the energy factor will further accentuate the differences that separate the landowners from others.

A comprehensive, multidisciplinary, comparative cost-benefit analysis of alternate energy sources would attempt to assess the social as well as the economic impacts on the introduction of new policies and programs. The standard cost-benefit approach cannot appraise social impacts for several reasons: social variables frequently cannot be translated into monetary values; benefits from a program frequently take a long time to realize; groups that receive benefits may not be those who pay the costs; and benefits for one group may be considered socially harmful to another. (36) Social impact studies employing a general systems perspective attempt to model the contribution of input, (e.g., development projects); direct impacts (e.g., demographic and economic changes); and indirect impact (e.g., social structural changes) as well as their separate and joint contributions to the social-quality-of-life.

Aspects of nonconventional energy sources merit further study employing economic and social systems methods and concepts. These include assessments of:

- fiscal incentives
- import of plastic for solar stills
- impact of solar distillers on irrigation in draught area, and public health levels of the subregions population

- decentralized fertilizer production
- subsidies to cover the cost (U.S. $50) of hooking up households to electric distribution systems, and
- the distribution and utilization of land.

Formulations of energy policy in Greece show that such an approach is not merely academic. In its Report On the Energy Policy to Greece, 1977 prepared under the aegis of the National Energy Council, Ministry of Coordination and Planning, the basic goal of its solar energy policy is described in the following terms: (37)

> ...to maximize the participation of solar energy in the energy balance of the country at the fastest possible rate, subject to the constraints relating to investment and technological capabilities and potential, as well as the comparative social cost associated with solar applications.

More recently, an assessment of energy needs in developing countries recognizes "... the crucial social and developmental context of any intervention..." (38), although purely technical energy system solutions are frequently possible. In the same vein, two engineers recently acknowledge that in comparing alternative energy sources political considerations and psychological barriers for change must be considered in addition to energy availability, rate of production, life span of source, environmental and safety considerations, and economic competitiveness. (39) Finally, while social equity and economic efficiency are frequently perceived as contradictory requirements in conventional economic policy analyses, the opportunity to bypass petroleum may facilitate new conceptualizations of social equity and economic efficiency in developing countries. (40)

Table 9.5. Credit and Production by Groups of Areas - Brazil 1970

Credit - Crs$ 4,144,187 thous. Production - Crs$ 24,967,914 thous.*

Area groups (hectares)	% of total	Source of credit Govern.	Private	r. govern./private	% of total	r. credit/production
Less than 10	5%	3.3%	1.7%	r 1.9	18%	r 0.27
10 - <100	33%	26.3%	6.7%	r 3.9	40%	r 0.82
100 - <1000	42%	34.8%	7.2%	r 4.8	29%	r 1.45
1000 - <10,000	16%	12 %	4 %	r 3.0	11%	r 1.45
Above 10,000	4%	2.3%	1.7%	r 1.3	1.8%	r 2.22
TOTAL	100%					

---

*The production value was calculated over the Cr$ value of the following types of production, as individually mentioned in the census: <u>animal</u>, <u>vegetal</u>, <u>bovinos</u>, <u>asininos</u>, <u>muares</u>, <u>bufalinos</u>, <u>aquinos</u>, <u>ovinos</u>, <u>suinos</u>, <u>caprinos</u>, <u>coelhos</u>, <u>ovos</u>, <u>aves</u>, <u>leite</u>, <u>la</u>, <u>casulos de bicho de seda</u>, <u>mel</u>, <u>e cera de abelha</u>.

The Cr$ values refer to 1970.

Source: Data elaborated from Censo Agropecuario de 1970.

REFERENCES

(1) Eletrobras. 1978. Fontes Alternativas de Energia Eletrica. pp. 7-12. Brazil. Rio de Janeiro.

(2) Secretaria de Planejamento da Presidencia da Republica, 1974. Chapt. 8. 11 Plano Nacional de Desenvolvimento. Brasilia.

(3) This recent attitude was made evident by a project conducted by IBDF titled: Zoneamento Ecologico da Regiao Nordeste para Experimentacao Florestal, for the purpose of studying which arboreous types would be adequate for certain climatic sectors in the region.

(4) Planejamento & Desenvolvimento. Ano 5, no. 55, dez. 1977.

(5) Ibid.

(6) Reforestation includes planting eucaliptus and pine trees in the semiarid areas of the Northeast, because they are among the most profitable arboreous alternatives, but neither one is geoclimatically suited for the areas mentioned.

(7) For a comprehensive analysis of the various interdisciplinary factors affecting the viability of sun-cookers, as well as their advantages, disadvantages, and technical information, see: Torres, Cleantho C. 1974. Fogoes Solares para Uso Domestico na Regiao Semi-arida Brasileira. In Boletim LES, Semestre 11, Ano 1, Joao Pessoa.

(8) See Veja. 1978. agosto 9, p. 9.

(9) Ibid., and Emerson Freitas Jaguaribe and Cleantho Torres. 1974. Consideracoes sobre a Aplicacao de Destilacao Solar no Nordeste Brasileiro, in Boletim LES, Semestre 1, Ano 1, Joao Pessoa, UFPb.

(10) Pereira, Armand F. 1978. The State of Agribusiness in Brazil. Citibank, Banking Management Group. p. 25. Rio de Janeiro.

(11) Harrois-Moni, F. 1976. Science et Vie, Article on technology. Vol. 708, Sept.

(12) Information gathered from interviews, and from the publications of Projeto Sertanejo, Polonordeste, and EMBRATER.

(13) Analyses of the economic trends based on the findings of the national census conducted by Brazilian Institute of Geography and Statistics (PNAD/IBGE) have shown decreases in the buying power of the majority of the population, especially the bottom strata.

(14) Ministerio do Interior. 1977. Projeto Sertanejo: Manual para 1977. p. 7. Brasilia.

(15) Planejamento & Desenvolvimento. 1976. Ano 3, no. 35, abril 1976, pp. 49-50.

(16) These types include native xerofilas such as faveleira, licuri, oiticina, as well as sorgo, milheto, gergelim, and girassol.

(17) Ministerio do Interior. 1976-77. Projeto Sertanejo, and Estado da Paraiba. Governo Federal. Polonordeste: Primeiro Balanco do Polonordeste na Paraiba - junho 1976 - junho 1977.

(18) Ibid. This document only referred to the quality of the underground water in eleven of the sixteen existing project centers.

(19) Equipe de Destilacao Solar. 1978. Destilacao Solar Convencional: Desempenho e Custos. Joao Pessoa, UFPb, julho 1978.

(20) For the technical details of the units see Emerson Jaguaribe and Cleantho Torres. See also Torres, C., Yurevic, and Rodrigues de Araujo. 1978. Destiladores Solares no Nordeste Brasileiro: Perspectivas de Viabilizacao. Joao Pessoa, UFPb. Paper presented at the 2nd Latin American Congress on Solar Energy.

(21) See Torres, Yuryevic and Rodrigues de Araujo, pp. 6-8.

(22) Ibid. p. 8. See also Hay. 1972. The Solar Era: Part 3 - Solar Radiation; Some Implications and Adaptations. Mechanical Engineering, Oct. 1972, pp. 24-9. This author states that "solar stills are the cheapest means for desalting quantities of less than 50,000 gallons of saline water per day in areas of reasonable sunshine, and production costs are currently (1972) about US $3.50 per 1000 gallons." Although such costs vary according to local conditions, i.e. price of inputs, and quality of water, Prof. Cleantho Torres (UFPb) does not believe this figure is a realistic one.

(23) See Torres, C., Yuryevic, and Rodrigues de Araujo. p. 9, and Equipe de Destilacao Solar. p. 6.

(24) Centro de Technologia Promon. 1976. Boletim Informativo. Vol. 1, No. 2, dezembro 1976, p. 4.

(25) Ibid.

(26) Eletrobras. 1976. Maguinas Eolicas para Geracao de Energia Eletrica. junho 1976, pp. 1-2. Rio de Janeiro.

(27) See Torres, C. 1978. Eletricidade Obtida por Via Solar. Joao Pessoa, UFPb, jan. 1978, pp. 17-8. Paper presented at the 1st Pan American Meeting of Electrotechnical and Electronic Engineers. Salvador.

(28) Ibid., p. 18.

(29) Eletrobras. A Usina de Cacoes. fev. 1977. Rio de Janeiro.

(30) Bagacu is another culture from which alcohol and coal can be derived, but it is predominant in northern, rather than northeastern states.

(31) See Eletrobras. Fontes Alternativas de Energia.

(32) See Ministerio da Agricultura. 1977. Perspectivas da Agricultura Brasileira. Brasilia.

(33) See Pereira, Armand F. p. 9.

(34) Mears, L.G. 1978. Brazil's Agricultural Energy Program Moving Ahead. Foreign Agriculture, U.S. Dept. of Agriculture, July 17, 1978, pp. 5-7.

(35) Hall, Anthony L. 1978. Drought and Irrigation in North-East Brazil, Cambridge: Cambridge University Press.

(36) See Olsen, Marvin E. and Merwin, Donna J. Toward a Methodology for Conducting Social Impact Assessments Using Quality of Life Indicators, in Finsterbusch, K. and Wolf, C.P. eds. Methodology of Social Impact Assessment. 1977. Stroudsberg, Penn.: Dowden, Hutchinson and Ross, pp. 43-63.

(37) Ministry of Coordination and Planning, National Energy Council. 1977. Report on the Energy Policy of Greece 1977. December, 1977, p. 47. Athens, Greece.

(38) Palmedo, Philip F. et. al. 1978. Energy Needs, Uses and Resources in Developing Countries. Policy Analysis Division, National Center for Analysis of Energy Systems, BNL 50784, March, 1978. Upton, N.Y.: Brookhaven National Laboratory.

(39) Khalil, T.M. and Arias, A. 1978. The Economics and Policy of Alternative Energy Sources - A Review. In Veziroglu, T.N. and H.H. Hiser, eds., International Symposium-Workshop on Solar Energy, June 16-22, 1978. Cairo, Egypt.

(40) Warkov, S. 1978. Community Characteristics Predicting Public Interest in Household Solar. Paper presented at International Symposium-Workshop on Solar Energy, Cairo, Egypt, June 17, 1978. Also see Morrison, D.E. Equity Impacts of Some Major Energy Alternatives, in Warkov, S. ed., Energy Policy in the United States: Social and Behavioral Dimensions. 1978, pp. 164-194. New York: Praeger Publishers.

III

Food Production

Introduction to Part III

All five papers of this section are concerned with aspects of nontraditional food production through the agency of microorganisms. C.A. Shacklady rejects the term wastes in relation to what he terms organic residues, since wastes suggests nonvisibility and conceals resource potentialities. He reviews our present situation with regard to both carbohydrate conversion and lignocellulose degradation.

Keith H. Steinkraus likewise surveys the whole range of possibilities, citing many impressive examples. He also discusses various novel mushroom cultivations, the preparation of meat substitutes by texturing flavoring methods, using microorganisms and the growth of single cell proteins (SCP) on edible substrates.

The paper by J.T. Worgan is still more general in his attempt to demonstrate the complementary relationship between bioconversion and the traditional agricultural paths to food production. He discusses methods for improving agricultural production, texturing foods, and bioconversion for both animal feeds and direct human consumption.

Murray Moo-Young describes the Waterloo Process for the growth of SCP from a substrate of waste carbohydrates in a factory-scale aerobic fermentor.

The final paper of the group, by Kazem Behbehani and colleagues, gives a detailed account of comprehensive work in Kuwait on SCP production reached by seven different paths. This paper is marked by the serious attention paid to the socioeconomic implications of the large-scale use of these methods.

10 The State of the Art of Bioconversion of Organic Residues for Rural Communities

C.A. Shacklady

"When I use a word," Humpty Dumpty said in a rather scornful tone, "it means just what I choose it to mean, - neither more nor less."

Lewis Carroll, Through the Looking-Glass

The terminology used in the title of this paper lends itself to a variety of interpretations. For that reason it is desirable to define the sense in which the terms are used and the context to which they are applied.

Organic residues. An alternative way to expressing this could be agricultural and agroindustrial residues. Residue is preferred to waste since the latter implies that a material is of no further use. The object of the program from which the title of this paper is derived is to minimize waste and to demonstrate the extent to which these residues can form a renewable source of more useful products.

Bioconversion. While it is true that every bioconversion involves the use of microorganisms, the total process is not necessarily exclusively biological. Examples will be quoted in which chemical and physical treatment are combined with biological ones, to make a process effective or increase its effectiveness.

Rural communities. This term includes areas which are nonurban but not typical villages. In some countries, there are rural sites for the processing of agricultural crops where large quantities of residues may be produced; while these are not rural communities in the generally accepted sense, in this paper they will, nonetheless, be regarded as such.

THE ROLE OF THE UNITED NATIONS UNIVERSITY (UNU) IN BIOCONVERSION

In its Charter, the UNU is charged with addressing itself to "pressing global problems of survival, development, and welfare." It has three programs through which it is attempting to discharge this obligation: Human and Social Development (HSD); World Hunger (WH); and Use and Management of Natural Resources (NR).

The obvious relationship between World Hunger and the proper use of Natural Resources has inspired a joint WH-NR activity of the UNU. It is well known that the greatest degree of hunger and the greatest accumulation of organic residues both occur in the developing countries.

What may be less well known is the proportion of the major agricultural crops consumed directly by man in relation to residues. Disregarding grass and related crops of which the direct nutritional use by men is zero, 60 percent of the roots and tubers is consumed directly, 40 percent of the grain crop, 15 percent of the oilseed crop, and 10 percent of the sugar crop. Thus, by simple subtraction, it appears that 40, 60, 85 and 90 percent respectively of these crops must be regarded as residues as far as their direct use by man for nutritional purposes is concerned.

Some indication of the quantities involved are suggested by the following estimates. In 1974, cereal straw production in Asia alone amounted to 607 million tons. When combined with the further 207 million tons from Africa and Latin America, this represents almost half the world's production of straw.

The residues in Africa, Latin America, and Asia from cassava, bananas, citrus fruits, and coffee were estimated to be 124 million tons, almost 95 percent of the world total of residues from these crops, whilst 72 percent of the total world residue from sugarcane is found in these regions, amounting to 83 million tons. So, not only are the proportions impressive, but the absolute quantities are very considerable.

In addition, but even more difficult to estimate, is the enormous quantity of manure from the world's 9,500 million head of domesticated livestock of all types. Approximately 38 percent of these animals are in Africa, Asia, Latin America, and the Near East. The significance of such huge estimates lies in the fact that most - if not all - of these residues represent potentially valuable and renewable sources of raw materials for processing into more valuable products. The object of the UNU program with which we are concerned is to reduce to a minimum the element of waste and to encourage the fullest use of the residues.

RESIDUES: RESOURCES OR WASTE?

The UNU is concerned primarily with two uses for organic residues. One is in the production of biogas, the other is as a source of animal feed, or food for direct human consumption.

Biogas production is already established as a rural community project in India and Southeast Asia, where thousands of small production units are in operation at scales as small as individual farms or smallholdings. The process is one in which organic material is <u>digested</u>

by microorganisms in the absence of air; this anaerobic fermentation produces a mixture of gases, of which the dominant one is methane. It represents the harnessing by man of a process which has occurred in nature from earliest times.

Methane is the term used by organic chemists for the gas originally known as marsh gas or, by coal miners, firedamp. It occurs naturally by the anaerobic decomposition of vegetation in swampy areas, and by a similar process in the formulation of coal and oil. In the latter case, it constitutes a gaseous hydrocarbon with a high calorific value when burned, and is the major constituent of natural gas.

In theory, almost any organic residue could be used as the starting point for biogas production. In practice, however, the bulk of it comes from the fermentation of animal manure. In India, in particular, dried cow dung has been - and is still - used as a fuel, but this has the disadvantages of being both totally destructive of the manure, and productive of pollution when used in an enclosed space. Biogas production from manure gives a much cleaner source of heat, light, and power, with an undigested residue suitable for recycling as fertilizer.

Although the equipment is neither complicated nor expensive by the standards of industrialized countries, it is still beyond the reach of some communities. Consequently, efforts are now being made to reduce the capital cost of an installation by using cheaper materials for the gas holder than steel, with which most have been made to date. Thus Seshadri, in Madras, is experimenting with polythene sheeting as a geodetically constructed bamboo frame while in Indonesia, a precast concrete shell is being used.

Where social mores allow, the fermenter may be charged with human excrement as seems to be the practice in China.

Biogas production is, therefore, true bioconversion of an organic residue and, being applicable to rural communities, falls within the scope of the UNU program. It is, however, a nonnutritional use of the residues. Its relevance to the world hunger program is that it represents a source of energy, and all of the bioconversion processes which result in food or feed products require an input of energy of one kind of another.

Residues used for nutritional purposes as food or feed all require some treatment involving a biological step, if they are to be used to their best advantage. This might be done directly or indirectly, the indirect method being to improve the quantity and quality of the livestock products available. In the present state of knowledge and because of man's attitude to his food, there is little doubt that the indirect route, via the animal, is the one which is likely to predominate. It is probable, however, that the production or improvement of animal feed ingredients will constitute a major part of the bioconversion program. But this will, by no means, exclude attention being given to the production of food for direct human consumption when this is found to be feasible and acceptable.

STATE OF THE ART

A definitive announcement on the state of the art of bioconversion of organic residues can be found in the words used by Dr. Johnson to describe second marriages, a "triumph of hope over experience."

The term bioconversion may itself be slightly misleading in that it might imply the total conversion of the organic residue, whereas what is achieved in a number of cases is only a partial transformation of the residue resulting in an improvement in its nutritional value. The neologism bioamelioration might be more appropriate in such cases. Nonetheless, whether the transformation is partial or complete, the objective is to make the residue more useful as a source of food or feed. In almost every case, this is effected by using the residue as a medium for the growth of microorganisms by either a fermentation or a photosynthetic process.

Food production. Processes for fermenting residues by fungi to produce food exist in many countries as exemplified by such preparations as tempe in Southeast Asia and gari in West Africa. These are small scale processes employing traditional methods. From time to time the processes fail to produce the expected result, and research is in progress to improve their stability by gaining more basic knowledge of the behavior of the organisms in a variety of conditions. It should be remembered that by definition bioconversion deals with living entities, mocroscopically small, but nonetheless alive. These living entities have, within certain limits, the ability to adapt to changes in the environment in which they find themselves, just as do the macroscopic life forms with which we are more familiar. In the process of adapting, they may alter their nutritional or toxicological characteristics, which is one of the major problems to be considered in the development of biological conversion processes, whether for food or feed.

In theory, it is possible to further expand and diversify present production of fermented foods. However the mere production of a food is no guarantee of its use unless it conforms also to the social customs and the food tastes of the population.

Considerable interest is now being shown in the use of composted agricultural residues as a growth medium for mushroom production, the spent compose having a further use as a fertilizer and soil conditioner. Interesting as these developments may be, the significance of their effect in quantitative terms on the vast tonnage of residues existing in the developing countries may not be very great in the foreseeable future.

Feed production. Whereas many routes have been suggested for converting organic residues into animal feed ingredients, it is difficult to find examples of research projects or bench studies which have a practical application.

For the purpose of our program we have suggested a purely arbitrary classification of the projects as follows:

1. Projects which are already established and working on a village, community, or industrial scale.
2. Projects which have advanced to the stage of pilot plant operation.
3. Projects based on those in 1 or 2 which have already been proven but for which the plans for a particular area remain to be implemented.
4. Projects based on sound theoretical considerations which have been demonstrated on an institute scale and on the prepilot plant scale.

One process that we should consider as falling into the first category, but which might appear at first sight to be outside the definition of bioconversion, is the alkaline treatment of straw, now finding increasing application in both industrialized and developing countries. In countries with a well-developed agriculture, straw is not used very much for feeding ruminant animals, because of the availability of medium to good quality roughages such as hay and silage. In developing countries, it of necessity forms a much more important feed material. Due to its high lignocellulose content, the digestibility of the organic matter is low, about 40-45 percent. Even for the ruminant, straw is, therefore, a very poor quality roughage. A simple treatment with dilute alkali can increase the organic matter digestibility to 68 percent - a considerable improvement in nutritional value. Alkali renders the straw more susceptible to attack by the microorganisms in the rumen - which is in effect a fermentation vessel. The net result is a true bioconversion carried out inside the animal instead of in an external fermenter. This process is, of course, confined to the ruminants, and does not apply to animals such as the pig or fowl with simple stomachs. Nevertheless, because of the large number of cattle, sheep, and buffalo in the developing countries, the large amount of cereal straw available, the simplicity of the process and its adoption on an increasingly wide scale it must be regarded as belonging to the first category of our classification. It is, incidentally, one example of the chemical/biological type of process to which reference was made in the early part of this paper.

A further example of the remarkable adaptability of the ruminant animal as a bioconverter of organic residues is found in its ability to use dried or ensiled poultry manure, poultry litter, and residues from the fruit processing industry as a feed material. Any consideration of the state of the art of bioconversion of organic residues, and any program to advance its application should, therefore, always take into account the role of the ruminant. However, for the over 2000 million single structured animals in the developing countries, an increase in the nutritional value of residues requires a microbiological treatment external to the animal.

As far as is known, relatively few such treatments have been developed to a stage that would justify their inclusion in the first category. The Pekilo process as described by Linko (1), and a fermentation process described by Forage (2) seem to be operating on a commercial scale. The former produces a filamentous fungus on degraded cellulose originally from the wood pulp processing industry, the latter a single cell protein (SCP) on citrus residues; an earlier project on carob bean residues has apparently been abandoned. While both of these procedures reveal an advanced state of the art, the authors' comments on the complexity and cost of the processes raised some doubts as to their applicability to typical rural communities. They should, perhaps, be regarded as ancillary to the industries from which the residues are derived.

Similar considerations apply to an operation developed near Piven, in Bulgaria. Maize grown in the surrounding area is brought to a factory in which compound feeds for animals are produced. The maize husk residues are hydrolyzed with sulfuric acid, and the hydrolysate is used as the substrate for yeast (Candida tropicalis) production in Lefrancois type fermenters. The annual output of dried yeast is around 25,000 tons, all of which is used in the feeds. Once again, the operational complexity and the utilities required would seem to be beyond the resources of most rural communities - at least on the scale of the Piven operation. In this case, as is frequently evidenced in countries with a centrally controlled economy, it is difficult to arrive at a realistic assessment of the unit cost of production of the single cell protein.

In a very comprehensive report, Standon (3) cites an Amazonian village industry which uses cassava as a material for SCP production, but no details are given. The same report states that a process of wood degradation is operated by farmers in an evergreen rain forest area, where the breakdown of the wood is effected by naturally symbiotic microorganisms to produce a feed for cattle, but details of the process and location are lacking. (4) If they could be confirmed, the process would presumably qualify for the first category classification.

Turning from fermentation processes, methods of residue utilization by photosynthetic mechanisms should be considered. In practice, at present, this means the growing of microalgae on waste water. This is naturally best suited to areas in which sunlight is not a limiting factor. Considerable attention is being paid to algal cultivation in India, Southeast Asia, the Middle East, and parts of Central America. Among others, Shelef in Israel, Venkataraman in Mysore, and Clement in Mexico have described processes for algal production. Shelef's process is intended to form part of an integrated, bioregenerative system. At the time of writing, it was somewhat difficult to determine whether these processes have been developed to the extent that would justify their inclusion in the first category or, more properly, in the second category.

Projects which would seem to fall into this latter category are all related to fungal production. A report from the Denver Research Institute (5) refers to a pilot plant in El Salvador in which an Aspergillus Oryzae is grown on coffee wash waters, and also one in Cedar Rapids, Iowa, designed for the fungal processing of 3 million gallons of residues per day from the wet milling of maize. This report was produced in 1974, and the project was designed specifically to develop processes applicable to the conditions in less technically advanced countries.

Another project which has advanded to the pilot plant stage is that of the Lord Rank Research Centre in England. This process uses starchy or sugary residues as the growth medium for a Fusarium fungus. It was suggested that this would be applicable to areas in which such residues occurred as a result of cereal milling or fruit processing. However, there does not appear to be any recent evidence of development beyond the pilot plant stage. Our own observation of the pilot plant suggested that the degree of control necessary to ensure satisfactory performance might be beyond the technical resources of a rural community, although it could conceivably have been linked to the type of operation described by Linko and Forage. It is also understood that the product is intended for direct consumption by man, which may have presented some problems that would not have been associated with an animal feed ingredient.

There is believed to be a pilot plant in Thailand in which the starchy part of cassava forms the substrate for SPC production. While further details are lacking at present, it is believed that the plant has advanced to the stage of incipient commercialization.

In summary there seem to be relatively few projects which could be unequivocally placed in the second category. It is not surprising, therefore, that even fewer processes fall into the third category. It is not known if any projects reported to be in the pilot plant stage have been selected for full-scale operation elsewhere.

The fourth category comprises those small scale projects which have been demonstrated as potentially applicable to either a more general or larger scale.

Srinivasan and Chen, at Louisiana State University, have described one such process based on the fungal conversion of bagasse cellulose -a residue in the sugar cane industry - to a product of higher protein content, which is claimed to be applicable to other cellulose/starch sources.

This may, perhaps, be regarded as typical of the several processes mentioned by Stanton, the essential principle of which is the treatment of cellulosic or, more generally, lingocellulosic wastes by chemical or biological means to produce a substrate more readily utilized by microorganisms, which could be fungi, yeasts, or bacteria.

Although certain of the basidiomycetes indigenous to the tropics have been shown to possess lignocellulolytic activity, neither these nor the fungi capable of degrading cellulose seem to have been applied except on the experimental scale. The conversion of lignocellulose to glucose by chemical means seems to offer economic advantages, according to the information available at present.

Two other experimental projects are worthy of note. One, according to Sundhagul, is under development in collaboration with the Bangkok Microbiological Resources Centre (MIRCEN), of which she is the Director. This project uses the leaves of cassava as a substrate for fungal production. The other, described by Senez, is the so-called semisolid fermentation of cassava by a fungus. In this case the fungus is codried with the residue after a partial degradation of the cassava starch. The entire result, with its increased protein content, is intended for use directly in animal feeding.

While it is difficult to pass a judgment on the possible successful application of the above, it is even more difficult in the case of the fifty category projects, for which little or no experience exists as a guide. In theory, the use of basidiomycetes or other classes of fungus, which could convert native lignocellulose to carbohydrate without other expensive or complex treatments, seems attractive. Even more attractive would be organisms which could convert residues to nontoxic, high protein biomass rapidly and completely, but the existence of such organisms remains to be demonstrated.

Similarly if, as claimed by Standon, many communities already apply classical fermentation procedures to starch or starchy residues, it might be considered that these could constitute the basis for processes in which similar but not identical substrates were employed. One could continue this line of speculation and suggest that methods for fermenting sugary residues might be developed from those being used for more refined sugar products, but it must be recognized that this at present is no more than speculation.

One suspects that in many instances the bioconversion process has been regarded as an end in itself. That this is not - or should not be - the case should be self-evident. The ultimate objective, with the exception of biogas production, is the provision of more food for man either directly or indirectly via the animal. Consequently, a bioconversion program which does not go beyond the actual process must be regarded as incomplete. It is necessary to demonstrate that the products resulting from any process are suitable both toxicolically and nutritionally for the purpose for which they are intended. In most cases, there is very little evidence that this has been accomplished at all, and in the few in which it has been attempted, the published evidence would not meet the requirements of the most liberal regulatory authorities in the devloped world.

There may be a number of reasons for this omission, ranging from a failure to appreciate the need for such evidence, to a realization of the need, but the absence of facilities to meet it.

Of the various possible organisms that might be employed, the impression remains that fungi of one kind of another are the ones most favored. On the face of it, fungi seem to have some advantages over yeasts and bacteria for the ease of processing, but may present greater problems regarding toxicity or their nutritional value. The production of mycotoxins could be a very real danger, and this emphasizes the need for care in the selection of organisms, design of the equipment, and operation of the process.

Certain of the yeasts and bacteria have been evaluated more thoroughly than the fungi, but they may not be so suitable as organisms in nonsterile conditions. The establishment and maintenance of aseptic fermentation is neither easy nor cheap.

Lignocellulosic residues which, in terms of dry matter content, constitute the largest single type of residue all seem to require multistage processing comprising mechanical, chemical, and biological steps. Chemical treatment might be replaced by microbiological degradation if improved strains of fungi with lignocelluloytic activity could be developed to effect this much more rapidly than now appears possible. This could be a rewarding line of research, and one which need not be transferred to an industrialized country to be counducted effectively. The next stage, that is the fermentation of the partially degraded cellulose, is theoretically open to a number of options according to circumstances.

The handling of starchy and sugary residues might appear simpler, but the large volumes of liquid effluent may present extra problems of disposal.

One of the major problems to be overcome is the translation of bioconversion research into practice. It is one thing to conduct a fermentation process involving the growth of a microorganism in the controlled conditions of a laboratory. It is something quite different to operate this on a practical scale in conditions, such as environment, substrate, and personnel, which are less easily controlled; this requires technology as distinct from simply technique.

Microbiology is clearly central to bioconversion processes, but it is becoming increasingly evident that a multidisciplinary approach is needed in order to bring the basic work of the microbiologist to practical fruition. This will involve the participation of engineers familiar with fermentation technology, specialists in nutrition and toxicology, together with those having an appreciation of the socio-economic aspects of the problem. Somewhat belatedly this is being recognized and accepted.

Reference has been made earlier in this paper to algal production in a bioconversion program. There is some traditional use of algae in Mexico and Africa, for example, but the deliberate cultivation of algae for food or feed is still in an early stage of development. The most advanced systems appear to be beyond the financial or technical resources of the average rural community. Attempts, nonetheless, are being made as in India to simplify and adapt projects to village technology, although it is too early to judge the success of those which have already been started.

There appears to be very little published information on the economics of the various forms of single cell protein, which might result from the bioconversion processes under study, the exceptions consisting of those reported by Linko and Forage. This is not surprising in view of the stage of development and scale of operation of the majority of projects. Standard economic evaluation is not wholly appropriate in estimating the value of these processes. How, for example, does one place an aesthetic value on an improved environment or an enhanced quality of life resulting from indigenous sources? What is it worth to be more independent of other communities, or countries, in vital areas of food and feed? These are some of the factors, imponderable but real, that must ultimately be considered in assessing the value - as distinct from the economics - of all development in this area.

It would be misleading to suggest that the art is in a highly developed state. It is our objective to advance the state by stimulating research in areas in which it is most urgently needed; to disseminate the information which exists and which will become available as this research is applied; to open up channels of communications between those working in this field, and to support soundly based projects with material and technical aids, including the provision of training where necessary and appropriate.

This review must be regarded as inadequate simply because the field is so wide and the work so fragmented that it is not possible to be aware of - much less to cover - every piece of research, pure or applied, which may have a bearing on it. With the interest in many quarters now being shown, it is likely that progress in the future will be more rapid and that articulating some of the problems will bring us somewhat closer to some of the solutions.

REFERENCES

(1) Linko, M. 1977. New Feed Resources, FAO Animal Production and Health, Paper No. 4, pp. 39-50, FAO Rome.

(2) Forage, A.J. Ibid, pp. 119-206.

(3) Stanton, R. 1977. Microbiological Conversion of Wastes. UNEP/FAO/1554/12, Rome.

(4) Stanton, R. Ibid.

(5) Blackledge, J.P., Church, B.D. and Miller, J.M. 1974. Denver Research Institute. Proposal No. INT 7502/C 7504, August 1974.

11 Production of Microbial Protein Foods on Edible Substrates, Food By-Products and Lignocellulosic Wastes

Keith Steinkraus

> Some of the Third World's best crops may be waiting in the poor man's garden, ignored by science. Merely to have survived as useful crops suggests that plants are inherently superior. They are already suited to the poor man's plot and to his mixed farming, his poor soil, his diet, and the way of life of his family and village. (1)

This statement by Dr. Noel Vietmeyer confirms our own experiences with indigenous fermented foods. It was not until the Western World started its research and used Indonesian tempe, for example, that the topic achieved sufficient prestige for local administrators and scientists to support and institute research in its development. The gold mine of information on methods the developing world itself has evolved at the village level to feed people on minimal incomes has only recently been discovered. It would be a great mistake not to make maximum use of such experience. However, we should also recognize the part prestige plays in the acceptance of foods. As soon as the Western World adopts a poor man's or a village food, that food takes on an enhanced prestige, and it is much more likely to become accepted.

TOWARDS SOLVING THE WORLD'S NUTRITIONAL PROBLEMS

No country can hope to sustain its necessary development if that development is not accompanied by adequate nutrition for its people. And yet hunger and poverty go hand in hand today in a great part of the developing world, where millions have to support their families on less than $1 per day. The poor are generally compelled to be vegetarians. They consume on the average a pound to a pound and a half of cereal grains per day. They need nutritious, low cost meat substitutes that are acceptable as staples in the diet.

The Green Revolution has resulted in a vast increase in worldwide productivity of rice and wheat; and farmers the world over will produce still more food if they can sell it for a profit. However, we have no way at present of improving the economic status of the millions of malnourished people. Although food now is generally available, many people simply do not have the money to buy it. Thus, we have to look to alternative ways of increasing the food supply, or modifying the distribution of cereals and legumes between animals and man.

On a worldwide basis, about 400 pounds of cereal grains are available per person per year (2). In the developing world, the cereal grains are generally consumed by humans. In the United States, however, of the approximately 2000 pounds of cereal grains that are available per person per year, only about 200 pounds of grain are consumed directly in foods, such as bread, cereals, etc. The rest is used for animal feeds and alcoholic beverage production. If Americans alone were to become vegetarians, releasing the grain presently fed to animals, we could feed approximately another 800 million people a basic cereal diet.

Americans and other Westerners are not at this point likely to become vegetarian, but there are some interesting developments in the Western World that will eventually favor our becoming more vegetarian, for example the development of meat analogues from soybeans. (3) Meat analogues are an industrial term for meat substitutes or synthetic meats made principally from plant proteins. The basic technique is to extract soybean protein and concentrate it to above 90 percent purity. The protein is then extruded through platinum dies and chemical baths to form very fine filaments similar to hair, which are then combined to form a fibrous meatlike texture. Meat flavors and fats are added. Synthetic bacon bits (BACOS, General Mills, Inc., Minneapolis, Minnesota) are already on the market. Synthetic hamburger bits used widely in chili and other souplike dishes are also on the market. Synthetic roast beef, ham, chicken, etc., have been developed for the market.

Swift and Company, Chicago, Illinois, has developed a process for producing extruded soy nuggets mixed with favorable flavors. As the material emerges from the extruder, it develops a puffed structure, becoming a chewy, meatlike nugget. Such meat analogues are very likely to be an important addition to the diet in the future. They can reduce the need for real meats and provide meat-eating consumers with a way of directly consuming legumes in an acceptable form.

The Miller, Rank, Hovis, MacDougall Research group in England produced a mold mycelium based meat analogue. In their process, they grow an edible mold (Fusarium sp.) on low cost starchy substrates, adding inorganic nitrogen (for synthesis of protein) and minerals to produce a type of single cell protein (SCP). The mold mycelium, which provides the fibrous meatlike texture, is grown in tanks, recovered by filtration, flavored with meat flavors and fats to produce another type of meat analogue (4,5). The process is particularly adapted to production of synthetic chicken breast meat. This process has been licensed by a large American company and eventually the mold mycelium meat analogues are likely to appear on the American market. They are already being market tested in Europe.

These mold mycelial based meat analogues are produced by a highly sophisticated technology. At present they are entirely beyond the economic means of the poor in the developing world. But this is true also of all canned, frozen, and most dehydrated foods that are so important in the developed world. Thus, we must look elsewhere if we expect to contribute to improving nutrition among the poor.

MICROBIAL FARMING: SINGLE CELL PROTEIN (SCP) PRODUCTION

SCP production on inedible substrates such as hydrocarbons is one of the great developments in modern applied microbiology. (6) Single cell protein consists of cells of bacteria, yeasts, mold, or algae containing respectively up to 80, 50, 40, or 40 percent protein on a dry weight basis. SCP production requires no arable land; it can be produced in the desert. While the grasses such as elephant grass and alfalfa double their cell mass in from two to three weeks, bacteria and yeasts double their cell mass in from two to four hours. Thus 1000 kilograms of yeast doubling its cell mass in two hours can produce 12,000 kilograms of new cells containing 6000 kilograms of protein in a twenty-four hour period. The selected microorganisms use hydrocarbons as a source of energy for growth, and inorganic nitrogen for synthesis of protein. Their remaining nutrient requirements are minerals and a sufficient supply of oxygen (7).

Microbial farming, or SCP production, was so promising that it was estimated that by the 1980s, 3 percent of the total protein produced in the world would be in the form of SCP (8). The SCP would have been used primarily as animal feed, thus releasing vast quantities of cereal grains and legumes for use in feeding humans.

Unfortunately, the cost of petroleum unexpectedly rose so high that production of SCP on hydrocarbons can no longer compete with the cost of producing soybeans or fishmeal.

Because of the limited supply of petroleum for energy and its consequent cost, it is unlikely that it can serve as substrate for economical SCP production in the future. However, production of SCP on lignocellulose, the world's largest reserve supply of renewable carbohydrate, could become an efficient alternative.

At present, the major practical converters of cellulose to useful products, such as milk and meat, are the ruminants - sheep, goats, and cattle. They have bacteria in their gut that can hydrolyze cellulose to glucose which, in turn, is used by the bacteria for energy to synthesize proteins from inorganic nitrogen, and can be supplied in forms such as urea. The animal then digests the bacteria and synthesizes milk and meat proteins. Thus, the ruminants themselves are SCP fermenters.

Cellulose is not digested by the human but, as a major component of fiber, it does play a role in motility of the gastrointestinal tract.

Hydrolysis of cellulose outside the ruminant is at present too slow to be a practical method of producing SCP. However, many laboratories are working on the problem, and it is likely that cellulose hydrolysis may become rapid enough to permit cellulose to be utilized in the future as a major energy source for the production of SCP.

Processes have already been developed to raise the protein content of straw to as high as 30 percent by growing a celluolytic mold on it. This improves the straw as an animal feed.

It is possible also to use cellulose or lignocellulosic wastes, such as waste paper, cotton waste, straw, wheat, or rice bran, and go directly to a human food. This application has already been developed to a high degree in the production of mushrooms in Asia. (9,10,11) Mushrooms contain 2 to 5 percent protein on a fresh weight basis, and from 30 to 47 percent protein on a dry weight basis. (12)

As much as 1.25 kilograms of fresh mushrooms can be produced from 1 kilogram of dry straw. In Hong Kong, there is an estimated 30,000 tons of cotton waste per year. This can serve as a substrate for production of approximately an equal weight of fresh mushrooms.

The padi mushroom is grown by many farmers in Asia using rice straw as a substrate. Thus, the Asians have demonstrated to the world a practical way to transform lignocellulosic wastes directly to highly acceptable human food. It literally is growing a type of microbial protein (SCP) directly on cellulosic waste as a nutritious, delicious human food.

The padi and the oyster mushrooms can be grown by rather simple conditions. Paper or cotton are shredded. Straw can be trimmed, or coarse ground, or used directly. Five percent wheat or rice bran, and 5 percent $CaCO_3$ are added, along with a sufficient amount of water to raise the moisture content to about 60 percent. This requires that approximately 1500 milliliter water be added per kilogram of lignocellulosic waste. The substrate should then be steamed for 30 minutes. Alternatively, the substrate can be composted in heaps in which microbial activity results in the temperature rising to about 55^oC. Then the substrate is cooled and inoculated with the mushroom spawn. The spawn is the desired mushroom species grown on soaked, sterilized wheat grains, corn kernels, or rice straw. Approximately 160 grams of spawn is added to each kilogram of starting (dry weight) substrate. Within a few weeks under tropical temperatures and humidities, several flushes of fresh mushrooms are produced (13).

The developing countries in Asia are already expanding their own use of mushrooms in the diet. Taiwan is producing canned mushrooms for export. Last year Americans consumed 163,000 metric tons of mushrooms, 22 percent of which were imported. (14)

PRODUCTION OF MICROBIAL PROTEIN (SCP) ON EDIBLE SUBSTRATES

Asia also leads the way in growing microbial protein on edible substrates and converting food by-products, such as oilseed presscakes, to human food by fermentation. It was Asia that taught the world how to convert vegetable protein to meatlike flavors in the form of soy sauce (shoyu) and Japanese miso-soybean paste. (15,16)

Indonesians introduce meatlike textures into vegetable substrates. A prime example is Indonesian tempe in which soybeans are soaked, dehulled, given a short cook, cooled, inoculated with a mold Rhizopus oligosporus, wrapped in wilted banana or other large leaves, and fermented from thirty-six to forty-eight hours, during which time the white mold mycelium knits the soybean cotyledons into a tight cake, which can be sliced thin and deep fat fried, or cut into chunks and used in soups. (17,18,19).

Tempe, a major meat substitute in Indonesia, is produced daily by small factories in the villages. Containing nearly 47 percent protein, it is very nutritious and, in fact, kept thousands of Westerners alive in Japanese prisoner-of-war camps during World War II. The mold not only introduces texture, it also solubilizes the proteins and lipids, making them more digestible, and releases a peppery flavor, which adds to the nutty flavor of the soybean substrate. Riboflavin content doubles, niacin increases almost seven times, pantothenate decreases slightly, thiamine unfortunately decreases, but surprisingly vitamin B-12 is found in nutritionally significant amounts (20).

One of the problems of vegetarian diets is that humans generally obtain their vitamin B-12 from animal products, such as milk and meats. Vegetable foods generally do not contain significant vitamin B-12 activity. It was found that a bacterium present along with the mold is responsible for the vitamin B-12 activity in tempe (21). If the fermentation is carried out with the pure mold, the tempe does not contain B-12 activity. If the bacterium is present, the tempe will contain as much as 150 mg B-12 activity per gram. Thus, this single food provides both protein and vitamin B-12 for vegetarians.

There are at least five vegetarian communes in the United States today (for example, The Farm, Summertown, Tenn.) where tempe has been adopted as the major protein source, replacing meat in the diet. In California, Nebraska, and Canada (Toronto) there are at least six small factories producing tempe commercially. The acceptance of this Indonesian food technology in the United States suggests that the technology could also be extended to developing countries in the world, thus improving the diversity and nutritive value of the diets of the poor. It has already been demonstrated that the tempe process can be used to introduce texture in other substrates made not only from soybeans but wheat and other cereals as well. (22) The vitamin B-12 bacterium has been used to raise the content of vitamin B-12 in Indian idli made by fermenting a batter of ground soaked rice and black gram dahl with

Leuconostoc mesenteroides. (23) Thus, the world has a technique for introducing texture and vitamin B-12 into vegetarian foods.

The reader will note a similiarity between the Miller, Rank, Hovis, MacDougall meat analogue process and the tempe process. In both cases, the texture is derived from mold mycelium; but the former process is sophisticated and relatively costly, while the latter is low cost technology.

Quick-cooking foods are appreciated worldwide. Fuel is costly. The tempe fermentation reduces the cooking time for soybeans from six hours to about thirty minutes boiling prior to fermentation and ten minutes boiling, or four to five minutes deep fat frying at 190 degrees C of the final product prior to consumption.

SCP can easily be produced using starch as a source of energy, and feeding the organisms minerals and inorganic nitrogen. In fact, this is the basic process used by Miller, Rank, Hovis, MacDougall to produce mold mycelium for the production of meat analogues. The question then can logically be raised, why not grow edible microbes on starchy foods such as rice and cassava, sacrifice a portion of the calories for energy to grow the microorganisms, and then having raised the protein content, partly through synthesis of SCP and partly through sacrifice of some of the total starch, consume the whole product as a new food? The answer is that the Indonesians have already done this in foods called tapé ketan (from rice) and tapé ketella (from cassava). The major fermenting organisms are Amylomyces rouxii, a mold, and at least one yeast, such as Endomycopsis burtonii, which grow together in the substrates, not only raising the protein content but raising the thiamine content three times, selectively synthesizing lysine, the first limiting amino acid, and producing acids, alcohol, and esters which result in a flavor highly acceptable to those consuming the resultant product. (24) The protein content of rice can increase to as high as 16 percent, and that of cassava can reach 4 to 8 percent. With only 1 or 2 percent protein, cassava in its unfermented state cannot possibly supply the consumer with enough protein. Yet millions of the world's very poor use cassava as a major staple food. In the form of tape ketella, the protein quantity and quality of cassava are both improved.

The Indonesians have thus demonstrated to the world how to use microbes to raise the protein quantity and quality of high starch foods by fermentation. This process could be expanded and extended to other countries for the benefit of the world's poor and hungry.

The Indonesians also have shown the world how to convert food by-products, such as peanut and coconut press cakes which the Western World has traditionally fed to animals, to human quality foods called ontjom and bongkrek. They have done this by use of the basic tempe process. The press cakes are hydrated, coarse ground, steamed, cooled, and inoculated either with the tempe mold or Neurospora intermedia. The mold overgrows the particles knitting them into tight cakes that can be sliced or cut into chunks and used in soups (25). These products are low cost protein-rich meat analogues. The basic changes are similar to those that occur during the tempe fermentation. In addition, it has been found that the content of aflatoxin always present in peanut press cake is reduced. (26) The strains of Neurospora intermedia also contain cellulases, which reduce the natural fiber content of the peanut or coconut press cake.

The indigenous fermented food processes are a gold mine of scientific knowledge that can be tapped for the advantage and progress of all mankind. They not only contribute to Western food science, but are processes suitable for low cost production of foods at the village level with acceptable flavors, textures, and nutritive values for the hungry and poor all over the world. If mankind wants to improve nutrition among the poor, it must closely examine the possibilities offered by indigenous fermented foods.

REFERENCES

(1) Vietmeyer, N. 1978. Poor people's crops. Agency for Int. Development, Washington. Agenda 1 (8): 12.

(2) Brown, L.R., and Eckholm, E.P. 1974. The changing face of global food scarcity. Social Education. 38, 640.

(3) Smith, A.K., and Circle, S.J., eds. 1972. Protein Products as Food Ingredients. Soybeans: Chemistry and Technology I. Proteins, pp. 365.

(4) Spicer, A. 1971. Synthetic proteins for human and animal consumption. Vet. Record, 89, 482 (1971a).

(5) Spicer, A. Protein production by microfungi. Tropical Sci., XIII, 239 (1971b).

(6) Shacklady, C.A. 1970. Single cell proteins from hydrocarbons. Outlook on Agriculture, 6, 102.

(7) Lipinsky, E.S. and Litchfield, J.H. 1970. Algae, bacteria, and yeasts as food or feed. Critical Reviews in Food Technology, 1, 581.

(8) Wells, Jeremy. 1975. Analysis of potential markets for single cell proteins. Paper presented at Symposium on Single Cell Protein, American Chemical Society Meeting, April 9, 1975. Philadelphia, PA.

(9) Chang, Shu-Ting. 1972. The Chinese mushroom. Chinese University of Hong Kong.

(10) Chang, Shu-Ting. 1977. Cultivation of the straw mushroom (Volvariella volvacea). UNESCO/UNEP/ICRO/CSCHK/CUHK Regional Training Course on Cultivation of Edible Fungi (Mushrooms) Laboratory Manual. Chinese University of Hong Kong.

(11) Eger, G., Eden, G. and Wissig, E. 1976. Pleurotus ostreatus -

Breeding potential of a new cultivated mushroom. Theoretical Applied Gen. 47, 155.

(12) Kurtzman, R.H. 1975. Mushrooms as a source of food protein, Nutrition and Clinical Nutrition, I. Protein Nutritional Quality of Foods and Feeds. Part 2. Quality Factors. Am. Chem. Soc. Symposium on Chemical and biological methods for protein quality evaluation. Atlantic City, N.J., 1974.

(13) Chang, Shu-Ting. 1977. op. cit.

(14) Hayes, W.A. 1978. Edible mushrooms. L.R. Beuchat, ed., Food and Beverage Mycology, pp. 301-333. Avi Publishing Co., Westport, Conn.

(15) Yokotsuka, T. 1960. Aroma and flavor of Japanese soy sauce. Advances in Food Research Vol. 20, pp. 75-134. Academic Press, New York.

(16) Shibasaki, K. and Hesseltine, C.W. 1962. Miso fermentation. Economic Botany 16, 180.

(17) van Veen, A.G. and Schaefer, G. 1950. The influence of the tempeh fungus on the soya bean. Doc. Neer. Indones. Morbis Trop. 2, 270.

(18) Steinkraus, K.H., Hwa, Yap Bwee, Van Buren, J.P., Provvidenti, M.I., and Hand, D.B. 1960. Studies on tempeh - an Indonesian fermented soybean food. Food Res. 25, 777.

(19) Hesseltine, C.W., Smith, M., Bradle, D., and Kjien, K.S. 1963. Investigations of tempeh, and Indonesian soybean food. Deve. Ind. Micro. 4, 275.

(20) Steinkraus, K.H., Hand, D.B., Van Buren, J.P., and Hackler, L.R. 1961. Pilot plant studies on tempeh. Proc. Conf. on Soybean Products for Protein in Human Foods. NRRL. USDA, Peoria, IL Sept. 13-15, p. 75.

(21) Liem, I.T.H., Steinkraus, K.H., and Cronk, T.C. 1977. Production of vitamin B-12 in tempeh - a fermented soybean food. Appl. & Envir. Micro. 34, 777.

(22) Wang, H.L., and Hesseltine, C.W. 1966. Wheat tempeh. Cereal Chem. 43, 563.

(23) Parekh, L.J. and Steinkraus, K.H. 1977. Unpublished data.

(24) Cronk, T.C., Steinkraus, K.H., Hackler, L.R., and Mattick, L.R. 1977. Indonesian tape ketan fermentation. Applied and Envir. Micro. 33, 1067.

(25) van Veen, A.G. and Steinkraus, K.H. 1970. Nutritive value and wholesomeness of fermented foods. Ag. and Food Chem. 18, 576.

(26) van Veen, A.G., Graham, D.C.W., and Steinkraus, K.H. 1968. Fermented peanut press cake. Cereal Science Today 13, 96.

12 Resources and Their Development for Maintaining World Supplies of Food

J.T. Worgan

The world population is increasing by 60 to 70 million per year, and despite all the measures being taken to prevent it, it would be unrealistic to assume that this increase will not continue for the next 20 to 30 years. The magnitude of the task of maintaining and increasing food supplies is illustrated by the estimate that 900 million tons of food per year are currently consumed by the world population. Apart from a relatively small proportion of foods harvested from the wild, such as fish, this huge quantity of material is produced by agriculture.

RESOURCES FOR AGRICULTURAL PRODUCTION

Air, water, sunlight, and arable land are the essential resources required for agricultural production. Air and sunlight are readily available, and when water is provided by artificial irrigation systems, these are dependent on input of support energy. Support energy, in addition to sunlight, is also used extensively in technological agricultural systems for the manufacture and use of mechanical aids, transport vehicles, fertilizers, weed killers, and insecticides. In all but the most primitive agricultural systems, input of energy is involved. Energy and arable land are, therefore, the two critical resources required for agricultural production, supplemented as are all production systems by human effort.

Resources of Land

Estimates indicate that approximately half the world's arable land was under cultivation in 1970. Thus, if the average food output per unit area does not increase, the supply of arable land will become critically limited as the world population approaches double the 1970 population of 3,500 million soon after 2000. Land reclamation may add to the world's resource of arable land but this will be offset by the continuing depletion of agricultural land by erosion, and urban and industrial development.

In other words, there is considerable uncertainty about the supply of land and whether it will be sufficient to meet the world's food demand in the future, even after the introduction of more productive agricultural systems. Such systems tend to rely on extensive inputs of support energy, and possibly will endanger the long-term fertility of the soil. This critical problem of the ability of land to produce sufficient food in the future raises the important additional question of whether the large scale cultivation of crops to produce alternative fuel sources or raw materials for industry will be feasible.

In view of the possibility that land for food production may become critical within a period of twenty years, it is worth considering whether alternative systems to agriculture are feasible.

There are only two possible systems. Raw materials, other than those from plant cultivation, which would compete with agriculture for land, can be made sufficiently available only by means of the following:

- Total synthesis of the components of food from the raw materials of carbon dioxide, water, and nitrogen, supplemented by relatively much smaller amounts of elements such as phosphorous and sulfur.
- By conversion of the world's store of organic materials, i.e., the fossil fuels.

However, with the exception of algal culture and the biological conversion of the fossil fuels, all the alternatives within these two categories would require energy input of a far greater magnitude than possible from agricultural systems as described below. Without an enormous increase in the world's energy resources, agriculture will, therefore, remain the main source of the world's food supply. This means that if a crisis in food supply is to be avoided, every effort should be made to improve agricultural production and to use the output from agricultural systems more efficiently.

Energy Input to Alternatives to Agriculture

Energy input is essential for all possible production methods. In order to compare the energy efficiencies of the various systems, E values have been estimated where E is the unit of energy input per unit of energy in the food product. Where an energy input from sunlight is involved this is not included in the E values, and is also omitted from E values which refer to agricultural production. If the food products are not specified, it is assumed that the system would provide a nutritionally balanced diet, the composition of which would consist of 10 percent protein, 10 percent fat, and 80 percent carbohydrate. The energy value of foods with this composition is 4620 kcal/kg.

Vitamins are required in very small quantities relative to the bulk components of the diet. They can all be manufactured by industrial processes and, in relation to the total requirements, significant amounts are currently being manufactured. Neither raw materials, manufacturing capacity, nor energy resources are liable to be limiting factors in the production of sufficient vitamins to supplement foods from either agricultural or alternative systems of food production.

The synthesis of all components of food, by chemical methods from the readily available raw materials of carbon dioxide, water and nitrogen, is feasible. Only the synthesis of carbohydrate has not been established as a technically viable process. The energy required for such a system is considerable, and is estimated at a value of 33E. By combining chemical and biological methods of synthesis, the energy requirement is reduced, although there is less control over the composition of the food product. For the chemical synthesis of methanol, for example, followed by its conversion to yeast or bacterial biomass with a high protein content, a value of 14E is estimated. Biological synthesis by the agency of the single celled algae has been investigated, and from data reported for an experimental cultivation system, a value of 2.8E is estimated. There is, however, the possibility of improvement in the technology of cultivating and harvesting the algal cells, which could result in a considerable decrease in the energy input required for this system.

Chemical processes for the conversion of fossil fuel raw materials to food are technically feasible, and fats, amino acids, and vitamins are being manufactured on a large scale. Since the raw materials contain stored energy derived from the process of photosynthesis in prehistoric times, the energy input to the system is considerably less than what is required for a system of total synthesis. The E value, which includes the fossil fuel raw material input, is estimated at 6.5E. Biological conversion of the fossil fuels has been extensively investigated in recent years, and processes for conversion by bacteria, fungi, and yeast have been developed. The E value for the production of microbial biomass from petroleum is estimated to be 3.1E. Although the processes developed have concentrated on the production of products with a high protein content and have been termed single cell protein, biomass with a high fat content can be produced by adjustments in the culture media and conditions of growth.

All the alternative systems discussed have the advantage over agriculture in that they do not require the use of arable land. The value of 2E for agricultural production, listed in table 12.1, is for a system with a high proportion of animal sources of food in the diet, and when a considerable amount of energy is used to replace human effort. A value of 1E is considered, therefore, to be more representative of agricultural systems. With the exception of algal culture and the biological conversion of the fossil fuels, all other systems have E values much greater than that of agricultural production. Although the E values given are only approximate estimates, they are considered to indicate the relative order of magnitude of the energy consumption in the various systems. For the chemical synthesis of food, the value of 33E would involve nearly 50 percent of the total current consumption of energy in the United States. The E value for the biological conversion of the fossil fuels could probably be reduced by technical improvements, and is of the same order of magnitude as a technological system of agricultural production. However, the future supply and the competing demands for the fossil fuels indicate that this system could only provide a minor supplemental supply of food. Algal culture differs from all other systems by requiring a large area of land, because of its need for exposure to sunlight. The nature of the land surface is not critical, and algal production does not need to occupy arable land. Since the E value could probably be reduced to a level comparable with that of technological agricultural systems, it is suggested that research and development on algal culture should be intensified. The product may be used as a source of food, or it could provide a source of biological raw materials for industry.

Table 12.1. Energy Consumption in the Production and Processing of Food (USA, 1970)

	Energy input / Energy of food output
Agricultural production	2.0
Food processing	3.2
Retail distribution, home storage and cooking	3.1
Total	8.3

METHODS FOR IMPROVING AGRICULTURAL OUTPUT

Production systems, other than those of arable land and natural supplies of water agriculture, can be considered to be dependent on the input of the two fundamental components: energy and human effort. If all the input of energy and human effort involved in a production system are added together, the resources required for the production of one unit of product can be expressed as energy and labor densities. For a technological agricultural system, the input of man-hours is small although the total amount of energy used is considerable. At the other end of the scale, labor input is high and, when applied to food production in an unfavorable environment, the product may not be sufficient to sustain in normal health the number of people involved in the production process. This situation applies in many areas of the developing countries.

An intermediate level of technology, originally proposed in economic terms by E.F. Schumacher, can also be defined as the optimum combination of labor with energy to produce the essentials for the survival of a healthy human population.

In the developing world, priority should be given to improving the productivity of the small farming unit, which is the main source of food supply. An increase of 20 percent in the productivity of the subsistence farmer would be sufficient to prevent most of the malnutrition which currently occurs. Some examples of the ways in which productivity could be increased follow.

There are specific periods in the crop production cycle when there are peak demands for labor. These critical periods determine the productivity of the system. The provision of simple tools to aid the farmer during these critical periods, such as a hoe or a scythe, can improve his overall productivity. Farming methods involving legumes in crop rotation, or the interplanting of legumes with cereals can increase yields without destroying the fertility of the soil. In the developed countries, crop rotation methods have tended to decline due to the specialization of crop production, and the availability of artificial nitrogen fertilizers. Improvements in the quality of seed available to the small farming unit can produce a significant increase in crop yields.

These few examples are sufficient to indicate that a considerable increase in the output of food could be obtained from areas where the productivity is low without resorting to methods which require high inputs of support energy. The knowledge and appropriate technical aid required to prevent the current occurrence of malnutrition is therefore available. The need is to disseminate this information, and provide the technical aid where it will be effective.

Methods for Making More Effective Use of Agricultural Output

In the affluent countries, the emphasis on the application of food technology is to produce more sophisticated products to attract the consumer, frequently at the expense of the nutritional value of the product. In the developing countries, a considerable proportion of the food supply is wasted because of poor storage conditions and the lack of methods of preservation. There is, therefore, a need in the future to apply more appropriate technologies to derive the maximum nutritional benefit from the output of agriculture.

In areas in which protein malnutrition prevails, optimum mixtures of cereals and legumes in the diet can improve the nutritional quality of the protein intake. In theory, it is not essential to include animal protein in the diet to maintain perfect health. However, in view of the uncertainty of this theoretical concept, particularly in relation to the provision of vitamin B 12, it may be advisable to include a small proportion of food from animal sources in diets. The proportion required is much smaller than that which prevails in Europe and North America, where no benefit to health is derived from the consumption of excessive quantities.

A reduction of 20 percent in the consumption of animal protein by the United States would release sufficient land to feed 100 million people on a cereal diet. Unfortunately for the food supply problem, human beings do not confine their consumption of food to their physiological need, and in nearly all cultures food from animal sources is valued and consumed, wherever it is available, in quantities greater than are essential to meet nutritional needs.

In the current world economic system, the excessive consumption of food from animal sources is liable to continue in the more affluent societies, in spite of the need for increased food supplies in the poorer areas of the world. Meat, in addition to being the main commodity consumed, also places the greatest demand on land use for the provision of livestock feed. Several recently developed technologies can be applied to reducing this demand, either by producing meat substitutes, or by providing alternatives to forage crops as sources of feed for livestock.

TEXTURED FOODS

The texturing of plant proteins to simulate meat is now a well-established process, which has been applied most extensively to soya protein. The loss during protein conversion is insignificant when compared to the loss of over 90 percent for the process of conversion by ruminants and of 75 percent for conversion by nonruminant livestock. The texturing process primarily involves a rearrangement of the structure of protein particles, and is a process which requires a relatively low energy input when compared to other processes in the food chain. It is interesting to note that in response to a similar food crisis, which arose when the rapid increase in urban population occurred during the early development of the industrial revolution, the texturing of vegetable oils and fats into margarine was developed to satisfy the demand for a product to simulate butter.

CONVERSION OF WASTES TO LIVESTOCK FEED

It is estimated that less than one-quarter of the biomass produced by the growth of crop plants is consumed as food. Large quantities of wastes, or underutilized materials, remain on the farm and further quantities occur during the processing of food and other biological raw materials. These wastes represent a largely untapped source of materials for conversion to livestock feed. Although a small proportion has some value as livestock feed in the form in which it occurs, the main bulk of these wastes are either indigestible, have very low nutritive value, or contain harmful substances which prevent their use as food.

From the wastes which contain a substantial proportion of protein, separation of the protein is probably the most effective method of utilization. Estimates indicate that the annual production of residues containing protein which remain after extraction of oil from the oilseeds is approximately 20 million tons, and in the past a substantial proportion of this material has been wasted or underutilized. Processes have been developed, or are being investigated, to enable this potential supply of protein to be made available for use as food or livestock feed. Within the past two years, several units for the extraction of protein from leafy materials have been established in the United Kingdom.

Most other wastes, according to their composition and the form in which they occur, can be divided into the following three categories:

- Solid fibrous wastes which occur mainly on the farm or at the site of primary processing. These have a low moisture content, are biologically stable, and can be stored and used for conversion in an even flow throughout the year. Examples are cereal straws, sugar cane bagasse, and sunflower heads.
- Solid nonfibrous wastes. These usually have a high moisture content, and deteriorate rapidly unless they are dried. Examples are fruits and vegetables rejected because of quality standards, and the peelings and other tissue removed during food processing.
- Liquid wastes. These contain dissolved or suspended organic matter, and occur as effluents from the processing of foods and other biological raw materials. They are biologically unstable and deteriorate rapidly. Examples are molasses, soya whey from the texturing process, and liquid wastes produced during the extraction of palm and olive oils.

The fibrous wastes consist primarily of lignocellulose. Because of the protective effect of lignin and the fibrous structure of cellulose, they are difficult to digest even by ruminant livestock. Treatment with alkali solutions, such as sodium hydroxide, separates lignin, and decreases the extent of the fibrous structure of cellulose. The nutritive value of cereal straws as a source of feed energy for ruminants can be increased several fold by this treatment, and a process applying this principle has been recently established in the United Kingdom.

CONVERSION OF WASTES BY MICROORGANISMS

Waste can be converted by microorganisms into biomass with a high nutritive value for use as livestock feed or, in some cases, for human consumption. Species of bacteria, fungi, and yeasts have been investigated. Most wastes require to be supplemented with nitrogen, which is essential for the production of protein; however all the species investigated are capable of using ammonium salts as their source of nitrogen. The carbon source is the main component required, and it is the chemical composition of the carbon compounds in wastes, which determines the type of microorganisms which can be used for conversion.

Yeast species are less versatile in the range of organic compounds they can use for growth, and molasses is one of the few wastes on which food yeast (Candida utilis) can be grown. Some bacterial species will grow on most wastes; however the cells are difficult to harvest, and due to their content of nucleic acid, they may cause problems if they are used for food.

For these reasons, we have investigated fungal species in our studies. Many fungal species produce a wide range of enzymes, and are capable of growth on most waste materials. Fungal biomass has the advantage of having a cohesive matted structure that can be harvested by simple filtration methods. In pilot plant studies, sufficient quantities of the biomass of several fungal species have been produced for feeding trials with rats, pigs, and poultry as test animals. No adverse symptoms have been observed, and the nutritive value of the biomass as a source of protein is equivalent to that of plant protein concentrates, such as soya meal.

Theoretically, the maximum yield of microbial biomass from carbohydrate compounds is approximately 60 percent, and 50-55 percent is considered to be the best possible practical yield. However, the difficulties associated with the digestion of fibrous wastes also apply to their conversion by microorganisms. For the fungal conversion of a fiber waste from the manufacture of cellulose pulp, the enzyme activity of the microorganism was increased by growing the inoculum by surface culture on a fiber slurry. When this inoculum was introduced into the main growth vessel, rapid conversion of the cellulose fibers to fungal biomass occured. The yield and protein content are reported in Table 12.2. For the conversion of the sunflower heads, discarded after removal of the seed, 20% of the growth medium from a previous batch was added as a source of enzymes. Rapid conversion took place of this fibrous waste to fungal biomass. Yields are reported in Table 12.2. As an indication of the quantities of this waste available, 750,000 tons are discarded annually in Turkey.

The solid nonfibrous wastes are easier to convert to fungal biomass. More than 20 percent of the banana crop is discarded for quality reasons. We have investigated conversion of the whole banana, including the stem and skin, since separation would be uneconomic.

Yields for both protein and fat production are also given in table 12.2.

The effluents from the processing of many biological materials contain dissolved or suspended organic matter, which causes extensive pollution if these effluents are discharged without treatment into lakes, rivers, or the sea. The Biological Oxygen Demand (BOD), which is a measure of the extent of pollution, may be one hundred times greater than that of the effluent from an urban community. The activated sludge process is the main method which is used for effluent treatment. The product consists of the biomass of a mixed population of microorganisms, the composition of which is not controlled, and for which there can be no guarantee of the absence of harmful micro-organisms or toxic substances. The controlled growth of a fungal culture in the effluent reduces the BOD, and can be carried out with equipment similar to that used for the activated sludge process. It will have approximately the same energy consumption. The fungal product is suitable as livestock feed or, in some cases, as a source of food for human consumption.

Table 12.2. Yields of Fungal Biomass from Wastes

Waste	Yield per hundred parts of waste	Protein	BOD reduction
Cellulose pulp fibers	51	31%	
Sunflower heads	42	36.5%	
Effluent from palm oil extraction	28g/liter	11g/liter	90%
Waste bananas	54	31%	
Waste bananas	36	22% fat	

All of the processes for the microbiological conversion of wastes would make more effective use of these bioresources if the products were to be used directly for human consumption instead of passing as feed via the animal food chain. The technologies are available for converting the biomass of microorganisms to acceptable food products. Textured protein fibers have been prepared from the protein of yeasts and bacteria, while the fungal biomass of several fungal species has a texture, when it is harvested, similar to that of pressed chicken meat. From these materials, flavored food products, similar to those developed with textured soya protein, could be produced. However, due to the extensive and expensive testing required to establish the safety of these products for human consumption, it will be several years before they are likely to make any contribution to food supplies.

An indication of the energy consumption of these fungal processes can be assessed from data reported for the process for the growth and harvesting of yeast biomass for which a value of 1.7 E is estimated, where E is the unit of energy input per unit of energy in the food product. For a fungal process, the energy consumption will be similar except that less energy will be required for harvesting. Modifications to the standard process for growing yeast, on which the above estimate was based, could reduce energy consumption. By sterilizing the growth medium at a low pH value, the temperature and time required are considerably reduced. We found that the most heat resistant bacterial spores in several wastes were sterilized by heating for three minutes at 43°C at a pH value of 0.45. The acid growth medium can be subsequently neutralized with ammonia, which provides nitrogen as a nutrient.

In the standard fermenter equipment used for growing microorganisms, air is pumped into the growth vessel to provide oxygen. To maintain the culture in a homogeneous state, the vessel is fitted with a mechanical agitation system. This type of vessel was used in the yeast process referred to above. By applying the principle of an airlift system, a growth vessel has been developed in which the air introduced as a source of oxygen is the only agitation required. In this airlift fermenter, fungi have been grown on a variety of wastes. Yields, rates of growth and, where appropriate, BOD reduction were the same as those in a mechanically agitated vessel. Theoretical calculations reported in the literature show that the energy input required to operate an airlift fermenter will be one-third that required for a mechanically agitated vessel. Although the extent of this reduction has to be established for a full-scale process, there is no doubt that an airlift fermenter will have a lower energy input. Taking into account the aspects discussed above, the energy consumption for the production of fungal biomass from wastes will be less than 1.7E.

Where liquid wastes have to be treated to prevent pollution of the environment, the fungal process, which yields a product that contributes to the food supply, has an obvious advantage. The first large-scale application of this principle has recently been established in Finland for the treatment of wastes from the manufacture of cellulose pulp.

SUMMARY AND CONCLUSION

In the foreseeable future, agriculture will remain the main source of the world's food supply. Resources are currently available for agriculture to provide an adequate supply for the world population. Malnutrition among a large section of the population is, therefore, the result of the maldistribution of resources or the knowledge to apply them most effectively.

Within the next twenty years, if the world population continues to increase at the present rate, the supply of arable land will become critical. The conservation of arable land should therefore be given priority by all governments. Measures must be taken to disseminate the knowledge and technical aid, which will enable the less productive farmers to increase their output, and research methods for improving agricultural production should be intensified.

Food supplies could be used more effectively to meet nutritional requirements by applying more appropriate methods of food processing. The consumption of foods from animal sources, which makes a large demand on arable land use, could be reduced in the world's affluent societies without any adverse effect on the health of the population. This change is more likely to be accepted if products which simulate animal foods are made available from plant raw materials.

Huge quantities of wastes are produced annually from agriculture and the subsequent processing of food and biological materials. These wastes are the world's main underutilized bioresource. The feasibility of converting many of these wastes to livestock feed, without the application of large input of energy, has been demonstrated. The products could replace forage crops, and release land for food production. Some of these products may be suitable as food for human consumption. Research and development is needed; however, to establish the safety of their use in the human diet. The quantity of waste is sufficient for a limited period of years to provide raw materials for industry, or materials for conversion to biosources of fuel. However, when resources for food production become critical, priority may need to be given to the use of wastes for food or feed production.

In the economic system which prevails in most of the world, current supplies in relation to demand determine the priorities, and no account is taken of the depletion of resources which may become critical in the future. Food is a commodity for which adequate supplies are essential to ensure the survival of a healthy population. Every effort, therefore, should be made to ensure that methods are available to improve agricultural production and make more effective use of our agricultural output.

REFERENCES

The following are articles by the author that give details on the information on which this chapter has been based.

Hockenhull, D.J.D., ed. 1968. Culture of the higher fungi. Prog. in Ind. Microbio 1, p. 74. London: Churchill.

British Food Manufacturing Research Association. 1973. Utilization of agricultural and food industry wastes. Byproducts of the Food Industry, Symposium Proceedings No. 16. England: Leatherhead.

Porter, J.G.W., and Rolls, B.A., eds. 1973. World supplies of proteins from unconventional sources. Proteins in Human Nutrition, p. 44. London: Academic Press.

Jones, J.G.W., ed. 1973. Protein production by micro-organisms from carbohydrate substrates. The Biological Efficiency of Protein Production, p. 339. Cambridge University Press.

Single Cell Protein. 1974. Plant Foods for Man 1, p. 99.

Bourne, A., and Steele, F., eds. 1975. Food production methods and their potential for increasing food supplies. The Man Food Equation, p. 179. London: Academic Press.

Proceedings of the International Food Industries Congress. 1975. Intermediate Technology for food utilization in Developing Countries, p. 123. London: Food Trade Press.

Duckman, A.N., Jones, J.G.W., and Roberts, E.H., eds. 1976. The efficiency of technological systems of food production. Food Production and Consumption, p. 215. Amsterdam: North Holland Pub. Co.

Birch, G.G., Parker, K.J., and Worgan, J.T., eds. 1976. Waste from crop plants as raw materials for conversion by fungi to food or livestock feed. Food from Waste, p. 23. London: Applied Science Publishers.

Norton, G., ed. 1978. Protein production by micro-organisms. Plant Proteins, p. 191. London: Butterworths.

Symposium on New Food Sources for Animal Production. Feeding value improvement of byproducts by micro biological processes. University of Cordoba, Spain (In press.)

13 A New Source of Food and Feed Proteins: The Waterloo SCP Process

Murray Moo-Young

Protein malnutrition, environmental pollution, and energy shortages are growing socioeconomic problems in many parts of the world. The utilization of waste biomass to produce edible products of SCP (single cell proteins) could help to alleviate all these problems simultaneously. Biomass is a renewable bioresource and occurs universally in vast quantities as agricultural and forestry residues or surpluses, in such forms as straws, corn stover, sugarcane bagasse, animal manures, wood sawdust, paper residues, pulp mill sludges, cassava, banana, and yam. Various biomass-to-SCP conversion processes have been proposed. (1) At present, the Waterloo SCP process is one of the few which appears to be economically feasible for developing countries. (2,3) A brief description of this process is given below.

THE WATERLOO SCP PROCESS

This process is based on the mass cultivation of certain yeasts or fungi in a factory-controlled aerobic fermenter, using waste carbohydrates as the main carbon nutrient. The yeast is grown in liquid-substrate fermentation systems on sugars produced by acid hydrolysis of the carbohydrate material; the fungus is grown in solid-substrate fermentation systems on the carbohydrate materials after preliminary softening and/or partial delignification of the material by thermal or thermochemical treatment. Supplementary nutrients for the culture are supplied by air and animal manures or fertilizer blends. A contamination-free culture is maintained by using low pH, sterile air and/or low moisture conditions. For energy conservation, anaerobically predigested manure is used, whereby methane fuel gas is produced as a by-product which is integrated into the overall process energy requirements. The processing water is recycled, and the pollution potential of the original raw materials is virtually eliminated. Application of the process for on-site or near-site farm operations is illustrated in figure 13.1.

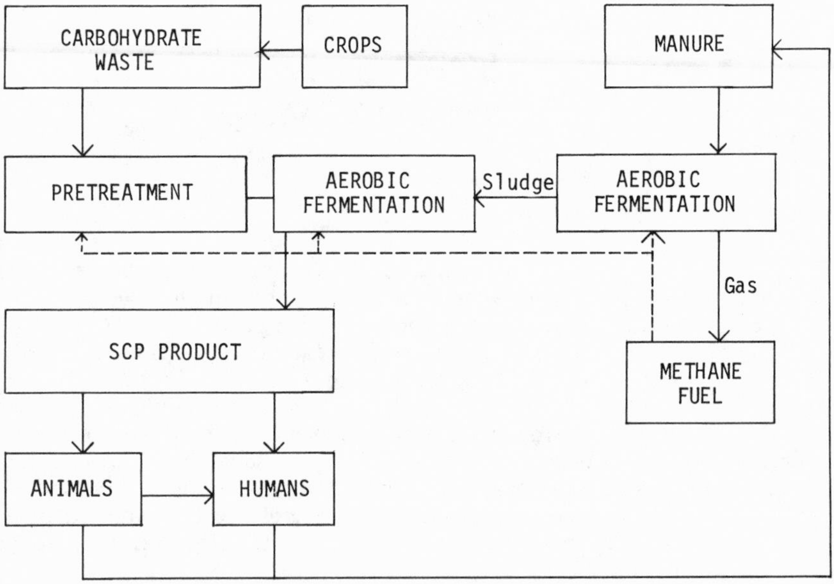

Fig. 13.1. Energy-conserving farm application of the Waterloo SCP process in waste biomass utilization.

Innovative features of the process include: novel scum-free tubular fermenters (4); a technique for enhancing fermentation productivity with inexpensive polymer additives (5); use of a new thermotolerant cellulolytic organism (6); energy-conservation by optimal integration of multicomponent aerobic-anaerobic fermentation systems. (7) These inventions are protected by various patents allowed or pending, and their commercial applications are controlled by the University of Waterloo Research Institute.

Extensive laboratory tests have already established that the process is technically feasible and is flexible in exploitation. Pilot-plant tests are in progress to check the economic viability for several operational strategies which have been derived from computer simulations of the process.

PRODUCT QUALITY

There are two basic varieties of the protein product. One variety contains a new cellulolytic fungus, Chaetomium cellulolyticum; it is recovered by simple filtration and drying as gray fibrous solids having a pleasant mushroomlike odor, and a protein content of up to 45% DM. Table 13.1 shows that the protein has a good amino acid profile compared to soya protein, and the UN-FAO Reference protein. Preliminary feeding trials with rats indicate that the product is suitably nontoxic, digestible, and nutritious in feed rations. Pathological examinations also show no malgrowth formations in the test animals.

Table 13.1. Essential amino acid profile (in %DM) of protein in the WAT-SCP products compared with soybean and the FAO reference proteins

Essential Amino acid	Fungal Product	Yeast Product	Soybean Meal	FAO Reference
Threonine	6.1	5.6	4.0	2.8
Valine	5.8	6.3	5.0	4.2
Cystine	0.3	0.7	1.4	2.0
Methionine	2.3	1.2	1.4	2.2
Isoleucine	4.7	5.3	5.4	4.2
Leucine	7.5	7.0	7.7	4.8
Tyrosine	3.3	3.3	2.7	2.8
Phenylalanine	3.8	4.3	5.1	2.8
Lysine	6.8	6.7	6.5	4.2
Tryptophan	-	1.2	1.5	1.4

The other variety of the product is based on a well-known fodder yeast, Candida utilis, whose amino acid profile is also given in the table. It is already established as an excellent feed or food supplement. The product is recovered by centrifugation and drying as an off-white powder or cream (as required), with a weak maltlike taste and odor, and a protein content of up to 55% DM.

The nonprotein components of both SCP product varieties are mostly carbohydrate and fat, which are also useful in feed and food rations.

Both are also rich in vitamin B complex. With cellulosic raw materials, forage-grade cellulose can be programmed into the technology for the production of complete protein-carbohydrate ruminant feed rations. Some lignin may be left in the product as fiber-aid roughage in diets.

PROCESS ECONOMICS

The process economics will depend on the scale and location of operation, the product composition, and state, etc. A computer program has been developed, which allows economic assessments of the process for a variety of scenarios of practical interest. For example, our present results, based on the utilization of straw and manure residues, indicate that the process is economically attractive for the near-site farm cooperative production and distribution of a complete protein-carbohydrate feed ration required by the equivalent of 1,000 or more head of cattle. (3) Similarly, with the increasing pressures on the pulp and paper industries to curb environmental pollution, the process appears to be economically attractive for the upgrading of waste clarifier sludges into the SCP products.

The Waterloo SCP Process becomes increasingly attractive for the future, and for Third World countries, when a trade off is made between the availability of renewable biomass resources and the rising costs of protein.

REFERENCES

(1) Moo-Young, M. 1976. A survey of SCP production facilities. Process Biochem. 11, No. 10, pp. 32-34.

(2) Moo-Young, M. 1977. The economics of SCP production. Process Biochem. 12, No. 4, pp. 6-10.

(3) Moo-Young, M, Daugulis, A.G., Chahal, D.S., and Macdonald, D.G. 1979. The Waterloo Process for SCP Production from Waste Biomass. Proc. Biochem. 14.

(4) Moo-Young, M., van Dedem, G., and Binder, A. 1979. Design of scraped tubular fermenters. Biotechnol. Bioeng. 21, pp. 593-607.

(5) Elmayergi, H., Scharer, J.M., and Moo-Young, M. 1973. Effects of polymer additives on fermentation parameters in a culture of *A. niger*. Biotechnol. Bioeng. 15, pp. 845-860.

(6) Moo-Young, M., Chahal, D.S., Swan, J.E., and Robinson, C.W., 1977. SCP production by *Chaetomium cellulolyticum*, a new thermotolerant cellulolytic fungus. Biotechnol. Bieng. 19, pp. 527-538.

(7) Moo-Young, M., Moreira, A., Daugulis, A.J., and Robinson, C.W. 1979. Bioconversion of agricultural wastes into animal feed and fuel gas. Biotechnol. Bioeng. Symposium Series, vol. 8, pp. 19-28.

14 Bioconversion Systems for Feed Production in Kuwait*

K. Behbehani, I.Y. Hamdan, A. Shams, N. Hussain

Kuwait is a petroleum-rich desert country located to the northeast of the Arabian Peninsula. A large fraction of the country's population dwells in Kuwait City, which imports much of its food, and must produce most of its potable water by evaporative desalinization. The Kuwait Institute for Scientific Research (KISR) has established programs devoted to increasing the self-sufficiency of Kuwait in terms of agricultural commodities, water, and manufactured goods. Inasmuch as Kuwait and its neighboring countries are blessed with an abundance of proven oil and natural gas reserves, as well as solar energy, one method of improving self-sufficiency is to discover, develop, and apply bioconversion systems, as well as to apply solar technologies to a maximum extent. Such technologies, when developed, would then provide the essentials of wealth after petroleum ceases to be a major source of national income.

Modern techniques for the economic production of poultry and livestock require strictly controlled conditions, and feeds that have

---

* The authors would like to express their thanks to KISR research staff, whose research reports formed an important part of this contribution, and to Dr. G. Hamer for his help in the preparation of this paper.

been compounded on a least-cost basis. Compounded feeds, which normally contain between 10 and 30 percent protein on a weight basis, are designed to satisfy the entire nutritional requirements of the fowl or animal to be fed. The bulk ingredients in all compounded feeds are cereals. The main function of cereals is to provide energy, but they also provide a low level of protein. Protein is, of course, the key functional ingredient in compounded feeds, and the available amino acid profile of the protein largely determines the performance characteristics of the feed. The traditional protein-rich ingredients used in feeds are oil seed meals, in particular soya bean meal.

Intensive poultry and livestock production in Kuwait and much of the Middle East is totally dependent on imported ingredients for feeds. Cereals are obtained from a number of sources with wide geographical distribution, but soya bean production for export is largely restricted to the USA and Brazil. Soybeans and soya bean meal are traded on a commodities basis, and considerable price fluctuations occur as a result of small actual or predicted fluctuations in supply and demand. (1) The instabilities in protein supply and pricing have acted as a major stimulant for the development of alternative protein sources. Fish meal is well established as a protein ingredient in feeds, but its production is declining, as the human food sector utilizes an increasing percentage of the essentially constant total world fish catch. (2)

A second major alternative is offered by Single Cell Protein (SCP), (3) produced directly by the growth of microorganisms on hydrocarbons, petrochemicals, and waste carbohydrates, or photosynthetically on carbon dioxide. The following production routes have been proposed for SCP:

(a) The growth of yeasts or bacteria on n-alkane or gas oil. (4)

(b) The growth of yeasts or bacteria on methanol. (5)

(c) The growth of bacteria on natural gas. (6)

(d) The growth of yeasts on ethanol. (7)

(e) The photosynthetic growth of algae on carbon dioxide. (8)

(f) The growth of yeasts or fungi on carbohydrates or cellulose. (9)

(g) The growth of yeasts or fungi on industrial waste liquors. (10)

These routes are presently at various stages of research, development, or commercialization in numerous organizations throughout the world. The routes that are assessed to be of initial interest in Kuwait are (a), (b), (c), and longer term route (e).

In Europe, North America, and Japan the production of biomass for animal feed from either hydrocarbons or petrochemicals has lost much of its commercial attractiveness. However, the situation is different in the major oil exporting countries, particularly as the quantities of feedstock required for self-sufficiency in animal feed protein production are small when compared with the total production of hydrocarbons at present and for many years to come. Further, hydrocarbon fractions that are unsuitable for export can either be used as feedstocks or converted into appropriate feedstocks for SCP production.

ESTABLISHED RESEARCH AND DEVELOPMENT

An integrated SCP research and development program was established at KISR, in 1977, to investigate the SCP technologies researched and developed by other organizations. Its major aims were to determine the suitability of these technologies, and the need for any necessary modification to suit Kuwait's conditions. The activities comprising its integrated program were:

(a) The assessment of the technoeconomic feasibility of those SCP production routes that are of potential application in Kuwait.

(b) The isolation of microorganisms obtained from other sources, so as to select the most suitable process microorganisms for Kuwait's conditions.

(c) The determination under Kuwaiti conditions of the nutritional performance of SCP produced at KISR relative to products from other organizations, studying its stability and biochemical integrity, and its performance in preliminary toxicological safety tests.

(d) The construction, commissioning, and operation of an SCP pilot plant facility at KISR, in order to produce products for nutritional and toxicological evaluation, and to provide a center for the education and training of personnel in biotechnology.

Although KISR's program had already been established, its objectives are consistent with the recommendations of the OAPEC Petro-Protein Expert Committee Meeting held at the OAPEC Secretariat in Kuwait in March 1977.

To date, research has been undertaken on three of the four major areas proposed for study. The progress and achievements can best be summarized under the following subsections.

Technoeconomic Feasibility

In order to assess Kuwait's domestic requirements for food and feed, a 20-equation econometric model has been constructed. The model can be used to forecast the future consumption of eggs, poultry, dairy products, and beef and, concurrently, the demand for animal feed protein to 1985. The model has been subjected to alternative self-sufficiency assumptions for food production, and on this basis the potential requirement of SCP for compounded animal feeds is found to range from 30,000 to 50,000 tons per annum by 1985. Assuming that the economic plant capacity for SCP production will be 100,000 tons per annum, an exportable surplus of 50,000 to 70,000 tons per annum should be available. The potential SCP importing countries are Egypt, Iraq, Lebanon, Saudi Arabia, Sudan, Jordan, Syria, Iran, India, and Pakistan.

On the basis of per capita income elasticities of demand for food, reasonable assumptions concerning future income and population growth, and SCP inclusion levels in animal diets, the total potential requirements for SCP in the countries listed as possible importers will be between 1.1 million and 1.5 million tons by 1985. On the weak assumption that Kuwait will be able to command 5 percent of this market, it should be possible to dispose of excess production by exporting the SCP surplus to these countries.

A cost evaluation model has been constructed in order to assess both the capital and the manufacturing costs of SCP. Preliminary results indicate that for a 100,000 ton per annum plant, using the bacterial/methanol route, and erected in 1980 at a capital cost of U.S. $ 117 million, the production cost of SCP will be U.S. $ 512 per ton. Assuming a return on investment of 15 percent, the product selling price will be U.S. $ 689 per ton. (Sensitivity analyses on both the capital and the manufacturing costs are being undertaken to determine the competitiveness of SCP with conventional animal feed proteins, and the extent of Government subsidy required by the plant.)

Isolation and Physiology

Most microorganisms proposed as potential process cultures for SCP are mesophilic in nature; i.e., their optimum temperature for growth is between 20° and 40°C. For a process operating in Kuwait, the use of such cultures will require expensive refrigerated cooling systems if sensible productivities are to be achieved. Estimates indicate that refrigeration represents some 11 percent of the capital costs, and some 12 percent of the variable costs of the n-alkane-based process, so that seawater cooling is preferred. With this in mind, the culture isolation program undertaken at KISR has been directed towards the isolation of those thermotolerant or thermophilic microorganisms from the Kuwaiti environment that can grow well between 40° and 55°C, employing rather more imaginative isolation techniques than those used in conventional isolation exercises. The vast majority of work to date has been directed towards methano-utilizing microorganisms, with particular emphasis on methano-utilizing yeasts. The more limited work directed towards n-alkane-utilizing microorganisms has only recently started, and it will include work on gaseous and volatile liquid fractions as well as on the waxy n-alkanes.

One promising methanol-utilizing yeast that grows well in batch culture at 42°C has been isolated and identified as a strain of *Hansenula polymorpha*. Previous studies on *H. polymorpha* have indicated that 42°C is the maximum temperature for growth of this yeast, and at such temperatures the carbon based yield coefficient is depressed.

In work at KISR, it has only been possible to perform batch-culture experiments, but with the new facilities now commissioned, a process research program utilizing continuous flow culture techniques is now under way to determine the true potential of this yeast and other isolates (including both mono and mixed cultures of bacteria) with respect to other methanol-utilizing cultures. The subjects of immediate investigation involve temperature sensitivity, maximization of the carbon based yield coefficient, and microorganism nutrition and fastidiousness.

It is not, of course, the objective of this program to select cultures isolated solely from the Kuwaiti environment. If cultures from elsewhere offer more advantageous processes and product quality characteristics, they will be adopted for subsequent process development studies instead of locally obtained cultures.

Nutritional Evaluation

No nutritional studies on KISR-produced SCPs have yet been performed nor, in fact, will they be performed until the pilot plant facilities become operational. In studies to date, the emphasis has been placed on the relative evaluation of those SCP's produced by multinational industrial organizations under Kuwaiti conditions. Three products have been subjected to examination:

(a) Toprina from BP Proteins Ltd, an n-alkane grown yeast.

(b) Pruteen from ICI Ltd, Agriculture Division, a methanol grown bacterial mono culture.

(c) A product from Shell Research Ltd, a methane grown bacterial mixed culture.

The three SCPs were subjected to chemical and biological analysis, and their nutritive quality was assessed by substituting them for soya bean meal in conventional poultry rations. The lysine levels in all three SCPs were either equal to or exceeded that of soya bean meal, confirming the compatibility of the SCPs with commonly used cereals. The sulfur amino acid levels relative to soya bean meal were lower in the cases of Toprina and Pruteen, and higher in the case of the Shell product.

In both these and other tests, feed consumption was directly proportional to body weight gain. No variation in either feed efficiency or total protein efficiency was observed. Gross examination of the soft tissues of broiler chicks fed diets containing SCPs showed no abnormalities, although chicks fed bacterial SCPs tended to have slightly enlarged livers. None of the SCPs tested gave marked increase in the nucleic acid levels in the breast and thigh muscles of chicks, and absolute levels were far below the level safe for human consumption.

Pilot Plant Facility

The objectives of this facility were stated earlier. Essentially, as much process oriented research work as possible will be carried out in bench-scale fermenters in order to economize on the quantities of materials required, and facilitate the operation of the program. However, it will be necessary to further examine and test certain process engineering solutions, and process optimization alternatives on larger scale equipment. In addition, it is critical for the development of the project to provide moderate quantities of on-specification product for the KISR evaluation program; the same applies for the nutritional and toxicological work to be carried out by other laboratories charged with establishing the safety and functionality of SCP produced by KISR.

Further, pilot plant equipment, operated under realistic production conditions in an integrated manner, is a prerequisite for the proposed training program in biological process technology envisioned for both Kuwaiti and regional personnel.

Various options were open to KISR for initial development work, but it was decided to concentrate activities on an Effigas Fermenter of 1500 liter capacity, and on the appropriate ancillary equipment for continuous flow operation at moderate and high production rates. The Effigas Fermenter is a mechanically agitated fermenter, for which particularly favorable gas-liquid transfer characteristics are claimed. The sequence of process operations envisaged is entirely conventional. The preparation facility will be such as to permit the use of either hydrocarbon or petrochemical carbon feedstocks; sterilization will be possible prior to fermentation, and the product will be harvested by centrifugation after flocculation. The product produced will be dried prior to subsequent storage and use with a Niro Spray Dryer.

The scale of operation was based on the requirements of the product testing program and projected productivity of the fermenter. The KISR testing program will require 10 kg dry SCP per day per (calendar) year, and it is anticipated that approximately another 5 kg per day per (calendar) year will be required for the product. SCP production in the pilot plant will be on a continuous basis (24 hours per day, 7 days per week), but it is anticipated that during the first year of operation the pilot plant will only produce output of the required specification 120 days in the year. Further, although operations will be on a 24 hours per day basis, it is not expected to harvest material for more than 12 hours per day. In addition, a 20 percent loss during harvesting can be anticipated. On the assumption that an average productivity of 2.5 kg per m^3 per hour can be achieved during the first year of operation, it can be estimated that production will be 2765 kg, or 75 percent of KISR requirements. However, in subsequent years of operation an average productivity of 3.5 kg per m^3 per hour would probably be realistic, and production of on-specification product will proceed for 180 days per year, resulting in a total production of 5806 kg, or 6 percent in excess of total KISR and other predicted requirements.

Obviously, a certain amount of flexibility is involved here. For example, the harvesting period can be extended when necessary to meet extra requirements. In addition, it is not the intention to commence with the nutritional evaluation program of KISR product on the first day of production. Some initial stockpiling will be both necessary and desirable, and hence the problem of initial shortfall in production would be effectively solved.

FUTURE RESEARCH AND DEVELOPMENT

In view of the very favorable position that Kuwait has with respect to solar insolation, the potential of photosynthetic routes for SCP production through the cultivation of microalgae on waste waters, and recycled animal/poultry waste (in completely integrated feedlots) has been considered at KISR.

The proposed process is shown in fig. 14.1. In this process, the waste water is purified and many of the dissolved nutrients are converted to high-protein microalgae. Microalgae can be harvested and are potentially useful for animal feed and/or fertilizer.

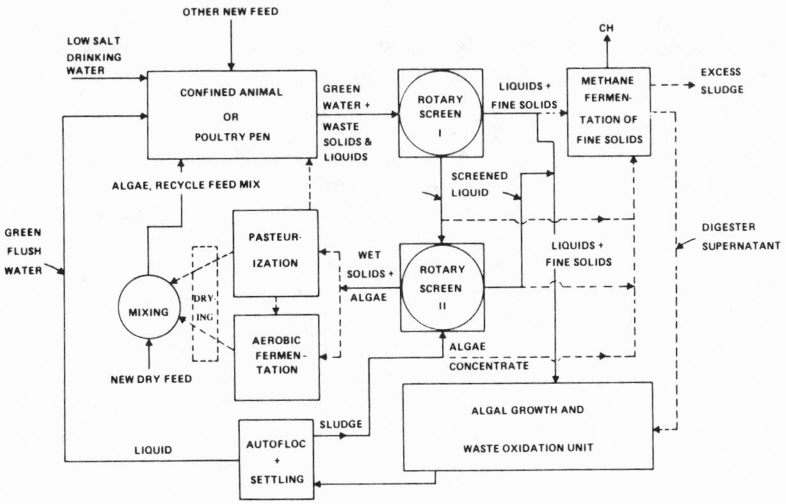

Fig. 14.1. Animal waste-algal-bacterial treatment and nutrient recycling system. (Dotted lines indicate alternative pathways.)

When microalgae are grown only on the wastes of feedlots (as opposed to municipal wastes), the potential is high for direct recycling of nutrients, and improved efficiency of fixed nitrogen utilization in the feedlot. For example, in conventional feedlot nitrogen-utilization efficiency is rarely more than 20 percent, whereas in completely integrated feedlots of the type shown in fig. 14.1, the nitrogen utilization efficiency can approach 80 percent or more.

Because of emphasis on other priorities in the United States, and a tendency to put feedlots in remote areas, no further work has been done on completely integrated poultry-algal-bacterial systems in the United States or elsewhere, even though such work is desperately needed. Therefore, in addition to fulfilling an important need for developing waste treatment and nutrient recycling processes in Kuwait, the output of these experiments will have international importance and will, no doubt, be given international attention.

The objectives of this program are to develop optimum designs for Kuwait, and operational procedures for large-scale integrated nutrient recycling systems involving poultry (or animals), algae, and bacteria. Studies will concentrate on the degree to which the wastes will be treated, the degree to which odor and fly breeding are controlled, and the extent to which nitrogen and other nutrients can be recycled. Also to be studied are new processes for algal separation, concentration, and processing in relation to the digestibility and protein utilization efficiency of algae, recycled feed, and new feed mixtures. Toxic metals, such as lead and cadmium, and biological toxicants such as ergot will be monitored as well. The technical and environmental costs and benefits of having algal cultures above the chicken pens will also be examined.

Output from this system will be information that can be used to design feedlot systems that treat (feedlot) wastes, are free from the nuisance of odors and flies, and permit recovery and recycling of protein nitrogen and other nutrients that would be lost in ordinary feedlots. Other important outputs will be information on algal productivity, and solar energy conversion efficiency through growth of algae on feedlot wastes, methods of processing feedlot waste solids and algae (to maximize nitrogen recovery and digestibility), development of improved algal harvesting procedures, and information on the toxicology and microbiology of completely integrated feedlot systems. The benefits and costs of utilizing the pen roof as the algal culture vessel will be observed throughout the experiments.

SOCIOECONOMIC CONSIDERATIONS

Controlled microbiological production of biomass is an economical process for the provision of energy, feeds, and fertilizers. In countries short of energy, developed as well as developing, biodigestion plants are proposed as a means of overcoming the problem of energy supplies. For example, the Ford Foundation has sponsored an economic evaluation of biodigesters for American farms to combat the uncertainties in availability and price of energy for farmers.

In contrast, Kuwait is not facing uncertainties regarding the supply of energy, nor is it confronting an excess of organic waste. However, it is interested in bioconversion processes for the production of protein and other products.

Until very recently, economists were rejecting the economic merits of energy production from renewable resources as very expensive; but due to a change in market factors, as well as utilization of life cycle costs and other comprehensive methods, such rejections, based on back-of-envelope calculations are less often heard. Production of protein from organic material is facing the same economic criticism today. As stated earlier, the production cost of SCP in Kuwait is considered high and so has been dismissed as uneconomical for the time being.

Uncertainties facing food economics at the global level are by no means of smaller magnitude than those concerned with the energy market. The demand factor in the Middle East is of special peculiarity, since the meat consumption in that part of the world is still one-sixth that of the United States level, while the per capita income is growing fast and approaching United States levels. Thus, the derived demand in the area will be fast growing. Most of the forecasts, even without considering the dynamism of such a factor, are not optimistic that supply of protein feeds for this region is going to suffice in satisfying the demand for meat.

By utilizing bioconversion systems as a means of converting the most abundant organic materials, a country like Kuwait can overcome uncertainties about this factor in its food industry. Our estimate at KISR indicates that converting about 1 percent of our flared gas will produce about 100,000 tons of SCP per year, which will satisfy Kuwait's need in protein feed (about 30,000 tons), and enable the country to export 70,000 tons to neighboring countries. Economically speaking, this is viewed as a bond against uncertainties in the food market. Considering that Kuwait has to import more than 90 percent of its food requirements, and thus has a dependency rate higher than any oil importing country has on energy imports, the value of such a bond in time of crisis is considerably high. Assuming a life cycle of n years for a given plant, then the stream of annual output will have a market value of:

$$S_1, S_2, \ldots, S_n.$$

If we compare the capital cost of the plant plus its operational cost with these returns, its economic merits can be seen clearly. To compare the cost with return, we use a life cycle present value system. Since the uncertainties facing the world food market are quite high, a rather high escalation in market price for this commodity is certain.

This can be noted in most of the econometric studies made on the subject, which place the expected rise in food prices above the inflation and discount rates. In such cases the present value of the microbiologically manufactured feed will be an increasing function over time. This can be written simply as:

$$P.V. = \sum_{t=1}^{n} S_t \left(\frac{1+i}{1+r}\right)^n,$$

where

$$S_1 = S_o \left(\frac{1+i}{1+r}\right), S_2 = S_o \left(\frac{1+i}{1+r}\right)^2, ---, S_n = S_o \left(\frac{1+i}{1+r}\right)^n,$$

and where S_o is the present market value of the annual output of the plant, i is the expected rise in the real price of protein feeds (here we assume a given annual rate, but in a thorough investigation the rate would change based on economic scenarios foreseen over years), and r is the real discount rate prevailing in the market. The present value curve of the life cycle cost of the plant will not be as steep as the curve representing the present output value of the plant. This is due to the fact that the incremental cost in components will increase with the general level of inflation. The relationship between these functions is shown in fig. 14.2 below.

In fig. 14.2, OC is the capital cost of the plant CC_n is the present value of operational cost over n years, and OS_o is the current market value of the output of the plant.

As can be seen, the accumulated present value of all returns is negative until year g where the two curves cross; from then on, the present value of economic gain increases at an increasing rate. The present value of net gain during the life of the plant is indicated by ε_c and ε_s.

The above calculation is a microeconomic evaluation, and does not include the total contribution of such a process to the national economy. The spin-off effects of value added gains of indigenous economic activity, such as for the SPC project, will probably add to its economic validity. Moreover the economic value of homegrown feeds is hards to quantify at a time of global food crisis.

CONCLUDING REMARKS

The research and development program established at KISR seeks to examine how the various proposed SCP technologies can best be adapted for efficient operation in both Kuwait and the Gulf region. The multidisciplinary approach employed has proven successful thus far, and it seems probable that important contributions towards the ultimate objective of SCP production in Kuwait will be made. The facilities that have been constructed are such that advanced training programs in biotechnology can also be undertaken now, so that properly trained technical personnel for future SCP manufacturing ventures will be available when the need for them arises.

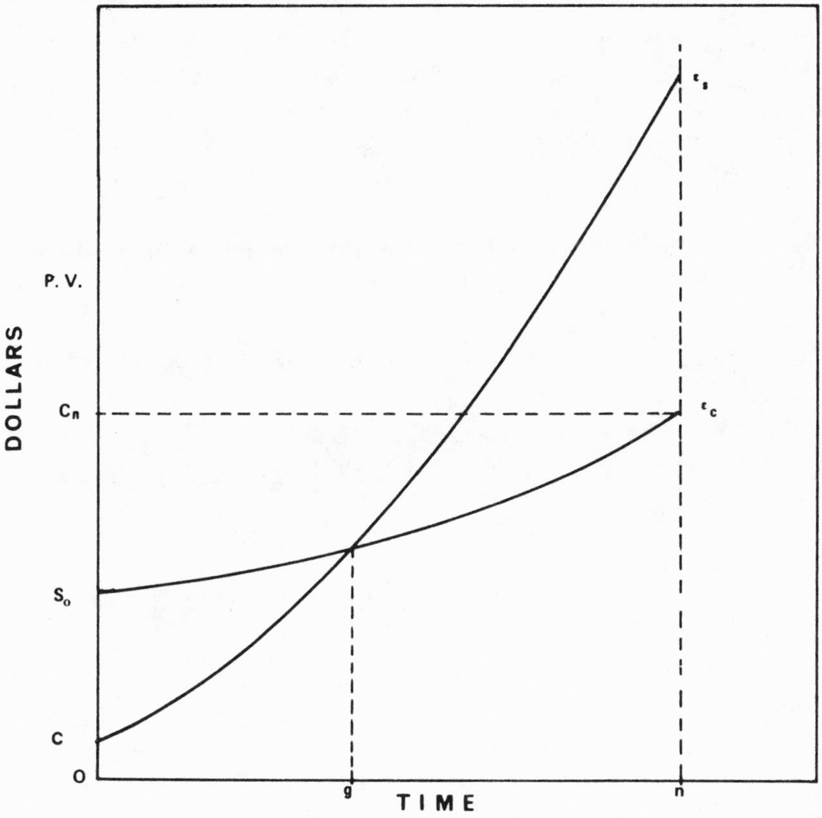

Fig. 14.2. Present value of life cycle cost of and return for protein production by biodigestion process.

REFERENCES

(1) Teweles, R.J., Harlow, C.V., and Stone, H.L. 1974. The Commodity Futures Game. p. 337. New York: McGraw-Hill.

(2) Food and Agriculture Organization. 1970-76. Yearbooks of Fishery Statistics, Fishery Commodities. Rome: FAO publications.

(3) M. I. T. 1968. In Proceedings of the First M. I. T. Symposium on SCP. Cambridge, Mass.: M. I. T. Press, 1966.

(4) a) Champagnat, A., Vernet, C., Laine, B., and Filosa, J. 1963. In Proc. 6th World Petroleum Congress. 4 : 259.

b) Champagnat, A. 1964. Impact. 14 (2) : 119.

c) Laine, B., Vernet, C., and Evans, J. 1967. In Proc. 7th World Petroleum Congress. 8 : 197.

d) Laine, B. 1972. Canad. J. Chem. Engng. 50 : 154.

(5) a) Cooney, C.L., and Levine, D.W. 1972. Adv. Appl. Microbiol. 15 : 337.

b) MacLennan, D.G., Gow, J.S., and Stringer, D.A. 1973. In Proc. Roy. Australian Chem. Inst. 40 (3) : 57.

c) Faust, U., Prave, P., and Sukatsch, D.A. 1977. J. Ferment. Technol. 55 : 609.

d) Ballerine, D. 1978. Rev. Inst. Franc. Petrole. 33 : 111.

(6) a) Hamer, G., Heden, C.G., and Carenberg, C.O. 1967. Biotechnol. Bioengng. 9 : 499.

b) Klass, D.L., Iandols, J.J., and Knabel, S.J. 1969. In Chem. Engng. Prog. Symp. Ser. 93. 65 : 72.

c) Hamer, G. and Norris, J.R. 1971. In Proc. 8th World Petroleum Congress. 6 : 133.

d) Hamer, G., Harrison, D.E.F., Topiwala, H.H., and Gabriel, A. 1976. Inst. Chem. Engrs. Symp. Ser. (44) : 565.

(7) Masuda, Y. 1974. Chem. Econ. Engng. Rev. 6 (11) : 54. Japan.

(8) a) Clement, G., Rebeller, M., and Trambouze, P. 1968. Rev. Inst. Franc. Petrole. 23 : 702.

b) Clement, G. 1971. Inst. Pasteur Lyon. 4 : 103.

(9) a) Imrie, F.K.E. and Vlitos, A.J. 1973. In Proceedings of the Second M. I. T. Symposium on SCP. Cambridge, Mass.: M. I. T. Press, 1975.

b) Anderson, C., Longton, J., Maddix, C., Scammell, G.W., and Solomons, G.L. 1973. In Proceedings of the Second M. I. T. Symposium on SCP. Cambridge, Mass.: M. I. T. Press, 1975.

c) Humphrey, A.E., Moreira, A., Armiger, W., and Zabriskie, D. 1977. In Biotechnol. Bioengng. Symp. (7) : 45.

(10) a) Jarl, K. 1969. Food Technol. 23 : 1009.

b) Romantschuk, H. 1973. In Proceedings of the Second M. I. T. Symposium on SCP. Cambridge, Mass.: M. I. T., 1975.

IV

Systems for Food and Energy Production

Introduction to Part IV

The three papers of this section are generally concerned with the same possibilities as those of the previous section, while taking a rather more systemic approach and with a greater concern for energy considerations. The paper by R. Anderson, C-G. Heden, and L. Williams discusses two research programs of an integrative character in relation to both food and energy output in total biomass utilization; both use algae as an important agent for solar energy capture. The first program emphasizes the energy analysis approach, and the second the bio-engineering constraints.

M.N. Alaa El-Din presents an extremely interesting account of the practices and research on bioconversion in China, where population pressure has stimulated sustained attempts to recycle organic wastes to the maximum possible extent.

With the paper of Oswald Roels, the subject turns to the marine environment. He discusses the St. Croix experiments on the upwelling of nutrient waters from the deep sea by artificial means, using the thermal differential between tropically warmed surface water, and cold deep water. Only a small proportion of the total energy generated is required to drive the pumps which bring the cold, nutrient charged waters to the surface.

15 The Potential of Algae in Decentralized Bioconversion Systems

R. Anderson
C-G. Heden
L. Williams

In recent years, there has been a rapidly growing interest in recycling agricultural waste materials. Recycling methods involve a wide range of techniques to convert organic matter into food, fodder, fertilizer, and fuel. At the grass roots level, opportunities have been noted in China, where there are two million biogas units, and in Korea and India, which have thirty thousand of such units each. (1,2a) Brazil's efforts to reduce its dependence on imported oil has led to experiments at the highest level of government decision-making, which involve adding fermentation alcohol to gasoline. (2b) Several intergovernmental agencies, such as FAO, UNEP, UNESCO, and UNU, are launching ambitious training and research programs in the area. And some nongovernmental organizations, such as IFIAS, have contributed studies that underline the importance of fields such as enzyme engineering (3,4), and systems integration. (5)

This paper will briefly review two such research programs. Both use algae as an important energy capturing device. The first is a cooperative effort which emphasizes a comparative energy analysis of various combinations of simple approaches. The second is aimed at delineating the outer limits that bioengineering sets to integration.

THE NEED FOR LOCAL RECYCLING OF FOOD, FODDER, FERTILIZER, AND ENERGY

In the energy field, the hazards of depending on large systems and the wish to achieve increased self-reliance have produced a growing R & D effort, but the emphasis has been on economy-of-scale, and on large nuclear, wind, and wave power systems, geothermal devices, or gigantic energy plantations. Strong arguments, however, can be put forward in favor of small-scale systems (6), since those may be particularly relevant to rural development in poor countries.

Normal agriculture is, of course, the backbone of any rural system, but the addition of a few specific fermentation and energetic processes could make a big difference. One must include physical, solar, and nonsolar devices, photoelectric cells, solar heat collection for water heating, distillation and pumping, windmills, solar ponds, and many more items in a carefully integrated system if the full potential of each component is to be reached (fig. 15.1). The integrated solar systems which IFIAS will analyze will combine, depending on need and suitability, all of the presently common biological and physical solar technologies, plus research developments.

IFIAS is launching this solar energy program for two major reasons. First, it is not clear how much practicality lies in all the optimistic talk about solar energy, posing the following questions: How many of these devices or processes are worth considering for rural (or urban) development? Can a rural community use solar energy to provide its energy needs? Are biogas digesters really worthwhile? If one counts the nonsolar energy costs of algae cultivation, is there a net energy gain or loss? The answers are probably yes, but the hard eye of energy analysis goes back to its inception when two conferences were held to establish the methodology. (7,8) This new project is a continuation of that effort.

Secondly, the benefits of systems integration have till now been largely neglected. Is the biogas digester a hybrid seed planted on unfertile soil? Fertile soil may mean integration of biogas into a system in which waste heat is available from another process, and the sludge and CO_2 from combusted gas can be used for mass algae culture, agriculture, water purification, etc. This looks at the system via the biogas, but it is simply one of many examples - a system means that one cannot look at simply one of the many elements.

Integration also implies a system which simultaneously provides for all basic needs. It means more than just providing for one need, i.e., not food without improved health, or fertilizer without sufficient water.

The critical feature of an integrated system is that the net benefit (measured in any one of several units) is greater than the sum of the benefits of each component in isolation. Waste becomes a misnomer.

IFIAS decided to determine if a rural community can energize its own development with solar energy. The aim is not just another solar energy project, but rather the building of a platform for the cooperation between a few groups prepared to single-mindedly evaluate the potential of integrated solar systems for development. The energy analysis group is headed by Dr. Malcolm Slesser, of the Energy Analysis Unit of Strathclyde University, Glasgow, and will work directly with two experimental communities at two different levels of technology. Dr. C.V. Seshadri, of the Shri A.M.M. Muragappa Chettiar Research Center of Madras (India), is committed to low level technology in a village using local manpower and resources almost exclusively. Dr. Shelef, of the Technion in Haifa, Israel, will extend his laboratory and energy independent kibbutz experience to a more typical farm coopera-

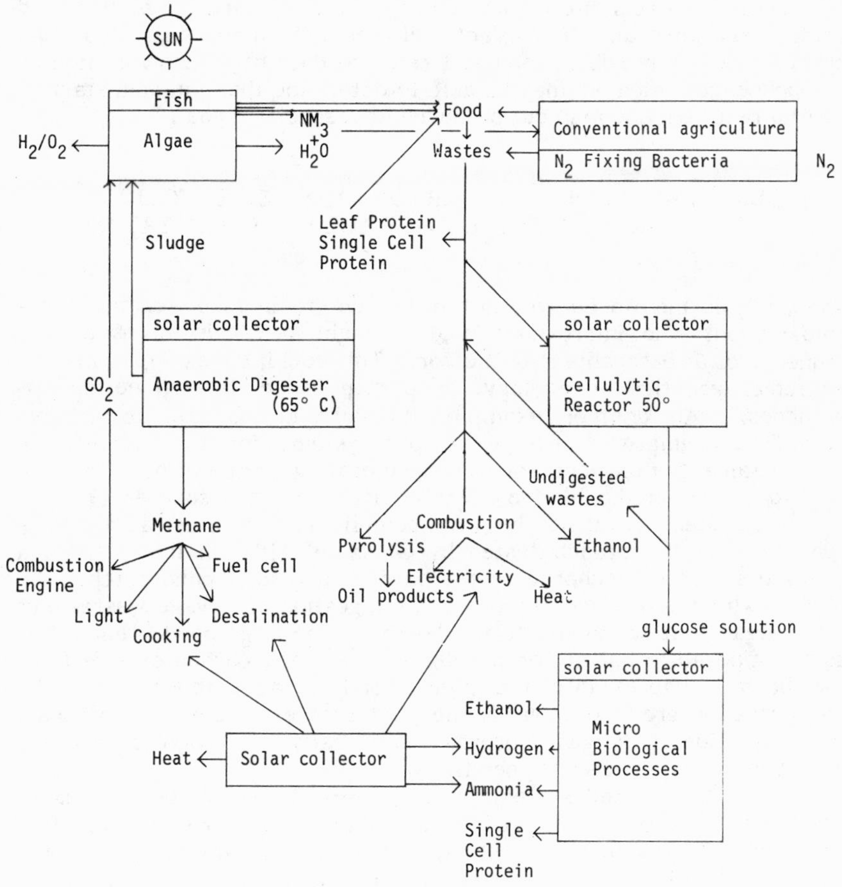

Fig. 15.1. Advanced integrated system for food, fuel, and nutrients.

tive, a moshav. This will employ technology at a moderate level of capital cost. Each of these groups will determine the potential of integrated biosolar systems for providing net energy to a rural community.

To permit a realistic evaluation, this study is partly analytical and partly experimental. If, in fact, self-reliance in the basic food and energy needs is possible - and self-reliance does not mean isolation or independence - then we may be able to determine the minimum starting capital required, and map out pathways to a specified goal.

BIOENGINEERING FOR CARBON DIOXIDE RECYCLING AND INTEGRATION FOR LOW-GRADE HEAT UTILIZATION

The analysis mentioned will not only have to include existing technologies but also improvements that might be achieved as a consequence of a reasonable R & D effort. This could, for example, involve microbial genetics or ecology, or perhaps novel bioengineering approaches. An another example, it might be possible to achieve considerable improvements by simple systems for the damping of temperature fluctuations, or for accelerating photosynthesis by the addition of carbon dioxide from fermentations or other sources. (9)

Such systems need not be very complicated, as illustrated by the submersed tent approach tested by G. Shelef. (10) In this system, a tentlike structure anchored to the bottom of a solar pond catches the biogas, which is produced by anaerobic digestion of sewage wastes plus some algae that sediments to the bottom. The large pond volume acts as a temperature buffer for the digester, and the carbon dioxide from the biogas diffuses into the algae pond as a consequence of the concentration gradient towards the photosynthetic zone. In this way, the heat value of the gas improves substantially in addition to providing a portion of the algae's CO_2 needs.

More sophisticated systems making use of combustion engines to produce CO_2, as a byproduct of delivering electricity or solar collectors to support thermophilic digestion, remain to be evaluated from the energetic point of view. Actually, their indirect use as an energy source, for example as fodder or fertilizer, might well prove to have the most significant effect on a community's energy balance.

ALGAE AS A RAW MATERIAL FOR LIQUID FUEL AND CHEMICAL PRODUCTION

Until recently, algae have mainly been studied as potential sources of fodder, food, and biogas. Now, interest is being focused on special algal species or growth conditions which permit the production of useful products like fodder protein simultaneously with useful basic chemical products such as glycerol, (11) lipids, (12) or starch. (13) These types of systems offer several opportunities for diversification, and could be of considerable interest in the context of a gradual industrialization starting at the village level.

An entirely microbial route to ethanol could be very useful as a locally produced liquid fuel in developing areas. Algal starch can probably be converted to ethanol using conventional hydrolysis and yeast fermentation, but we have been especially interested in bacterial fermentations yielding ethanol from the glycerol-rich algal biomass, which can be produced using the halotolerant algae Dunaliella. Although algal growth and glycerol production is a relatively simple matter, (11,14) the ethanol fermentation, using Klebsiella, has thus far been made to achieve only about half of its theoretical yield. (14) It is expected that further microbiological and biotechnical research will lead to greatly improved yields.

Although the proposed algae-to-ethanol system is probably not of economic interest in most countries with access to cheap starch or molasses, it could be of interest in many places lacking these agricultural products, especially in arid regions with seawater or saltwater resources. This process is illustrative of the many possibilities for integration among biological and solar energy processes. The recovery of biogas from fermenter effluents, the nearly complete recycling of nitrogen and especially the recycling of CO_2 to the extent possible are all essential features of the integrated process proposed here (fig. 15.2). In addition, the utilization of solar energy for thermophilic digestion, and for driving the distillation of the ethanol (requiring only a slight concentration to achieve the $100^{\circ}C$ bottom temperature) seem attractive.

Although the process described here is only hypothetical, research is continuing on several of the individual parts, and it is hoped that basic research in the microbiology and engineering of such systems, as well as the energy analyses mentioned earlier, will continue to progress and eventually lead to a better understanding, and a more widespread application of algal based integrated systems to aid rural development.

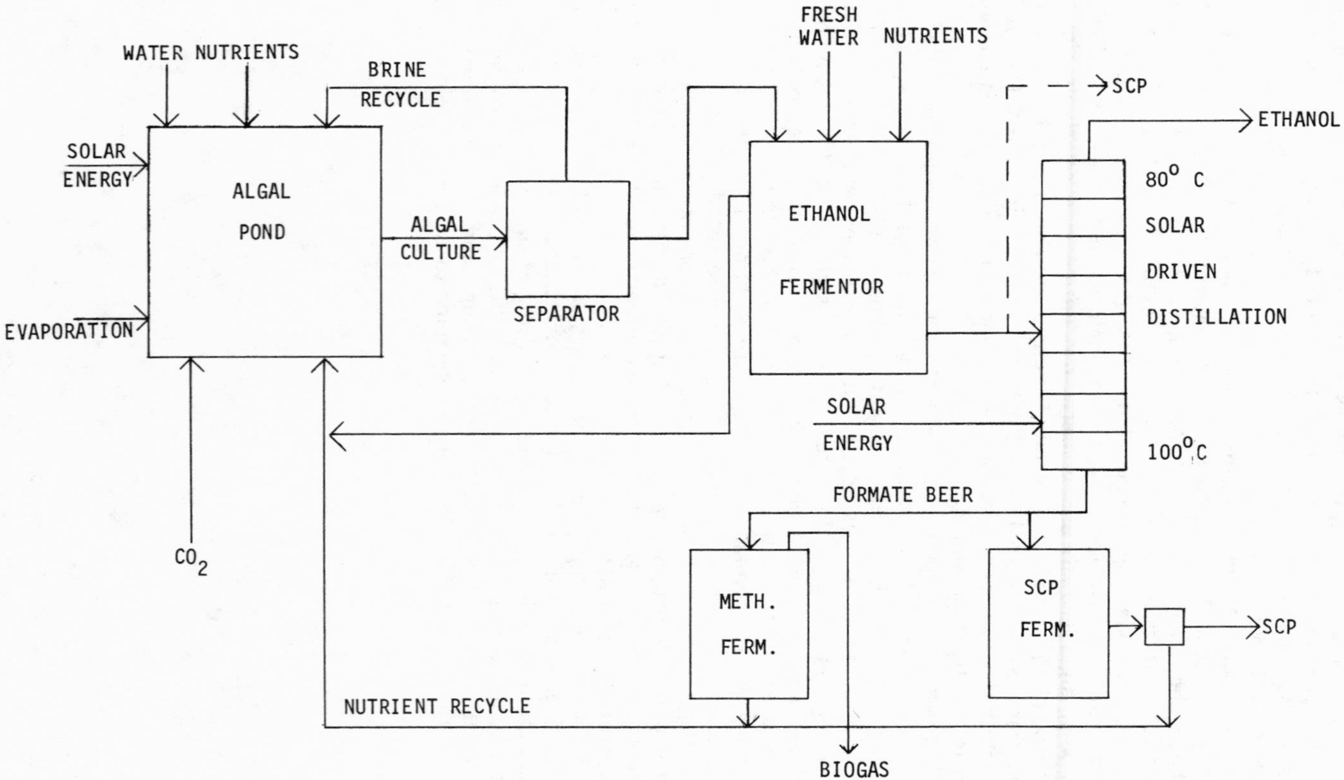

Fig. 15.2. Integrated process for the recovery of biogas from fermenter effluents.

REFERENCES

(1) Smil, V. 1977. Intermediate energy technology in China. Bull. Atom. Sci. 33(2), 25-31.

(2a) Da Silva, E.J., Olembo, R., and Burgers, A. 1978. Integrated microbial technology for developing countries; springboard for economic progress. Impact. Sci. Soc. 28:159-182.

(2b) Da Silva, J.G., and Serra, G.E. 1978. Energy balance for ethyl alcohol production from crops. Science 201, pp. 903-906.

(3) Heden, C-G. 1977. Enzyme engineering and the anatomy of equilibrium technology. Quart. Rev. Biophys., 10, pp. 113-135.

(4) IFIAS. Socioeconomic and Ethical Implications of Enzyme Engineering. Summary and Final IFIAS Report No. 15.

(5) Anderson, R. 1979. Biological Paths to Self-Reliance. New York: Van Nostrand Reinhold Co.

(6) Heden, C-G. 1978. Innovative technologies for a future society, Scott-Bader lecture, 1978, Nov. 4, 1978. (In press.)

(7) International Federation of Institutes for Advanced Study. 1974. Energy Analysis Methodology Workshop I. Ulriksdol Slott, Solna (Sweden).

(8) IFIAS. 1975. Energy Analysis Methodology Workshop II.

(9) Heden, C-G. 1978. Integration - the key to decentralized energy management. Biochem. Soc. Meeting, London, Nov. 8-10, 1978.

(10) Shelef, G. 1978. Production of microalgae as part of a waste water treatment. 1st Int. Conf. on Production and Use of Microalgae Biomass. Acre, Israel, Sept. 17-22, 1978.

(11) Avron, M. and Ben Amotz, A. 1978. Glycerol, B-carotene, and dry algal meal production from Dunaliella. 1st Int. Conf. on Production and Use of Microalgae Biomass. Acre, Israel, Sept. 17-22, 1978.

(12) Aaronson, S., et al. Microalgae as a source of chemicals and natural products, ibid.

(13) Pirt, M.W., and Pirt, S.J. 1977. Photosynthetic production of biomass and starch by Chlorella in chemostat culture. J. Appl. Chem. Biotech., 27, pp. 643-650.

(14) Williams, L.A., et al. 1979. Solar bioconversion systems based on algal glycerol production. In Symposium on Biotechnology in Energy Production and Conservation, to be published in Biotech. Bioeng. Symposium Series 1978/79.

16 Recycling of Organic Wastes in Agriculture

M.N. Alaa El-Din

There is nothing in the world that is absolute waste. This notion should be a guiding principle for every country's resources policy, and should be especially emphasized for those developing countries in which chemical fertilizers are expensive and in short supply. This paper concentrates on the Chinese experience in the recovery and reuse of waste materials, for nowhere is there an overall recycling program of organic wastes in agriculture as complete as in China.

Following the instructions of Chairman Mao, "Turning the harmful into the beneficial," the Chinese place great emphasis on recovering and reusing all organic waste materials for manure, fodder, and energy. About 70 percent of the plant nutrients needed for crop production are gained from organic manures, and only 30 percent from chemical fertilizers. A very efficient system for recycling organic wastes has been developed by the Chinese to meet the huge demand for nutrients needed to fertilize their some 130 million hectares of arable land (1), some of which produces two to three crops per year. This system is summarized in fig. 16.1.

Plants are either ploughed directly back into the soil (green manuring), or are used for making composts (water plants, and some legumes), or are fed to man, farm animals, silk worms, and fish. Organic wastes from the urban population are city garbage, night soil, sewage and kitchen refuse from hotels, restaurants etc. Kitchen refuse is, in fact, usually fed directly to pigs that are raised in the suburban areas that surround cities. Night soil and sewage are either used directly as liquid fertilizer, or indirectly after passing a biogas cycle for gaining fuel gas, which is converted to electrical energy in small generators.

Garbage is collected and composted, and used for organic manuring. In rural areas, the wastes of man and animals are usually recycled together. Processing methods, however, vary. High temperature compost and stable manure are of the same composition, i.e., night soil,

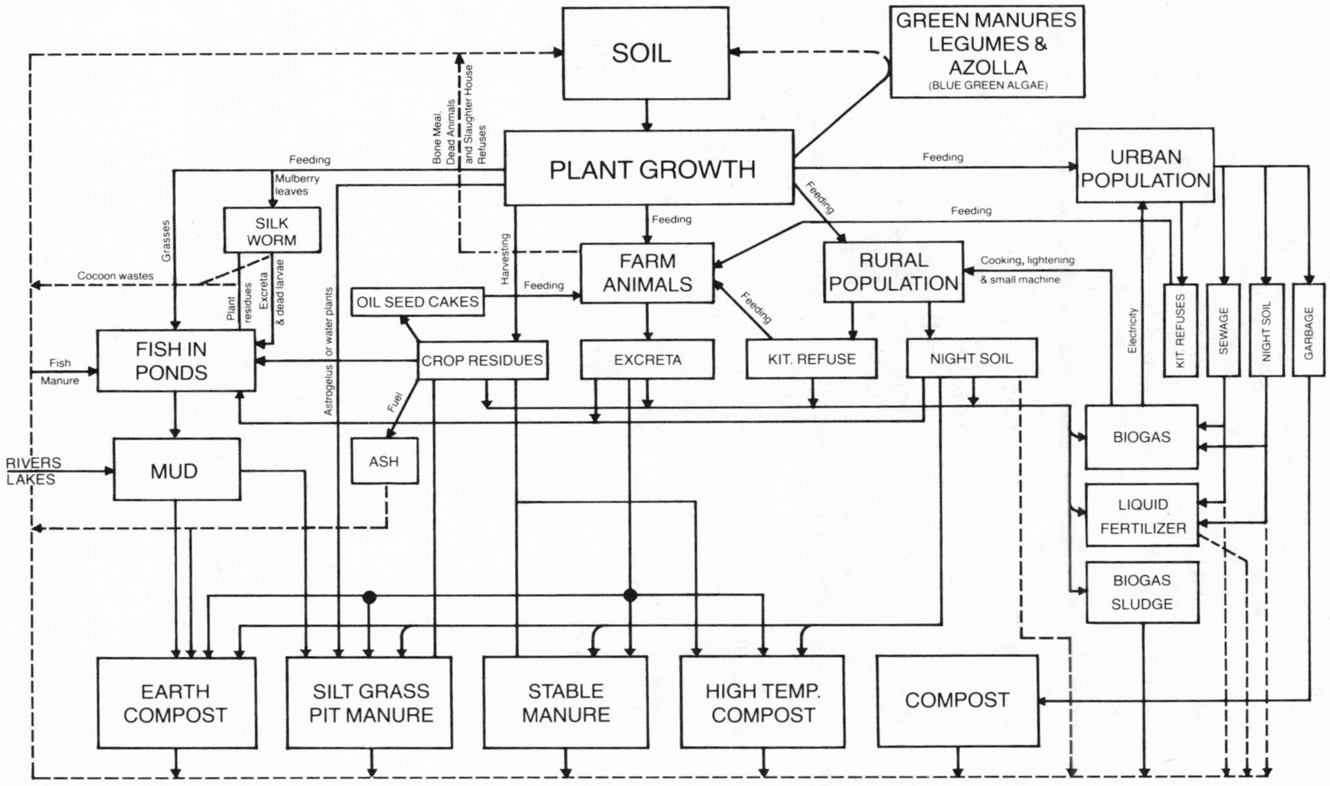

Fig. 16.1. Recycling of organic wastes in The People's Republic of China.

crop residues, animal droppings; however the high-temperature compost reaches 70°C., while the stable manure remains only slightly warm at 40°C. Silt grass pit manure and earth compost also have more or less the same composition, but the former is prepared under anaerobic conditions, while the latter under aerobic conditions.

Production of biogas from organic wastes in rural areas has other uses, namely, cooking, lighting, driving small scale power generators, improving the manuring value of the organic wastes, and killing off offensive odors and parasites present in the wastes.

Night soil is also directly used for fertilizing either with or without pretreatment. Such pretreatment would consist of three chamber storage tanks to destroy hookworm, and schistosame ova. Oil seed cakes are either fed to farm animals, or used directly for manuring. Farm animal wastes, like bone meal, dead animals and slaughter house refuse are usually directly applied to the soil.

In south China, there is a perfect recycling system. Fishes are bred in small man-made ponds close to sugarcane fields; mulberry trees are widespread since silk is a part of the commune enterprise. Leaves from the sugarcane and cocoon wastes (uneaten mulberry leaves, warm dung, and killed pupae taken from cocoons) go into the fish ponds. Water plants are grown on about 50 percent of the water area of the ponds, and these are used for feeding pigs raised in conveniently located pig barns; the pig manure, in turn, is washed into the fish ponds. Latrines are also built so that human excreta goes directly into the fish ponds. Mud from the bottom of these ponds, rich in organic matter, is then collected, and applied either directly to sugarcane, or for making earth compost. Some information concerning the quantity, nutrient content, and absorption rate of these nutrients from the common organic manures in China is presented in table 16.1; the status of organic manures in China today is, in fact, probably somewhat higher than indicated. What follows is a description of the main methods used in China for recycling organic wastes.

GREEN MANURING

Chinese farmers regard the green manures as natural food for rice crops and they have long been using a large variety of green manuring crops. The area allocated to green manure crops increased in 1976 from 1.3 million hectares after liberation to 6.6 millions. Moreover about 50 percent of the 10 million hectares of water area used for aquaculture in China is cultivated with water weeds (3), which are also used for green manuring. The main green manure crops cultivated in China are:

Leguminous Plants

Astragalus sinicus	(chinese milk vetch)
Vicia villosa	(hairy vetch)

Table 16.1. Application of Organic fertilizers in China [2].

Manure	Millions of metric tons (1966)	% of total nutrient applied as fertilizer available to plant (1966)	Nutrient content %				Absorption rate %
			N	P_2O_5	K_2O	Total	
Night soil	299	35	0.6	0.2	0.3	1.1	45
Pig manure	245	18	0.5	0.4	0.5	1.4	20
Large animals	257	21	0.6	0.3	0.8	1.7	20
Compost plant residues	53	4	0.3	0.2	0.6	1.1	30
Oilseed cakes	5	8	7.0	1.3	2.1	10.4	65
Green manure	102	19	0.4	0.1	0.4	0.9	65
River, lakes, pond* Mud	73	1	0.18	0.15	0.5-0.6	--	10

*FAO study Tour, May 1977, Personal Communication.

Source: Kang Chao, Agricultural Production in Communist China (1949-1965) (University of Wisconsin Press, 1970).

Vicia fabe	(broad bean)
Vicia sative	(alfalfa lucerne)
Melilotus officinalis	(yellow sweet clover)
Crotalaria juncea	(sunhemp)
Phaspeolus aureus	(golden gram)
Sesbania cannabina	(seasbania)

Water Weeds

Alternanthera philoxeroides	(water niseria)
Eichhornia crassipes	(water hyacinth)
Pistia stratiotes	
Azolla pinnata	(duck weed)
Anabaena sp. } Nostoc sp. }	Nitrogen-fixing blue green algae.

Four systems of green manuring are followed:

- A green manure crop is sown and ploughed back into the same field.
- It is harvested and applied to other fields (three to four times as big).
- It is cut and mixed with straw, mud, and pig manure, and put into a pit for preparation of the famous silt grass pit manure, which will be discussed later.
- It is interplanted with early rice so as to be used as green manure for the following late rice. Sesbania cannabina is used for this last system, and yields more green material and fixed nitrogen than other legume crops used for green manuring and even more than forage and grain legumes, as illustrated in table 16.2. Sesbania cannabina is known to be resistant to drought acidity, alkalinity, and flood. The fertility of land which has been under Sesbania is very much improved; the soil becomes rich in humus and looser, and this stimulates the microbial activity in the soil.

Water plants, like Alternanthera, Pistia and Eichhornia, are considered as weeds in many countries. In China, however, these water weeds are cultivated on the surface of lakes, rivers, fish ponds, and flooded areas, and are used for organic manuring, either directly or indirectly, through silt grass pit manure. They are also used for feeding pigs, rabbits, and ducks.

Table 16.2. Yields of green matter, nitrogen, protein and the rate of protein production of various green manure, forage and grain legume crops.

Crop	green material (ton/ha)	nitrogen yield (kg/ha)	Protein yield (kg/ha)	growth period days	rate of protein production, (kg/ha/day)
Alternanthera Philoxeroides[4] (Lake)	225-375	344-572	2147-3572	365	5.9-9.8
Eichhornia Crassipes (land)[5]	87.5	122	761		
(on sewage water)[6]	250	348	2174	365	6.0
Sesbania cannabina[4]					
(intercropped with early rice)	15-22.5	38-124	519-775	30	17.3-25.8
Azolla pinnata					
KIANGSU--CHINA[4]	157.5	431	2679	100	26.8
VIETNAM [7]	200-700	547-821	2319-5131	365	9.4-14.1
Trifolium Alexandrinum					
4 Cutting + grains (tops + roots)		298	1872	200	9.4
Tops only		223	1396	200	6.5
Glycine max[8]					
grain + straw + roots		363	2269	180	12.6
Grain + straw only.		325	2031	180	11.3

Azolla pinnata duck weed is a water fern with nitrogen-fixing blue green algae Anabaena azollae occupying the cavities in its leaflets; it is grown and used in China for green manuring, for feeding pigs and ducks, and for making composts. It is more popular in the northern parts of China because the optimum temperature for its growth lies between 20-28°C. Practices for cultivation, fertilization, and protection of Azolla against diseases and pests are also well established. The following methods for applying Azolla have been noted.

Growing Azolla for green manuring. The fields prepared for rice cultivation are flooded and inoculated with Azolla plants at the rate of 7.5 tons per hectare. After five to ten days, Azolla grows and reaches the suitable intensity (22.5 tons per hectare). The water is then drained, and the Azolla mat is ploughed in using a 12 h.p. walking tractor. After this, the field is flooded again and left for a further growth cycle of Azolla (no further inoculation is needed). The soil is, thereby, put under an intensive program for improving its fertility. Alternatively, rice seedlings are transplanted to these fields. In this case Azolla will grow again and the water surface between seedlings will be covered with Azolla within ten days, reaching the intensity of 22.5 tons per hectare. This is then buried in the soil by hand. This process is usually repeated twice or even three times.

Growing Azolla as a nitrogen fixation factory. In this case Azolla is grown and harvested up to ten times on the same field within 100 days. It is seeded at the rate of 7.5 tons per hectare to the flooded field. After ten days about 15 tons per hectare are harvested, and 7.5 tons per hectare are left as seeds for the following growth cycle. The Azolla yield within 100 days is about 157.5 tons per hectare of green material and is usually used for feeding pigs, rabbits and ducks, for inoculation of other fields, and for making silt grass pit manure together with the other components of this type of manure. The benefits realized from applying Azolla are summarized in table 16.3. It is clear from Table 2 that growing of Azolla yields a quite respectable quantity of green material within a short time (100 days), while Sesbania cannabina, which has the highest N-fixation capacity among leguminous plants (542 kilograms of nitrogen per hectare per year (9), only produces 15-22.5 tons per hectare of green matter within 30 days of complete field occupation. The rate of protein production by Azolla pinnata is still higher than by Sesbania cannabina. The yield and nitrogen gains of Azolla is, however, much higher in China than it is in Vietnam.

The following advantages arising from intensive application of Azolla have been reported:

- Increase of the organic matter content (from 1.3 to 2.8 percent) and nitrogen content of the soil (0.09 to 0.29 percent).
- Improving soil structure.
- Saving of at least 38.3 kilograms of nitrogen per hectare in rice cultivation.
- Increased productivity and grain weight.

Table 16.3. Benefits Realized from Various Application Methods of *Azolla pinnata* in China.*

Application methods	Green material	N	Nitrogen	fertilizers
	tons / ha	kg / ha	Ammonium sulfate kg/ha**	Urea kg/ha***
a) In rice fields				
Ploughing under only.	22.5	61.5	306.0	133.0
Ploughing and burying once.	45.0	122.0	612.0	266.1
Ploughing and burying twice.	67.5	183.6	918.0	399.1
Ploughing and burying three times.	90.0	244.8	1,224.0	532.2
b) As N-fixation factory				
10 times harvest within 100 days.	157.5	428.4	2,142.0	931.3

* The yields of nitrogen are calculated according to information from Chinese colleagues that the N-nutritional value of 500kg *Azolla* = 8 kg of the usually used fertilizer ammonium bicarbonate (17 %N), this means 2,72 kg N / ton fresh *Azolla*.

** as ammonium sulfate containing 20 % N.

*** as urea containing 46 % N.

- When applied in addition to chemical fertilization, yield increases by 15 percent over results using chemical fertilization alone.

Production of inoculum of nitrogen fixing blue green algae containing a mixture of Nostoc sp. and Anabaena sp. has been attempted. This would be distributed to rice fields, but the process is still at the research level. Research is currently underway at the Agricultural Research Institute, in Nanking, under sterile conditions (fig. 16.2).

After several steps of scaling up, 750 kilograms of fresh algae are spread per hectare of rice field. The algae grows and reaches 7.5 tons per hectare within 10-15 days. At temperatures higher than 30°C, the yield of algae could reach as much as 15 tons per hectare.

BIOGAS AND BIOGAS MANURE

Biogas generation in China takes place in special digesters. The process involves the microbial anaerobic fermentation of a mixture of organic wastes (up to 10 percent solid material and 90 percent water) made up of crop stalks, pig manure, night soil, and kitchen refuse. The gas produced (methane, 50-70 percent, and carbon dioxide) is combustible and used for cooking, lighting, and powering internal combustion engines, thereby saving 70 percent of diesel oil. The manure obtained from biogas is richer in nitrogen content (due to lower N-losses), more in quantity than that obtained by conventional composting (lower carbon respiration due to anaerobic reactions), and free from pathogens and parasites normally present in the digesting materials (e.g. in night soil and in pig manure). Odors are killed during the anaerobic digestion and storing of slurry (see fig. 16.3). In 1972, China began a massive well-organized campaign to popularize the technology of biogas production. In 1976, there were 410,000 biogas plants in the country. The vast majority of these were located in just a few counties. (10) Wuching county (Kiangsu), for example, was reported to have set up 60,000 digesters. By 1978, it has been estimated that some 5 million units have been set up. Technical problems, e.g., temperature, hydrogen ion concentration, C:N ratio, and dilution rate are now under control.

About five basic designs of biogas digesters have been constructed in different localities. Their general feature is that the gas holder and digester are combined in one unit (fig. 16.4), and placed under ground so as to maintain a constant temperature at a higher degree. The gas holder is the brick dome-shaped cover of the digester itself. The household biogas unit is about 3.5 meters in diameter and 3 meters deep, the digester being twice as deep as the gas holder. It is made of bricks using a mixture of 5 percent lime and 95 percent earth. The walls are given a thin plastering (about 3 centimeters) with cement. The cost of construction (without labor charges) is reported to be 50 Yuans ($25). In comparison with the Indian Gobar-Gas system, the Chinese system has the following advantages: the plant can easily be

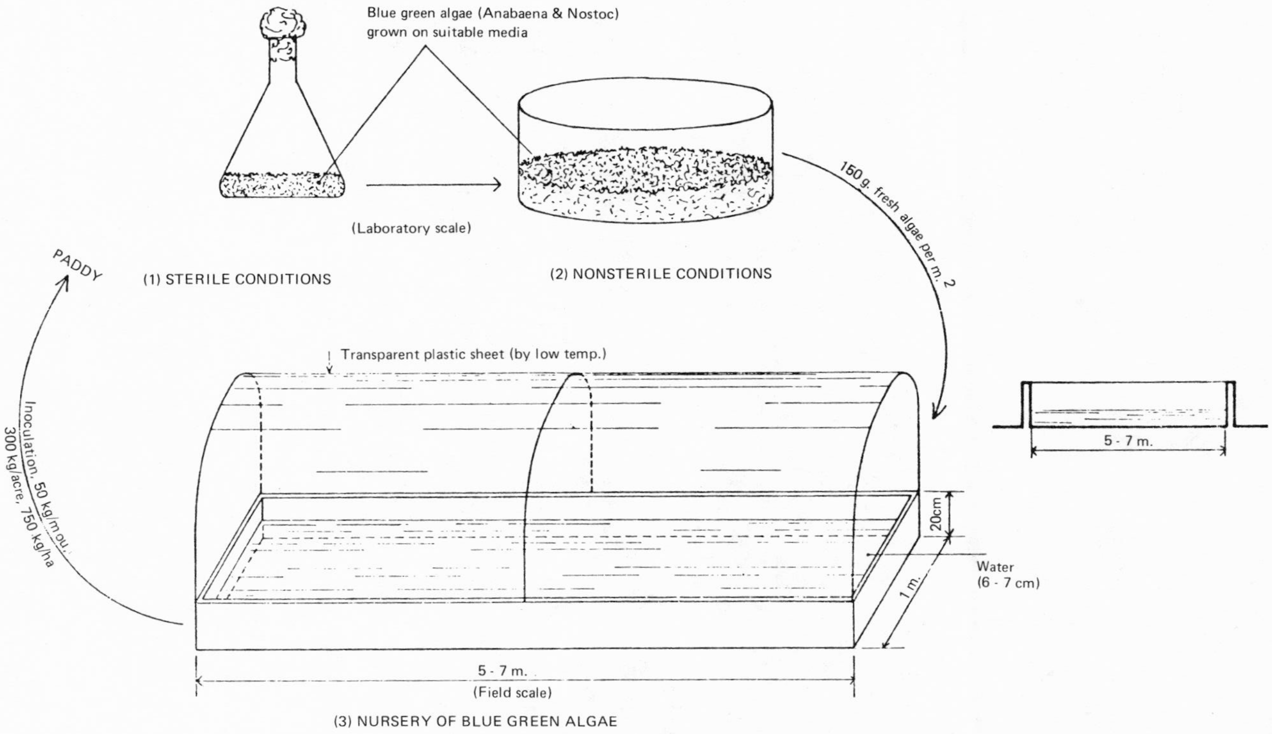

Fig. 16.2. Inoculation of paddy with blue green algae, Nanking (Kiangsu).

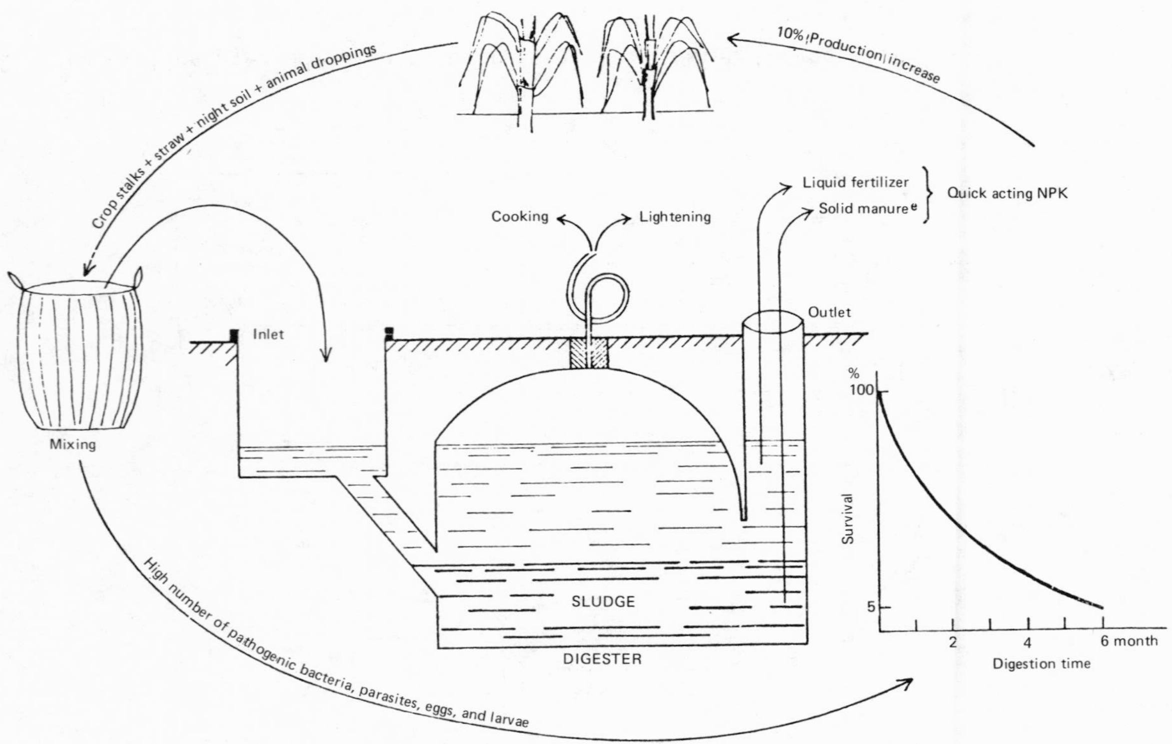

$$C_6H_{10}O_5 + 2H_2O \xrightarrow{\text{Anaerobic fermentation}} 3CH_4 + 3CO_2$$

Fig. 16.3. Biogas cycle in China.

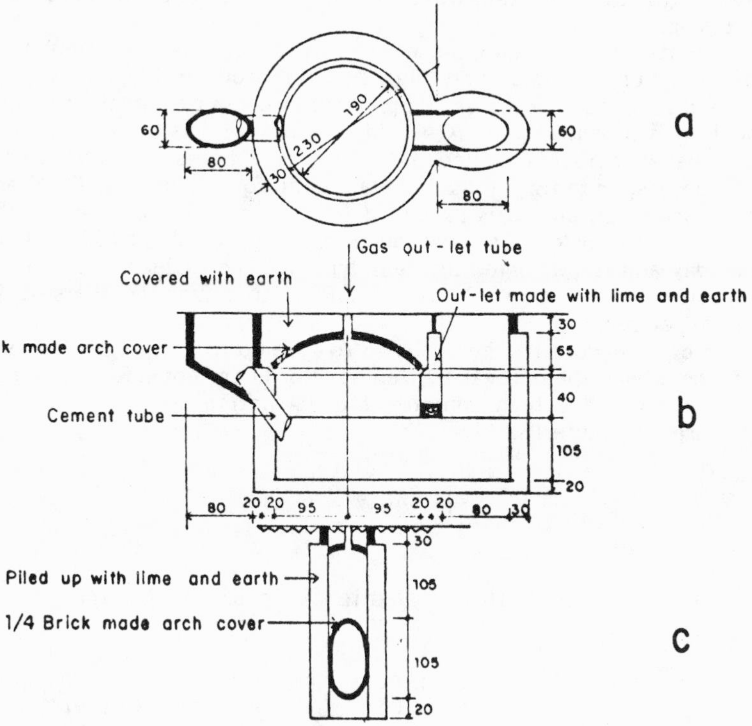

Total volume: 6.42m^3, fermentation chamber: 5.06m^3, arch: 1.36m^3.
a) Front elevation drawing
b) Longitudinal profile
c) Longitudinal profile

Fig. 16.4. Biogas unit no. 3 made with lime and earth.

---

constructed by peasants; it is less costly to construct and maintain; it is easier to sustain a suitable temperature as the whole system is under ground, and the digested sludge is removed only twice a year compared to daily in the Indian system.

The 10 cubic meter biogas plant generates about 5 cubic meters of gas per day, which is sufficient to supply a Chinese family with enough gas for cooking and lighting during the digestion period (about 6 months). Moreover, 10 cubic meters of sludge and 14 cubic meters of effluent per year are also produced. The sludge is used either directly as manure, or indirectly for making humic acid fertilizers. It is usually heaped, plastered, and kept till needed. The effluent is used directly along with the irrigation water, or stored in tanks for application as top dressing.

Plants up to 60 cubic meters are built collectively to recycle wastes of hospitals, schools, and piggeries to produce biogas for cooking, animal feed, fueling water pumps, farm processing machinery, and small scale power generators. One cubic meter of gas is enough to run an internal combustion engine of 1 h.p. for 2 hours, a 3-ton truck for 2 kilometers, or to light a 60-100 watt lamp for 6 hours. In Fu-Shang city near Shanghai, biogas is produced from night soil alone in big 45 cubic meter septic tanks. Gas is produced at a rate of about 230 cubic meters per day and is converted into electricity. The effluent remaining after digestion, which takes 22 days, is sold to commune members at 5 yuans ($2.5) per ton.

Biogas manure has been shown to give up to 17 percent higher yields of wheat than the equivalent weight of ordinary compost. This could be attributed to the high content of quick active nutrients in the biogas manure (see table 16.4).

Table 16.4. Nutrients in Biogas Manure

	Content in ppm			Content in %	
	N	P_2O_5	K_2O	Organic matter	Humic acid
Effluent	500	15	2000	------	------
Sludge	650	40	9400	35	9
Soil fertilized with effluent	140	31.2	212		
Soil fertilized with stable manure	93	33.8	156		

ORGANIC MANURES

Compost made of city garbage. City garbage is collected and transported out of the cities, and dealt with in one of two ways:

- o It is taken to rural areas, where it is mixed with night soil, rice straw, and animal droppings, and put in piles 5 meters long, 2 meters wide and 1 meter high. There it is plastered with silt and after a high temperature composting process (up to 70°C.) a high quality organic fertilizer is produced.
- o It is taken to the treatment site of the municipality where it is put into closed compost bins (2x2.5x2.3 meters) for a 25 day composting period (70°C* is also reached). The compost produced contains 0.2-0.37% N, 0.15-0.50% P_2O_5, 0.37% K_2O and 15-20% organic matter. It is then applied at the rate of 15 tons per hectare of cropland.

Night soil. The use of human excreta for fertilizing is a traditional practice in Southeast Asian countries and specially in China. It is considered a good source of plant nutrients. To avoid spreading debilitating diseases, the Chinese farmers are exhorted to store it in properly designed three-tank fermentation systems (fig. 16.5) over a period of one month in the summer, or two months in winter, before application. This destroys the kinds of parasites that cause diseases, such as schistosomiasis, ancyclostomiasis, and enterobiasis. Application of the treated night soil is applied to cropland at a reported rate of 75 cubic meters per hectare.

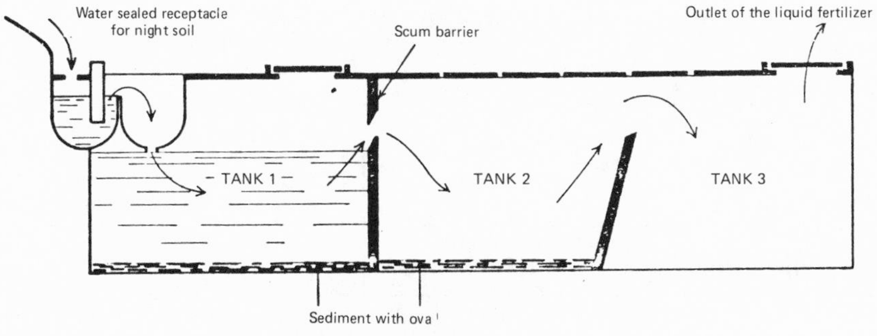

Fig. 16.5. Three-tank fermentation system for treatment of night soil in the countryside, Malu Commune (Shanghai).

Another way of recycling human excreta without danger is to pass night soil through a biogas production cycle, using it for making high temperature compost and/or silt grass pit manure. Collected night soil from cities is transported by boats to rural areas, where it is either directly used with city garbage or crop residues for making high temperature compost, or stored for two weeks in pits having a capacity of 70 cubic meters. These pits are covered with polyethylene sheets. Sewage from urban areas with sewers is used for irrigation, usually after passing a sewage treatment process using activated sludge techniques. Public latrines are built over fish ponds wherever it is possible, so that night soil is used for feeding fish.

Pig manure. The Chinese peasant regards a pig as a costless fertilizer factory moving around on hooves. One pig has an annual yield of over three tons of manure, which means that China now produces at least 780 million tons of pig manure per year.

According to estimates of Chinese agronomists, the application of the manure produced by 20-30 pigs per year could result in the same increase of rice yield as one ton of ammonium sulfate, namely three tons of rice. Pig manure is prepared by private owners in deep pits mixed with straw, crop stalks, grass, and mud. In collective pig raising, the manure is made by:

- Washing the sties. The liquid manure is then mixed with water weeds and grasses, and stored in covered pits until needed; in some cases the liquid manure is distributed by boat to fields alongside the stream; or
- Mixing pig excreta (40 percent) with dried fine mud (60 percent), and storing the mixture in manure sheds (see table 16.5).

Table 16.5. Composition of Pig Manure

Source	% of O.M.	N %	P_2O_5%	P %	K_2O%	K%
Pig manure (fresh)	15	0.6	0.4	0.18	0.44	0.37
Urine	2.8	0.3	0.12	0.05	1.0	0.83
Pig manure (air dried)	34.3	2.12	0.98	0.43	2.45	2.03
Pig manure (stable, using straw or litter)	34.0	0.48	0.24	0.11	0.63	0.52

The prepared pig manure is applied either directly to crops as top dressing (in liquid form) at the rate of 8 tons per hectare of cropland, and as base dressing (in solid form) at the rate of 80-100 tons per hectare of cropland; or indirectly, when pig manure is used for making other kinds of manures, e.g., silt grass pitmanure, high temperature compost, and biogas manure. The rates of pig manure applied through these manures are 7.5, 10 and 15 tons of pig manure per hectare of cropland respectively.

Draft animal manure. Livestock provide an important source of fertilizing agents since the total number of cattles, water buffalos, horses, donkeys, mules, and camels has been increased from 59.8 million in 1949 to 95 millions in 1972, and the number of sheep and goats has also increased from 42.4 millions in 1949 to 148.2 millions in 1972. (11) A cow or a buffalo provides about 9 tons of manure per year, containing 0.3% N, 0.25% P_2O_5 and 0.10% K_2O. The dung is carefully collected from stables, shelters, and pathways, and is used for the preparation of high temperature compost, silt grass pit manure, and for production of biogas, as previously described for pig manure.

Silt or mud from rivers, lakes, and ponds. In areas such as the Yangtse and Pearl River deltas which are covered with water ways, silt is an important source of fertilizer. The extensive use of it, incidentally, helps in desilting water ways which suffer from high siltage rates, e.g., the Yangtse River has a siltage rate of 2.26 pounds per cubic foot, which is 27 times greater than the world average. The Nile River has a siltage rate of only 0.065 pounds per cubic foot. (12)

The high siltage rate of rivers in China gives some idea of the high rate of soil erosion. Silt is either used as is at a rate of 600-700 tons per hectare in sugarcane fields and banana plantations, or in the form of silt grass pit manure at a rate of about 225 tons per hectare per year. This can be considered as a way of recovering the fine particles taken away from the soil by heavy rainfall. (See table 16.6).

The silt is collected manually or by mud suckers, and is often applied either directly to sugarcane fields, mulberry beds, and to the stands of banana plantation at the rate of 600-700 tons per hectare. Otherwise, it is used for making silt grass pit manure, earth compost, and for covering heaps of composts (garbage, sludge, etc.,) to avoid multiplication of files. The beneficial effect of the silt is attributed to its plant nutrient content (e.g., ammonical N in the silt is reported to be 2 to 3 times greater than in the soil), and to its capacity to help retain soil moisture and improve soil structure.

Silt grass pit manure or mixture. This type of manure is widespread in areas with high rates of rainfall (e.g., Kiangsu and Shanghai). The manure is prepared in round or rectangular pits, 1.5 meters deep with a capacity of 8 to 10 tons of manure (fig. 16.6). The constituents -7.5 tons river silt, 0.15 ton rice straw, 1.0 ton pig or other animal manure, 0.75 ton grass (astragalus), or water weeds, and 0.020 ton superphosphate - are laid as 15 centimeters thick layers in the pit, saturated with water, covered with silt, and fermented for three months. Three turnings are carried out during this time. The anaerobic fermentation

Table 16.6. Nutrient Content of River Silt

	River Silt (Si Chiao, Kwantung)	Lake (Tai Lake, Kiangsu)
Organic matter %	3.3	5-8
Content of N%	0.18	0.25
P_2O_5%	0.15	0.50
P%	0.07	0.22
K_2O%	0.50-0.60	0.91
K%	0.42-0.50	0.76

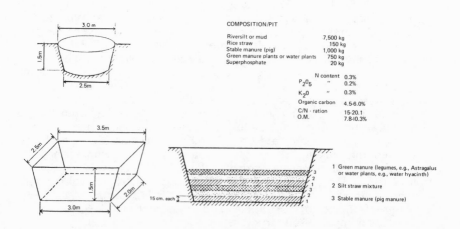

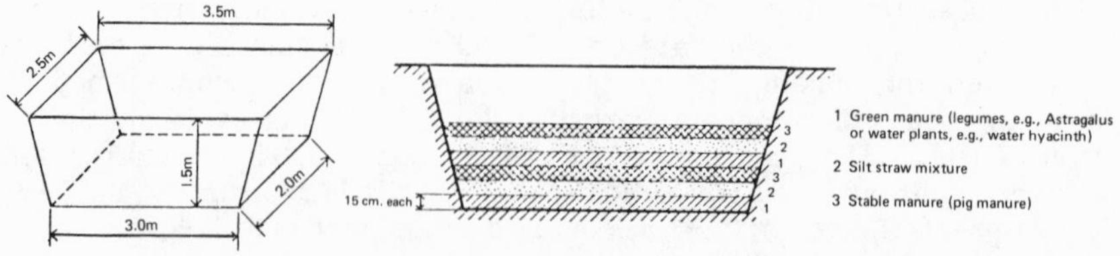

Fig. 16.6. Silt grass mixture or pit manure, Yueh Chi Commune, Wu County (Kiangsu).

and the use of silt and straw reduce the N-losses to a minimum. The manure produced contains 7.8-10.3% organic matter, 0.3% total N, 0.20% P_2O_5, 0.09% P, 0.50% K_2O, 0.25% K and has a C:N ratio of 15-20:1. Silt grass pit manure is applied three times per year at the rate of 75 tons per hectare of cropland (225 tons per hectare per year).

Earth compost. This kind of compost is widespread in dry, warm areas, such as Kwantung. It is always prepared under sheds to avoid losses of nutrients caused by sun and rain. The main component of this type of manure is river silt (at least 60%) which is collected, dried, and then ground by special mills. The compost is prepared according to the following methods:

- The ground mud (60 percent) is mixed with pig manure (40 percent), made to a heap and kept in a shed until needed. Application rate is 7.5 tons per hectare of cropland.
- Fresh animal droppings and night soil are first mixed with ash in the ratio of 3:2, then this mixture is mixed with mud in the ratio of 2:3, and piled in 10 alternate 15 centimeter high layers.
- Garbage enriched with superphosphate at the rate of 0.5 kilograms per 100 kilograms of garbage is mixed with equal portions of night soil. The product is then mixed with mud in the ratio of 2:3 and heaped under roof as described previously.

High temperature compost. Many successful methods for making high temperature compost have been developed by Chinese peasants. The most common methods use more or less the same constituents, that is, chopped crop stalks, garbage or agricultural wastes, night soil, animal manures, superphosphate, and water; these are made into heaps for decomposition by aerobic, thermophilic, microbial processes. The differences between these methods are in the form of heap and in the aeration systems. In Tachai (Shansi province), they turn and mix the pile after two weeks to maintain the high temperature (60-70°C) for a longer time. In Chao county (Hopei), the aeration is ensured by inserting hollow bamboo sticks in the heap crosswise while piling. The bamboo sticks are taken away after plastering the heap, keeping the 10 centimeter holes intact (see fig. 16.7). The holes are then sealed with mud when the temperature rises to 65°C. In Tahei county (Hopei), huge bunches of maize stalks are inserted while making the heap so as to provide aeration. The composition of the product is reported to be 20 percent organic matter, 0.5 percent nitrogen, 0.3 per cent P_2O_5 and 0.6 - 0.7 per cent K_2O. Application rate is generally 90 tons per hectare per year.

Other organic manures. Oil seed cakes made from the seeds of soybean, peanut, rapes, cotton, sesame, tea, and tung nut constitute the major part of this kind of manure. Together they add up to about 10 percent of the organic manures in China; this includes fish manure, silk cocoon wastes, bone meal, dead animals, slaughter house refuses, etc.

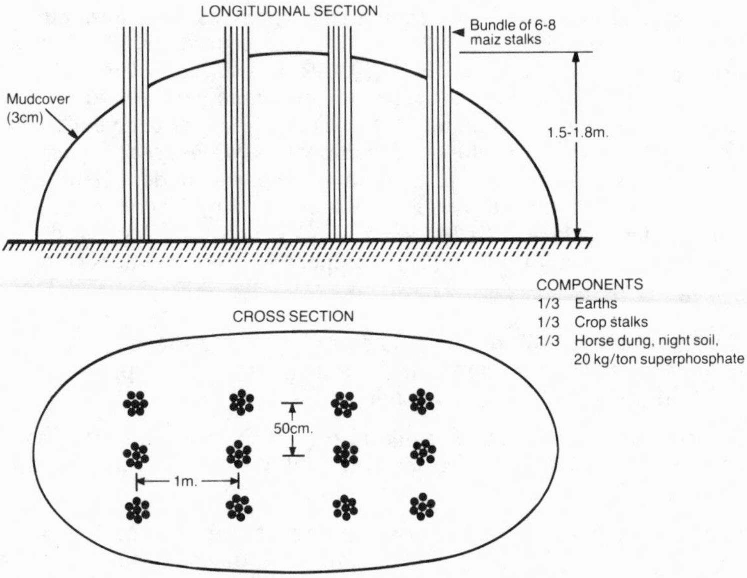

Fig. 16.7. High temperature compost heap. (Using maize stalks for ariation) Tung Shaoyng Production Brigade, Tahei County, (Hopei).

REFERENCES

(1) FAO report of the Regional office for Asia and The Far East. 1976. Learning From China. Page 1, Bangkok.

(2) Chao, Kang. 1970. Agricultural Production in Communist China (1949-1965). University of Wisconsin Press.

(3) Tapiador, D.D., Henderson, H.F., Delmendo, M.N., and Tsutsui, H. 1977. Freshwater Fisheries and Aquaculture in China. A Report of the FAO Fisheries Mission to China, April 21-May 12, 1976, FAO, Rome.

(4) Chinese information during the FAO study tour on Recycling of Organic Wastes in Agriculture. 1977. April 28-May 24, 1977. China.

(5) Harley, J.L. 1976. Scientific Visits to China Under Arrangements between the Academia Sinica and the Royal Society, 12-28 July, 1975; parts III-VIII, The Royal Society, London.

(6) Abu-El-fadl, M. 1960. Organic Manures and Processing of Plant and Animal Wastes. Page 232, Lagnat Elbayan Elaraby, Cairo. (In Arabic.)

(7) Boswinkle, E. 1976. Strengthening of the Institute for Soils and Fertilizer Research of Vietnam, Technical Report of FAO.

(8) Alaa El-Din, M.N. 1977. Recycling of Organic Wastes in Agriculture in China. Technical report presented to the Agriculture Research Center, Ministry of Agriculture, Egypt, (In Arabic.)

(9) Nutman, P.S., ed. 1976. Symbiotic Nitrogen Fixation in Plants, Cambridge University Press.

(10) Finger, T. and Bachman, D. 1976. China's energy policies and resources development. Report to a seminar, June 2-3, 1976, p. 5, Stanford University, CA.

(11) U.S. Department of Agriculture, 1974.

(12) Trangar, T.R. 1970. A Geography of China, page 220.

17

The Production of Food, Energy, and Fresh Water from the Sea Through Artificial Upwelling*

Oswald A. Roels

The limited supply and high cost of arable land, fresh water, and petroleum mean that it is essential that we explore alternative methods to provide the world's people with new sources of water, energy, and food.

The scarcity of arable land necessary to increase food production naturally points to the vast area of the oceans as the world's largest collector and storage system of solar energy, particularly in tropical and subtropical latitudes.

The world's oceans cover approximately 70 percent of the earth and, therefore, receive more than twice as much solar energy as do the land masses. In contrast to most other solar energy collectors, they retain and can yield the stored energy during the night as well as in the day; however, we do not now utilize most of this stored heat. Furthermore, the quantity of animal protein presently harvested from the tropical seas is small. Although the surface layers of the tropical oceans receive far more solar energy than temperate land areas due to the greater light intensity and the higher angle of incidence of the solar radiation in the tropics, these waters do not produce very much plant

---

* The St. Croix Artificial Upwelling experiments referred to in this paper were supported by the United States Department of Commerce, National Oceanic and Atmospheric Administration, Office of Sea Grant, the Caesar Kleberg, G. Unger Vetlesen, and H.E.B. foundations. The author gratefully acknowledges the collaboration of his colleagues in the Artificial Upwelling Project: Ludo Van Hemelryck, Dr. S. Laurence, Dr. K.C. Haines, Paul McDonald, Marian Trout, Judith Sunderlin, Leo Aust, Al Lang, William Tobias, R. Widdowson, R. Railey, O. Francis, P. Markowitz, V. Railey and Paul Tucker, without whose dedicated collaboration the St. Croix experiment would not have been possible.

material because of the lack of nutrients (nitrate, phosphate, etc.) needed for autotrophic photosynthetic plants to grow. As a result of this low plant production, the animal populations in the tropical seas are disappointingly small. The sea produces only about 5 to 10 percent of the protein now consumed. Our fish catch from the oceans has stabilized at 1970 levels, and overfishing of many species (e.g., whales, herring, and sardines) is depleting the natural stocks. (1)

Crisp (1975) (2) has calculated that the open ocean, which covers 90 percent of the surface area of the world's oceans, produces only 0.7 percent of its fish, whereas the coastal zones with 9.9 percent of the ocean's area produce 54 percent of the fish, and the upwelling regions with only 0.1 percent of the surface area of the world's oceans produce 44 percent of the fish. This is due to the lack of nutrients in the surface layers of the open ocean, the nutrient input from the land in the coastal zone, and the nutrient supply from deep water in upwelling areas.

This natural phenomenon of high biological productivity in upwelling areas (i.e., areas of the oceans where deep ocean water rises to the surface as a result of natural forces) has stimulated our research in Artificial Upwelling. Artificial Upwelling utilizes sunshine and deep ocean water as raw materials to produce fresh water, high quality animal protein and energy. Its protein production potential exceeds that of most land-based agricultural systems, and is not dependent on petroleum for fertilizer and energy.

Artificial Upwelling can derive mechanical energy, and/or fresh water from the temperature differential between the warm surface water and the cold deep water in the tropical and subtropical oceans. Only a small proportion of the total energy generated is required to drive the pumps to bring the deep water to the surface. The deep water is also rich in nutrients (nitrate, phosphate, and silicate) compared to surface water, which can be used as fertilizer to produce plant biomass for marine food chains. In a small land-based pilot plant on the north shore of St. Croix (U.S. Virgin Islands), the author and his colleagues have demonstrated the technical feasibility of plant and animal protein production based on deep seawater. Numerous paper studies have analyzed the engineering and economic feasibility of power generation and fresh water production by desalination from the sea's temperate differential.

UTILIZATION OF THE TEMPERATURE DIFFERENTIAL IN THE TROPICAL OCEAN

Energy Production. The ocean's waters are horizontally stratified and the deep ocean water is uniformly cold. In many tropical areas, the temperature difference between the sun-warmed surface layer and the deep cold water is 20°C throughout the year. This temperature difference can be utilized to create mechanical energy by inserting a suitable heat engine between the warm and cold layers; such an engine would have a low Carnot efficiency because of the small temperature difference, but the resource is practically inexhaustible, and it is renewable because it is powered by the sun.

The concept of utilizing the temperature differential in the sea, to run a heat engine and generate electrical power, is credited to d'Arsonval (1881). (3) Claude (1930) (4) constructed and operated a plant to generate electrical power from this temperature differential on the north shore of Cuba. The plant's operation was short-lived because of trouble with the cold water pipeline, but Claude demonstrated that the process was technically feasible. Since that time, numerous paper studies (Anderson and Anderson, 1966; Lockheed, 1975; TRW, 1975) have shown that such a plant can be constructed utilizing present-day technology. (5,6,7) There are wide variations in the projections of the cost of the power produced by such sea thermal power plants. These plants could use the open or Claude-cycle process, in which the warm water is evaporated under reduced pressure to drive a turbine. Downstream from the turbine, the water vapor is condensed either by a spray of cold deep seawater, or in a more conventional heat exchanger, where the vapors, cooled on the outside of the condenser and with cold deep water on the inside, produce fresh water. The latter variation, producing power as well as freshwater, is sometimes referred to as the hybrid open cycle. In the closed cycle process, an intermediary fluid such as ammonia, freon, or propane, is evaporated by the warm surface water and condensed by the cold deep water. The closed cycle is advantageous because the working pressures are greater and therefore allow for conventional turbine design. However, this system requires very large and expensive heat-exchangers between the working fluid and the warm and cold water. The open cycle avoids this problem, but requires a large turbine capable of efficient work at low pressures, and has problems with dissolved gases in seawater. Other problems with Ocean-Thermal Energy Conversion (OTEC) plants include corrosion and biofouling, but the general consensus is that the technical difficulties can be solved.

Roels, et al. (1978) have discussed the electrical power yield from such a system. (8) The energy available from the resource is best expressed in terms of cubic meters of deep water used, since long and large diameter pipelines must be installed to obtain the deep water, and because pumping is expensive. For a cold source at 280°K and a warm source at 300°K, the maximum theoretical efficiency n_{max} for full utilization of the resource is:

$$n_{max} = \frac{1}{2} \left(\frac{300}{280} - 1 \right) = .0357$$

and the maximum available energy W_{max} is:

$$W_{max} /m^3 = k\Delta n_{max} = 2.99 \times 10^6 \ J/m^3$$

where K = specific heat of water = 4.187×10^6 J/(°K m^3)

Van Hemelryck (1975) has discussed a Rankine-cycle plant, which makes optimal use of this resource. (9) At the limit for an optimal plant, the discharge temperature of the cold water (T'_c), and that of the warm water (T'_h), should be equal ($T'_c = T'_h$). Further, assuming a three-stage (multiple evaporation) plant and a surface water:deep water ratio of 3:1, he has shown that with a ΔT of $20^{\circ}K$ the theoretical output would be 1.642×10^6 J/m^3, neglecting irreversible losses associated with operating the equipment. Because net yield will depend upon various economic factors and the actual design of turbines, pumps, and heat-exchangers, a precise estimate of usable energy from this process cannot be made.

For a proposed open cycle plant at Abidjan, Ivory Coast, Salle and Capestan (1956) estimated a gross energy production of about 1.0×10^6 J/m^3 of deep water. (10) A 100 MW plant would thus require approximately 3.15×10^9 m^3 or 3.15×10^7 m^3/MW/year. In contrast, a recent closed cycle design commissioned by the United States Energy Research and Development Administration would require pumping 7.3 times more deep water, 5.7×10^{10} m^3/year to achieve a gross output of about 250 MW or 2.3×10^8 m^3/MW/year. (11) Anderson and Anderson (1965, 1966) estimated that a 33 MW net plant (37.6 MW gross), producing 302 kW/m^3/sec, would require 6.5 percent of the gross power production for pumping. (12) For a plant of this size, pumping costs would therefore be 1.96×10^4 J/m^3. This cost would undoubtedly decrease for larger plants.

The cost of the deep sea water is a major factor in OTEC plants. There are presently great discrepancies in the estimates made by different authors of the amounts of deep sea water required for power generation. Thus, Salle and Capestan (1956) estimate that 3.15×10^7 m^3 deep seawater/MW/year are required (13), Lockheed (1975) estimates 2.28×10^8 m^3/MW/year (14) and Anderson and Anderson (1965, 1966) calculate 1.04×10^8 m^3/MW/year. (15) These differences are due to the ratio of surface water to deep water the different designers propose to use, and the degree of warming of the deep seawater projected in the heat-exchangers in the plant. Thus, most United States proposed designs foresee warming the deep water by only $1^{\circ}C$ to $2.3^{\circ}C$ in the heat-exchangers. It would appear that there is considerable room for optimization of these projected OTEC power systems since there are variations in deep water requirements of almost an order of magnitude, as between the Salle and Capestan and Lockheed projections.

Both shore-based sea thermal power generating plants (OTEC plants) and floating plants are under consideration. A shore-based plant would have to be located in a coastal area in the tropical ocean between $20^{\circ}N$ and $20^{\circ}S$, where a steep offshore slope brings deep water with a temperature of $20^{\circ}C$ below that of surface water close to shore to minimize the cost of the pipeline. Moreover, the longer the pipeline, the more the cold water will warm up in transit to the plant. The advantage of shore-based plants is that the power transmission from the plant to consumers utilizes existing technology. Steep offshore slopes are rather exceptional along the edges of the continents, which frequently have wide continental shelves. Many oceanic islands rise steeply from the ocean floor and have steep offshore slopes. In a survey of the coastline between 20°N and 20°S, 291 coastal areas have been identified where 1000 meters deep water is less than 5 kilometers offshore. In some of these coastal areas, water with a year round temperature of 20°C below that of the surface water is no more than 300 meters deep, requiring pipelines of only about 1000 meters in length to bring it to a shore-based plant.

Floating OTEC plants are under consideration. In these plants, the deep seawater pipeline would be suspended from a floating platform that could drift with the currents or be self-propelled and thus graze the ocean for power generation. Some of these plants could have shorter deep water pipelines than shore-based plants, but face problems of power transmission to shore, or of utilizing the power in energy intensive industries constructed on the floating platform carrying the power plant.

Fresh Water Production by Desalination

Van Hemelryck (1975) has discussed the theoretical limits of fresh water production based on the temperature differential between surface water and deep water in the tropical oceans. (16) The author considers the case in which equal volumes of warm surface water and cold deep water are utilized in the desalination plant, and concludes that the theoretical maximum limit of fresh water production in a single stage system is 16.7 liters per cubic meter deep water used. In a dual stage system using twice as much surface water as deep water, the theoretical limit would be 33.3 liters fresh water per cubic meter of deep water pumped.

The same author has calculated that if a ratio of surface water to deep water of 3:1 is used with a ΔT of 20°C, the theoretical maximum fresh water production from a three-stage system would be 58.3 liters of fresh water produced per cubic meter of deep seawater utilized. However, there will be irreversible losses which are inversely proportional to the size and thus the capital cost of the installation. The fresh water output for a given deep water flow is therefore mainly dependent on a tradeoff between the optimum size of the plant and the irreversible losses. This optimum may vary considerably from one project to another, resulting in different yields of fresh water per cubic meter of cool deep seawater.

Van Hemelryck assumes that 40 liters of fresh water per cubic meter of deep seawater can be produced in a plant using three times as much surface water as deep water and a ΔT of 20°C.

Othmer and Roels (1973) described the design of a hybrid open cycle sea thermal power plant producing both electricity and fresh water. (17) This plant was designed for a deep seawater flow of 3,262 m^3 per minute with an output of 7,180 kilowatt net, and a fresh water production of 6 million U.S. gallons of fresh water per day corresponding to 4.9 liters fresh water per cubic meter of deep seawater pumped. It should be taken into account, however, that in this hybrid open cycle, the water vapor would be utilized for power generation prior to condensation for fresh water production.

It appears unlikely that fresh water produced in this way would be cheap enough for use as irrigation water. Moreover, the deep ocean water provides a fertile medium for aquaculture, and could produce more plant protein per unit surface area than comparable surfaces devoted to conventional agriculture: i.e., it would be better to make deep sea water ponds for mariculture than to irrigate farmland of comparable area. However, fresh water production for domestic and individual use based on the sea thermal difference could be very advantageous in certain locations.

Other Cooling Applications

The cold deep water can be utilized for other cooling applications, such as air conditioning, ice making, and for condenser cooling of fossil fuel or nuclear power generating plants. By utilizing the cold deep water in the condensers of the power plants, thermal pollution can be avoided and the plant's efficiency can be increased slightly.

UTILIZATION OF THE DEEP WATER NUTRIENTS FOR MARINE PROTEIN PRODUCTION

After its utilization in the condenser of a sea thermal power generating plant, a desalination plant, or an air conditioning system, the deep water is unaltered except for its temperature, and can be utilized as a source of nutrients and as an excellent growth medium for mariculture. Indeed, the deep water is free of parasites, pollutants, predators, epizoites, epiphytes, and disease-bearing organisms for mariculture crops.

The technical feasibility of Artificial Upwelling mariculture has been demonstrated in a small plant on the north shore of St. Croix, U.S. Virgin Islands (17° 47'N, 64° 48'W) in the Caribbean Sea. The site on St. Croix was chosen because there the ocean reaches a depth of 1000 meters, approximately 1.6 kilometers offshore. Three polyethylene pipelines, each 1,830 meters long and 6.9 centimeters I.D. in diameter, were installed in 1972, and have brought deep water to shore continuously since that time; the present deep water flow is 250 liters/min. The deep water is pumped into two 50,000 liter (13,000 gallons) pools. Diatoms grown in these pools are started from laboratory cultures, then cultured in 757 liter (200 gallon) tanks, which are used to inoculate the pools. One diatom, Chaetoceros curvisetus Cleve (STX-167), can be grown in continuous culture in unsupplemented deep water at turnover rates of up to 1.5 pool volumes per day. The pool cultures are pumped continuously into shellfish tanks at metered rates, depending upon the feeding activity of the shellfish. The system also contains a hatchery, in which the clam Tapes japonica (Deshayes) is regularly produced, a larvae-setting area for juveniles, an experimental shellfish area used to determine optimum feeding rates, animal density, etc., and a pilot shellfish rearing area used to test results of small-scale studies and for preliminary economic determinations. Food to these areas can be supplied from the pools or from a wide range of algae grown in 10 elevated 2,000 liter culturing vessels (reactors). In addition, a separate set of ten 2,000 liter reactors is used to study the possibility of maintaining continuous cultures using a surface-water inoculum. Table 17.1 gives the concentration of the major nutrients necessary for algal growth present in deep and surface water at St. Croix.

Table 17.1. Nutrient Concentration in the Deep (870 m) and Surface Waters North of St. Croix, U.S. Virgin Islands

	Nutrients (μg-atom/liter)				
	(NO_3+NO_2)-N	NO_2-N	NH_3-N	PO_4-P	SiO_4-Si
Surface Water (3km Offshore)	0.2	0.2	0.9	0.2	4.9
870-m Deep Water	31.3	0.2	0.7	2.1	20.6

The yearly temperature range in the shellfish tanks is 22-29°C. Ten species have been screened for growth and survival in the St. Croix system. Eight species grew well, and reached market size quickly. They are the European oyster (Ostrea edulus), the Pacific oyster (Crassostrea gigas), the Pacific oyster for the half shell trade (C. gigas, Kumamoto variety), the Japanese little neck clam (Tapes japonica), the Southern clam (Mercenaria campechiensis), the F_1 clam (a cross M. campechiensis x M. mercenaria), the bay scallop (Argopecten irradians), and the Japanese pearl oyster (Pinctada martensii).

The spiny lobster, Panulirus argus, has been reared on culled shellfish. Hypnea musciformis, a carrageenan-producing red seaweed, doubles its weight every three days by stripping ammonia (an animal excretory product) from the shellfish tank effluent.

Primary Production

One of the main goals at St. Croix is maximal algal productivity. Since inorganic nitrogen (nitrate, nitrite and ammonia) is the limiting nutrient for algal growth in deep sea water, we have expressed our algal production in terms of protein per hectare, based on the efficiency of conversion of the inorganic nitrogen, dissolved in the deep sea water, to algal protein. The latter is dependent upon internal (or species-specific) variables, as well as upon external variables, such as temperature, nutrient concentration, dilution rate, pool depth, and light.

In the pools at St. Croix, *Chaetoceros curvisetus* regularly attains a concentration of 25 µg-atom protein nitrogen/liter. Since the inorganic nitrogen concentration in the incoming deep sea water is 32 µg-atom per liter, this represents a conversion of deep water dissolved inorganic nitrogen to phytoplankton protein nitrogen of over 78 percent.

The St. Croix pools have been operated in pilot plant fashion for the last two years. Between July 6, 1977 and July 6, 1978, 811 g protein/m^2 was produced in the pools, corresponding to a protein production of 8.11 tons/hectare/year. During this period, the pools were *active* for 83 percent of the time. The 17 percent down-time was due to culture collapse, necessitating emptying the pools, refilling, reinoculating, and cell growth to the required density in batches before the pools could be switched back to continuous culture.

In the present St. Croix system, the cultures are nitrate-limited and not light-limited. In a commercial operation, one would try to approach light-limitation to exploit the available sunlight to the maximum and, therefore, construct deeper pools. To maximize the phytoplankton protein which can be produced per unit surface area and per m^3 of deep water, the optimal pool depth and turnover (dilution) rate of the pools should be determined. Farmer (1976) studied productivity of *C. curvisetus* (STX-167) at St. Croix in outdoor cultures in 80 centimeters deep 2,000 liter vessels as a function of the culture turnover rate and light intensity. (18) Light intensity was controlled through the use of neutral density screens, which regulated the surface light intensity of the cultures at 3, 20, 30, 46, or 100 percent of the natural sunlight intensity (I_o) on the beach in St. Croix. Light attenuation in each culture was determined at sunset and sunrise each day by measuring subsurface and bottom light intensities in the pools. Four different deep water flow rates were used for each light condition: 0.25, 0.70, 0.95, and 1.20 turnovers/day.

From the results of those cultures with a surface light intensity of $0.3 \times I_o$ only, pool depth, light attenuation, turnover rates, and hence productivity values for an optimized algal system were constructed. (19) It must be emphasized that an *optimum* set of algal pool parameters (depth vs. length and width) must take into account economic factors, such as cost of excavation, maintenance, etc., and, therefore, that depth which provides the maximum production per unit surface area may not be the best in terms of capital, operating, or maintenance costs. Thus, for a pool depth of 4.88 meters, good light attenuation is achieved and a compromise between depth and productivity is reached: 6.99 g protein/m^2/day with a pool turnover rate of 0.8/day. This would correspond to a plant protein production of 23 tons/hectare/330 days. The maximum productivity within the explored range is obtained with a 7.10 meter pool depth at a turnover rate of 1.2/day and yields 8.42 g protein/m^2/day. This would correspond to a plant protein production of 27.8 tons/hectare/year. It has been estimated that 3 meter-deep pools would be more likely to be utilized on a commercial scale, and would represent a compromise between cost and productivity per unit surface area. Such a pool, at a turnover rate of 0.75/day, would yield 16.7 tons of phytoplankton protein per hectare/year. These extrapolations are based on many assumptions and have to be verified experimentally.

Those achieved (8.1 tons/hectare/year in a 1 meter deep pool), and projected protein yields ranging up to 27.8 tons/hectare/year for deeper pools should be compared to the protein yields of alfalfa, which is land-based agriculture's highest protein producing crop, and yields 0.71 tons of plant protein/hectare/year (20) with intensive use of fertilizers and mechanized systems.

A number of problems remain to be solved in the primary production step of Artificial Upwelling mariculture for large scale application. The duration of the continuous phytoplankton cultures should be increased and culture collapse, requiring emptying of the pools and restarting of the cultures with fresh inoculum, should be avoided. The algal productivity in deeper pools should be tested experimentally because all St. Croix data are based on 0.8 or 1 meter pool depth, and the extrapolations to deeper pools are based on shading of the surface of the 0.8 meter culture vessels, and the determination of the optical density of the culture in 0.8 or 1 meter depth. The influence of materials of construction to be used in the deep water system, such as pipelines, pumps, heat exchangers of the sea thermal power plant, etc., on phytoplankton productivity should also be determined.

Secondary Production

The algae produced in the St. Croix mariculture system have been used as food for filter-feeding shellfish: clams, oysters, and scallops. The conversion efficiency of deep sea water nitrate-nitrogen to algal protein-nitrogen averaged 70 percent. Conversion efficiencies of phytoplankton protein-nitrogen to clam meat protein-nitrogen (<u>Tapes japonica</u> was used) of 31-35 percent were achieved in relatively short term (36 days duration) experiments. (21) During actual pilot scale experiments at the St. Croix Marine Station over a one year period, growing several populations of <u>Tapes japonica</u> from seed to market size, a conversion efficiency of 22 percent of total photoplankton protein-nitrogen produced in the pools to clam meat protein-nitrogen was achieved, with the animals ready for market after 56 days in the hatchery, and 224 days in the pilot plant. This should be compared with plant protein to animal protein conversion ratios of 31 percent of cows' milk production, and 6.5 percent of feedlot beef production.

Recently, work has been started in St. Croix to determine the feasibility of raising other marine animals than filter-feeding shellfish in the system. Very promising results have been obtained in rearing a small crustacean, Artemia salina, the brine shrimp, in the system. These organisms, in turn, can be used as food for a wide variety of marine animals, and could lead to three step food chains.

Some problems remain to be solved prior to the final design of large scale Artificial Upwelling mariculture systems. The conversion efficiency of different species of animals at the secondary production level should be tested. A food chain to penaeid shrimp should be investigated, and the influence of materials of construction of the deep water system and OTEC plant on growth and survival of the secondary producer contemplated should be determined, especially for the larvae and juveniles.

LARGE SCALE APPLICATIONS OF THE ARTIFICIAL UPWELLING CONCEPT

What then is the extent of the thermal resource? The total surface area of the world's oceans between 20°N and 20°S is approximately 1.25×10^{8} km^{2}. If we assume that the surface mixed layer averages 50 meters depth in this area, then the total heat source for sea thermal power generation would amount to 1.25×10^{14} $m^{2} \times 50$ m = 6.25×10^{15} m^{3}. The cold source in the tropical oceans is, of course, vastly greater: the average depth of the tropical oceans is 3,500 meters, and it can be safely assumed that cold enough water occurs from a depth of 1,000 meters down to the ocean floor. Assuming that 1 percent of the total volume of the warm mixed layer of the tropical oceans were utilized per year to generate power (1 percent of 6.25×10^{15} m^{3} = 6.25×10^{13} m^{3}), and that the ratio of warm surface water to cold deep water utilized in these sea thermal plants would be one to one, then the total power generating capability of these plants would be 5×10^{5} MW if the sea thermal power plant requires 3.75 m^{3}/sec deep water per MW of net electrical power produced.

If 1 percent of the water in the mixed layer were used daily, the net power produced would be a staggering 2×10^{8} MW or 200 Terawatt. The total United States power generating capacity in 1976 was 2 Terawatt, and the world capacity in that same year was 6.2 Terawatt. (22)

The potential impact of the operation of such plants on the heat budget of the sea has been studied. Martin and Roberts (1977) have calculated that if one hundred 200-MW plants with a total capacity of 0.02 Terrawatt operated in the Gulf of Mexico for 30 years, the sea surface temperature would drop 0.05^{o}C, and the deep cold water region below the cold water intake would warm 0.8^{o}C. (23) If one thousand 200-MW plants with a total capacity of 0.2 Terawatt operated in the

Gulf, the sea surface temperature would drop 0.3°C during the first two years, and remain fairly constant thereafter. However, the deep water in the region below the cold water intake would warm continuously at a rate of about 0.3°C per year. These calculations are based on the utilization of 8.5 m^3 of total sea water pumped per second per MW of power produced. The high rate of warming of the deep water was caused by the fact that the model the authors used to make their predictions does not allow for the removal of this heat input to the deep water from the Gulf by the currents. It might be expected that cold deep water from the Caribbean would seek to displace warm water at an equivalent depth in the Gulf. Hence, the thermal resource available for a very large scale OTEC in the Gulf may depend upon the rate of this exchange of deep water between the Gulf and the Caribbean.

The Potential for Marine Protein Production

In our discussion of the thermal resource, we have assumed that if 1 percent of the warm mixed layer of the tropical oceans were utilized per year to generate power, and if the ratio of warm surface water to cold deep water utilized in sea thermal power plants would be 1:1, these plants would then utilize 6.25×10^{13} m^3 deep ocean water per year. The potential mariculture yield of this deep water flow would be 750 million tons of clam meat per year, based on actual deep water nutrients to clam meat conversion achieved in the St. Croix system (12 g of Tapes japonica fresh weight clam meat produced mer m^3 of deep water utilized in the system). This production should be compared to the total world meat production (veal, beef, mutton, lamb, pork, poultry, game) for human consumption of 118 million tons during 1975, and to 67 million tons of fish produced in the world in the same year. (24)

To achieve this production would require 8.3×10^6 hectares, or 83,000 km^2. This surface area is only 0.07 percent of the total surface area of the tropical oceans which cover 125 million km^2.

Since presently contemplated OTEC plants will warm the deep water up by only approximately 1° in the heat exchangers, with perhaps an overall 2°C warming of the deep water over its in situ temperature, the deep water will generally be denser than the surface waters due to its considerably lower temperature, and will sink rapidly back to its depth of density equilibrium. To utilize this deep sea water in a mariculture operation, it would be necessary to contain the deep water in ponds or bays on or near shore for land-based OTEC plants or in some kind of floating structures, which would maintain it near the surface of the ocean where it is exposed to sunlight, for OTEC plants floating in the open sea. It appears, therefore, that we are a long way in our technological developments from very large open ocean mariculture farms, and that the shore-based option appears far more feasible in the near future.

Winer and Nicol (1977) have examined the cost of electrical energy transmission from floating OTEC power plants. (25) They calculated that for an undersea cable, linking a 200 MW plant to shore at a distance of 100 miles, the cost of transmitting the power to shore would amount to approximately one cent per kilowatt hour, and that such cables are not currently state of the art.

Therefore, the most likely economic solution for the utilization of deep sea water lies in shore-based sea thermal power plants, in which the deep ocean water can be used in land-based mariculture systems after its discharge from the power plant condenser.

Economic Considerations

In 1975, reports of two OTEC systems sponsored by the Division of Solar Energy of the United States Energy Research and Development Administration (ERDA) were published, with preliminary estimates of the capital investment required, and the bus bar cost of electrical power generated. ERDA has specified closed cycle, large (100MW or more) floating ocean thermal energy conversion power plants in their request for proposals.

Trimble et al. (1975), of the Lockheed Missiles & Space Company, reported that a 160 MW net output OTEC floating power plant could deliver energy at a bus bar cost of less than three cents per kilowatt hour, and that the capital cost of the plant would be $3,615 per kilowatt capacity installed (exclusive of the cable to shore). (26)

R.H. Douglass (1975), of the TRW Company, estimated that for a 100 MW floating sea thermal power plant using the closed cycle (utilizing ammonia as the working fluid) the system cost would be $2,100 per kilowatt capacity installed, and that the bus bar cost would be between 3.5 and 5.8 cents per kilowatt hour. (27) These cost estimates should be regarded as preliminary, and if OTEC cost estimates follow the same development as most estimates for other new technologies, they are probably too low.

Table 17.2 compares estimated gross revenues of a shore-based combined OTEC-mariculture plant that would produce 1 MWe net, and utilize 3.75 m^3 deep ocean water/MW/sec. The mariculture plant would receive the deep sea water, after its use in the power plant.

The comparison between the power yield and the meat yield from the same volume of deep sea water in table 17.2 is over-simplified since a 1 MW power plant would probably be uneconomical and considerable economies of scale can be realized in much larger power plants. If the entire deep sea water flow from such large power plants were utilized in mariculture systems, the production of marine animals would be so great that marketing problems may arise.

However, the combined utilization of the ΔT and the nutrient content of deep water in the tropical ocean could be economical, and would contribute to solving shortages of food and energy now faced by humanity.

Table 17.2. Annual Gross Dollar Value of Products From a Combined OTEC-Mariculture System Using the Same Deep Water Flow of 3.75 m^3/sec

System	Product	Assumptions	Unit Price	Gross Sales Value
OTEC	1 MWe	90% of Time on Line	4¢/KWH Bus Bar	$ 315,360
Mariculture	1,693T Shellfish	42% Meat	$1/LB Meat	1,564,200
	Whole Wet Weight	711 T Meat	(=$2.20/Kg)	

REFERENCES

(1) Mayer, J. 1976. The dimensions of human hunger. Scientific American, 235(3):40-49.

(2) Crisp, D.J. 1975. Secondary productivity in the sea. In Productivity of World Ecosystems. National Academy of Sciences, Washington, D.C.

(3) Arsonval, d' 1881. Revue Scientifique, Sept. 17.

(4) Claude, G. 1930. Mech. Eng., 52(12):1039.

(5) Anderson, J.H. and Anderson, J.H., Jr. 1966. Thermal power from seawater. Mech. Eng., Apr., pp. 41-46.

(6) Lockheed Corp. 1975. Ocean thermal energy conversion (OTEC) power plant, technical and economic feasibility. Vol. 1, National Science Foundation, RANN, SE/G1-C937 /FR/75/1.

(7) TRW Systems Group, 1975. Ocean thermal energy conversion. Vols. I-V, National Science Foundation, Contract C-958.

(8) Roels, O.A., Laurence, S., Farmer, M., and Van Hemelryck, L. 1978. Organic production potential of artificial upwelling marine culture. Process Biochemistry, February, Vol. 12, No. 2, pp. 18-23.

(9) Van Hemelryck, L. 1975. Energy aspects of artificial upwelling. Seminario Internacional de Surgencias, Nov. 18-19, Univ. del Norte, Coquimbo, Chile, pp. 43-60.

(10) Salle, M. and Capestan, A. 1957. Travaux anciens et recents sur l'energie thermique des mers. Soc. Hydrotechn. de France, Quartr. Jour. de l'Hydraulique, Paris, 13-15 June (1956); La Houille Blanche II: 702-711 (1957).

(11) Lockheed Corp. 1975, op. cit.

(12) Anderson, J.H. and Anderson, J.H., Jr. 1966, op. cit.

(13) Salle, M. and Capestan, A. 1957, op. cit.

(14) Lockheed Corp. 1975, op. cit.

(15) Anderson, J.H. and Anderson, J.H., Jr. 1966, op. cit.

(16) Van Hemelryck, L. 1975, op. cit.

(17) Othmer, Donald F. and Roels, Oswald A. 1973. Power, fresh water and food from cold, deep-sea water. Science, 182(4108):121-125.

(18) Farmer, M. 1977. Doctoral Dissertation, Biology Department, City College, New York, N.Y.

(19) Roels, O.A. et al., 1978, op. cit.

(20) Pimental, D., Dritschilo, W., Krummel, J., and Kutzman, J. 1975.

Energy and land constraints in food protein production. Science, 190:754-761.

(21) Roels, O.A. et al., 1978, op. cit.

(22) UN Monthly Bulletin of Statistics, 1978.

(23) Martin, P.J. and Roberts, G.O. 1977. An estimate of the impact of OTEC operation on the vertical distribution of heat in the Gulf of Mexico. In Proceedings, Fourth Annual Conference on Ocean Thermal Energy Conversion (OTEC), Mar. 22-24, pp. IV-26. La.: New Orleans.

(24) FAO. 1976. The State of Food and Agriculture, 1975. FAO, United Nations. Rome.

(25) Winer, B.M. and Nicol, J. 1977. Electrical energy transmission for OTEC power plants. In Proceedings, Fourth Annual Conference on Ocean Thermal Energy Conversion (OTEC), ed. George E. Ioup Mar. 22-24, pp. III-26-III-33. Univ. New Orleans.

(26) Trimble, L.C., Messinger, B.L., Ulbrich, H.G., Smith, G., and Lin, T.Y. 1975. In Proceedings, Third Workshop of Ocean Thermal Energy Conversion (OTEC), ed. G.L. Dugger. May 8-10, pp. 22-38. Texas: Houston.

(27) Douglass, R.H. 1975. Ocean thermal energy conversion; an engineering evaluation. In Proceedings, Third Workshop on Ocean Thermal Energy Conversion (OTEC), ed. G.L. Dugger. May 8-10, pp. 22-38. Texas: Houston.

V

Bioresources for Energy and Chemical Feedstocks

Introduction to Part V

This group of eight papers reflects the present interest in finding renewable energy sources, and it is significant that a high proportion are concerned with bioenergy substitution for fossil fuels in the United States. The first paper by Alex Alexander makes a strong case for the creation of energy plantations based on sugarcane in developing tropical regions and using the total product, especially its fiber component, rather than cultivating essentially for sucrose. S. Kresovich and his colleagues make a somewhat similar plea for the cultivation of sweet sorghum with regard to the United States energy economy. They indicate that recent genetic research and improved methods of cultivation have greatly increased the yield possibilities sufficiently to make sorghum a major and economic source of ethanol.

The papers by M. Scholl and collaborators and by Bart Lucarelli and Richard L. Meier offer interesting assessments of the extent to which biomass energy production can provide for the needs of the United States and of California, respectively. The conclusions of these two papers, which are rather optimistic, are based on a total use of the bioresources, including forestry wastes, agricultural residues, municipal wastes, and the harvest from terrestrial energy farms, possibly augmented by fresh water algae, and marine kelp farms. Both papers stress the economic, legal, and political constraints, and stress the need for early policy decisions. The papers by Paul Bente and by John Zerbe and Andrew Baker are to some extent addenda to the two more general papers previously mentioned in providing more detailed information on the potentialities of wood as a major energy source in the United States.

The contribution of I.V. Berezin is of a quite different character. It describes the basic work in the University of Moscow on electron transfer by means of immobilized enzymes, with potential application to the construction of biological fuel cells for the direct conversion of hydrogen to electricity.

The final paper of the group, by Harry W. Parker, deals with the potentialities of the biomass in producing feedstocks for the chemical industry rather than for energy production as such. This thoughtful contribution takes account of the competing uses for the limited biomass, and recognizes that petroleum will, in all probability, be available for petrochemical use after it has ceased to be used generally for combustion, and hence, while promising, he suggests that the manufacture of organic chemicals from bioresources via the methanol, ethanol, and methane is likely to evolve slowly.

18 The Potentials of Sugarcane as a Renewable Energy Resource for Developing Tropical Nations

Alex G. Alexander

Sugarcane is a renewable energy source, whose potential value to both industrialized and agrarian nations is only beginning to be recognized. It is the world's finest living collector of sunlight, and one which operates 24 hours per day on a year-round basis. (1) More than any other plant, sugarcane has perfected the art of harvesting the radiant energy of sunlight, and of storing this energy in massive quantities in the form of fermentable solids and fiber. In tropical regions, it has been grown for centuries as a source of sweeteners and fermentation substrates for the production of rum. Although less productive when removed from the tropics, sugarcane has sustained sugar industries in both northern and southern latitudes, where growing seasons range from 7 to 10 months duration. (2)

It seems ironical that so much emphasis has been placed on sucrose, while the bulk of the sugarcane plant has been generally ignored. Sugarcane has a natural tendency to produce fiber rather than sugars; in fact, a majority of Saccharum species and subspecies excel in producing new tissues while having little or no capacity for making sucrose. Even the commercial hybrid sugarcanes are inclined to utilize their sugars in support of growth processes when water and nutrient supplies are sufficient. Historically, the fiber from such plants has been underutilized, or not used at all.

During the mid-1970s, (3, 4) sugarcane began to be recognized as a total biomass candidate from which fuels and chemical feedstocks would compete, or supplement the traditional sugar and molasses products (table 18.1). The petroleum embargo of 1973 was partially responsible for this, but there are other powerful forces of change that began to be felt by the sugar industry at about this time. World sucrose prices, hovering between 10 and 13 cents per pound, exclude any possibility of profit when production costs are reckoned at 16 to 18 cents per pound. In Puerto Rico, production costs have increased to about 28 cents per pound. The development of nonsucrose sweeteners is

Table 18.1. Types of sugarcane and potential energy contributions

Species	Product	Potential Feedstock for Time-Frame: Near Term	Long Term
Wild *Saccharums*	Fiber	Boiler Fuel	Boiler Fuel Gasification Fermentation (Fuel)
Hybrid *Saccharums*	Fiber	Boiler Fuel	Boiler Fuel Gasification Fermentation (Fuel)
	Sugars	Fermentation (Fuel) Fermentation (Rum)	Fermentation (Fuel) Fermentation (Rum)

progressing rapidly at a time when new roles for natural sugars are being identified in the petrochemical industries. (5) At some future date, ethylene and a series of other chemical feedstocks presently derived from petroleum may be largely obtained from fermentation ethanol. In this connection, bagasse could conceivably be used as a gasification feedstock for production of liquid and gaseous fuels. (3,6) Moreover, as a fermentation feedstock, the glucose residing in the cellulose and hemicellulose complexes of bagasse may soon become competitive with sugars extracted by conventional milling operations.

Powerful social and economic changes are also occurring in tropical regions, where sugarcane had long reigned as King. In Puerto Rico, for example, within a period of about 40 years, sugarcane has declined from the Island's principal industry and largest employer to a heavily subsidized and bankrupt industry losing over 30 million dollars annually. It is essentially a government-owned operation in which the profit incentive is stifled and monetary losses are not personally accountable. For the Island's internal economy it provides jobs for an otherwise unemployable labor force, and supplies some of the molasses for the rum industry.

Agricultural planners have favored the conversion of some sugarcane lands to food production as a means of curtailing Puerto Rico's purchases of food from the United States mainland. This policy was never wholly sound in view of Puerto Rico's heavy reliance on imported energy, but it seemed reasonably safe prior to the oil embargo of 1973.

Today, the economic scenarios for food and energy are completely reversed, with energy costs more than double those of food, and the gap between them widening rapidly. When viewed in this perspective, sugarcane poses two new tasks for sugarcane researchers and agricultural planners responsible for its development:

- Sugarcane should be reevaluated as an energy plantation crop in which total biomass, rather than sucrose, is the prime objective. This does not mean that four centuries of production experience must be discarded, but a whole range of constraints imposed on the plant by King sugar will be lifted when energy becomes the principal salable commodity.

- Agricultural planners in tropical nations must carefully weigh the merits of energy-planting versus food-planting on available land resources. In particular, climatically-favored energy crops, such as sugarcane, must be weighed against technologically-favored food crops produced in temperate regions. The advantages of purchasing food from friendly suppliers, as opposed to energy purchases from indifferent or potentially hostile suppliers, must also be considered.

GROWTH AND SUGAR PRODUCING POTENTIALS OF *SACCHARUM* SPECIES

The original commercial sugarcanes, the official sugarcanes, belonged to the species *S. officinarum*, otherwise known as noble canes or garden canes. (7,8) These plants were cultivated by early man, while their more primitive relatives were left untouched in the wild. Virtually all commercial canes today are interspecific hybrids bearing large germ plasm dosages from *S. officinarum*, together with contributions from *S. robustum*, *S. sinense*, and *S. spontaneum*. (9)

(a) Origin of Sugarcane. There are several theories regarding the origin of *Saccharum* species, but the original ancestor probably evolved on an ancient land mass that connected Australia with southeast Asia. (1) This *Saccharum* prototype, probably a diploid, is either extinct or has totally introgressed with other genera of tropical grasses. *Saccharum* species still extant in the region include *S. spontaneum*, *S. robustum*, *S. sinense*, *S. edule*, and *S. barberi*. Each of these groups represents large evolutionary advances over the original ancestor plus a range of growth and sugar-producing capabilities.

The land mass which joined Australia with Southeast Asia was periodically inundated, so that insular and continental conditions alternated to produce a kind of botanical caldron favoring the evolution of both diverse and highly-adaptive plant forms. *Saccharum* species were in continuous competition with other herbaceous plants, and introgressions with other genera of tropical grasses probably occurred. (7,8) This intermingling was aided by a *Saccharum* propensity to cross with other plants at both the interspecific and intergeneric levels.

The Saccharum characteristic of producing a mobile photosynthate in the form of sucrose, and translocating it rapidly to sites of utilization, may have offered a competitive advantage over species having starch as the main end product of photosynthesis. (1) In any case, the species S. officinarum began to attract the attention of primitive man roughly 20,000 years ago in the region of present-day Malaysia. Plants having soft, thick stems, and a perceptively sweet taste were grown in village gardens for chewing. Some of these canes, the products of unknowing but long-term selection processes, were eventually adopted for commercial production. These are commonly identified as the noble canes. They began to be replaced by interspecific hybrids early in the present century. Today they are used mainly for breeding purposes. (9)

(b) Breeding Constraints in the Genus Saccharum. The capacity of sugarcane to cross with other plants at both the intergeneric and interspecific levels vastly increases its long-term potential as a biomass energy source. However, several important genetic and physiological constraints have operated to prevent this potential from being realized. A widespread belief today that the many existing sugarcane varieties are ready and waiting to meet future demands on sugarcane as a renewable energy source is quite erroneous. The genetic base of commercial cane hybrids and parental types is, in fact, precariously narrow, consisting of perhaps five or six gametes from the many hundreds that reside in the Saccharum germ plasm pool. At the genetic level, the female parent (usually a form of S. officinarum) frequently contributes the somatic chromosome number (2n) to the interspecific cross, while the male parent contributes the gametic number, (n) to produce 3n progeny having a higher chromosome number than either parent. (10) This has enabled cane breeders to intensify desirable attributes as a short-term objective, but the long-term effect has been to create excessively high polyploidy within the genus. Parental canes having high polyploidy (usually octaploids or higher) are reluctant to receive new germ plasm contributions. Moreover, under these conditions, chromosomal segregation and recombination does not proceed in accordance with Mendelian laws of inheritance as they apply to diploid plants.

Sugarcane breeders are further confronted with a physiological problem, that is, with poor flowering syncronization among different Saccharum species. (1,11) A majority of wild Saccharum types, (S. spontaneum, S. sinense, S. robustum), which carry the bulk of untested germ plasm, tend to produce tassels from six weeks to four months earlier than the noble canes and commercial hybrids. As a consequence, the breeder can only rarely make crosses involving new germ plasm. Such crosses would utilize the very latest flowers from the early-tasseling plants and the earliest flowers from late-tasseling plants. Ordinarily, however, the breeder has had to be content with repeated reshuffling of the same old germ plasm from late flowering commercial hybrids.

Breeding constraints in the genus Saccharum are so severe that no crossing at any level was known prior to the present century. Efforts to break such restrictions have not generally been successful, nor has it been possible to bypass conventional breeding to any appreciable extent through techniques of cell and tissue culture. (12,13) Nonetheless, the *Saccharum* germ plasm pool is such a rich and varied source of genetic material that the eventual breaking of these constraints should quickly lead to new recombination types that will make museum pieces of present-day varieties.

(c) *Outlook for Sugarcane as an Energy Crop*. Analysts of sugarcane agriculture, and of the changing petrochemical and chemical-sweetener industries, perceive a considerably modified future role for sugarcane. This stems from the plant's increasing recognition as a valuable and renewable energy resource, rather than strictly a provider of sugar and molasses. From the cane breeder there is a greater need than ever before for improvement in both sugar and fiber producing hybrids. The most striking changes can be expected in about five major categories of hybrid characteristics:

- Increased yields of sucrose and total fermentable solids.
- Increased yields of fiber and total biomass.
- Increased responsiveness to intensive cultivation on prime lands.
- Increased responsiveness to extensive cultivation on marginal lands.
- Increased habitat expansion into subtropical and temperate regions.

In regions such as the continental United States, sugarcane has never really felt at home. Here, the expansion of the plant's habitat is a critically important factor. A northward extension of the effective climate range, by as little as 80 or 100 miles, would vastly increase the nation's sugarcane acreage. This would not be an unreasonable request of the cane breeder once the problem of breeding constraints has been solved. In tropical areas with suitable climates but only limited land resources, new varieties are needed that will respond to intensified propagation. This is particularly true with reference to increased plant densities, increased harvest frequencies, and more efficient use of water and nutrient inputs.

In all climatic zones, a new emphasis can be given to marginal lands that formerly were too dry, too saline, or too steeply contoured for development as the traditional sugar plantations. This type of agriculture is a form of *low till*, or minimum tillage farming in which relatively low yields are offset by low expenditures of production input. Fiber, rather than extractable sugars, would be the primary product. In all probability, the superior sugarcanes here will derive from the rugged, wild forms of *Saccharum* that previously served only as germ plasm sources. Some of these, particularly clones of the species *S. spontaneum*, *S. robustum*, and *S. sinense*, have survived in the wild for several hundred million years without care or management in any form.

One must remember that energy rather than refined sucrose will be the principal salable product of sugarcane planted as a renewable energy source. However, even if sucrose is totally replaced by chemical sweeteners, the fermentable solids extracted from sugarcane will still be of very considerable importance to future energy planters. In nations such as Brazil, the fermentation substrates from sugarcane will be needed in producing fermentation ethanol. This, in turn, will be used as a motor fuel, a fuel additive, and as a feedstock for production of ethylene and other industrial compounds presently derived from petroleum. In Puerto Rico, where rum sales are a major source of Island revenue, sugarcane molasses will be needed in the production of alcoholic beverages. It is in this context that we ask the cane breeder for new hybrids having "increased yields of fermentable solids". This is indeed a difficult request on a per plant basis, since we can no longer afford to manage sugarcane solely in the interests of sugar. What we are really asking the breeder to do is to give us new varieties that will, at least, maintain present sugar yields under cultural conditions heavily slanted in favor of total biomass rather than sucrose.

However, it should be stressed that the cultivation of sugarcane for energy rather than sucrose will have a predictably negative impact on extractable sugars, if we rely solely on present-day varieties. The simple truth is that sugarcane is more adapted to produce fiber, while for centuries we have concentrated on producing sugar. To optimize fiber, we will have to manage sugarcane in a manner unheard of in the days when sucrose was king.

A case in point is sugarcane's pronounced responsiveness to nitrogen and water, two major inputs that traditionally could be offered only at the expense of sucrose. Even the sweetest of commercial sugarcane hybrids will tend to produce new tissues rather than sugar, if they are given access to water and nutrients in a suitable temperature regime. Studies in Puerto Rico have shown that to fertilize heavily with nitrogen beyond the second month of the new ratoon crop can produce plants still trying to grow at 10 to 12 months, that is, at a time when they were supposed to be ripening or accumulating sucrose in vegetatively inactive stems. (1) Similarly, it was never possible to maximize irrigation when sucrose alone was the desired product. To do so, particularly in the later stages of the crop cycle, would promote the inversion of stored sucrose for use in revitalized growth and respiratory processes.

One could continue with discussions of row spacing, harvest frequency, soils management, and other production input, which have always been slanted in favor of sucrose rather than total biomass. In the selection of varieties from available sources, the sugar planter has had to be biased in favor of sweet canes with high sucrose yields as their main attribute. The author has seen many high tonnage varieties relegated to maintenance plots, as little more than conversation pieces, because they produced disproportionately more fiber than sucrose. So much bagasse has been produced in the past with so little effort to maximize this potential. Without question, this capacity for making biomass can be vastly increased once the decision is made to plant sugarcane for energy rather than sucrose.

The high biomass yields of conventional sugarcane are widely recognized, but until quite recently there was little demand for the fibrous residues (bagasse) produced by cane milling operations. Mill engineers saw some advantage in burning bagasse to provide process heat for sugar factory operations and the generation of electrical power; however, its use as a boiler fuel consumed only a fraction of the available supply, and no alternate uses of any appreciable magnitude were ever developed. There was some reluctance to use bagasse even as a boiler fuel as long as fuel oil could be purchased at around two dollars per barrel. The optimal tonnage potentials of sugarcane as a fuel source, therefore, remained an open question.

In a botanical sense, an individual cane plant has a relative growth rate about equal to field corn, sweet sorghum, and sunflower, but such rates are relative only when measured over a short period of time during the plant's grand period of growth. As an agronomic crop, sugarcane is equalled by few plant species, if any. This relates in part to the long duration of its rapid growth phase, and the profusion of stems that emerge from a single crown during the course of a year. As do most herbaceous species, sugarcane has two growth phases; the first a highly visible tissue expansion phase, and a second phase, in which dry matter (fiber) accumulates with little outward change in the plant's size. The second phase is especially productive in sugarcane, but this productivity relates closely to the large volume of green stems developed during the period of rapid tissue expansion.

In today's sugar industry an annual yield of 40 green tons per acre (about 10 dry tons) would be regarded as a good average yield for any region (sugarcane yields are ordinarily expressed in short tons. A dry ton refers to oven dry material containing about 6 percent moisture). Isolated plantings yielding 60 green tons or more per acre year would be common, as would poorly managed plantings producing 20 or 25 green tons. In Puerto Rico, island-wide yields average about 35 green tons and 9 dry tons per acre in a cropping year of 10 to 12 months duration. By way of comparison, a good yield of dried forage grasses under temperate conditions would be in the order of 4 or 5 tons per acre, and harvested within a growing season of about 5 months. At present, the Fuels From Biomass Branch of DOE is emphasizing woody plants (silviculture or forestry species) as a potentially favorable source of biomass for the continental United States. (14) With optimal management, such species might produce 4 to 6 tons of woody material per acre in growing seasons, ranging from about 5 months in the northern states, to 8 months in the southeast.

The sugarcane production values noted above can be vastly increased when total biomass rather than sucrose is the principal product. In Puerto Rico, for example, initial attempts to maximize tonnage produced a three-fold increase over the average yield for the Island sugar industry (table 18.2). These increases resulted from several straightforward changes in the plant's management, including: (a) selection of a high-tonnage variety; (b) increased fertilization; (c) use of narrow row centers; and (d) inclusion of trash in the final yield computations. Of these changes, the increase of plant density resulting

Table 18.2. Sugarcane Biomass Potentials in Puerto Rico

Sugarcane Status	Estimated Dry Tons/Acre, For Year - 1978	2000
PR Industry Average	9	12
Partially Maximized For Biomass	29	35-40
Fully Maximized For Biomass	35-40	40-50

from narrow row centers (50 vs 150 centimeters) was the least effective and most costly option. Only about two dry tons were gained in this way. The superior variety (PR 64-1791), together with increased fertilization (300 lbs N per acre year vs 150 lbs), raised dry matter production to about 23 tons per acre year. An additional six tons were gained by collecting trash, i.e., aged leaf and leaf sheath tissues that have desiccated and detached from the stalk. These materials were formerly burned prior to cutting the cane as a means of easing harvest operations, and to lessen the extraneous matter being shipped to the mills. In an energy-planting operation trash becomes a valued product.

Both the varietal and fertilizer variables have yet to produce maximum possible yields. More important, the growth of sugarcane's plant crop (first year yields) is considerably less than that of the ensuing ratoon crops. It is reasonably certain that production levels can be raised to the order of 35 to 40 dry tons per acre year. It must be emphasized that these levels are attainable with existing varieties and production technologies. Beyond this lies a large but unknown potential for higher yields. Unfortunately, these yields must await the breaking of serious genetic constraints, which to date have severely handicapped the sugarcane breeder. It is not unreasonable to expect that yields approaching 50 dry tons per acre year will eventually become possible.

Table 18.3. Puerto Rico's Expenditures For Petroleum; 1967-1977*

Year	Expenditure $US (Millions)
1967	14
1970	30
1974	202
1976	854
1977	1,100**

* External Trade Statistics, Commonwealth of Puerto Rico.

** Projected.

FOOD PLANTING VS ENERGY PLANTING IN THE TROPICS

To this point we have discussed sugarcane's potential as an energy crop as opposed to a sugar crop, but equally important is the role that sugarcane will play in tropical regions where energy-planting must soon compete with food-planting. While year-round growth potentials are commonly accepted in tropical regions, many tropical nations have limited land, water, and technological resources. These, in turn, are being studied for ways to provide food and clothing for typically large human populations. It is not surprising that government planners feel obligated toward maximum development of domestic agriculture, while minimizing foreign expenditures for food. However, with an increased mechanization of agriculture, coupled with industrial development and higher living standards, the need for energy in these regions is also mounting. Within this context, the cost increases for fossil energy since 1973 have superimposed a new, and perhaps more severe demand, on agricultural resources. This demand is for the land and water resources that could be diverted from food production to the planting of domestic biomass energy.

Puerto Rico's energy problems are much farther advanced than those of most underdeveloped tropical countries. Nonetheless, they are typical problems in many important respects.

For most of her 450-year history, Puerto Rico was an agrarian society largely self-sustaining in its food production. It was a totally undeveloped society, with poverty widespread among all but a small upper class. This structure began to change slowly at the close of the nineteenth century, as sugar plantations became increasingly centralized under foreign ownership. An historic decision was made by the Puerto Rico government during the 1940s in an effort to break the old pattern of poverty and social stagnation that afflicted most of the Island's population. From this point onward, industrialization was stressed as the principal means of employment. Foreign industry and investment, mainly from the United States, was attracted to Puerto Rico with generous tax and marketing incentives. Under the title Operation Bootstrap, Puerto Rico's labor force became her principal resource, and the Island experienced nearly two decades of a rapidly-rising standard of living, coupled with an increased dependence on foreign supplies of food. She was totally dependent on foreign suppliers of fossil energy to sustain both her new industries, and her rapidly-rising living standards.

Although hailed as a social and technological success, Operation Bootstrap left Puerto Rico precariously dependent on external sources of food and energy. The food dependency was the first to alarm government planners, and it must be remembered that this was both an unnatural and an embarassing situation for a recent agricultural society. A good example of this is seen in rice, a Puerto Rican food staple, which for years had been produced locally. By 1976, virtually all rice was imported from the United States mainland at a cost of about 38 million dollars. (15) This seemed to be an enormous price to pay for a single food commodity. By this time also the sugarcane acreage had shrunk to about 140,000 acres, an area less than half that planted during the sugar industry's peak years. Government planners took steps to reestablish a local rice industry on some of the lands formerly occupied by sugarcane. Efforts were also made to establish local dairy and poultry industries, and to expand production of fruits, vegetables, and starchy root crops.

Attempts to revitalize Puerto Rico's agriculture proceeded haltingly during the 1960s and early 1970s. There seems to have been a clear reluctance among the younger generation, and among Puerto Rico's most talented business managers, to become involved in the occupation of their ancestors. Equally important, the Island was not well suited to a mechanized, highly technical and competitive form of agriculture which characterized the model farming practices of the United States mainland.

While the food dependency was embarassing and somewhat costly, the oil embargo of 1973 spotlighted an energy dependency with vastly more sinister implications for Puerto Rico's future. Within one decade, Island expenditures for foreign oil increased from about 14 million dollars to 1.1 billion dollars (table 18.3). These expenditures continue to rise with no prospect whatever that the cheap oil during Operation Bootstrap will ever again be available. Moreover, Puerto Rico can pay the petroleum price only by curtailing further industrial development, and a broad range of governmental and social services. Unfortunately, Puerto Rico has no immediate choice but to pay what is asked, since she has no fossil energy resources of her own. With a food dependency, the worst that could happen is that Puerto Rico would continue to purchase food from the United States, a country with which it shares a common citizenship, form of government, and national defense. With an energy reliance on foreign suppliers, the worst that could happen is a total collapse of her developed life-style, and a loss of her national independence.

By 1977 Puerto Rico's outlay for imported petroleum had exceeded her total expenditures for food by a factor of two (table 18.4). Economists are further disturbed by the realization that all petroleum expenditures represent a leakage from the Puerto Rican economy, that is, these were dollars that would not reenter the local economy. Regarding food purchases from the United States, some consolation lies in the fact that these dollars have a way of returning via a series of federal programs. Perhaps the most disturbing aspect of the exorbitant energy costs is a general failure of agricultural planners and news media to perceive that the food and energy costs imbalance even exists. Hence, the extensive losses experienced in trying to produce sucrose have prompted the response to regard the sugar industry as a lost cause. This reaction, even if well-meaning, has failed to consider that it would amount to throwing away one of the Island's few assets at hand for combating her energy crisis.

Recently, the author was asked to estimate the energy-producing potential for sugarcane in Puerto Rico, and the costs for developing this potential over a ten-year period. By 1988, under a critical need scenario (critical need scenario for an insular society without fossil energy resources might suggest a World War III situation, in which steamship contact is cut off, or under heavy constraint. Or, it could simply arise from an increase of fossil energy costs to a level which cannot be paid without decisively injuring the structure of a developed society, a situation which is, in fact, rapidly threatening Puerto Rico), Puerto Rico could produce at least 20 dry tons of bagasse per acre year on a planted area of approximately 300,000 acres. Assuming an energy content of 16 million Btus per dry ton, this represents a biomass energy value in the order of 0.10 quadrillion Btus, or 0.10 quads. The equivalent electrical energy content amounts to some 10 billion kilowatt hours, a figure exceeding the combined power sales for home, commercial, and industrial uses in Puerto Rico during 1974. Electrical power production, in turn, consumed about 31 percent of the Island's total energy expenditures. This fraction amounted to just over 200 million dollars (1974 US dollars).

Development costs cannot be estimated with great precision, but ball park figures are available for the primary cost input, such as land and water resource development, a sugarcane biomass breeding program, an agronomic research program, equipment modifications, and mill modifications. Cost estimates based on 1978 dollar values over a ten-year period amount to 90 to 100 million dollars (table 18.5). It

Table 18.4. Puerto Rico's Payments for Imported Food and Petroleum; 1977

Commodity	Estimated Value* $US (Millions)
Food	500
Petroleum	1,100

* External Trade Statistics, Commonwealth of Puerto Rico, 1977.

Table 18.5. Estimated Costs for the 10-Year Development of PR Sugarcane Resources for Biomass Production

Resource	Development Costs 1978-1988 ($ US)
Land (300,000 acres at $30/acre)	9,000,000
Water (400,000 acre ft at $150/ft)	60,000,000
Breeding (200,000/year)	2,000,000
Mill Redesign (at 200,000/mill)	1,400,000
Equipment Modifications	15,000,000
Other	5,000,000
Total:	92,400,000

should be noted that a $10 million per year development bill for a native energy program amounts to less than 1 percent of Puerto Rico's present annual expenditures for foreign oil. Moreover, dollars invested in the Island's agriculture have a multiplier value of about 3.5, that is, they are spent over and over again locally, whereas Puerto Rico dollars invested in OPEC oil constitute a total loss (leakage) from Puerto Rico's economy.

A consideration then of decisive importance to Puerto Rico is the fact that she still retains the basic framework of a sugarcane industry, an industry that can be modified to produce a large portion of her total energy needs. Puerto Rico's policy-makers must very carefully ponder the question of whether or not Puerto Rico can still afford to plant food as a means of avoiding expenditures for mainland produce. Key factors to consider include the following:

- The United States mainland food supply is not becoming exhausted, whereas fossil fuels must eventually run out;
- Puerto Rico's economic, political, and cultural ties with the mainland are strong and becoming stronger, but her ties with OPEC nations are a perpetual question mark;
- Food commodities critical to the Puerto Rican diet, such as rice, beans, and vegetables, can be produced far more effectively by mainland growers, while just the opposite is true of climate-oriented energy crops such as sugarcane;
- The technological hardware needed for large-scale energy planting already exists in Puerto Rico; and
- Puerto Rico has four centuries of ingrained experience with sugarcane.

The last point is perhaps the one most overlooked in present-day planning for Puerto Rico's future. The history of sugarcane in Puerto Rico is virtually synonomous with the history of the vast majority of Puerto Ricans, notwithstanding the cosmopolitan personalities one finds today in San Juan or New York. From the sixteenth through the nineteenth century, the sugarcane in Puerto Rico can be interpreted as a study in the tyranny of a plant over a society. (16) This dovetailing of the development of a plant and a people did not really begin to disintegrate until the 1940s. (17) Perhaps, after all, La Cana still has a vital, if not so sweet a role to fulfill in Puerto Rico's future.

REFERENCES

(1) Alexander, A.G. 1973. Sugarcane Physiology. A Study of the Saccharum Source-to-Sink System. Amsterdam: Elsevier Publishing Company.

(2) Van Dillewijn, C. 1952. Botany of Sugarcane. Waltham, Mass.: The Chronica Botanica Company.

(3) Capturing the Sun through Bioconversion. 1976. Conference on solar energy utilization through biomass conversion. March 10-13, 1976. Washington Center for Metropolitan Studies, Washington, D.C.

(4) Vlitos, A.J. 1977. Annual Report, Tate & Lyle Group Research and Development, Philip Lyle Memorial Research Laboratory. England: Reading, Berks.

(5) Lipinsky, E.S., McClure, T.A., Nathan, R.A., Anderson, T.L., Sheppard, W.J., and Lawhon, W.T., 1976. Systems Study of Fuels from Sugarcane, Sweet Sorghum, and Sugar Beets. Vol. II. December 1976. Agriculture Considerations. Battelle-Columbus, Columbus, Ohio.

(6) Alich, J.A., and Inman, R.E., 1974. Effective utilization of solar energy to produce clean fuel. Final report, NSF grant to the Stanford Research Institute, Grant No. 38723, June 1974. Menlo Park, Calif.

(7) Brandes, E.W., and Sartoris, G.B., 1936. Sugarcane: Its origin and improvement. USDA Yearbook of Agriculture, U.S. Govt. Printing Office, pp. 561-611. Washington, D.C.

(8) Artschwager, E., and Brandes, E.W. 1958. Sugarcane. Agricultural Handbook No. 122, U.S. Govt. Printing Office, Washington, D.C.

(9) Stevenson, G.C. 1965. Genetics and Breeding of Sugarcane. London: Longmans, Green and Company.

(10) Price, S. 1961. Cytological studies in *Saccharum* and related genera. VII. Maternal chromosome transmission by *S. officinarum* in intra- and inter-specific crosses. Bot. Gaz. 122: 298-305.

(11) James, N.I. 1970. Photoperiodic control of flowering in the Florida sugarcane Program. Sugar y Azucar, January, 1970.

(12) Nickell, L.G., and Torrey, J.G. 1967. Crop improvement through plant cell and tissue culture. Science 166: 1068-1070.

(13) Nickell, L.G. 1964. Tissue and cell cultures of sugarcane; another research tool. Haw. Plant. Rec 57: 223-229.

(14) Biomass Production Section, Second Annual symposium on Fuels From Biomass. 1978. June 20-22. Troy, New York.

(15) External Trade Statistics. 1977. Commonwealth of Puerto Rico.

(16) Golding, M.J. 1973. A Short History of Puerto Rico. (In English.) New American Library, Inc. (Mentor).

(17) Mintz, S.W. 1960. Worker in the Cane. New Haven: Yale University Press.

19 Sweet Sorghum: A Renewable Source for Energy for the United States*

S. Kresovich
D.R. Jackson
W.T. Lawhon

Because of our country's effort to find alternative sources of energy, renewed interest has been placed on sweet sorghum as a source of renewable energy. Battelle's Columbus Division, along with the U.S. Department of Agriculture (USDA) Sugar Crop Field Station at Meridian, in Mississippi, the University of Florida, Louisiana State University, and Texas A & M University are investigating sweet sorghum as a renewable source of energy and fiber. Preliminary results indicate that sweet sorghum has great potential in the United States, both in the Midwest and the South. Because of its adaptability and high-yielding potential, sweet sorghum could contribute three quads of contained energy by the year 2000. (1) This amount of energy would be produced from sweet sorghum in the form of approximately 25-30 billion liters of ethanol. The majority of this energy would originate in the midwestern cornbelt states.

Production of sweet sorghum in the midwestern United States is not unprecedented. From 1870 to 1920, the midwestern states contributed 40 percent of sorghum syrup produced in the United States (U.S. production peaked in 1920 with 50 million gallons). (2) After 1920, syrup production dropped because: (1) varieties of sweet sorghum were highly susceptible to leaf anthracnose and stalk red rot; and (2) most varieties were low in sucrose content. (3) Because of these difficulties, sweet sorghum syrup production dwindled to about 2.5 million gallons per year through the 1960s. (4) These problems, however, have been overcome through research in varietal breeding, and selection by the USDA group at Meridian, in Mississippi.

Recently, the value of fiber produced by sweet sorghum has been

---

* The authors gratefully acknowledge that this work was supported in part by the U.S. Department of Energy Contract W-7405-ENG-92, Task 77.

recognized as having great importance in making sweet sorghum viable as an energy crop. The fibrous sweet sorghum crop could possibly be used as: (1) a source of combustible energy to make liquid motor fuel production more energy self-efficient; (2) a source of combustible energy to generate electricity for sale to the electric grid system; and (3) a source of fibrous products that can help reduce the net cost of fermenting sugars.

In this presentation, the goal of the authors is to present an overview of the cultural practices and economics which will occur as sweet sorghum is grown with energy as the end product.

CULTURAL PRACTICES

The yield and quality of sweet sorghum for energy production are affected by a number of cultural practices (i.e., row spacing, fertilizer application rates, and date of planting), and environmental conditions (i.e., soil type, solar radiation, precipitation, and length of growing season).

Row spacing. Total biomass yields of sweet sorghum are very high for a crop with a growing season of 110-180 days. The introduction of narrow-row spacings have further increased the yield potential of sweet sorghum. Yield increases in total biomass and fermentable sugars have ranged from 25 to 100 percent with narrow-row spacings. Reported yields of sweet sorghum grown under experimental conditions range from 22-44 metric tons of dry biomass per hectare in Texas, 30-31 metric tons per hectare in Louisiana, 23-25 metric tons per hectare in Mississippi, and 15-26 metric tons per hectare in Ohio. (5) Fermentable sugar yields also increased proportionally (table 19.1). In addition, because of improved cultural practices in Ohio, 1978 dry matter yield levels will reach 38 metric tons of dry matter per hectare. Thus, experimentally, we are approaching a yield level necessary for making sweet sorghum a viable energy crop. (1). These production levels were achieved using varieties which were bred for sucrose production as the primary goal. As breeding and selection for fermentable sugars and fiber becomes the goal, yield levels may further increase.

Varietal development. The USDA Sugar Crop Field Station at Meridian, in Mississippi, is presently the principal organization in the United States undertaking varietal development of sweet sorghum. It has a repository of over 4,600 varieties. This station is engaged in a relatively low level of effort, with a research staff composed of one plant breeder, an agronomist, and a pathologist. However, sweet sorghum yields have increased from this effort. For even greater yield increases, the ingenuity and funding used to make dramatic improvements in corn, sugar beets, and sugarcane should be applied to sweet sorghum.

Fertility. Unlike most other high yielding crops, sweet sorghum does not require large amounts of nitrogen fertilizer. No yield response has

Table 19.1. Sweet Sorghum Production of Biomass and Fermentable Sugars with the Use of Narrow-Row Spacings

Location	Yield[a] (t/ha)	Total Sugar (t/ha)
Texas	22-44	5.0-8.3
Louisiana	30-31	(b)
Mississippi	24-25	2.8-5.5
Ohio	15-26	(b)

(a) Oven-dry weight basis.

(b) No data avilable.

Source: Lipinsky et al., 1978b. (5)

been shown for nitrogen levels of over 45 kilograms per hectare. (6,7). The general fertilization requirements of sweet sorghum in Mississippi (4) are 45 kilograms per hectare each of nitrogen (N), phosphate (P_2O_5), and potash (K_2O). Fertilizer application rates for sweet sorghum are much lower than for corn, which requires 168-224, 84, and 112 kilograms per hectare of N, P_2O_5, and K_2O, respectively. However, these tests have only been conducted with sweet sorghum at row spacings of one meter. Increased planting density may correspondingly require increased fertilizer rates. More research is needed in this area. Lower fertilizer input will greatly increase the economic feasibility of sweet sorghum production for energy by lowering the dependence on petroleum resources.

Harvesting. New planting techniques developed to increase yields of sweet sorghum will cause changes in harvesting techniques and equipment. Narrow-row plantings of sweet sorghum cannot be harvested with current equipment. This problem is compounded by the increase in fresh weight tonnage of the crop.

As with other cultural practices, harvesting equipment and techniques are highly dependent on the technology employed for juice extraction and fiber separation. The completion of a successful transition of material from field to processing site requires a harvester that fulfills the needs of both the producer and processor. Future equipment must be designed to achieve maximum efficiency for the integrated production system. Thus, the following questions will need to be answered:

- Will whole plant harvesting be required with selective separation of plant parts?
- How long should the stalk parts be?
- Will seed heads be processed with the stalks, leaves, or independently?
- Can current equipment be modified to meet the requirements of narrow rows?
- How much of the crop residues should be returned to the soil?

As production and processing practices further develop, a better picture of harvesting equipment and technique will emerge.

ECONOMIC ANALYSIS

A summary of the yield and cost goals for narrow-row plantings of sweet sorghum is shown in table 19.2. By the year 2000, the goal for fermentable sugars from sweet sorghum will be \$0.077-\$0.095 per kilogram. However, the cost for fermentable sugars decreases as the entire plant biomass is utilized. Under this alternative, the cost goals for sweet sorghum's fermentable sugars are \$0.051-\$0.062 per kilogram. In order to realize these costs, it is important that the assumed by-product credits can be realized.

By the year 2000, the cost of ethanol from sweet sorghum is estimated at \$0.24-\$0.32 per liter (table 19.3). The potential ethanol production per hectare will be about 5,000-6,000 liters from sweet sorghum. Due to the great adaptability of sweet sorghum, total ethanol production from all sweet sorghum could conceivably reach 25-30 billion liters by the year 2000.

SUMMARY AND CONCLUSIONS

Sweet sorghum can be a source of renewable energy in the United States. A great deal of research and development will be needed, however, to optimize the production aspects of the crop. Salient points of this presentation are:

- Dry matter yields of sweet sorghum range from 25-45 metric tons per hectare.

Table 19.2. Yield and Cost Goals for Close-Spaced Sweet Sorghum in the Southern United States, 1980 and 2000

	1980 Sweet Sorghum	2000 Sweet Sorghum
Yield (Metric tons per hectare)		
Fresh weight		
Stalks	47-57	70-85
Total biomass	64-78	95-117
Dry weight		
Stalks	16-20	24-30
Total biomass	23-28	33-41
Fermentable sugars (stalks only)	6.0-7.5	9-11
Combustible organic material		
Stalks	9-11	13-16
Total biomass	15-19	23-28
Costs Utilizing Stalks Only ($ per hectare, unless otherwise noted)		
Total costs per hectare	1070-1310	1175-1435
Credit for fibrous byproducts	180-22	265-320
Fuel value of residual combustible organic material	99-110	130-160
Net cost of fermentable sugars		
Dollars per hectare	805-905	780-950
Dollars per metric ton	118-144	78-96
Cents per kilogram	11.9-14.5	7.7-9.0
Costs Utilizing Entire Plant		
Total costs per hectare	1025-1255	1080-1320
Credit for fibrous byproducts	180-220	265-320
Fuel value of residual combustible organic material	220-270	330-400
Net cost of fermentable sugars		
Dollars per hectare	630-770	490-600
Dollars per metric ton	93-113	50-60
Cents per kilogram	9.2-11.4	5.1-6.2

Source: Lipinsky et al., 1978b.

- Fermentable sugar yields of sweet sorghum range from 5.0-8.5 metric tons per hectare.
- Methods for increasing yields and decreasing unit cost of fermentable sugars include:
  1. Use of narrow-row spacing
  2. Varietal development for energy and fiber production
  3. Reduction of fertilization levels
  4. Develop efficient harvesting equipment and techniques.
- Goals for the year 2000 include a total production of 25-30 billion liters at a cost of \$0.24-\$0.32 per liter.
- Production must be integrated with processing and conversion to optimize the system.

Table 19.3. Goals for Year 2000, Assuming Ethanol Production from Sweet Sorghum

Sweet Sorghum	Goals, Year 2000
Yield	5,100-6,200 liters per hectare
Area under cultivation[a]	5,000,000 hectares
Total production	25-30 billion liters
Cost[b]	\$0.24-\$0.32 per liter

[a]Includes midwestern United States.

[b]In 1980 dollars.

Source: Lipinsky et al., 1978b.(5)

REFERENCES

(1) Lipinsky, E.S., Kresovich, S., McClure, T.A., and Lawhon, W.T. 1978a. Topical Report on the potential benefits and technology development costs for sugar crops as an energy source. To the Fuels from Biomass Branch, DOE.

(2) Walton, C.F., Jr., Ventre, E.K., and Byall, S. 1938. Farm production of sorgo sirup. USDA Farmers' Bulletin No. 1791, Washington, D.C.

(3) Coleman, O.H. 1970. Syrup and sugar production from sweet sorghum. In Sorghum Production and Utilization. Published by Avi Publishing Co., P.O. Box 670, Westport, Connecticut.

(4) Freeman, K.C., Broadhead, D.M., and Zummo, N. 1973. Culture of sweet sorghum for sirup production. USDA Agricultural Handbook No. 441, Washington, D.C.

(5) Lipinsky, E.S., Kresovich, S., McClure, T.A., and Lawhon, W.T. 1978b. Sugar crops as a source of fuels. Volume I, Agricultural research, and Volume II, Processing and conversion research, DOE.

(6) Lyons, E.S. 1957. Effect of plant spacings and fertilizers on the yields of sorgo. USDA Report ARS 34-2.

(7) Matherne, R.J. 1970. Sweet sorghum growing in Louisiana. USDA Report CR-39-70.

20 Potential of Bioresources for Energy in the United States

M. Scholl
D. Salo
J. Henry

Bioresources as a source of energy are technically practicable, available, and in many applications economically competitive. The analyses leading to these conclusions supported by the MITRE Corporation and others are based primarily on socioindustrial and economic assumptions characteristic of our present United States environment. Many of the results, however, may be applicable to other developed and developing countries with concentrated or centralized energy load centers.

Bioresources as an energy feedstock will vary significantly in price as a function of the type of resource, growth conditions and productivity, accessibility and collectability, storability, and transportation requirements. Today, for example, the residues of the wood products industry in the eastern United States may be purchased for as low as $0.53 per million Btu., while logging residues in the western United States may be as high as $3.63 per million Btu. Agricultural residues such as manures are available from feedlots for less than a $1.00 per million Btu., while field crop residues are as high as $2.67 per million Btu.

In the near term, it is estimated that between 9 and 10 quads per year (one quad equals 10^{15} Btus.) of bioresources are available for energy use within the United States. These resources come primarily from wood and municipal solid waste. It is expected that the wood resource availability will decrease over the next ten years as more of this resource finds application in higher-value-added wood products. Before the turn of the century, however, terrestrial energy farms may begin to increase the net bioresource availability for energy, with the potential of supplying on the order of 14 quads per year by the end of the first quarter of the twenty-first century.

Bioresources may be used as feedstock to power process steam boilers, generate electricity, and produce fuels, such as low- and medium-Btu. gas, charcoal, synthetic oils, alcohol, and fuel pellets. The estimated price of these energy products will vary as a function of feedstock cost, plant size, and improvements in conversion technologies (see table 20.1). Based on conversion processes presently available, fuel pellets, manufactured by densifying wood, at $2.00 per million Btu. seems to be the most economically attractive fuel product derivable from raw biomass. Although slightly less convenient to store and transport than conventional fuel such as coal, pelletized wood has the advantage of low ash content, and compatability with present coal combustion technology. Process steam, electricity, and low Btu. gas also seem to be near competitive with present day conventional technology in many parts of the United States. Improvements in thermochemical, pyrolytic and hydrolysis processes expected over the next 10 to 20 years may bring other products into an economically competitive range.

The bioresources considered in this review include forest resources, agricultural resources, municipal solid waste, land based energy farms, and marine or aquatic energy farms.

In the present context, the forest resource includes all unused mill residues generated by the forest products industries, logging residues, annual mortality, surplus growth, and noncommercial timber. Agricultural residues include farm surpluses, farm residues, food processing residues, and manures. Municipal solid wastes are also included under bioresources. Land- or water-based energy farms will probably be large scale operations producing biomass in various forms solely for its fuel and/or feedstock value.

BIORESOURCE PROPERTIES AND PRODUCTS

Bioresource systems possess some unique features which distinguish them from other solar technologies.

Bioresources are produced when solar energy is collected and converted into plant material. This stored energy can be released through a series of processes which include:

- Direct combustion to produce process heat and electricity.
- Thermochemical gasification to produce fuel gas or synthesis gas.
- Thermochemical liquefaction to produce liquid fuels.
- Fermentation to produce ethyl alcohol.
- Anaerobic digestion to produce Synthetic Natural Gas (SNG).

Not only can bioresources be converted to a large number of energy products, but the feedstock is renewable, and the conversion processes and resulting products are relatively clean. They are potentially attractive alternatives to fossil fuels.

Bioresources also have limitations which must be considered - for

Table 20.1. Estimated "Plant-Gate" Selling Prices for Energy Products from Wood (Assumes Feedstock Cost of $1.00/10^6 Btu)

PRODUCT	PLANT SIZE ODT/D*	PRODUCT COST $/10^6 Btus
Electricity	850 (~ 50 MW)	11.80 (~ 40 mills/kWh)
	1700 (~ 100MW)	8.80 (~ 30 mills/kWh)
Process Steam	170	4.00
	850	4.00
Low-Btu Gas (LBG)	170	3.80
	850	2.70
Charcoal	850	4.90
Charcoal/Steam Credit	850	2.10
Char, LBG, Fuel Oil	140	2.50
	580	2.00
Methanol	850	7.60
	1700	6.20
Fuel Pellets	300	2.00

*Oven dry tons of wood feedstock per day.

instance their low energy density. The energy content of a given volume of wood, grain, municipal solid waste, or kelp is considerably less than that of fossil fuels. This characteristic is responsible for resource management problems which result in relatively high acquisition and utilization costs.

Several potential sources of biomass, such as terrestrial and aquatic energy farms, are now being developed. As a result, it is generally thought that the magnitude and character of the bioresource will change with time as follows:

- In the near-term, 1975-1995, agricultural and forest resources will constitute the bulk of the biomass fuels;
- In the midterm, 1995-2025, terrestrial energy farms will become the major source of biomass; and
- In the long-term, after 2025, aquatic and terrestrial energy farms will be the major source of biomass.

Near-Term Period (1975-1995)

Several research analysts have estimated the potential availability of all bioresources in the near-term period. A summary of results is presented in table 20.2. Potentially available resources include:

- wood residues, surplus commercial timber, and noncommercial timber
- surplus grains
- surplus sugar
- agricultural and food processing residues including manures
- municipal solid waste (MSW)

The potential resource is considered to be that portion remaining after existing demands for food, feed, forest products, and internally consumed fuel have been satisfied.

The availability of certain agricultural bioresources such as grain and sugar is the least reliable since annual supply and demand for these commodities can vary dramatically. Most agricultural residues are presently returned to the land for their nutrient and soil conditioning value. The amounts of these residues reported in table 20.2 are the amounts produced annually. If they were removed for fuel purposes, it would be necessary to increase current fertilizer applications. Furthermore, the extensive removal of these residues can create serious soil erosion problems in many areas.

Table 20.2. Potential Annual Availability of Bioresources in the Near Term*

	1975/76				1995			
	Million Dry Tons	%	Quads	%	Million Dry Tons	%	Quads	%
WOOD:								
Surplus Growth	184		3.1		26		0.4	
Forest Residues	102		1.7		131		2.2	
Mortality	87		1.5		98		1.7	
Noncommercial	87		1.5		0		0	
Mill Residues	13		0.2		3		0.1	
Other	51		0.9		51		0.9	
TOTAL WOOD	524	50	8.9	54	309	33	5.3	39
GRAINS:								
Corn	18		0.3		0		0	
Wheat	18		0.3		0		0	
Soybeans	0		0		14		0.2	
Sorghum	0		0		0		0	
Other	11		0.2		11		0.2	
TOTAL GRAINS	47	4	0.8	5	25	3	0.4	3
AGRICULTURAL RESIDUES:								
High Moisture	115		1.7		150		2.3	
Low Moisture	239		3.6		260		3.9	
Trash/Hulls	6		0.1		8		0.1	
Manures	47		0.6		65		0.8	
TOTAL AGRICULTURAL RESIDUES	407	39	6.0	37	483	52	7.1	51
MSW	75	7	0.7	4	99	11	0.9	7
TOTAL RESOURCES	1,055	100	16.4	100	922	100	13.7	100

*Calculated from data supplied by Battelle/Columbus Laboratories, The MITRE Corporation/Metrek Division, Midwest Research Institute and SRI International and based on consumption projections by the U.S. Department of Agriculture

It is estimated that the potential availability of bioresources* in the near-term for wood, grains, sugars, and agricultural residues will show that:

- 10 quads will include relatively dependable supplies of wood and municipal solid waste;
- more than half of the total resource in the form of wood;
- almost 40 percent of the resource in the form of agricultural residues, the removal of which must be carefully considered on a site-by-site basis;
- surplus grain and sugar crops do not contribute significantly to the resource base.

* The potential annual resource base is currently about 16 quads. By 1995, the resource base will have decreased to about 14 quads annually due principally to increased use of potentially available wood for forest products. A conservative projection of wood and municipal solid waste availability for 1995 is about 6 quads annually.

The distribution of various bioresources estimated by U.S. Department of Agriculture (USDA) Farm Production Regions is presented in table 20.3 for 1975 and 1995; it shows that wood is concentrated in the eastern and western parts of the United States; grain sugar, and other agricultural resources are primarily available in crop producing regions, such as the corn belt; and municipal solid waste is a potential resource in most large urban areas.

The near-term utilization of bioresources will to a large extent depend on the relative costs of bioresource materials and other fuels. Illustrative costs expected for near-term bioresources are presented in table 20.4. The costs shown in this table include:

- A production and/or collection cost. In the case of standing timber, a stumpage value is included. The cost of agricultural residues includes a product cost (straw, hay), or a nutrient value cost (manures).
- A transportation cost for an average distance of about 40 miles from the point of utilization.

In terms of cost per million Btu., wood and municipal solid waste appear to be the most attractive resources. In many areas of the country, the projected cost of these resources is competitive with coal. These two resources are also attractive from an energy balance point of view. The net energy ratios (the energy contained in the fuels to the energy expended in their acquisition) are 28 for wood, and 18 for municipal solid waste.

Agricultural trash/hull and manure resources are the next most attractive resources from a cost perspective. Their net energy ratios are 52 for trash and 5 for manures. The total potential energy

Table 20.3. Potential Regional Availability of Bioresources in the Near Term (1975-1995)
Million Dry Tons/Year

USDA REGIONS	WOODS	GRAINS	SUGARS	AGRICULTURAL RESIDUES	MSW	TOTAL	PERCENT OF NATIONAL TOTAL
			1975				
Northeast	76	0.8	0	4	26	107	11
Southeast	79	1.3	0.3	6	7	94	10
Appalachian	79	1.2	-	-	-	80	8
Lake States	42	6.9	0.1	28	6	83	9
Corn Belt	15	16.6	0	110	13	155	16
Delta States	53	2.2	0.2	18	3	76	8
Northern Plains	3	11.1	0.1	80	-	94	10
Southern Plains	19	3.2	0	24	5	51	5
Mountain	77	2.0	0.3	22	3	104	11
Pacific	81	1.7	0.7	23	13	119	12
Total US:	524	47.0	1.7	315	76	963	100
			1995				
Northeast	38	0.4	-	5	31	74	9
Southeast	43	0.8	0.7	8	12	65	8
Appalachian	37	0.7	0	-	-	38	5
Lake States	24	3.7	0	39	7	74	9
Corn Belt	8	9.3	3.6	164	17	202	24
Delta States	29	1.4	0.6	30	4	65	8
Northern Plains	2	5.4	0.1	75	-	83	10
Southern Plains	11	1.6	0.6	31	8	52	6
Mountain	51	0.9	0.3	21	4	77	9
Pacific	66	0.8	0.5	25	16	108	12
Total US:	309	25.0	6.4	398	99	838	100

Table 20.4. Estimated Cost of Near-Term Bioresources
(1977 Dollars)

	1975		1995	
RESOURCE	$/Dry Ton	$/Million Btu	$/Dry Ton	$/Million Btu
Wood:				
Eastern U.S.	9-13	0.53-0.76	10-15	0.59-0.89
Western U.S.	14-62	0.82-3.64	20-67	1.18-3.94
Grains:	107-146	7.13-9.73	89-123	5.93-8.20
Sugars:				
Cane and Beets	45-59	2.96-3.88	94-133	6.18-8.75
Sweet Sorghum	--	--	43-50	2.69-3.21
Agricultural Residues:				
High/Low Moisture	38-40	2.53-2.67	38-40	2.53-2.67
Trash/Hull	16	1.01	16	1.01
Manures	12	0.92	12	0.92
MSW	6	0.67	6	0.67

contribution of these resources is, however, very small (table 20.2). Acquisition costs of other bioresources are relatively high. They are also characterized by low energy ratios in the range of 3 to 6.

Thus, from a quantity, cost, and availability viewpoint the wood and municipal solid waste present the most attractive near term bioresources development. Other bioresources can also be expected to contribute to energy supplies, but the input will probably be smaller and more dispersed.

Midterm Period (1995-2025)

Terrestrial energy farms could contribute to the national bioresource base by 1995. Silvicultural or agricultural biomass farms are expected to be large-scale operations producing biomass solely for its energy or chemical feedstock value.

Silvicultural energy farms will be used to grow closely planted hardwood trees on a rotation schedule of less than ten years, and will rely on intensive management practices to optimize yields.

The potential contribution of silvicultural energy farms to the national biomass resource is strongly dependent on two major factors - the land area which can be devoted to energy farms without encroaching on other land uses, and the actual annual productivity of the farms. In a systems study conducted for the Department of Energy, MITRE has assumed that up to 10 percent, or about 325 million acres of the forest, pasture and range, and forage cropland, which meet prescribed minimum standards, could be devoted to silvicultural energy farms. Two levels of productivity were assumed. For the period around 1990, today's productivity of about 8 dry tons/acre-year has been assumed. Productivity in the twenty-first century has been projected to be about twice that of today, due to improved biomass crops and management practices. These assumptions have been used to estimate the expected contribution of silvicultural energy farms to national bioresources between 1995 and 2025. The results are shown in table 20.5 by USDA Farm Production Regions.

Agricultural .energy farms, in contrast to normal agricultural operations, will produce fuel rather than food, feed, and fiber. Farm management will be modified to optimize biomass yields, rather than farm commodity yields. Little used or presently unused strains of grain crops and plants, such as kenaf, giant reed, or cattail could replace currently grown crops. Yields comparable to those estimated for silvicultural farms can be projected for herbaceous crops as well. The land areas identified as potential areas for silvicultural energy farms could also be used for agricultural energy farms. Problems associated with agricultural biomass farms include soil management and crop storage. Nevertheless, the possibility of growing herbaceous crops for fuel uses is a distinct possibility in certain regions of the nation.

A recent survey by the USDA suggests that about 100 million acres of noncropland have a high to medium potential for conversion to

Table 20.5. Availability of Biomass from Silvicultural Energy Farms (1995-2025)

REGIONS	MILLION DRY TONS/YEAR	QUADS/ YEAR	MILLION DRY TONS/YEAR	QUADS/ YEAR
Northeast	19.0	0.32	33.0	0.65
Southeast	53.0	0.90	95.4	1.62
Appalachian	35.2	0.60	66.0	1.12
Lake States	27.0	0.46	54.0	0.92
Corn Belt	35.2	0.60	66.0	1.12
Delta States	38.0	0.65	68.4	1.16
Northern Plains	6.3	0.10	12.6	0.21
Southern Plains	41.4	0.70	73.6	1.25
Mountain	0	0	0	0
Pacific	7.0	0.12	14.0	0.24
Total US	262.1	4.45	488.0	8.29

cropland. Most of this potentially available land is located in the mountain states and Northern and Southern Plains. If 10 percent of this area were converted to agricultural energy farms, the midterm supply of biomass could be increased by 0.5 to 1.0 quads/year in 1995 and 2025. The likelihood of using this land to grow energy crops is small, however, because of environmental constraints and competing uses.

The data presented in table 20.5 show that most of the energy farm resource expected to become available in the 1995-2025 period is expected to be located in the eastern United States. The cost of producing biomass on silvicultural energy farms has been estimated at $20 to $30 per dry ton, or $1.20 to $1.30 per million Btu. in 1995, and $17 to $20 per dry ton, or $1.00 to $1.20 per million Btu. in the year 2025 (1977 dollars). It is likely that these costs, if realized, would permit bioresources to compete with coal in most parts of the country.

Long-term Future (After 2025)

Aquatic biomass production systems are long-term prospects. Insufficient data are available at present to estimate their potential impact on the nation's energy supply. Various estimates suggest that 4 quads or more of algae, kelp, or other aquatic plants could be produced annually. This resource is a particularly attractive feedstock for the production of synthetic natural gas through anaerobic digestion, but numerous questions regarding production and conversion costs remain unanswered. Such aquatic systems, however, may present many interesting options for combined energy, food, and fiber production.

SUMMARY OF PROSPECTS

Assuming that an aggressive policy of developing terrestrial energy farms is initiated early enough, the bioresource could be maintained at close to 10 quads per year through 1995. In light of expected genetic and farm management improvements, the potential bioresource could subsequently reach about 15 quads/year by 2025. The establishment of aquatic energy farms could continue to increase the annual bioresource to almost 19 quads per year.

Reaching this potential will require policy decisions which encourage: the more extensive use of near-term resources, such as wood for process heat, electricity in the forest products and other industries, and municipal solid wastes; the continuation of research and development in conversion processes, such as pyrolysis, thermochemical gasification and liquefication, acid hydrolysis, enzyme hydrolysis, anaerobic digestion and combined systems; the establishment of terrestrial energy farms as soon as possible; the improvement of yields through breeding programs and improved crop management; and the investigation of aquatic production systems.

discussed herein, distributed utilization in rural and village environments is a distinct possibility. In the United States context, such applications are likely to make a relatively small contribution to national energy demand, although contributing a substantial one to local energy supply. Significant rural village biomass energy use in developing nations is likely.

In such situations, however, care must be taken to develop a program in which the long-term productivity of the soil is maintained. Thus, even in rural or village environments, managed silvicultural or agricultural biomass production is necessary.

21 The Potential for Using California's Biomass Resources for Energy Production

Bart Lucarelli
Richard L. Meier

This effort is part of a larger study conducted at Lawrence Berkeley Laboratory (LBL) that is looking into the feasibility of California meeting its energy needs from renewable resources. (1) To an important extent, it may also be viewed as a regional test of the Amory Lovins hypotheses regarding a "soft energy path. (2) The LBL researchers have assessed the resource potentials for renewable energy in California (wind, solar, hydro, geothermal, and biomass), and have matched the output from these resources against projected energy demand.

In estimated future energy demand, the LBL team has taken into consideration the potential for energy conservation and the effects of increased population and economic growth. In the scenario for the year 2025, one major constraint was identified: liquid fuels will be insufficient to meet demand in the transport sector. If the projected shortfall is to be closed, some exotic form of biomass, such as kelp or fresh water algae, will need to be developed. The alternative would be the importation of coal-derived liquid fuels.

Table 21.1 presents the demand/supply balance net potential. This partial supply/demand balance provides the content for planning the utilization of biomass in California.

CALIFORNIA'S BIOMASS RESOURCE BASE AND ITS ENERGY POTENTIAL

For this study, five categories of biomass have been independently investigated. They are:

- wood wastes (mill residues and logging slash)
- agricultural residues
- municipal wastes (solid waste and sewage)

Table 21.1. Energy Supply/Demand Balance - Distributed Energy Systems Future, 2025 (trillion Btu)

	Electricity	Heat < 350°F	Heat > 350°F	Liquids
On-Site Solar				
Residential, Commercial and Agriculture		616		-
Paper Industry	40	53	11	-
Other Industries	132	498	383	-
Geothermal	330			-
Hydroelectric	137			-
Wind	759			-
Total Supply	1398	1167	394	-
Total Demand	1099	1167	693	1765
Unmet Demand (+) Shortage (-) Surplus	- 299		+299	+1765

Source: Craig, et al., Distributed Energy Systems in California's Future: Interim Report, Vol. 1, 1978.

- Harvest from unirrigated energy farms
- feed grains (converted to alcohol)

We have estimated the energy content of the biomass production in California by locale, using county statistics (table 21.2). The typical thermal energy content of each kind of biomass sources is presented in table 21.3.

The conclusion that the future liquid fuels requirement are expected to exceed supplies can be seen by comparing the 2025 column in table 21.2 with table 21.1. Note that table 21.2 approximates that the portion of the net energy from biomass available at any price for the long run that could be converted economically into liquid fuel even by 2025 is somewhat less than the sum of the biomass available. Environmental regulations will enforce a further reduction. More important, the conversion losses to be experienced in conversion to liquid fuels are expected to be in the neighborhood of 50 percent, possibly more. The gap might be bridged with the aid of ocean-based kelp farms or fresh/water algae ponds. The wet biomass produced through photosynthesis can be fermented to yield methane (with some carbon dioxide), which can be converted catalytically into hydrocarbon fuels of all specifications. Liquid hydrocarbons, obtainable from fermentation, is another possible fuel for transport over the long term.

A comparison of the 1976 and 2025 columns in table 21.2 suggests that the annual production of collectible biomass will rise by only 25 percent in fifty years - from 0.8 to 1.0 quadrillion Btus. by year 2025. Table 21.4 shows the expected changes in composition of this output. Wood wastes are projected to increase sharply as a result of forest improvement programs that have already begun, but still need to be continued throughout the state. The waste from field crops are expected to increase from a more efficient use of irrigation water, and municipal solid wastes to decline in energy potential, because most of the paper, cans, and plastics are likely to be recycled prior to assembly at central points.

A consequence of these shifts in sources is that the northern portions of the State will increasingly become net energy producing areas, while the southern portions will tend to become net energy consuming areas. In addition, a troublesome seasonal bias emerges due to the harvesting of unirrigated energy farms, and the gathering of logging slash and crop waste. The seasonal feature will introduce some costs because of requirements for storage space.

COST OF COLLECTION AND TRANSPORT

In Table 21.6 we have summarized the cost of collecting and transporting each type of biomass in millions of Btus. Roughly eighty percent of the 2025 biomass potential could be available for energy conversion at a cost of $2.00 per million Btu. or less (in 1976 dollars). This cost should be competitive over time with the cost of Utah coal

Table 21.2. California Biomass Resources, 1976 and 2025 (Billion Btu)

Biomass Source	1976	2025
Mill Residues	23,036	27,844
Slash	112,973	268,072
Orchard Prunings	28,150	32,723
Field Crops	102,144	121,793
Veg. Crops	8,146	9,775
Dairy/Feedlot Wastes	54,305	76,027
Food Processing Wastes	3,938	5,514
Solid Wastes	165,495	133,140
Sewage Wastes	13,742	25,196
Feed Grains	43,391	61,588
Unirrig. Energy Farms	253,502	253,502
Total Biomass	808,824	1,015,175

Table 21.3. Fuel Properties of Different Biomass Resources

Biomass Resource	Higher Heating Value (Btu per dry pound)	Moisture Content (total weight basis) (%)	Ash Content (percent dryweight)
Wood Wastes			
Lumbermill wastes	9000	25%-50%	.5%-2.0%
Slash	9000	"	"
Precommercial thinnings	9000	"	"
Agricultural Residues			
Orchard prunings	8000	25%-50%	1%-2%
Field crop residues	7000-7500	15%-30%	20%
Vegetable crop residues	6500	50%	"
Dairy/Feedlot wastes	8500	70%	N.A.
Food processing wastes	6500	60%-80%	N.A.
Municipal Wastes			
Municipal solid wastes	4000-5000	20%-40%	
Municipal sewage wastes	8500	>80%	N.A.
Feed Grains	6500	N.A.	N.A.
Unirrigated Energy Farms (wood)	8000	20%-40%	1%-2%

Table 21.4. Biomass Resource Potential by Category for 1976 and 2025 (10^{12} Btu)

Category	1976	2025	% Change (Col. 2-Col.1) Col. 1
Mill residues	23	28	21%
Slash	113	268	137%
Orchard prunings	23	33	18%
Field crops	102	122	20%
Vegetable crops	8	10	25%
Dairy/Feedlot wastes	54	76	41%
Food processing wastes	4	6	50%
Municipal solid wastes	166	133	20%
Municipal sewage wastes	14	25	70%
Feed grains	43	62	44%
Unirrigated energy farms	254	254	0%
Total	809	1037	28%

Table 21.5. Biomass Resource Potential by Season of Availability, 1976
(10^{12} BTU)

Category	April 1-May 31	June 1-Sept 15	Sept 15-Nov 30	Dec 1-Mar 30
Mill Residues	5.75	5.75	5.75	5.75
Slash	16.95	33.90	45.20	16.95
Orchard Prunings	---	---	---	28.00
Field Crops	---	40.80	61.20	---
Vegetable Crops	2.40	2.40	1.60	1.60
Dairy/Feedlot Wastes	13.50	13.50	13.50	13.50
Food Processing Wastes	.40	2.00	1.20	.40
Municipal Solid Wastes	41.50	41.50	41.50	41.50
Municipal Sewage Wastes	---	3.50	3.50	3.50
Feed Grains	---	21.50	21.50	---
Unirrigated Energy Farms	127.00	127.00	---	---
Total	207.50	291.85	194.94	111.20
Avg. Monthly Output	103.8	83.4	78.0	28.0

Table 21.6. Cost of Collecting and Transporting California Biomass

Biomass Category	Range of Collection & Transport Costs (1976 $ per million BTU)	Biomass Yield 1976 (billion BTU)	Biomass Yield 2025 (billion BTU)
Wood wastes			
Slash & thinnings	$1.10-$1.65	113.0	268.1
Mill residues	$ .45-$1.00	23.0	27.8
Agricultural Residues			
Orchard prunings	$ .50-$1.30	28.2	32.7
Field crop residues	$2.00-$11.70	102.1	121.8
Vegetable crop residues	$2.00-$11.70	8.2	9.8
Dairy/Feedlot wastes	0	54.3	76.0
Food processing wastes	0	3.9	5.5
Municipal Wastes			
Solid wastes	(-) $.55	165.5	133.1
Sewage wastes	0	13.7	25.2
Feed Grains	N.A.	43.4	61.6
Unirrigated Energy Farms			
Mechanical harvest	$ .95-$2.00		207.1
Manual harvest	$2.60-$8.40	46.4	46.4
Total	N.A.	808.8	1015.2

delivered to a conversion site in California. For example, the Pacific Gas and Electric Company (PG&E) estimates the current costs of Utah coal delivered by unit train to a Northern California site at $1.22 per million Btu. (3). These costs are for Utah coal obtained from PG&E-owned mines. PG&E estimates that the real cost for Utah coal from its own mines will increase to $4.66 per million Btu. by 2000. It is difficult to predict how the real costs of collecting and transporting biomass to conversion sites may change. However, the projected costs for Utah coal suggests that biomass will become increasingly competitive as an energy feedstock.

PROPERTIES OF CALIFORNIA'S BIOMASS RESOURCES AND THEIR SUITABILITY FOR ENERGY CONVERSION

Numerous energy conversion processes exist which can convert biomass into usable energy. These processes can be conveniently separated into three categories:

- Direct combustion process
- Thermochemical processes (pyrolysis, gasification, catalytic conversion)
- Biological processes (anaerobic digestion, enzymatic hydrolysis)

These processes can produce a variety of energy and chemical products (see table 21.7).

Properties of each biomass resource, such as higher heating value, moisture content, and ash content, will have an important bearing upon the suitability of each resource for specific conversion processes. In table 21.3, we list these three characteristics for each type of biomass. For comparison purposes, Utah coal is estimated to have roughly a 4 percent moisture content, an 8 percent ash content, and a higher heating value of 12,800 Btu. per pound (3).

Although Utah coal has a lower moisture content and higher Btu. contents, most forms of biomass have a lower sulfur content (not shown in table 21.3), which will improve the economic attractiveness of converting biomass into usable energy.

THERMAL EFFICIENCIES AND REVENUE REQUIREMENTS FROM PRODUCT SALES

The efficiency and cost of biomass conversion for each process will vary depending upon the scale of the plant, costs of the biomass feedstock, its moisture content, the financing method, and rate of interest used to construct each plant. For this draft, we have not attempted to

Table 21.7. Summary of Eleven Conversion Processes - Thermal Efficiency and Revenue Requirements from Product Sales

	Process	Products	Thermal Efficiency	Revenue Requirements from Conversion Products ($ per million Btu)* Regulated Utility Basis	Unregulated Utility Basis
1.	Direct Combustion	Electricity	21%	$5.25	-
2.		Steam	76%	$3.20	-
3.		Steam and Electricity	76%	$3.55	-
4.	Gasification	Char and Low/ Intermediate Btu gas	70-80%	$4.00	-
5.	With Methanation Cycle	Methane	63%	$7.45	-
6.	With Methanol Synthesis Cycle	Methanol	57%	$8.85	$12.80
7.	Pyrolysis	Oil and Char	74%	$3.15	$ 3.86
8.	Catalytic Liquefaction	Oil	55%	$6.35	$ 8.70
9.	Anaerobic Digestion	Methane/Fertilizer	33-63%	N.A.	N.A.
10.	Enzymatic Hydrolysis With Ethanol Conversion	Ethanol	17%	N.A.	N.A.
11.	Fermentation	Ethanol	37%	N.A.	N.A.

*Assumes a plant capacity of 1000 dry tons of feedstock per day, a feedstock cost of $1.00 per million Btu ($18.00 per dry ton of wood) and a feedstock moisture content of fifty percent. A capacity factor of 80% was assumed for electric generating technologies, 90% for all others.

Source: S.K. Kohan, 1978; Clarence G. Gouleke, 1977.

systematically determine how these factors will affect system performance.

We do have, nevertheless, some preliminary data for these important process parameters, which suggest some interesting possibilities. These data which were obtained from a report prepared by S. K. Kohan of Stanford Research Institute (SRI International) for the Department of Energy, are presented in tables 21.7, 21.8, 21.9, 21.10, and 21.11. (4) Table 21.7 lists the thermal efficiencies and revenue requirements per million Btu. of product sold for a number of thermochemical, direct combustion, and biological processes. The SRI data assumes a plant capacity capable of handling 1000 dry tons per day of wood feedstock at a 50 percent moisture content. Plant capacity factors vary from 0.8 for direct conversion processes to 0.9 for all others. We have supplemented the SRI data to include biological processes such as anaerobic digestion, fermentation, and enzymatic hydrolysis for plants capable of handling 1000 dry tons per day of feedstock. (5) From these data we note that, for a regulated utility, revenue requirements per million Btu. of product would vary from $3.20 per million Btu. for steam to $8.85 per million Btu. for methanol.

For illustration purposes, the real cost of gasoline in 1975 was $3.45 per million Btu., or $0.45 per gallon. For methanol from wood wastes to compete with gasoline will require the real cost of gasoline to increase $1.15 per gallon.

In tables 21.8 through 21.11, we have listed additional economic data for two conversion processes, i.e., methanol synthesis and direct combustion. In these tables, we depict the effect that variations in feedstock cost, plant capacity factors, and plant scale will have on the revenue requirements from product sales by a regulated utility.

These data suggest that variations in feedstock costs may have a greater effect on process economics than scale of plant and plant capacity factors listed in the tables. For example, it would be almost as economical to construct a methanol synthesis plant of 500 tons per day feedstock capacity at a feedstock cost of $1.00 per million Btu. than to construct a plant of 3000 tons per day feedstock capacity at a feedstock cost of $2.00 per million Btu (see table 21.8). In other words, the added cost of transporting the biomass fuel supply to large scale conversion facilities may overwhelm the economies of scale from the larger plant.

The effect of variations in capacity factor on revenue requirements from product sales varies considerably from process to process. Nevertheless, within the capacity utilization range of 75 to 90 percent, it may still be more economical to operate at a lower capacity factor than to transport fuels from long distances to maintain optimal capacity factors. (see tables 21.9 and 21.11).

These hypotheses are tentative and require some detailed analysis to determine the cost tradeoffs between scale and feedstock cost, and capacity factor and feedstock cost. Such analysis would hopefully shed some light on the effect that seasonal availability and regional concentration of biomass may have on the economic feasibility of using biomass for energy production.

Table 21.8. Gasification with Methanol Synthesis Process - Effect of Variation in Feedstock Cost on Revenue Requirements from Sale of Methanol by Regulated Utility*
($ per million Btu)

Feedstock Costs		Revenue Requirements from the Sale of Methanol by Plant Size*		
$ per dry ton	$ per million Btu	500 tons per day	1000 tons per day	3000 tons per day
$ 9.00	$ .50	$ 8.69	$ 8.03	$ 6.90
$18.00	$1.00	$ 9.56	$ 8.90	$ 7.77
$27.00	$1.50	$10.43	$ 9.77	$ 8.64
$36.00	$2.00	$11.30	$10.64	$ 9.51
$45.00	$2.50	$12.17	$11.51	$10.38
$54.00	$3.00	$13.04	$12.38	$11.25

*Plant size listed by dry tons per day of feedstock input, assumes .9 capacity factor, 50% moisture content for wood feedstock.

Source: Adapted from S.K. Kohan, 1978.

Table 21.9. Methanol Synthesis Process - Effect of Variation in Plant Capacity Factor on Revenue Requirements from the Sale of Methanol

Capacity Factor (percent)	Revenue Requirements from Sale of Methanol for Different Feedstock Costs		
	$1.00 per million Btu	$2.00 per million Btu	$3.00 per million Btu
70%	$10.80	$12.16	$13.50
75%	$10.20	$11.64	$13.06
80%	$ 9.60	$11.15	$12.70
85%	$ 9.20	$10.84	$12.48
90%	$ 8.90	$10.64	$12.38

Source: Adapted from S.K. Kohan, 1978

Table 21.10. Direct Combustion Process - Effect of Variation in Feedstock Costs on Revenue Required from the Sale of Electricity and Steam by a Regulated Utility
($ per million Btu)

Feedstock Costs		Revenue Requirements from Sale of Electricity and Steam by Size of Plan		
($ per dry ton)	($ per million Btu)	500 tons per day	1000 tons per day	3000 tons per day
$ 9.00	$ .50	$3.40	$2.75	$2.76
$18.00	$1.00	$4.06	$3.55	$3.42
$27.00	$1.50	$4.72	$4.25	$4.08
$36.00	$2.00	$5.38	$5.05	$4.74
$45.00	$2.50	$6.04	$5.80	$5.40
$54.00	$3.00	$6.70	$6.55	$6.06

Source: Adapted from S.K. Kohan, 1978

Table 21.11. Direct Combustion Process - Effect of Variation in Plant Capacity Factor on Revenue Required from the Sale of Electricity and Steam by Regulated Utility
($ per million Btu)

Capacity Factor	Revenue Requirements from the Sale of Electricity and Steam by Feedstock Costs		
(percent)	$1.00 per million Btu	$2.00 per million Btu	$3.00 per million Btu
50%	$5.20	$6.08	$6.96
60%	$4.50	$5.53	$6.56
70%	$4.10	$5.27	$6.44
80%	$3.75	$5.07	$6.39

Source: Adapted from S.K. Kohan, 1978

CONCLUSION AND FUTURE RESEARCH DIRECTIONS

Based on this preliminary assessment of California's biomass potential, we reach the following tentative conclusions:

- As the prices of alternative fuels increase, biomass will become increasingly competitive as an energy feedstock. In 1976 prices, over 80 percent of the California biomass should be available at processing points at a cost of $2.00 per million Btu. or less.
- Seasonal availability and resource dispersal should not seriously reduce the economic feasibility of using biomass for energy production in the state, but will require that large amounts of seasonal fuel storage be carried out at processing plants.
- In the near term, biomass will be most economically used for producing electricity, low Btu. gas, and methane via anaerobic digestion and as a backup fuel for solar heated buildings.
- In the long-term, shortages of liquid fuels will probably dictate that the most profitable use of biomass be in the production of liquid fuels for the transport sector.

Given the preliminary nature of our findings, considerable research is still required to determine the economic and institutional feasibility of using biomass for energy production in California. As a result, we have identified the following questions and issues for future research:

- Other biomass resources
  - -- What are the resource potentials for kelp and algae farms in California?
  - -- What are the cost of production, collection and transport for these more exotic biomass resources?
- Economics of biomass conversion and location of conversion facilities
  - -- How do different means of finance affect the economics of each conversion process and the optimal scale of plant?
  - -- How does the dispersal of the state's biomass by county and the cost of transport for each type of biomass affect the optimal scale of plant by process for different regions of the State?
  - -- How does the cost of seasonal fuel storage requirements affect the cost of conversion and the optimal capacity factor for each process?
- Competing uses for biomass
  - -- What are the major competing uses for each biomass resource?

-- What are the sizes of these competing markets and the values of biomass in these markets?

-- How will these competing uses affect the availability of biomass for energy production?

- Institutional barriers to biomass use

-- What are the existing regulatory agencies and regulatory policies which control the production, exchange, and end use of biomass?

-- How will these agencies and policies affect the implementation of a biomass energy program in the state?

-- What new policies or changes in public policies are required to achieve commercial success for biomass energy program in the state?

-- What are the economic and environmental benefits and costs of these policy changes? Who will suffer? Who will benefit?

REFERENCES

(1) Craig, Paul P. et. al., 1978. Distributed Energy Systems in California's Future: Interim Report, Vol. 1. Prepared for the Department of Energy under Contract No. W-7405-Eng-48, March, 1978.

(2) Lovins, Armory, 1977. Soft Energy Paths Towards a More Durable Peace. Cambridge, Mass.: Ballinger Publisher Company.

(3) Pacific Gas and Electric Company, 1977. Notice of Intention: Fossil 1 and 2. Submitted to California State Energy Resources and Conservation Development Commision, December 1977.

(4) Kohan, S.K., 1978. Thermochemical Conversion of Biomass. Menlo Park: Stanford Research Institute, International.

(5) Golueke, Clarence G., 1977. Biological Reclamation of Solid Wastes. Emmaus, PA.: Rodale Press.

22 Bioproductivity and Biomass Potentials

Paul F. Bente, Jr.

Wood for energy is only one aspect of the broad and multidisciplinary topic of biomass, but there are a few points about the potential for wood which might be considered to be of overriding importance.

- U.S. forests and woodlands presently comprise an abundant, natural resource for energy and other products. This resource offers an even greater potential in the future.
- The technology for burning wood is well developed. It is in use to a much greater extent than any other alternate, renewable energy approach. Moreover, engineering improvements are well advanced for introducing a more efficient generation of woodburning equipment.
- If wood for energy is to achieve its potential, and have a significant effect in reducing imports of oil, commercialization incentives must be provided, emphasizing site-specific factors.

To help place our national needs in perspective, it should be noted that in 1973 the Arabs supplied 15 percent of total United States petroleum imports; for the first three months of 1978, this figure had climbed to 35.2 percent. In 1973, the Arab imports were 4.8 percent of total supplies; and by 1978 these were 15.5 percent.

THE WOODLANDS RESOURCE AND POTENTIAL

No one knows very accurately how much biomass this country has in the form of trees, but it is known that the amount is large. Department of Energy (DOE) estimates the standing forests to contain the equivalent of 300 Quads of energy. As a comparison, proven reserves of natural gas in the United States are 290 Quads. Oil reserves are only 200

Quads. In speaking of Quads (a quadrillion Btus.of energy), let us keep in mind that United States consumption of energy is now about 77 Quads per year.

This figure of 300 Quads is extrapolated from U.S. Forest Service estimates of the commercial timber, which is the so-called merchantable bole. This inventory does not include leaves, branches, bark, stumps, or roots of harvested trees generally left behind. Nor does it include noncommercial varieties, or small trees, or trees that are thinned out. Also excluded are dead and fallen trees, and crooked or so-called junk trees. In practice, we harvest the best and leave the worst. Small private woodlots are also omitted.

Some authorities say the DOE estimate is overly conservative. The vice-president for energy science of the Chase Manhattan Bank puts the figure at 1,157 Quads or nearly four times that of DOE estimates. This is more in line with estimates of annual growth made over a 15-year period on 20,000 acres (140-some plots) in three major types of forests in Maine. These measurements showed that the amount of biomass is about three times the amount of the commercially useful portion, and also that the total annual bioproductivity for the state of Maine is about nine times that of the annual commercially harvestable portion as estimated by the Forest Service (70 million vs. 8 million tons).

Bioproductivity can be increased by managing the woodlands. Trees can be optimally spaced when planted, or thinned to avoid crowding, thereby permitting a better growth for the remaining stock. Genetically improved stock can be used for replanting, while competitive, useless growth can be eliminated during restocking. Irrigation and fertilizer sometimes can be used. The U.S. Forest Service, at Rhinelander, Wisconsin, has made tests which show that with such techniques bioproductivity can be increased three to tenfold over that of highly productive natural stands.

There is great potential for adding to bioproductivity by silviculture. Our country has 250-300 million acres of land that could be used for growing trees. This land is not considered suitable for agricultural crops. It has more than 25 inches of rainfall per year on the average, and hence requires no irrigation. It has less than 17 degrees of slope, making mechanized operations practical. It takes about 6-7 million acres to raise about 1 Quad of wood per year. Thus, full utilization of this land offers a potential of 40 to 50 additional Quads per year. But we could put half this area into silviculture, and produce 25 more Quads. We should not wait for another oil embargo to consider that option.

DOE's more conservative figures estimate that the annual growth of United States woodlands is about 8.1 Quads. Of this, the equivalent of 1.8 Quads is turned into wood and paper products, 1.1 Quads is burned for energy production by the wood processing industry, and 5.2 Quads is not even used. The Chase Manhattan Bank figures assert that annual growth is about 35 Quads, and that 31.2 Quads eventually rots. In effect, 88 percent of the annual forest yield is not used by man.

There is a desperate need for a national inventory of the biomass resource and its bioproductivity, and for careful estimates of that portion which could be recovered at various levels of effort. There is also a need for better understanding of management practices (including the percent of productivity that can be removed) to maintain the long-term productivity of forests.

LEVEL OF COMMERCIAL USE

It is widely asserted that 1.3 Quads of bioenergy is used today. This is about 1.75 percent of the United State's energy consumption. About 1.1 Quads of this is used by wood processing industry burning its wood waste in boilers, thereby providing nearly half of the industry's energy needs. By contrast, all the energy thus far garnered from all the other solar energy approaches, excluding hydroelectric power, is less than 0.1 Quad. Calculated as heat released, as in resistance heating, hydroelectric power amounts to only 1 Quad (although, of course, it would take about 3.5 Quads of thermal energy, whether from biomass, or coal, or oil, or gas, to generate that much electrical energy). The 1.3 Quads of bioenergy is equal to 65 percent of the heat released in generating nuclear power. It is also equivalent to 7 percent of imported oil.

In August 1978, a special biomass panel called together by DOE claimed that these bioenergy consumption figures are both incomplete and out-of-date, in view of the recent rapid adoption of woodburning following the oil embargo. The panel set consumption at 2 to 3 Quads.

There is no doubt that in the northeastern states, woodburning has become common practice. A DOE spokesman stated that in a three-year period, the number of New England homes burning wood has increased from 4 to 24 percent. A 1976 statistic for Vermont revealed that 7 percent of homes use wood exclusively for heating; by 1978 the number had jumped to 18 percent. Maine is said to have shown a similar spurt, and has adequate supplies for heating 70 percent of homes with wood, using 3.6 cords per year per home. Nationally, some 750,000 woodburning appliances are being sold each year.

Industry is also shifting to wood as a fuel. Woodburning equipment of all sizes is commercially available. Examples can be found in the Bio-Energy Directory. Fluidized bed equipment to burn wood - a more recent development - is now also being offered commercially. This is suitable for larger scale operations and is growing rapidly in use. Combustion efficiency as high as 99.7 percent has been attained producing hot gases at a temperature of 1,475°F.

Pressurized, fluidized bed combustion equipment, which has been under development for nearly ten years, is now finally being installed for its first commercial use to drive a turbine to generate power. Temperatures of 1800°F are achieved by this combustion technique. The equipment is suitable for units producing 20 megawatts of power. The trick has been to filter hot gases under pressure, in order to avoid damaging the turbine buckets. In this procedure, burning wet wood is an advantage, for the steam derived from the excess water contributes significantly to the volume of gas driving the turbines.

The biomass panel referred to above estimated that energy produced by burning wood will grow to 5-6 Quads by 1985, and to 6-8 Quads by 2000, provided strong commercialization incentives are launched.

NEED FOR COMMERCIAL INCENTIVES

Burning wood is not the most convenient way to get energy. Furthermore, industry already has made large investments in equipment to burn fossil fuels. Incentives, therefore, are needed to convert industry to using wood, even though the supply in the area may be abundant. Balance of payments savings that could be accomplished by reducing imports of oil at nearly $15/barrel should more than offset the cost of a large incentive program to persuade industry to use wood as fuel. Thus far, our government has not provided any such incentives, although the practice is not without precedent. In the last sixty years, the federal government has spent at least $15 billion to stimulate oil, gas, coal, nuclear and other forms of electrical energy production. Some claim the figure is close to $500 billion.

Canadians, on the other hand, already use wood to the extent of 3½ percent of total energy consumption. Their government desires to increase this severalfold, and in July 1975 launched a strong program with funds designated to encourage industry to use more wood.

The Forest Industry Renewable Energy (FIRE) program allocated $140 million for use over a five-year period to contribute up to 20 percent of approved capital costs of systems using wood as energy. A companion program, Energy from the Forest (ENFOR), provides $30 million over a five-year period to implement large-scale use of forests, and provide greater amounts of fuel in the late 1980s.

To spur these two programs, a series of cost-shared, federal-provincial agreements will be set up involving a federal contribution of $114 million to be allocated over the next five years. The provincial contribution has not yet been announced. These agreements will be a significant force to apply expensive prototype technology on a broad scale.

In addition, a loan guarantee program is being instituted to encourage generation of electricity from wood and municipal waste. The first project of its kind is eligible for a guarantee of 50 percent of loan capital for a direct generating station and 66-2/3 percent for a cogenerating station. With the aid of these programs, it is considered possible that by the year 2000, the use of wood will make a 10 percent contribution to Canada's energy supply.

If we consider wood as a replacement for imported oil costing nearly $15/barrel, it would seem appropriate that the use of wood as a fuel, including procuring and delivering it, should be subsidized to the extent that the differential in price between wood and oil permits. This would doubtless accelerate the use of wood for energy purposes. As the volume of usage grows, per unit costs should decline so that eventually no subsidy would be needed. Wood as fuel would then attain its full potential.

Of all the solar technologies, biomass has the best opportunity to provide large benefits quickly even though use of wood will doubtless be site-specific, and widely dispersed. Though inconspicuous today, bioenergy will grow tremendously if commercialization incentives are provided. What better way is there to reduce dependence on imported oil, to help correct the imbalance of payments by keeping our energy dollars at home and to increase local employment?

23 Forest Resources for Producing Energy

John I. Zerbe
Andrew Baker

The prospects for using more forest wastes for energy production are becoming noticeably better in the United States. More and more wood-burning boiler installations are being placed in forest products' manufcturing plants, and other industries and institutions are planning to burn wood fuel. For example, a school district in Grand Marias, Maine, has converted from burning fuel oil to wood waste; and a utility in Burlington, Vermont, has recently passed a bond issue to finance a 50 MW generating plant using wood fuel. Many rural homeowners are avoiding high fossil fuel costs for domestic heating by burning wood.

Residues are the most promising near-term source of wood fuels, although other sources, particularly fuel plantations and forests managed for multiple products including fuel, could be more important in the long-term.

WOOD RESIDUES

Wood residues that are or could be used as fuel include mill residues, logging residues, noncommercial timber, dead trees, cull trees, and precommercial thinnings from timber stand improvement.

Roughly 80 percent of wood residues, and 60 percent of bark residues from primary manufacturing (excluding pulp and paper manufacturing) were used in 1973. These mill residues are used for paper, fiberboard, and particleboard manufacture, as well as fuel. However, there are still about 20 million ovendry tons of wood and bark that are generated, which are unused each year. The South probably has the largest volume of unused mill residues.

Residues in logging operations include wood, bark, and foliage from growing stock, nongrowing stock, and uncut, small or undesirable trees. Removable logging residues from harvesting operations, together with dead and cull trees, is estimated to amount to 145 million dry tons per year.

Another tempting source of wood is noncommercial timber. Total inventory of noncommercial timber is around 1,000 million tons. The annual increment from small noncommercial timber, and excess growth over cut, is estimated to be 230 million dry tons. In addition, about 20 million tons of soft woods and hardwoods are removed annually in the United States for such operations as timber stand improvement, land clearing, and changes in land use.

A further source of wood fuel is the urban forest. Municipal discards include significant quantities of dead shade trees, demolition waste, and used pallets. It is conservatively estimated that wood wastes and tree removals in urban areas amount to 70 million dry tons of material annually.

An estimate of unused wood from these sources is summarized in table 23.1. The total potential of 485 million dry tons annually would be equivalent to 8.3×10^{15} Btus. of energy (8.3 Quads) or 1.5 billion barrels of oil. If we assume that one-half of the 8.3 Quads could be made economically available, this is about 4.1 Quads, or 700 million barrels of oil. This compares to the current usage of wood for fuel to provide 1.1 Quads annually. (Table 23.2). The total of 5.2 Quads with the increase of 4.1 Quads would provide about 7 percent of our total National needs, if markets for the fuel were developed.

Forests might also provide wood fuel through intensive culture of biomass plantations. Forest Service research has shown that intensive culture can increase biomass yield five- to tenfold over conventional plantations and highly productive natural stands. The concept is dependent on development of hybrids with fast growing characteristics. For instance, stands of trees which normally produce about 1½-2 dry tons per acre per year in the colder parts of the country, could be converted to high growth stands and produce 8-12 tons per acre per year. In the South, higher growth is possible. The highest production rates are dependent upon optimized conditions of nutrients, water, and spacing. Possibilities for using waste such as pulpmill effluent as an irrigating medium are also being invested.

However, there are economic, space and ecological considerations which will always limit the practicability of fuel plantations. In economic terms, wood for fuel is always likely to take second place to its other uses; and to keep an average steam-electric plant going would require 300 square miles of growing space to supply the necessary wood fuel. Ecological considerations, such as the effect of harvesting large areas of land on watershed, wildlife, and esthetics, have yet to receive widespread comments from the public. Therefore, collecting residues from land harvested for other products seems more feasible than fuel plantations.

Table 23.1. An Annual Estimate of Unused Wood

	Million Dry Tons	
<u>Forest</u>		
1. Excess Growth and Small Noncommercial Timber	230	
2. Logging Residues, Mortality, and Cull Trees	145	
<u>Urban</u>		
1. Tree Removals and Wood Wastes	70	
<u>Other</u>		
1. Forest Products Industrial Waste	20	
2. Waste Wood from Land Clearing	20	
Total	485	(equivalent to 8.3 Quads)

Source: Based on resource data from The Outlook for Timber in the United States, Forest Service, USDA, FRR no. 20, July 1974.

Table 23.2. The Estimated Significance of Wood to the National Energy Budget

Item	Energy Equivalents	
	Quads	Million Bbls. Oil
1. Contribution of Wood for Energy if we Assume that One-Half of the 8.3 Quads Could Be Made Economically Available. (See Table 23.1)	4.1	695
2. Current Use of Wood and Wood Byproducts for Energy		
-- Use by Forest Industries	0.9	150
-- Wood for Home Heating and Miscellaneous Industries	0.2	35
Total*	5.2	880

*This represents nearly 7 percent of the National Energy Budget in 1978.

UTILIZATION PROBLEMS

The greatest problem in utilizing more wood for energy is its economic availability. Although tremendous amounts of forest residues are generated each year, harvesting, transportation, and processing involves cost of at least $20-$30 per ovendry ton. The challenge is to reduce these costs to make wood more competitive with fossil fuels. To this end, the Forest Service is encouraging work at several research stations. In the South at Alexandria, Louisiana, the Southern Forest Experiment Station is developing a mobile harvesting machine. It is being designed to clean up after logging operations, to chip accumulated slash, and to provide for efficient transfer of chips to vans for removal from the forest. The research is being sponsored cooperatively with the Forest Service by the Department of Energy and five forest products industries. The machine may be adaptable to areas outside the South, where slope of terrain and soil conditions are moderate.

Technology for combustion of wood is fairly advanced, although there is still room for improvement. An advanced burner for wet fuel, the Jasper-Koch suspension burner, is under development by Missisipi State and the Southern Forest Experiment Station. Dutch ovens, spreader stokers, fluidized beds, and oscillating grates in various sizes, factory fabricated or field-erected, are generally available. Combustion efficiencies may range from 60-80 percent. In some cases, wet fuel may be burned, or separate drying equipment may be installed before the combustor. It appears that burning wet fuel is generally more economical than drying. However, drying does impart a number of advantages, including easier pollution control, higher combustion efficiency ability to use smaller combustion equipment, and increased heating value per unit weight of fuel.

As a rough estimate, woodburning boilers and satellite equipment are estimated to cost $30-$35 per pound of steam per hour of output capacity.

An interesting approach to reduce costs of conversion of fossil fuel burning facilities to woodburning facilities is refinement of the wood fuel to make it compatible with existing equipment, thus, avoiding the costs of installing complete new boiler systems.

In some cases wood can be pelletized and burned in boilers designed for coal. One location where this is seen is at a hospital in Fort Steilacoom, Washington. Preparations are also being made for a similar operation at a prision in Stillwater, Minnesota.

Wood gasification might be used to generate a fuel gas for boilers designed to burn oil or natural gas. The Solar Energy Research Institute, in Golden, Colorado, estimates that a wood gasification unit might be installed in conjunction with an existing oil and gasburning facility at a cost of $8.00 per pound of steam per hour. However, wood gasification technology is not highly advanced, particularly in the United States.

In Europe during World War II, considerable use was made of gas from portable generators which operated mainly on wood. In Japan and other countries, so-call gasogens were also used. As soon as gasoline became available after the war, however, the wood gasogens were quickly retired.

So-called producer gas and water gas have had wide application in the United States, as well as abroad. However, the most common fuel for this type of gas was coal or coke. If the proper equipment for making a producer gas from wood were available, this might work well for use in conjunction with a gas or an oil burning boiler.

Several wood gasifiers are now being developed in the United States by small inventors, such as Forest Fuels, in Keene, New Hampshire, and Combustion Equipment Co., in Monroe, Wisconsin, as well as large conglomerates, such as Union Carbide, in Tonawanda, New York. More effort should be taken to put these promising units on stream.

Another problem in wood utilization for energy is the conversion of wood to liquid fuels. As may be seen from table 23.3, the most efficient way to use wood for fuel is to burn it directly. Generally, more petroleum could be saved if wood were burned in boilers in place of petroleum-based fuels, than if wood were converted to a liquid and used as a substitute for motor fuels. Nonetheless, it is necessary to improve the technology for liquifaction of wood so that emergencies may be met in the future. There is an even greater need for the technology in other countries, such as New Zealand and Brazil, which are lacking both coal and petroleum, but have a relative abundance of wood.

Three technologies for liquifying wood are commonly proposed: conversion to oil, ethanol, or methanol. The most progress in converting wood to oil has been made by the Georgia Institute of Technology, and the Department of Energy. At Georgia Tech, a low temperature pyrolysis process to produce a combination of oil, char, and gas has been developed. It is being demonstrated with a 50 ton per day pilot facility at a sawmill in Cordele, Georgia. At Albany, Oregon, the Department of Energy has a complex wood to oil pilot facility. It produces two barrels of oil per ton of dry wood. The plant is still being modified to optimize the process. It operates with wood flour and pressures of about 4,200 pounds per square inch.

The Forest Products Laboratory has a long history of work in wood saccharification and fermentation research for production of ethanol, glycerol, and other chemicals. The Madison wood dilute sulfuric acid hydrolysis process for producing ethanol from wood was used in a plant for production of ethanol at Springfield, Oregon during World War II, but the plant was never fully operational. It was dismantled when the war ended. Forty plants using this process essentially are operating in the Soviet Union. Other new technologies for producing ethanol from wood are being proposed. These include enzyme hydrolysis, which is being researched at various locations in the United States, and a new version of acid hydrolysis, at Purdue.

A difficulty in producing ethanol from wood is the fact that it can be synthesized readily only from the cellulose fraction. Even so, starch from grain is much easier to convert to glucose and ethanol than

Table 23.3. Comparative Energy Recovery from Wood

Compound	Yield/T OD (1)	Product Heat Value Btu	Total Potential Heat Value MM Btu/T OD
Wood Direct Burning	2,000 lb	8,500/lb	17.0
Charcoal	670 lb	12,500/lb	8.38
Oil	370 lb (2)	14,380/lb	5.32
Methanol	647 lb	9,788/lb	6.33

(1) T OD = tons, ovendry.

(2) 1.25 bbl or 52.5 gal based on 7 lb/gal and 42 gal/bbl

cellulose from wood. If the wood cellulose is used for ethanol, uses must also be found for hemicellulose and lignin to permit economic operation of a plant. Hemicellulose could be converted to furfural, xylitol, and other products, for which there are currently no large markets. Lignin utilization poses more obstinate problems. Various solutions have been proposed, including hydrogenation to phenol, gasification to producer gas, with upgrading to synthesis gas, catalytic conversion to methanol, and burning for fuel.

A more promising approach to the liquifaction problem appears to be gasification of the whole wood fraction to producer gas, optimization of the gas through a shift reaction to provide hydrogen and carbon monoxide in the ratio of two to one, to yield synthesis gas, and the conversion of the synthesis gas into methanol.

With existing technology, this process might result in an overall energy recovery in the output methanol, compared to the wood input of 38 percent. However, the weak link in the process, as with boiler fuel, is the gasification step. If methanol were produced, it could be used as a motor fuel directly, or it might be converted to gasoline with a catalytic high-yield process under development by Mobil.

Another alternative would be direct conversion of wood to gasoline from a synthesis gas. Such a process for coal is in effect in South Africa. In this case, the most pressing problem with wood would also be the gasification process.

Given the various alternatives for using forest resources for producing energy, mill residues are being converted to in increasing amounts, and Grantham (1) predicts that essentially all this readily available material will be used by the year 2000. Other residues, including slash from wood harvesting operations, mortality, noncommercial timber, thinnings from timber stand improvement and land clearing, and urban wood waste will also be used in increasing amounts. Contributions from fuel plantations will probably be minimal in the near future.

The greatest use of wood for fuel will continue to be in boilers for production of process steam and electricity, mostly in forest products manufacturing plants. Use of wood fuel for domestic heating will continue to grow, but its share of the total wood use for energy will probably remain at 15-20 percent. Use of wood fuel by utilities for power generation will make some gains in the short-term. Conversion of wood to liquid fuel, especially methanol, may turn out to be viable in developing countries, but an optimal process to gasify wood must first be developed. Such a process is also necessary to permit expedient conversion of oil and gas burning boilers to wood producer gas fuel.

REFERENCE

(1) Grantham, John B. 1977. Anticipated competition for available wood fuels in the United States. In Fuels and Energy from Renewable Resources, ed. by David A. Tillman, Kyosti Sarkanen, and Larry L. Anderson. Academic Press.

24 Functions and Properties of Immobilized Enzymes

I.V. Berezin

Immobilized enzymes provide a powerful tool for development of new chemical and biochemical processes in industry. Some enzymes are difficult and expensive to prepare, so their preservation and stability in an immobilized form is important.

To obtain new information on immobilized enzymes, a systematic study is underway at the Moscow State University. A simple approach is used that consists of incorporating an enzyme into a dense polymeric matrix, which prevents unfolding of the tertiary structure of the enzyme protein. The result of experiments with the enzyme chymotrypsin, which has been entrapped in cross-linked polymethacrylate gel, confirmed this approach. (1) It turned out that with a gel concentration of about 25 percent, a very strong increase in enzyme stability occurred. At a 50 percent gel concentration, the stability of the enzyme was 10^5 times higher than it was when it was in solution alone. Experiments with light depolarization and kinetic measurements show the stabilization effect is a direct result of enzyme freezing in a polymeric matrix. These facts suggest the so-called multipoint interaction model of stabilization, in which an enzyme molecule entrapped in a matrix of gel establishes weak bonds (e.g., hydrogen bonds) with the elements of the matrix structure. Due to the density of the matrix, the surroundings of these bonds reinforces the strength of the enzyme molecule, and increases its stability. Experimental data have been obtained (1,2) to prove this model.

The reinforcement of the enzyme structure can also be achieved in a different way. Surround an enzyme molecule with a long polymeric molecule which has side groups capable of forming different kinds of bonds with the functional groups of the enzyme surface. In experiments of this kind, use can be made of the enzyme formate dehydrogenase of bacterial origin, and a copolymer of vinylpyridine and acrolein; the pyridinium side groups are partially acrylated by treatment with methyliodide. The resulting polymer contains the following side groups:

positively charged N-methylpyridinium, aldehyde, and hydrophobic pyridinium groups.

Formate dehydrogenase treated with this polymer remains soluble, but its stability increases very considerably. (3) For instance, the half time of decay of the soluble enzyme is about 30 hours, whereas when the soluble enzyme is entrapped in a polymer gel the half time of decay is over 1,000 hours. Experimental data indicate this kind of treatment gives rise to formation of a very tight complex, with an enzyme-polymer stoichiometry of 1:1 due to formation of covalent bonds (Shiff bases), ion pairs (carboxylic groups and methylpyridinium groups), and hydrophobic linkages (pyridinium groups). The final shape of the modified enzyme can be thought of as a protein globule wound around by a polymer molecule.

This type of stabilization is of interest in cases when a stable but soluble preparation is required. It is necessary to keep in mind that the specificity of such an enzyme can strongly differ from the original material.

Among the properties of special interest of enzymes entrapped in polymeric matrices are peculiarities of electrochemical processes, in which an immobilized enzyme can take part. This phenomenon is a detail of a more general process, which has been recently christened Bioelectrocatalysis. In general, bioelectrocatalysis deals with conjugation of biochemical and electrode reactions. Systems of reactions are in some instances very complicated, but recognition of biocatalytic contribution to the general process does not represent any difficulty.

For a simple case the following scheme is often valid. (4):

$$E + S \rightleftarrows ES \rightleftarrows E\ (\pm\ n\bar{e}) + P$$

$$E\ (\pm\ ne) \xrightarrow{\text{electrode}} E \pm n\bar{e} \quad \text{(electrode)}$$

Here, E ($\pm$ n$\bar{e}$) stands for the enzyme active center, which is an oxidized or reduced form. The overall result of these consecutive processes is reduction or oxidation of the corresponding substrates, (5) and generation of energy in the form of the electrode potential.

Owing to the high activity of the enzyme, the limiting step in this system is usually an electrode reaction. There are two possibilities to facilitate this process. First, use can be made of low molecular weight mediators. Mediators have to be good substrates for a given enzyme which can undergo rapid electrochemical conversion on the electrode. For instance, hydrogen (H_2) cannot be oxidized on a graphite electrode (E) at a normal potential. But, if hydrogenase (enzyme) is immobilized on an electrode surface, and a mediator (methyl viologen, MV) is introduced to the system, then hydrogen will undergo smooth oxidation at a reversible potential (5) The sequence of events is as follows:

$$E + H_2 \rightleftarrows EH^- + H^+$$

$$EH^- + 2MV^{2+} \rightleftarrows E + 2MV^+ + H^+$$

$$2MV^+ \rightleftarrows 2MV^{2+} + 2\bar{e} \quad \text{(electrode)}$$

The net reaction is oxidation of molecular hydrogen and generation of the electrode potential. This system can be regarded as a hydrogen fuel electrode. (5)

Despite good results which can be obtained with the use of mediators, in this case there are some drawbacks. Side reactions which might eventually destroy the mediator are the major ones. To avoid this, attempts are made to create a system in which direct transport of electrons between the enzyme active center and an electrode is possible.

For this purpose, use was made of a conductive polymeric matrix in which the enzyme hydrogenase of microbial origin was entrapped. (6) A complex formed by 1-polypropargylpyridinium and tetracyanochinodimethane was used as a matrix for immobilization of hydrogenase. The entrapment capacity of this matrix is very high. It is possible to immobilize up to 20 percent of hydrogenase (by weight) in this nonsoluble complex. If this enzyme-containing complex is brought into contact with a graphite electrode, hydrogen readily undergoes ionization at a reversible electrode potential. (6)

This approach is also valid in case of an oxygen electrode based on the use of the enzyme laccase, kindly provided to us by Professor B. Malmstrom (Gateborg Univ.). Laccase, immobilized on a carbon surface, is able to pick up electrons from an electrode and to channel them to oxygen molecules reducing these into water. (7)

In all the described cases, the intimate mechanisms of the direct electron transfer between the enzyme active center and a polymeric matrix or polymeric support is still to be understood. But, it is evident that this phenomenon may play a very important role in many biocatalytic and bioelectrocatalytic systems.

REFERENCES

(1) Martinek, K., et al. 1977. Biochimica et Biophysica Acta. 485: 13-28.

(2) Martinek, K., et al. 1977. Biochimica et Biophysica Acta. 485: 1-12.

(3) Dickov, M.M., et al. 1978. Bioorganic Chem. (USSR), (In press.)

(4) Varfolmeev, S.D., et al. 1978. In Proceedings of IFIAS Workshop on

Physico-Chemical Aspects of Electron Transfer Processes in Enzyme Systems. Pushchino-on-the Oka, USSR, pp. 144-151. Stockholm: IFIAS.

(5) Varfolomeev, S.D., 1978. Advances of Science and Technology. All-Union Institute of Scientific Information (USSR), eds.: V.L. Kretovitch, I.V. Berezin. Biological Chemistry 12, pp. 253-269.

(6) Varfolomeev, S.D., et al. 1978. Proc. Acad. of Sci. (USSR) (In press).

(7) Berezin, I.V., et al. 1978. Proc. Acad. of Sci. (USSR) (In press).

25 Expectations for Organic Chemicals and Polymers From Biomass Feedstocks

Harry Parker

Our dependence on fossil fuel began with the industrial revolution in the eighteenth century. Until that time, man's economy was based almost entirely on biomass. With the development of coal as a new and economical source of energy, low-energy biomass based societies were transformed into high-energy fossil fuel energized societies. More recently, our energy supplies have become dominated by petroleum and natural gas, which are even more economically produced and utilized than coal. Today, however, we must accept the fact that these more convenient sources of energy are in rather limited supply. At some time sources of energy other than fossil fuels must again dominate our energy supply.

The timing of this transition is still a subject of debate. Many individuals believe now is the time to make a rapid movement from dependence on oil and gas. To balance that argument, fig. 25.1, based on data by the U.S. Department of Interior, illustrates that there are many prospects for new petroleum reserves on a global basis. (1) The area in each rectangle is proportional to the estimated probability for oil reservoirs, while the dots represent the amount of drilling to date. Only the United States has experienced extensive drilling in relation to the potential for oil discovery. However, even if global depletion of petroleum and natural gas reserves are in the distant future, local concerns of economics and security may dictate development of nonfossil fuel sources.

This generation is not the first to consider the desirability of using biomass for fuel instead of fossil fuels. F.W. Junge, writing in 1908, noted that biomass could supply the needs for boiler fuel at that time instead of coal, in a chapter titled "The Rational Utilization of Low-Grade Fuels." (2) He also noted that continued addition of carbon dioxide to the atmosphere by burning coal could "exercise an influence on the temperature conditions of the earth far greater than is usually suspected." (3)

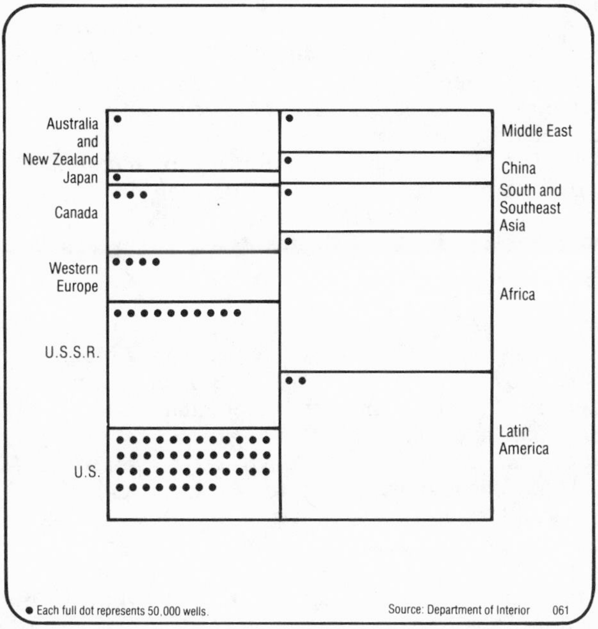

Fig. 25.1. Estimated opportunities for discovery of new petroleum reservoirs.

This paper is principally concerned with the utilization of biomass as a raw material for the production of plastics, fibers, rubber, and organic materials. It will be necessary to relate this particular topic to the total energy problem and to other uses for biomass.

UTILIZATION OF BIOMASS

The word biomass is an all encompassing term for recently grown plant and animal materials. The manner in which biomass is utilized is equally broad. The immediate concern of this paper is chemical conversion of biomass into polymers and organic chemicals. The dominant raw materials for the products are now petroleum and natural gas, therefore, they are frequently referred to as petrochemicals. Although plastics, synthetic rubber, nitrogen fertilizer, and organic chemicals have an essential role in modern society, only a small portion of petroleum and natural gas are feedstocks for these products, 6 percent in 1975. (4) One option which exists for a continued economical supply of petrochemicals is to conserve petroleum and natural gas for these purposes. This could be accomplished by government policy decisions, or by allowing prices to increase on oil and natural gas. At some prices, they would be too valuable for fuel, and would be used primarily for petrochemical feedstocks and lubricants. Another option, the production of petrochemicals from biomass instead of fossil fuels, is the emphasis of this paper.

Obviously, food is the most essential use of biomass, but wood and paper are also essential to society. Utilization of biomass for organic chemicals must consider these needs, as well as the utilization of biomass for energy. Fig. 25.2 illustrates the many routes for biomass utilization. Since wood can be burned on a large scale in an environmentally acceptable manner, there is little incentive to gasify it before combustion, except as a means of retrofitting existing furnaces designed for oil and gas. One reason for gasifying biomass, however, is to provide gaseous fuels for internal combustion engines. Biomass can then be used for transportation and operation of mechanical devices. The use of wood and charcoal-fueled gas producers on cars, busses, trucks, and tractors was widely demonstrated during World War II.

Charcoal is a convenient means to transport and utilize biomass as energy on a small scale, since it has a high heat of combustion, and burns without smoke. Biogas, anaerobic fermentation of biomass, can provide gaseous fuel. The disadvantages of biogas are slow production rates, and the limited portion of the biomass converted. If biogas is to compete on a large scale with other fuels, the residue must be used in a profitable manner.

Wood can be converted into gaseous and liquid fuels by reaction with hydrogen or carbon monoxide. Thi is a complex and expensive process, but no more difficult than similar processes being developed for coal.

CONVERSION OF BIOMASS TO PETROCHEMICALS

Two broad approaches are considered for the conversion of biomass into petrochemicals: chemical modifications of biomass into the desired products, and conversion of biomass to synthesis gas, a mixture of hydrogen and carbon monoxide. Additional chemical processing is then required to reassemble the synthesis gas molecules into the desired products. Some products which are available from these two procedures are illustrated in fig. 25.3.

Synthesis gas produced from hydrocarbon sources now provides essentially all of the ammonia and methanol produced today. This same technology can be adapted to the use of synthesis gas derived from biomass. Ammonia's major use is for nitrogen fertilizer and as such, it represents a considerable energy requirement to maintain our present levels of food production. It is reassuring to know that necessary nitrogen fertilizer needs can be met from biomass.

Methanol is a simple organic chemical which can be utilized directly

BIOMASS UTILIZATION

DIRECT USES	DIRECT ENERGY	CHEMICAL CONVERSION
- FOOD	- DIRECT COMBUSTION	- SYNTHESIS GAS PRODUCTS
- FIBER	- GASIFICATION	- CHEMICAL MODIFICATIONS
- WOOD	- CHARCOAL	- WOOD DISTILLATION
- ANIMAL RATIONS	- BIOGAS	
- RUBBER	- HYDROGENATION PROCESSES	
- DRYING OILS		
- GUMS AND RESINS		
- FERTILIZER		

Fig. 25.2. Methods to utilize biomass.

CHEMICAL CONVERSION
OF BIOMASS

SYNTHESIS GAS
(CARBON MONOXIDE & HYDROGEN)
REACTED TO CHEMICALS

- AMMONIA
- FISCHER-TROPSCH PRODUCTS
- METHANOL
  - FORMALDEHYDE
  - ACETIC ACID
  - FUEL
- METHANE

CHEMICAL
MODIFICATIONS

- CELLULOSE
  - PAPER
  - PLASTICS
  - FIBER
  - GUMS
  - ANIMAL RATIONS
- ETHANOL
  - FOOD
  - CHEMICALS
  - FUEL
- FURFURAL PRODUCTS
- STARCH PRODUCTS
- LIGNIN PRODUCTS
- SUCROSE CHEMICALS

Fig. 25.3. Products of biomass conversion.

as a fuel, or even converted into hydrocarbon fuels. It can be reduced to formaldehyde, which enters into the production of many polymer products. The Fischer-Tropsch process converts synthesis gas into a mixture containing a wide variety of hydrocarbons and oxygenated hydrocarbons, which must be processed for subsequent usage. This process utilizing coal was employed effectively in World War II by Germany, and is now in use in South Africa.

A major thrust of the DOE coal gasification program is the production of synthesis natural gas, methane, from coal via synthesis gas. It is also possible to produce methane from biomass by the same process, so methane is listed as a possible product in fig. 25.3.

Some research personnel are suggesting accelerated development of organic chemicals based on synthesis gas, so that synthesis gas can replace ethylene as the primary building block for organic chemicals.

Another route to a wide variety of organic chemicals is to employ acethylene as the building block. Acetylene can be produced from biomass by production of charcoal, employing the charcoal to produce calcium carbide. The calcium carbide is then reacted with water to produce acethylene. This option was not itemized separately in fig. 25.2 since it requires a large amount of electricity for the furnace which reacts lime with charcoal. It is not, therefore, expected to compete with the synthesis gas route. Locations with an excess of hydroelectric power might consider the process.

Chemical modifications of biomass are more varied and so the listing in fig. 25.3 is rather general. Paper is a major item in today's economy. Many other chemical modifications of biomass have significant usages. One product listed in fig. 25.3, ethanol, is most economically provided today by petrochemical sources, not biomass. However, ethanol, via fermentation of biomass, is sufficiently close to being competitive so that considerable debate regarding its potential is in progress.

Wood alcohol has been the common term used for methanol because its initial commercial source was the destructive distillation of wood. Several other organic chemicals were also produced by this procedure, such as acetone and acetic acid. For this reason, wood distillation is listed as a means for modifying biomass into various organic chemicals. The residue from wood distillation is charcoal, which has considerable value as a fuel, and as a reducing agent in metal smelting. Development of synthetic methanol via the synthesis gas process made the recovery of methanol, and other organics from wood distillation, uneconomical. (5) Today's charcoal production facilities burn the produced organics along with the gaseous products from charcoal manufacture. It is not expected that salvage of these organics will become economical in the future.

The two major routes to organic chemicals from biomass synthesis gas and chemical modification result in different products, but many of the uses of these products overlap. Figure 25.4 itemizes these advantages and disadvantages for the synthesis gas route. This procedure is flexible in that the synthesis gas molecules can be

ADVANTAGES	DISADVANTAGES
1. FLEXIBLE	1. HIGH ENERGY REQUIREMENTS
2. MINIMIZES SOLIDS PROCESSING	2. NOT PRACTICAL ON A SMALL SCALE
3. CONSISTENT WITH PRESENT TYPES OF TECHNOLOGY	3. HIGH INVESTMENT
4. LARGE SCALE OPERATIONS POSSIBLE	

COMPETITIVE OPTIONS

1. SYNTHESIS GAS FROM COAL
2. CONSERVATION OF PETROLEUM
3. HYDROGEN ECONOMY

Fig. 25.4. Synthesis gas route to chemicals from biomass.

---

reassembled to produce many products. The difficulty of large-scale processing of solid biomass must be solved only once: in the design of the synthesis gas reactor. The use of synthesis gas is consistent with today's technology, since synthesis gas is already being used on a very wide scale. The synthesis gas process can be easily utilized in very large processing facilities, which results in considerable savings in investment and labor in costs per unit of production capacity.

One disadvantage of the synthesis gas process is its high energy requirements. Approximately 30 percent of the heat of combustion contained in the biomass is used during its production, plus additional energy during the conversion to the desired products. Many conversion reactions release energy, but this energy must be salvaged at some expense and loss. The synthesis gas route requires many steps of gas compression, reaction, purification, and usually an oxygen plant to supply pure oxygen to the synthesis gas reactor. These technologically sophisticated steps cannot be economically accomplished on a small scale. Another result of this complexity is the very high investment required for production of chemicals via synthesis gas.

Coal can be employed as a feedstock for the production of synthesis gas more easily than biomass. The logistics of supplying coal to an economically competitive plant producing 5,000 tons per day or more of products will be easier than supplying the same amount of biomass. Removal of large amounts of sulfur contained in many coals can be accomplished for a rather low incremental cost over that required to remove the small amounts of sulfur contained in biomass, or low sulfur coal. In the future, coal fueled synthesis gas plants producing ammonia, methanol, and many derived products may be major chemical production centers, just as ethylene based centers exist now.

Another option which is available on a global basis is to produce ammonia and methanol with natural gas in remote locations, where there is little demand for the available natural gas. The methanol and ammonia can then be exported easier than liquified natural gas to the industrialized nations which are deficient in natural gas.

It can be expected that petroleum and natural gas will be available for conversion to petrochemicals for a longer time span than they can be employed for just their fuel value. This situation will result in ethylene and petroleum based aromatic chemicals remaining very significant factors in the organic chemical industry into the twenty-first century.

Several groups have proposed a possible hydrogen economy. Hydrogen as a chemical reactant is much more valuable than hydrogen as a fuel. Hydrogen can be converted into chemicals via the synthesis gas route, or in many cases by direct reactions.

The direct chemical conversion of biomass involves a wide variety of processes. Some procedures can be exceedingly simple, for example, treating plant residues with caustic to improve their digestibility by ruminant animals. Other chemical conversion processes for biomass can become quite complex. For this reason they must be practiced on a large scale, such as is practised in the paper and rayon industry. As shown in figure 25.5, the chemical modification of biomass has an inherent advantage of reduced energy input relative to synthesis gas, because the structure of the original biomass molecule is retained. Some biomass conversion processes can be practiced on a medium to small scale if they are simple. The conversion processes lack flexibility as facilities for one raw material and product can not be easily changed to other processing tasks. All ofthese chemical modification processes involve considerable solids handling, which is expensive, and must be adapted individually to each application. Since a portion of the biomass molecular structure is retained in the chemically modified product the quality of the raw material utilized is of considerable importance.

A ranking for the uses of biomass is given in figure 25.6. This ranking cannot be applied in an exclusive fashion. Although ranked last in terms of value, providing sufficient biomass for maintenance of soil quality is essential. Lands damaged from overgrazing and massive ecological changes resulting from the removal of forests are demonstrations of not properly acknowledging this necessity.

ADVANTAGES	DISADVANTAGES
1. MINIMAL ENERGY OUTPUT	1. LACKS FLEXIBILITY
2. MEDIUM SCALE OPERATION	2. MUCH SOLIDS PROCESSING
	3. CONSTANT QUANTITY OF FEED REQUIRED.

Fig. 25.5. Chemical conversion of biomass.

Even with food as a primary use for arable lands, considerable quantities of biomass residues are produced. These residues can be used in a wide variety of purposes listed in figure 25.6. The priorities and other factors result in obstacles to the utilization of biomass for energy and chemicals in figure 25.7. Development of processes for utilization of biomass residues make the supply and price of residues uncertain. Some, indeed, may currently have a negative value, i.e., a disposal cost. If a process is developed to utilize the residue, the original producer of the residue will expect to be compensated for it. Both weather and economic factors will influence the kinds of residues available, as food producers alter their crops for a maximum return on their primary product. These problems can be circumvented by intentional growth of biomass for energy or chemicals. The competition still remains for arable land between growth of food and growth of energy, or chemical feedstocks. The various trade offs in this competion must be demonstrated in the market place.

Established industries frequently produce multiple products such as petroleum refineries or smelters. The development of biomass chemical feedstock, or energy plantation, which also produces paper, wood products, and outdoor recreational opportunities will result in an initial difficulty of logically assigning the cost of its operation to each product. With this assigned cost, and knowing the market value of the products, management practices can be selected which maximize the return on the investment. Interest rates and projections of future market prices will be very important in these decisions, since growth of trees for lumber requires many years. Esthetics, politics, and social responsibility of the owners will also enter the management decisions.

Collection, storage, shipping charges for low bulk density, high moisture biomass feedstock places them at a considerable disadvantage compared to petroleum and coal. This inherent problem is being addressed. Processes to compress biomass are available, but they add

1. FOOD
2. MONOGASTRIC ANIMAL RATIONS
3. FIBERS
4. RUMINANT ANIMAL RATIONS
5. CHEMICALS AND PLASTICS
6. FUEL AND SYNTHESIS GAS
7. SOIL MAINTENANCE

Fig. 25.6. Ranking of biomass usages.

---

1. PRIORITY OF FOOD
2. UNCERTAINTY OF SUPPLY AND PRICE
3. COORDINATION OF MULTIPRODUCT SYSTEMS
4. STORAGE AND SHIPPING OF LOW DENSITY HIGH MOISTURE RAW MATERIAL
5. SEASONAL AVAILABILITY

Fig. 25.7. Difficulties regarding use of biomass for energy and chemicals.

10 to 20 dollars per ton to the cost of the biomass being processed. Planning for solar energy to dry biomass in the field or forest avoids the high moisture problem, but entails possible damage to the biomass during drying, and the investment in the feedstock being dried. Biological processes require high moisture raw materials, or even added water, but they result in products and residues, which must be distilled, evaporated or dried prior to utilization.

The problem of collection and transportation costs appears to suggest the advantage of small processing plants. The tremendous advantage of large processing facilities generally offsets increased transportation costs over moderate distances. When processed residue can be used near the point of generation, small processing plants may be favored. Examples of this situation are animal feeds prepared by chemical treatment of biomass residues, and gasification of biomass for internal combustion engine fuels on farms or ranches. Even these small scale possibilities remain to be demonstrated as economically attractive. In many ways Small is Beautiful but actually in many cases Big is Better in terms of economics for chemical processes.

EXTRINSIC LIMITS ON THE UTILIZATION OF BIOMASS FOR CHEMICALS

The principal extrinsic limit on the utilization of biomass for chemicals is that other raw materials may remain more economical. Aromatics and ethylene based on petroleum may even retain dominance as a building block for organic chemicals after petroleum has been priced out of the fuel market. These extrinsic limits suggest that biomass residues are best utilized as fuel for boilers. An exception would be chemical processes which effectively utilize the molecular structure of the biomass.

A premise contained in many discussions of alternative energy sources is that when the price of oil and gas reaches a certain level, the alternative energy source will become economically attractive. Analogous inferences could be made for biomass utilization as chemicals. Unfortunately, for processes employing alternative energy and feedstock sources, construction costs will rise as rapidly as the selling price of the energy or chemicals produced.

Data regarding the cost of construction and the cost of energy dating back to 1926 are plotted in figure 25.8. To have a consistent set of information, the data published by W. L. Nelson in the Oil and Gas Journal have been employed. (9) Industrial construction costs are similar for all process plants, including petroleum refineries, as priced by Nelson. In a similar manner all industries will seek to use the most economic fuel just as a petroleum refinery does. In the future, we might expect that coal would be used to fuel petroleum refineries when it is the least costly source of fuel. At that time the Nelson index would probably include the cost of coal in its energy cost calculation.

The data reported in figure 25.8 shows essentially a one-to-one correlelation regarding the cost of bulk energy for industrial operations and construction costs. The period from 1957 to 1969 indicates a constant level of energy costs, but the costs began to rise steeply prior to the Arab oil embargo in 1973. Energy costs and construction have now been restored to their historic one-to-one correlation. Many

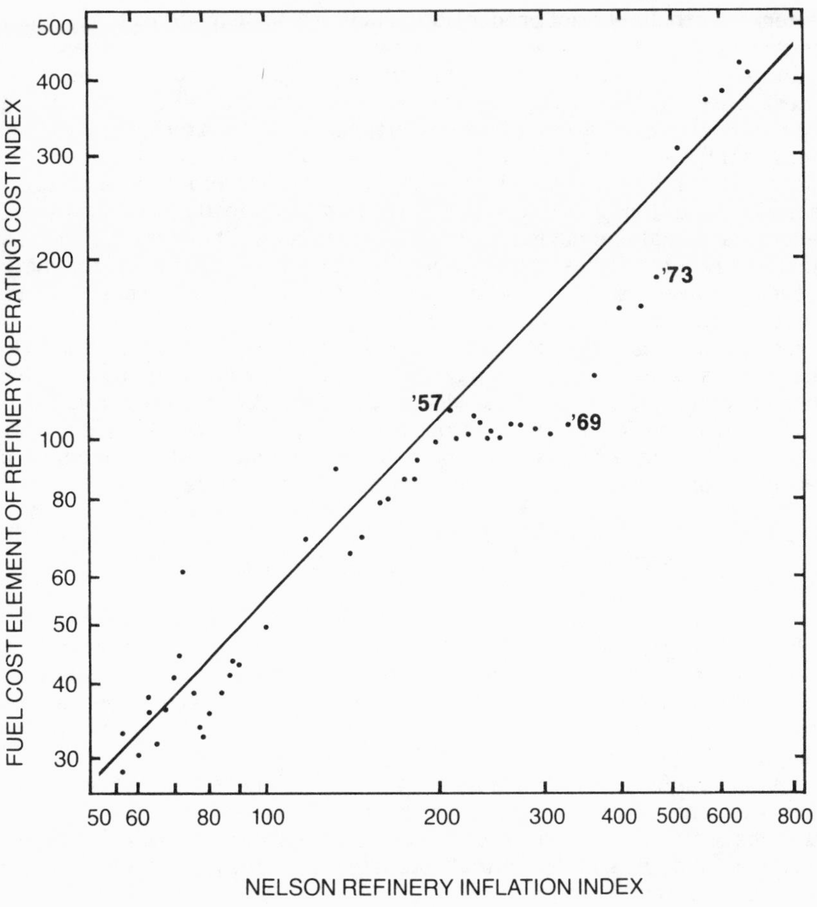

Fig. 25.8. Correlation of fuel cost and construction cost for petroleum refineries (Parker, 1977).

projections are made about future costs of bulk energy and construction costs, but in the author's opinion a continued one-to-one correlation is the most reasonable extrapolation. At every stage of mining, refining, fabrication, and actual construction there are significant energy requirements. For this reason, the cost of bulk energy and construction costs are tightly coupled. In addition, increasing retail energy costs result in increased wage demands, and therefore increased costs for labor.

The observed correlation between bulk energy costs and industrial construction costs suggests the following statement: Processes for alternative bulk energy production which are not economic today due to high investment costs will not be economic in the future due to the parallel rise of bulk energy costs and industrial construction costs. We must base our economy on the least costly source of bulk energy required for generation of electricity and manufacturing operations. Inevitable increases in the real cost of bulk energy must be compensated for by increases in productivity, or by default a decrease in standards of living. The most economical domestic sources of bulk energy are coal and nuclear power. Combustion of biomass residues can make only a small, less than 10 percent contribution to our bulk energy needs. Based on coal and/or nuclear power for bulk energy needs, several routes are available to provide convenience fuels such as gasoline and gas as needed. This need will be determined by the price consumers are willing to pay for these convenience fuels. The convenience fuels can be produced by synthetic processes, from oil shale, enhanced oil recovery processes in old oil fields, or by discovery and production of gas and petroleum resevoirs which cannot be economically exploited in the present energy cost structure.

EXPECTATIONS FOR BIOMASS UTILIZATION

The ideas expressed in this paper can be compressed into several brief statements, but it is more realistic to term these statements as expectations, not predictions or conclusions. Twenty years is a reasonable time period for extrapolation, since it is beyond normal planning and construction periods for new processes, but still yielding a reasonable amount of information on which to base the projections. The expectations will be stated for two circumstances. In one case there will be relatively open selection among various sources for energy supplies and organic chemical feedstocks. These expectations are itemized in figure 25.9.

The second circumstance in which projections are made for biomass utilization is one in which governmental policies dictate extensive use of renewable resources. These policy decisions can be positive action, such as tax and interest rate advantages to renewable resources, or negative actions regarding fossil fuels and nuclear power, such as selective taxation and excessive environmental constraints on coal and nuclear power. In some cases, specific prohibitions against traditional

1. BIOMASS WILL BE UTILIZED FOR BOILER FUEL ON A MODEST SCALE.

2. PETROCHEMICALS BASED ON ETHYLENE AND AROMATICS WILL RE-MAIN DOMINATE.

3. SYNTHESIS GAS GASED ON COAL WILL DISPLACE HYDROCARBON BASED SYNTHESIS GAS FOR AMMONIA, METHANOL, ETC.

4. EXPECT SOME RETURN TO DIRECT UTILIZATION OF BIOMASS MATERIALS -- COTTON, RUBBER, ETC.

5. SELECTED CHEMICAL MODIFICATIONS OF BIOMASS MAY BECOME MORE ATTRACTIVE.

Fig. 25.9. Twenty-year expectations for biomass utilization (open economic choices of energy sources).

---

1. BIOMASS WILL BE THE MAJOR SOURCE OF ADDITIONAL ENERGY SUPPLIES.

2. MAJOR INCREASES WILL BE MADE IN DIRECT USE OF BIOMASS -- COTTON, RUBBER, WOOD, ETC.

3. BOTH CHEMICAL MODIFICATION AND SYNTHESIS GAS ROUTES WILL BE USED TO SUPPLY "PETROCHEMICALS"

4. POSSIBLE DECREASE IN STANDARD OF LIVING

Fig. 25.10. Twenty-year expectations for biomass utilization. (policy dictated use of renewable resources).

energy sources, and specific requirements for renewable resources may be applied. Expectation for chemicals from biomass with governmental policy dictating use of renewable resources are given in figure 25.10.

In actuality, the governmental policies will be a compromise between the two cases discussed above. In many ways, these policies are determined more by social and political factors than by facts alone, since our society has developed an emotional attitude toward energy and the environment. In other cases, the important facts are not known. These uncertainties about governmental policy make decisions regarding investments in energy sources - either alternative or conventional - quite difficult. This uncertainty will in itself be a deterrent to continued availability of energy at a reasonable cost to the consumer.

The role of biomass materials in supplying feedstock needs, for what are now termed petrochemicals, can be expected to evolve rather slowly. The market place is the best guide to the best uses of biomass residues, and if it is desirable to intentionally grow biomass for energy and organic chemical feedstocks.

REFERENCES

(1) Oil and Gas Journal. 1976. April 3, 1976, p. 32.

(2) Junge, F. E. , 1980a. Gas Power. P. 473, New York: Hill Publishing Co.

(3) Ibid, p. 474, 1980b.

(4) O'Hara, J. B., Jentz, N.E., and Papso, J. E. 1975. Survey of Coal Liquefaction Products Including Suitability as Petrochemical Feedstocks, March 18, 1975, Seventy-Ninth National Meeting American Institute of Chemical Engineers, Houston, Texas.

(5) Baker, A. J., 1977. A History of the Charcoal Industry in the US, 11th Great Lakes Regional Meeting of ACS, June 6-8, 1977, Stevens Point, WS.

(6) Parker, H. W., and Whetstone, G. A., 1974. Fuels and Petrochemical Feed Stocks from Agricultural Wastes, Paper 53, Seventy-sixth National AIChE Meeting, March 10-13, 1974, Tulsa, Okla.

(7) Schumacher, E. F., 1973. Small is Beautiful, New York: Harper & Row.

(8) Parker, H. W., 1978. Nearly Available Energy Technologies. Invited Paper Second Annual Texas Energy Policies Conference, (1977 and 1978 data added), Texas Governor's Energy Advisory Council, March 28-29, 1977, Austin, TX.

(9) Nelson, W. L., 1978. Nelson Cost Indexes. Oil and Gas Journal, p. 125, October 2, 1978.

VI

Environmental and Productivity Considerations

Introduction to Part VI

The next two papers are concerned with the need to preserve and enhance the productivity of the soil and of the importance of microorganisms in this. The first of these, by Geoffrey Stanford is an interesting and amusingly written essay on the ecology of the soil system, seen as a mechanism of negative entropy which human intervention has threatened over the millenia and which, with the explosion of population, could impose a serious constraint to food production. The argument advances that with the increasing knowledge of the symbiotic relationships with the soil system, we are now in a position to stop the deterioration. The second paper, by Howard Worne, explores the same question in considerable scientific detail, and discusses many research approaches to the improvement of agricultural productivity through a new understanding of the role of soil micro-organisms.

The conference did not include a discussion of the environmental effects of a greatly increased, if not total, biomass utilization. This, of course, is related to the soil productivity question, but there are wider considerations. In most discussions of bioresource utilization, it is assumed that the environmental consequences will be beneficial. This may well prove to be true, but the matter deserves study, especially, perhaps, from the aesthetic point of view.

The final paper of the conference, by C.M. Barnes, presents a fascinating example of the use of spacecraft sensors and scanners of the environment in general, and the vegetable cover in particular. The case described was the scanning by satellite, coupled with computer acceptance of the information to environments and terrain of significance for insect control, specifically mosquitoes and screwworms. There is clearly great possibility for development in this field.

26 The Long-Term Productivity of Agricultural Soils

Geoffrey Stanford

Nature has been developing plant life for a tremendously long time before man came in to interfere - or, as we had intended, to improve. If we were to imagine that all life began just ten years ago, then man began one year ago, fire for cooking five days ago, agriculture one-and-a-half days ago, city life twenty hours ago, and modern scientific procedures only six minutes ago. On this scale we can see how very recent, indeed, is the use of chemical fertilizer in agriculture - about six minutes ago - compared to agriculture itself - one-and-a-half days, and compared to plant life itself ten years ago.

What has nature been doing all this time? Nothing less than a vast experiment in negative entropy; storing energy against the enormous forces of dissipation. If we dissipate energy faster than nature can store it, all life must perish, and man with it. So our task is to see whether we can indeed help nature to store more energy each year in the future than she has done in the past without our help. And - even more important - we must dissipate less each year than nature is storing; we must maintained a credit balance in the energy bank.

Let us take a look at how nature here on our earth has been transducing and storing sunlight energy from outer space.

TRANSDUCTION AND STORAGE OF SOLAR ENERGY

The way that green leaves store sunlight energy is simple in outline, even though extremely complicated in its elegant details. Basically, carbon dioxide in the air is combined with water from the soil by forcing out some of the oxygen, and gluing the remainder together with the energy packet. That makes sugar. But sugar is soluble, and will be washed away in the first storm. Several sugars joined together make starch, and that is not soluble. But it is soggy and flabby - just think of wet spaghetti; you cannot make trees out of that for it has no structural strength. So more sugars are added to make an even larger molecule in a long stringlike chain: that is cellulose. It has structural strength, like rope or cloth, but no rigidity. So it is embedded in lignin, much like glass wool is embedded in epoxy resin to make fiber glass, or steel wire is embedded in concrete to make reinforced concrete. With this structural rigidity achieved entirely out of sugar units (and each of these held together by energy), the plant can hold up its leaves, spread the chlorophyll in them, and trap more sunlight energy.

But one essential ingredient is missing from this simplified story: life. Sugar, starch, cellulose, lignin - all these materials are dead. The essential ingredient of life can only be breathed into them when nitrogen is added to the molecule - a protein is formed. Nitrogen originally comes from the air, but green plants have not managed to evolve a mechanism for trapping nitrogen as they have for trapping sunlight energy. Strangely, some much simpler organisms - bacteria - can do that. These bacteria live in the soil. They trap nitrogen from the air to make protein for their own life programs. When they die, their proteins are digested by other organisms, and eventually their nitrofixate finds its way to the plants. But this nitrofixing program is very expensive in terms of energy: it takes the energy from several hundred grams of sugar to fix just one gram of nitrogen. And there lies a problem: how do bacteria find that energy? They get it partly from sugars which are exuded into the soil by plant roots; partly by digesting dead roots themselves, and extracting the energy packet from the sugars which make up the cellulose in the root; and partly from the bits of leaves and twigs which rain down on the soil surface from the plants above. When they reach the ground, these are chewed up into myriads of small particles by a large variety of insects, and those particles are carried underground by others. Let us follow the fate of one of them.

THE SOIL SYSTEM

This particle is carried underground, perhaps by an earthworm. It passes through the gut, and is left behind in the burrow. Rain flows in, and washes it further along. It lodges against the soil wall. The individual grains which make up the soil are piled against each other, but with considerable air spaces in between. Each grain touches others around it at the contact points, but over most of their surface they form the walls of an interconnected gallery of air spaces. A film of water covers each grain, and rounds off the contact angle. As more and more water fills the soil, air is driven progressively out; as the wind and the sun pull out the water saturated air from the soil spaces, so more water evaporates into the fresh air that is drawn down, and soil water is lost. So there is a steady ebb and flow of water, a sort of tidal current, which is as irregular as the rain and the sunshine, as the warm of the day and the cold of the night. In this water film live the <u>soilorgs</u> -

bacteria, simple and complex yeasts, mobile nematodes and amoebae, and many other single-celled or simple animalcules, which have no formal digestive tract. They exude enzymes into the water around them, and those enzymes diffuse through the water, reach the detrital particle, and start to digest it. That releases soluble sugars and amino acids (simple proteins) into the water, and those can then be absorbed by the organisms.

This may seem a clumsy program - rather like throwing golf balls at a supermarket in the hopes of getting an orange - but since all the organisms are doing it, and are all producing different kinds of enzymes, they all stand to benefit: they are making for themselves a nutritious even if a watery soup. It is an example of a complex cooperative program - a higher order symbiosis. And it is the sugars that the bacteria obtain that provide them with the energy to power their nitrofixing programs. So they multiply, and fix more nitrogen to make more protein to multiply again. Eventually, the film of water in which they are living dries out, and they die. After the next rain, a new generation of organisms secretes enzymes, which digest the proteins of those now dead original soilorgs, and so they enrich the soil soup with more soluble amino acids, nitrates, and ammonia. Now the plant root can absorb these, and absorb the nitrofix that it needs.

This simple program has some interesting complications. For example, the cellulose which is being broken down to sugar and thus releasing energy is, as we have seen, embedded in a matrix of lignin. So the cellulose chain cannot be attacked along its entire length: the enzymes can only nibble away at it from each end. That makes a kind of slow-release effect. Further, since the lignin is biodegrading so much slower than the cellulose, a microtubule array is formed, and that holds water tenaciously against the pull of evaporation. But a root hair can penetrate that tubule and extract the water when it needs it.

Dead plant material - detritus - therefore has two important functions: firstly to provide an energy flow to soil microorganisms, and especially to the nitrofixers; and, secondly, to store water. But that is only a part of the story.

MACRONICHE AND MICRONICHE

This soil soup coats all the soil particles. When the water film is fairly thick, bacteria and other unicellular motile organisms can swim around freely in it. As the films evaporate, the soup becomes more viscous, and at the same time these smaller organisms become confined to the larger pools, which are held in the contact angles by capillarity. So, the ecological macroniche, which was represented by the sphere of food availability provided by the detrital particle, has now become broken up into a complex series of microniches, more or less isolated from each other in the contact angles. Yet, they are not totally isolated, because fungal threads, hyphae, can travel through a water layer which is thinner than their own diameter, and so they can extend from one microniche to another, digesting the dead bacteria, and transferring that food supply along their length; they can continue to exploit the macroniche long after it has been broken up into discrete microniches. Plant root hairs can do better than that: so long as the air spaces between the soil grains are fully saturated with water vapor they can travel far and wide, powered from above by sugars (and therefore energy) coming down from the leaves. And they can compete actively with the fungi for the food supply. Indeed, they have a further advantage: they can supply food by excreting sugars into the soil water, and so encourage nitrofixing bacteria all around them. The legume nodule is an extreme example of this, in which they enmesh the nitrofixers within their own root structure.

CRUMB STRUCTURE

These continuing cycles of growth and death of soil organisms, of synthesis and of digestion, make a soup which contains a significant amount of jellies. As the soil dries out, they coat the soil grains, and hold them apart. With the next rain they absorb the moisture, swell, and keep the air spaces open to absorb yet more water. This explains why a good mature soil absorbs water freely, while a newly formed sand dune rejects it. But, the jelly does more than that. It holds the soil grain against wind blow erosion, and also against raindrop bombardment. That mechanism is greatly reinforced by the threadlike nature of the dead fungal hyphae, which act as a network of microscopic ropes binding each grain to the next. Soilorgs, therefore, play another important role: they resist wind and water erosion, and stabilize the bare soil surface. But this vigorous program is dependent on an annual supply of fresh cellulose.

Cellulose is readily biodegraded, and its energies are quickly extracted: it represents spending money. Lignin is much more resistant to enzymatic action: it represents energy capital gain. So organic content of the soil is not necessarily the same as fertility. Fertility is short-term, cellulose-associated. It is tilth that is long-term, lignin-associated. And tilth, with its attendant character of crumb formation, is further assisted by the slow steady deposition of waxes and varnishes in the contact angle. Those are derived from the surface coverings of the leaves, and the cases of insects. They get there by dissolving the soil soup in a very dilute solution, and then precipitating out as that soup becomes more concentrated. Like lignin, they take a long time to biodegrade underground, but their strength is lost rather rapidly in daylight - which is one reason why plowing and harrowing can destroy tilth so rapidly.

ENERGY STORAGE AND LOSSES

All ecosystems tend to store energy. As they mature over thousands of years they approach climax character; year by year over the ages they store ever smaller annual increments, until eventually they tend to steady state. Much of the energy store is represented by nitrofix, jealously hoarded, carefully recirculated. Excessive export of nitrofix by farmers can be compensated for by adding chemical fertilizer - if it is available. But the annual recharge of energy - of cellulose - can only be made from plant detritus. Evidence of overexport of this annual recharge under a vigorous agricultural program can be masked for a short time by mobilization of lignin reserves. Overexport of native nitrofix can similarly be masked by taking from the substance of the soilorgs, which are dying out from lack of the annual cellulose energy recharge.

Under this program, the soil system as a whole and its components are driven into a cannibalistic program, and total reserves fall - the so-called endogenous program. This simple abuse of an ecosystem - as, for example, by overgrazing a prairie - is exacerbated by traditional agricultural tillage programs. Those leave the soil bare for much of the year. Certainly weed competition is removed, as well as water loss by evapo-transpiration from those weeds; further loss of water from the bare soil is conserved to some extent by the dust mulch which forms. But rainfall is not absorbed so effectively as under the weed cover; raindrops splash and erosion is increased many hundreds of times, dew distillation is lost to the atmosphere instead of conserved in the region, and surface heating of the bare soil encourages even faster biodegradation of the already scarce detritus. Nature tries to cover bare soil as quickly as possible - there are a whole range of plants which seem to be adapted especially for that. Some grow from seed exceedingly fast: during a quite short period they flower, set seed, and die. Their roots below ground represent a local, concentrated energy store; their shoots above ground, like dust, represent a widespread diffuse energy supply, which can collect under the leaves of another plant and provide a local surface mulch. Germination of this seed is usually triggered into activity by a rainshower.

At the other extreme is the very slow growing perennial plant. When times are hard it is nearly dormant, living on its reserves; when times are good it recharges its reserves but puts on very little growth. Over a long time, it can be seen to be growing slowly but surely. In between these two extremes exist a wide array of plants. At present our agricultural crops are chosen from the first extreme, and we control conditions to relieve stresses and prolong the growing period. These controls are energy-intensive, derived from oil supplies.

Some questions arise: Would we be wise to learn more about intermediate types, and thus keep the soil surface better covered? Over a hundred year period, or even over a ten year period, do weeds consume more waste than they conserve? Do they destroy an ecosystem more than they improve it? Does the farmer's dust mulch conserve long-term in the ecosystem better than weeds? Or is this a short-term raid on a complex long-term equilibrium capital improvement program?

Behind that complex of questions lies still another question which may be simpler to answer: Just how much export can an ecosystem support without loss of energy reserves? Does a given proportion of export stimulate compensatory replacement? Or is all loss an irretrievable loss - a reduction in the speed of progress in that ecosystem to climax steady state?

Obviously we would like to think that export is replaceable through further plant growth. There is some evidence, at least in a mixed ecosystem, that some export of some of the growth taken at some part of the life cycle does stimulate an increase in population. There is also some evidence that the total system sun/air/topgrowth/root/soil/water can provide a small surplus indefinitely. The condition seems to be that this increase is limited by the component in shortest supply - usually nitrofix, but often a micronutrient metal. The circumstance which most favors this stimulated production seems to be harvest before seed formation, or even before flower formation: that is, while juvenile and vegetative hormones are still circulating, and maturation hormones have not yet begun to be formed. In simplistic terms, it could imply that the plant strives to replace itself sexually, and that if the objective is thwarted, it will transfer its energy production to increasing its vigor here and now - either for vegetative survival or for a second attempt at forming sexual reproductive organs. And so, within reason, we can harvest both the first and second growths and export them.

STIMULATED PRODUCTION

Many clipping and grazing trials have shown that the annual biomass production of grasslands is greater under light export than under free growth without export. But that may be an incomplete finding, since in the absence of export, all of the production - seed, leaf and stem -is added directly or indirectly to the energy store of the total system. Grazing will keep the system as grassland, under grassland rainfall. Free growth may permit energy storage, and thus progression and conversion to shrub land and eventually to forest, and (under suitable circumstances) to induce a corresponding increase in rainfall. That this progression takes many centuries, and is normally too slow to be observed during the lifetime of a single man, does not mean that it is not occurring when the land is left alone, or that it cannot occur. Indeed, we know it often is occurring: witness a forest area which had been cleared for field crops by our grandfather, became farmed out, was rested to pasture, was overgrazed, and has recently been bought by a building speculator and allowed to lie fallow. This land reverts to woodland very quickly, even though the interval since it was last under forest may be fifty or more years, and presumably the soil circumstances, both live and dead, have changed enormously during that period.

The annual production of leaf tissue in a natural climax deciduous forest is much the same as in a natural prairie - 1-5 tons/ha. But the forest does not need to use any of its energy on nitrofixing: its own reserves, constantly recycled, can meet all its needs. The prairie grasses, on the other hand, are trying to store energy and also to nitrofix. Does this explain why the forest can put so much energy into its savings account - wood? And can we safely steal indefinitely from that savings account as long as we do not raid the current account and current working capital? Is this a clue to suggest we stop our efforts to grow annual crops for biomass fuel, and concentrate on woody tissue to maintain the energy reserves in the soil?

There is another intriguing question: Why do so many trees produce energy-rich seeds in quantities that are vastly greater than are needed to maintain the species? Is this a mechanism which stores energy (concentrated as oils) and nitrofix (concentrated as protein) over winter, inside that resistant seedcase? In early spring, before the deeper soil has warmed up and the leaves have unfurled, that seed germinates, and starts to photosynthesize. Is it trapping the CO_2 which is arising from the surface mulch as it also warms up? And when the tree has unfurled its leaves, and the forest floor becomes dark again, is the eventual death of that seedling an example of planned infanticide? Is it an elegant mechanism for overwintering some of the precious reserves, and for quickly recovering them through the roots when they are needed again for leafing out and for producing new shoots? This reasonable surmize is clouded by another observation: Often times these seeds are so badly infested with grubs that only a few survive. Can we safely compete with the grubs, and export the entire crop before they eat it?

GUIDING PRINCIPLES

With these considerations in mind, can we formulate some principles which we should follow to produce a surplus for our excessive populations? Firstly, should we conserve or increase the nitrofix reserves in the soilorg biomass? That we can do (in the absence of chemical fertilizer and the energy import that it represents) by planting legumes and other species of plants which are active nitrofixers. Secondly, should we provide to the soil an annual replacement of fresh cellulosics - at least two and preferably five or ten tons per hectare, per year, dry weight? This can either be provided from plant detritus produced on-site, or from city refuse, much of which is paper. And thirdly, should we maintain a continuous canopy over the soil, to protect it from the sun and wind during the summer, and from rain and flood during the winter? These conditions can be achieved by planting wind break and shelter belt trees across the line of the prevailing winds, and by growing rows of clump-type grasses along the contour instead of planting stolonic grasses broadcast. Many of these clump grasses are deeper rooted than the stolonics, and thus much more drought resistant. They have the further advantage that the cattle walk between the clumps as they browse and do not crush the tender growing tips.

Should we strive to combine some of these programs? Leguminous trees can be chosen in preference to nonleguminous, and fir trees (which have an active nitrofixing program of their own) in combination with hardwoods, depending on local conditions. And should we also take especial care to conserve the total nitrofix reserves of the region and its waters by carrying all the sewage waters from the cities out to the agricultural land, there to be stripped as they irrigate and recharge the deep aquifers?

STRATEGY

If we focus our attention each year on a given objective - harvesting hay, felling trees, growing corn, replacing nitrogen deficiency, irrigating - we blind ourselves to the true situation, which is to achieve an exceedingly long-term complex interactive shifting equilibrium. It is so complex that in the short-term, it seems to tolerate our abuses; but in the long-term, when we take advantage of that apparent tolerance, will it falter and die? Will dust bowl and desert supervene? History shows that they will indeed follow. To prevent it, we should abandon our attempts to maximize short-term profit by mining capital. We should stop trying to intervene with unit processes. We should study the entire system as a living, working entity. In particular, we should study the entire energy flow, direct and indirect; we should be careful that the portion that we divert for our own consumption would comprise a surplus to the energy budget of the region both short- and long-term. And we should do all that quickly on a global scale.

Vegetation, both forest and prairie, is disappearing, rainfall patterns are being disrupted, deserts are increasing all over the world. These are not diseases by themselves - they are only the evidence of a deeper disease - loss of biological energy reserves in the topsoil and in its vegetative mantle. It seems man has been consuming his own birthright ever since agriculture began 12,000 years ago. But the circumstances of that excessive consumption have changed forever. Until recently, we did not comprehend what was happening, or that we were the cause. Today we know, for the first time in the long history of man's evolution. Therefore, we have the power to stop, and the ability to save ourselves and our children, and we must stop.

27 The Role of Soil Microorganisms in Increasing Agricultural Productivity

Howard Worne

Soil is essentially composed of five components - mineral matter, organic matter, water, air, and a living population composed of highly interrelated groups of microorganisms consisting of bacteria, actinomycetes, fungi, viruses, protozoa, yeasts, algae, and other similar soil microorganisms, in addition to nematodes, rotifers, earthworms, and countless other forms of chitinous insect life. It is the interaction and balance of this myriad of biological life forms that helps to maintain the health of the soil.

Through the intercession of soil microorganisms, there appears to be several distinct and viable approaches for improving plant growth and yield. One is basically concerned with improving the availability of organic and inorganic nutrients, while the second is involved with the protection of plants from bacterial and fungal predators. In one instance, the desired effects are due to the increased activity of the soil microorganisms as the result of the addition of organic matter to the soil or to the rhizosphere. In the other, the activity of highly specialized microorganisms can fix atmospheric nitrogen and secrete inhibitory antibiotics, in addition to releasing inorganic matter from the soil and making it available to the plants.

ORGANIC MATTER

The ability of external forces to stimulate microbiological activity in the soil so as to increase the amounts of nitrogen, phosphorus, and other nutritionally important elements available to plants is of prime importance.

Organic matter in many of our soils has already been reduced to subnormal levels. Soil might be revitalized by the use of green manures, but when arable land is scarce, it is costly for the farmer to grow crops and plow them under for this purpose. Other sources of available organic matter therefore need to be developed, i.e., farm manures and nonfood wastes, such as straw, weeds, leaves, sludges, etc. The low nitrogen content of most of these materials may be compensated for during decomposition by the addition of sufficient fixed nitrogen to provide a balanced C/N ratio for microbial metabolic requirements. The microbiological conversion of huge and accumulating quantities of organic matter, such as sawdust, garbage, paper waste, and sewage sludge could also enhance the quality of currently deficient soil.

Organic matter also has a role in controlling the soil-born bacterial and fungal diseases of plants. The tremendous increase in the use of pesticides, herbicides, and other chemicals in agriculture has inhibited normal biological control, and allowed the possible absorption of these toxicants by the plants, leaving toxic residues on foods and feeds.

One of the best examples of biological control is that of nematodes by predacious fungi. In soils containing 2 percent organic matter, the concentration of nematodes may vary from 100,000 to 3,000,000 nematodes in the surface 6 inches of soil. A portion of the nematodes are free-living species that are not parasites on plant roots. However, many of the remainder are parasitic, and can be controlled as a result of the concentration of both organic matter and predacious fungi in the soil. Soils low in organic matter through analysis have been shown to contain low levels of predacious fungi and, as a result, the predatory nematodes are free to create serious problems, unless they are controlled through the application of chemical nematocides.

For example, significant reductions in the concentration of the pineapple root rot nematodes have been reported in Hawaii as a consequence of the explosive increases observed in the concentration and activity of predacious fungi following the incorporation of green pineapple plant residues into soil, which was heavily contaminated with predatory nematodes. These additives are able materially to reduce disease severity, even under field conditions.

By building organic matter in the soil through either green manuring, the addition of compost, or almost any suitable amendment, the substrate for the proper growth of the predacious fungi can be established in the soil.

The innoculation of the treated soil with a mixed culture, consisting of various types of predacious fungi, then establishes an overall network throughout the soil, which finally becomes a nematode trap. No definite functional niche has been established for the predacious fungal species, but they apparently participate in the microbiological balance in the soil, limiting the size and activity of the protozoa-nematode fauna. In an arid soil of low organic matter, inoculation would be successful, because it is first necessary to establish the organic matter on which the fungi can grow and form the necessary network.

Soil phytopathogens, with very few exceptions, have demonstrated they are more destructive to their host in sterile soil than in normal soil. In addition, it has been demonstrated that the virulence of known phytonathogens inoculated into sterile soil is significantly reduced if mixed cultures of the saprophytic microorganisms, normally found in the soil, are added to the inoculum. These and other relevant facts indicate that the normal saprophytic microflora in the soil are important for the management and control of various plant diseases. The heterogenous population of nonpathogenic soil microorganisms competes with, or antagonizes through selective antibiotic synthesis, the phytopathogens and, as a result, slows or inhibits their rate of spread. Because of the practical significance of the known pathogen-microflora interaction, numerous attempts have been made to alter the microbiological equilibrium in the soil.

There have been two major ways of biologically controlling phytopathogens: (1) The direct inoculation of the soil with active cultures of selected microorganisms, producing specific antibiotics effective against sensitive pathogens; and (2) the alteration of the soil environment to effect a transformation of the microflora, so that the biochemical and metabolic activities of the modified flora will be biologically destructive to the invading pathogens without concern for the actual mechanism of growth suppression.

To establish the validity of the first approach, microbiological isolates are selected on the basis of their ability to manifest antibiosis to the selected pathogens under laboratory conditions. The selected microorganisms are then evaluated to determine whether the experimental cultures are able to control the invasive bacterial or fungal pathogen in the absence of the normal competing microflora. Tests are also made to find out if the toxic factors secreted by the pathogen antagonists are produced under the conditions found in normal soil. Further studies, in which pathogens and the antibiotic producers are inoculated simultaneously into sterile soil planted with the susceptable plant host, have shown significant control of many plant diseases. For example, pythium infections have been controlled with various strains of trichoderma and streptomyces, while certain strains of antinomycetes will materially decrease the severity of root rot of wheat caused by the fungal pathogen Helminthosporium sativum.

Initial success in the use of special inoculants of antibiotic producing microorganisms, such as streptomyces, penicillium, trichoderma, and various members of the genus bacillus, has been achieved in the prevention of seed and seedlings invasion by pathogens. Significant numbers of highly active pathogen antagonists can be concentrated on the minute area of the seed surface where the pathogens must grow, and when nutrients that support this growth are relatively abundant. Thus, as an example, the damping off of the Scott's pine seedlings, caused by certain fusarium species, has been satisfactorily controlled by treating the seeds with spores of antibiotic secreting gliocladium, or penicillium strains.

Another innovative approach of great practical importance is the modification of the soil chemistry by admixing with the soil various organic soil amendments. Certain organic materials are capable of stimulating germination of fungal spores which, after vegetative growth, is followed by enzymatic lyses of the formed mycelium. If this metabolic stimulation and subsequent lysis can be accomplished prior to planting a crop susceptible to the particular fungi, the population of the predatory fungi can be reduced and a measure of control obtained. For example, the addition of chitin to soil has been shown to stimulate the development of chitinase secreting strains of mycolytic bacteria, which are quite active against Fusarium oxysporum, a widely occurring and an economically important phytopathogen.

THE PLANT RHIZOSPHERE AND PLANT GROWTH

Studies have shown that there are greater concentration of microorganisms in rhizosphere soil than in root-free soil. The root structure of the plant exerts a strong selective action on the microflora, which results in the predominance in the rhizosphere zone of gram negative rods, such as Pseudomonas fluorescens, various bacteria requiring amino acids to achieve optimal growth, bacteria such as azotobacters that are capable of vitamin and phytohormone synthesis, and bacteria capable of releasing bound phosphorus from the soil.

Qualitative and quantitative changes in the microbiological populations in the rhizosphere are also observed as a result of root structure and excretions. In fact, these rhizosphere microorganisms tend to express the usual characteristics associated with the general microbial population, which develops on actively decomposing green plant residue. This observation is quite comprehensible, since sloughed off epidermal and apical tissues and root excretions also represent the type of material which provides the nourishment for the microorganisms growing adjacent to the plant roots. Many factors influence the type and abundance of the root microflora, including the type of plant grown, the age of the plant, the moisture content of the soil, pH of the soil, cultivation practices and specific environmental factors, such as light and temperature. These factors have a significant effect on plant growth, and as a result of photosynthesis and subsequent translocation there is a direct influence on the type and character of the rhizosphere population.

It has been observed that the application of a variety of substances to the foliar areas of the plant may also exert a potent effect on the microbial population of its roots. For example, foliar sprays containing urea have been shown to increase the bacterial count on wheat roots, and conversely decrease the fungal population. The foliar application of zinc bacitracin, and other antibiotics after translocation reduced the concentration of bacteria in the rhizosphere, and increased the level of fungi. Of particular interest to those using foliar sprays is the possible secondary effect of various agricultural chemicals on the rhizosphere population immediately following their translocation and exudation from the roots, which can materially effect the plant metabolism and, thereby, the type and quantity of root excretions.

Various substances, such as 2, 4 Dichlorophenoxyacetic acid and

Alphamethoxyphenylacetic acid, have been detected in root exudates when foliar spray has been applied to plant leaves. This type of application has a distinct potential with regard to the control of rhizosphere populations with its subsequent effects on the health of the plant. For example, chemical substances that increase microbial activity in the rhizosphere would stimulate improved nutrient turnover in that area. Such additions may also provide a more effective microbiological barrier to root invasion by various predators and phytopathogens. As an example, it has been reported that applying urea to corn causes an increase in the concentrations of actinomycetes antagonistic to Fusarium roseum in the rhizosphere.

As soon as the rhizosphere has begun to develop, a multiplicity of interrelated microbiological reactions occur. Almost every conceivable interaction, including symbiosis, synergism, antibiosis, nutrient competition, cellular lyses, and parasitism may be detected in this concentrated and dynamic microbiological community. These functions are also directly involved in determining the type and concentration of the various microorganisms found in the root zone, which under highly competitive conditions results in the preponderance of certain of the microflora in the ecosphere, and the relegation of others to a less dominant position. Thus, these processes are of distinct importance in the establishment of the desired seed inoculants in the rhizosphere.

It has been determined that the root microflora exerts a number of beneficial effects on overall plant growth. There is an increase in the amount of CO_2 in the root zone, as well as an increase in the concentration of various organic acids which arise as a result of the metabolic activity of the microflora. These organic acids contribute, through chelation, to the solubilization of soil minerals, thereby improving the availability of inorganic nutrients, such as potassium, phosphorus, sulfur, calcium, iron, magnanese, zinc, etc. The liberation of insoluble phosphates by those strains of microorganisms capable of secreting phosphatase enzymes in the root zone has been recently evaluated. This broad spectrum enzyme activity helps to decompose organic substances excreted by the root, in addition to dead and dying root tissue, thus liberating and making available needed nutrients.

Nitrogen in the form of ammonia, arising from microbiological action, may be absorbed directly at the root interface by the plant or after biological conversions to nitrates. At the same time, through cocometabolism, these enzymatic reactions are capable through bioxidation of destroying phytotoxic substances that may affect subsequent planting of the same crop. Amino acids and vitamins are also produced by certain of the microorganisms that may accelerate plant growth in the early stages, and supply the plant with vital amino acids and vitamins, thereby improving the quality of plants for human and animal consumption. Plant growth stimulants, with their diverse and far reaching plant growth effects, are synthesized. And lastly, a microbiological obstruction, containing potent lytic and antibiotic substances, is provided to decrease root invasion by soil borne phytopathogens. The antibiotic activity functions not only in the root zone, but as a result of absorption and translocation. also helps to protect the plant from stem and foliar phytopathogens.

Another microbiological means of increasing plant growth is by utilizing microorganisms with special characteristics, as the ability to fix atmospheric nitrogen, to produce plant growth substances, such as auxins, gibberellins, or cytokinins, to elaborate antibiotic or cellular lytic substances, to excrete vitamins and amino acids, or to solubilize soil materials. These microorganisms occur naturally in many soils and, if available, may be stimulated to exert their particular and individual effects by using soil amendments. However, by the choice of selected microorganisms for specific end applications, a much greater measure of control can be achieved. This can be increased also by adapting microorganisms to crops, and with our knowledge of microbial genetics by breeding more effective microbes, whether for increasing nitrogen fixation, antibotic production, or substrate solubilization.

Since practical considerations preclude the general use of such microorganisms as general soil inoculants, seed treatment provides the simplest and most effective means of placing the desired microorganisms in the root zone, where they will do the most good. This controlled use of microorganisms is not only more specific, but is also more economical than animal manure applications or green manures.

There are two basic types of microorganisms involved in nitrogen fixation from the atmosphere. These are the symbiotic and the nonsymbiotic. The symbiotic nitrogen-fixing bacteria are the rhizobium, which are involved in the inoculation of legumes. In very fertile soil containing considerable quantities of nitrogen, however, it has been determined that rhizobial activity is minimized due to the fact that considerable quantities of nitrogen are generally available from the soil. Rhizobium legume inoculants have achieved their most notable success in land development programs on low grade soils. In arid soils requiring large amounts of nitrogen, legume inoculants in combination with other symbiotic microorganisms may be extremely important for both short- and long-term requirements.

In organic soils, it is often difficult to establish the desired rhizobia on plant root structures due to biological antagonism from other microorganisms in the rhizosphere, especially the antibiotic producing antinomycetes. The incorporation of various fungicides and insecticides in seed mixtures has been shown to significantly reduce rhizobial nodulation. With regard to herbicides, there has been signfificant investigative effort on this subject, and it has been shown that some of the herbicides are quite inhibitory towards proper nodulation, while others have little or no effect. Foliar spraying of nitrogen bearing nutrients, such as urea, may also have a strong effect on reducing nodulization, presumably by increasing the nitrogen level of the plant, and altering the carbon/nitrogen ratio in the root area.

Another important factor of nitrogen is the use of specialized bacteria, such as Azotobacter vinelandii, Bacillus polymyxa, Clostridium pasteurianum, and Pseudomonas fluorescens. For the azotobacters to fix nitrogen from the air, certain trace elements are necessary to stimulate this activity. Molybdenum and iron are the two main inorganic constituents of the nitrogenase enzyme complex that are necessary for nitrogen fixation. Humic and fulvic acids, which are produced by the biological decomposition of organic matter, also stimulate the metabolic activities of the azotobacters. The azotobacters produce various vitamins, more spefically thiamine, riboflavin, nicotinic acid, biotin, inositol, pantothenic acid, pyridoxine and vitamin B_{12}. The interrelationship of the azotobacters with various rhizobium exists because of the ability of the azotobacters to synthesize biotin, a vitamin growth factor that is essential for the growth of the rhizobium, the bacteria in the legume root nodules that mediate in the symbiotic transfer of atmospheric nitrogen to plants. The vitamins, because of their synergistic interrelationship, produce beneficial effects on the very important mycorrhizal fungi that form on plant roots, and help to make nutrients available to the host plant.

When azotobacters are in close proximity with various soil phytopathogens, the inhibitory toxicants secreted by the azotobacters are a potent pathogen antagonist. In addition to this vital antibiotic secreting activity, the azotobacters produce phytohormones, more particularly auxins, gibberellins, and cytokinins, which are potent stimulants to plant growth. The azotobacters exist in a symbiotic relationship with cellulose decomposing bacteria, particularly the cellulomas, utilizing their cellulolytic capability to supply available sugars for metabolic energy.

Azotobacters have symbiotic relationships with phosphobacteria that transfer phosphate from insoluble soil particles directly to the plants in a soluble form. Azotobacters and phosphobacters function more efficiently as a synergistic mixture than when each is used along. In addition, metabolic intracellular phosphate is released from the microoranisms after death in a form usable by plants. Since the life span of an individual bacterium is about 24 hours, this process is quite rapid. Azotobacters exist and function in a soil for which the optimum pH is from 7.2 to 7.6. In acid soils below a pH of 6.5, growth of the azotobacters is slowed, and nitrogen-fixation is totally inhibited. The discernable benefits of adding lime to the soil may be attributed primarily to azotobacter stimulation, rather than any direct feeding of the plant by the calcium in the lime. Since numerous studies show that these bacteria grow best under fields of grass of which corn is a member, a synergistics relationship between the two is suspected. Seeds treated with mercury and other fungicides, however, inhibit the azotobacter so the practice of planting untreated seeds is a definite plus.

In addition to nitrogen fixation, the two major contributions of these microorganisms are believed to be supplying organic substances that stimulate plant growth and improve the quality and yield of the crop and, very importantly, protection against phytopathogens. It will be noted that these effects are very much the same as those of the rhizosphere microflora except that they are presumably more intensified by seed innoculation. They are not designed to supplant normal fertilizer practices or protective measures.

Seed inoculation is seen as the main means of concentrating desirable microorganisms in the immediate vicinity of the plant root, so that the products of their growth and metabolism may be absorbed directly by the plant. To be successful, the inoculant must establish itself in this growth zone, and meet the intense antagonism from the native microflora. This is, no doubt, one of the most critical factors affecting successful seed inoculation. However, by utilizing special techniques, it is possible to develop mirobial and fungal strains that are able to resist this rather formidable competition, and to colonize the root and carry on their activities to the benefit of the plant. Their growth pattern can also be intensified by establishing favorable conditions for their continued expansion by using either soil amendments or foliar plant treatment. There is no doubt that many of the failures of seed inoculation in the past have been due to the fact that environmental conditions, such as moisture pH, organic matter, phosphate availability, and soil type, were not suitable for the inoculant.

To supply the demand for additional quantities of food for an expanding world population, it will be necessary to enhance agricultural productivity. In addition, more efficient methods must be developed for using solid wastes to rebuild the organic matter of the soils. This can only be accomplished with the help of a vast array of heterogeneous soil microorganisms that have the biochemical capability of converting compostable waste into rich soil-building humus. We must also adjust our present methods of fertilization so that we assist the soil microorganisms, and not hinder or destroy their basic biochemical capabilities. By considering soil as a living, functioning ecosystem instead of dirt, we can truly form a solid basis for constructing a biotic pyramid, in which the soil microorganisms exist in an efficient and a functioning, productive, and symbiotic interrelationship with plant life supplying nitrogen that has been fixed from the atmosphere, and with biological controls to prevent phytopredators from attacking the plants and reducing yields.

28 Satellites and Computer Systems to Aid in Insect Control

C.M. Barnes

Observing the major bioresrouces of earth by means of sensors aboard satellites and computing the total biomass with associated computer programs seems a real possibility in the decade immediately ahead. Such technology, considered a spin-off of the current space exploration program, will be of immeasurable importance to the present generation. Crop identification and yield predictions, not only for the United States but for all areas of the world, will serve to assist in accurately estimating the total food production available for increasing populations. Similar observations on timber, used in construction or for fuel, and the environment which alters their growth rate, are currently underway. The use of these modern devices for inventory comes at a propitious time in civilization, when it has been amply demonstrated that if mankind is to prosper, indeed survive, an adequate plan for use of our natural resources is mandatory.

Another important aspect of sufficiency is that of conservation. Each year disease and insects account for major losses in agricultural crops, animals, and people. Many of these diseases are related to the environment, and cover broad geographic areas which may be monitored by satellites or aircraft. While satellite data per se is not diagnostic, it can evaluate subtle factors indicative of disease. For example, the infrared signature of healthy foliage is generally different from diseased or dead plants, and valuable insight is derived from such observations. Insects multiply in proportion to ground temperature and moisture, and sensing those parameters aid in detecting their presence and potential for population expansion.

The National Aeronautics and Space Administration has been conducting pilot studies concerning the ability of spacecraft and airborne sensors to observe the earth and collect data considered important in the disciplines of environmental medicine, geographic pathology, ecology, and entomology. These studies refer to the usefulness of such data in insect and disease control programs.

Lectures, workshops, and seminars have been held with several groups, including local and international health workers, and environmental scientists. Research data was presented and attendees queried as to the value of these basic concepts for use of aerospace systems, as adjuncts to existing health and insect vector control procedures. The majority suggested that remote sensing data will be particularly appealing to agencies responsible for extensive disease control in developing countries having minimal public health facilities. International health organizations have requested technical assistance and liaison to combat specific problems in country development. Preliminary evaluations of their requirement makes one realize that, while significant progress has been made, there is still an inadequately developed technology for remote sensing applied to public health. Thus, it appears desirable to continue remote sensing research within the federal government and at university laboratories.

THE BIG VIEW IN MAPPING DISEASE

Dr. Barnett Cline, an epidemiologist, (1) has written that NASA's remote sensors give him new eyes to see more clearly the big picture of the geographic disease problems with which he contends. Indeed, because aircraft and satellite operate at such altitudes to permit a unique perspective, there is an opportunity to accurately encompass larger geographic areas, and to determine how certain physical features (swamps, estuaries, tidal flow, mountains, rivers, valleys, etc.) contribute toward the dissemination or natural control of disease processes (fig. 28.1, 28.2).

Mapping is important in geographic study of disease. Our experience within a southern Mexico test site indicates some of the difficulties of securing accurate, detailed maps for certain regions of the world. For example, the map location of specific villages, important as ground checkpoints, varied 1 to 10 kilometers from their actual location as determined by space imagery. Precision in mapping is important for many reasons, but particularly so if one is to use aerial delivery systems for insecticides or pesticides.

The World Health Organization considers detailed maps to be of primal importance in disease control. For example, the identification of grasslands and the location of their interface with forested areas in inadequately charted regions of Africa can be helpful in understanding the habits of simians which harbor several important human vital diseases of that continent (such as yellow fever).

Virologists at the USPHS Communicable Disease Center have commented on the value of remotely-sensed freshwater-saltwater interfaces seen from space. This zone supports ecologically the development of forest hammocks in Florida, and is well-known as the habitat of Culex atratus, the mosquito vector of a strain of Venezuelan encephalomyelitis virus (fig. 28.3).

Fig. 28.2. Color infrared photo of Texas City-Galveston, Texas area from NASA aircraft at 60,000 feet. Water quality (turbidity and flow patterns), mosquito breeding areas, industrial blight, shellfish harvesting areas are rapidly identified from this altitude.

Fig. 28.3. Vegetative hammocks at the freshwater-saltwater interface along the coast of Florida are known as breeding areas for the Culex atratus mosquito. Hammocks are readily identified by high altitude aerial photography and many times from space altitudes.

Preliminary work in the Trinity River basin of Texas has led to the hypothesis that the satellite images of the area can adequately define the breeding habitat of the salt marsh mosquito Aedes sollicitans. Perhaps 80 percent of this mosquito species is produced in only 10 percent of the terrain. If this is typical of other river basins of the world, where salt marsh mosquitoes may be serious vectors of disease, it appears possible to control major populations of these mosquitoes with insecticide release over proportionately smaller areas. The resultant savings in cost for spraying, as well as the value of releasing decreased quantities of insecticide to the environment, could be quite attractive. In both of these cases, it is obvious that satellites cannot see mosquitoes -rather, they can define terrain, geographic features, and the vegetative ground cover, which has been shown to be directly related to breeding habitat. The EROS Data Center (U.S. Department of the Interior) currently has NASA acquired imagery from many river basins in inventory. Some of these river areas undoubtedly contribute to local mosquito problems. It seems important to provide such data to health officials of the countries concerned.

Use of the Computer

Of equal importance to the large areas viewed by space systems is the capability for collection and reduction of remotely-sensed data by modern analytical methods. Due to the diversity and quantity of detailed information required to accurately assess the vagaries of disease habitat, it is essential that all potentially valuable data be collected, sorted, and presented to the investigator in formats which can aid in diagnostics and/or solution to the problem. Formats vary between the elementary to those of extreme sophistication. Sometimes black-and-white photography or simple computer printouts are adequate for the purpose. Occasionally, a false color coded presentation can separate different data on the same image, and do a superb job in explaining the relationships between them. This could mean that the more expensive color procedure may be more cost effective. Examples of information collected and formatted are temperatures, (including degree day sums), gross estimates of moisture conditions, terrain altitude, cloud cover, and vegetative cover.

For many purposes, not only must the data be synoptic, it must also be collected, analyzed, and distributed within an appropriate time frame, allowing responsible officials to develop a compatible disease management strategy. Modern computers and software have enhanced this capability. Scientists at the Johnson Space Center have demonstrated what can be done in at least one research and development program (the screwworm data system). This program evolved from a need to understand factors which cause the growth and decline of screwworm populations over all of Mexico. Routinely, this system provided 14 parameters of environmental data on a daily basis within five days after passage of the satellite. These data consisted of millions of bits of environmental measurements in a geographical region 760,000 square miles in size. The resolution used varied between 1 and 4 kilometers depending on the need for that particular information. The five-day delay was adequate for studies of this specific insect vector, (Cochliomyia hominovorax), which has a nominal 25-day life span. A 24-hour turnaround could have been provided if required for the problem (fig. 28.4).

Personnel at the Earth Resources Laboratory (ERL) at the NASA National Space Technology Laboratories are conducting a series of investigations to develop remote-sensing techniques that apply to the study of wetlands. For one of these investigations, an airborne 24-channel multispectral scanner was used to differentiate vegetation.

By using computer-determined vegetational classes, known relationships between plant species associations and the egg-laying habitats of the salt marsh mosquito were employed to outline the probable areas where mosquito control would be most effective. Thus, vegetational types could be analyzed for indications of positive or negative mosquito breeding terrain. Resolution in this case varies with the aircraft altitude, and may commonly be 3 to 20 feet.

In addition to multispectral electronic sensing, the Johnson Space Craft Center staff has investigated low altitude aircraft photographic sensors with spatial resolution of a few feet. These photographic sensors, operated with appropriate filters, can do creditable jobs in environmental analysis. If one can use light aircraft, the cost of precision photography for limited area surveillance is considerably smaller than with comparable electronic systems. This can be quite appealing to governmental entities with limited budgets.

Some Problems in the Use of Remote Sensing

A New Technology. One of the problems currently recognized as hindering the rapid development and dissemination of remote sending includes understanding the technology. Remote sensing is multidisciplinary in nature and utilizes the sciences of physics, electronics, data processing, photography, and systems engineers. In general, health scientists do not fully understand these disciplines. Training courses, workshops, and demonstration programs must be offered such that public health administrators can be trained and will be willing to include such adjunct, cost beneficial methods in their armamentarium.

Basic Costs of Instrumentation and Ground Truth. Data gathering and processing equipment is expensive. For laboratories without existing computer services and with limited resources, the initial investment required both in hardware and personnel has been found to be a definite constraint. Because the satellite sensor system views large areas and collects many data points, the expense of providing staff, transportation, and communications for the initial large scale ground truth verification of observed data may be almost prohibitive. On the positive side, one might say that never before has one been able

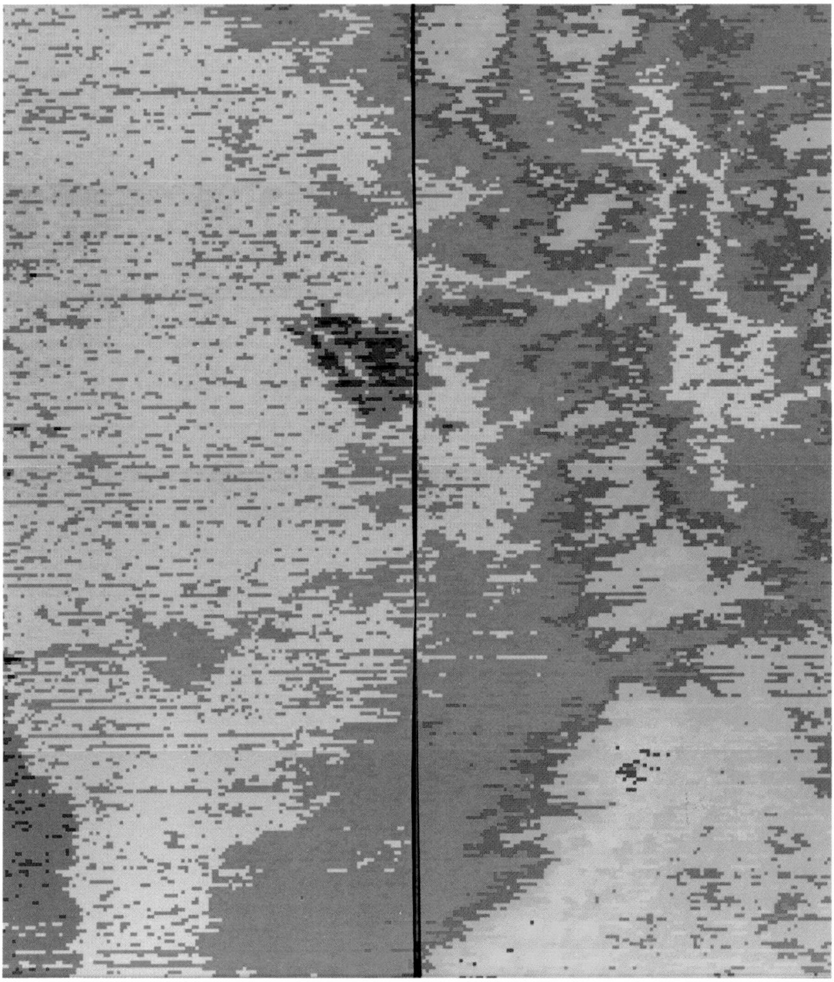

Fig. 28.1. An electronic false color image of an area in Central Veracruz, Mexico (approximately 200 x 300 kilometers) as seen with thermal sensors of ITOS II. The coastal plain is light blue blending to darker blue, green, and yellow of the mountainous highlands. Red dots (pixels) in the upper yellow are very cold areas of mountain of 6000 meters altitude. Lake Aleman is dark blue in the central plain, and the Tehuacan valley (light and dark blue in the lower left) can be seen as connected thermally with the coastal zone.

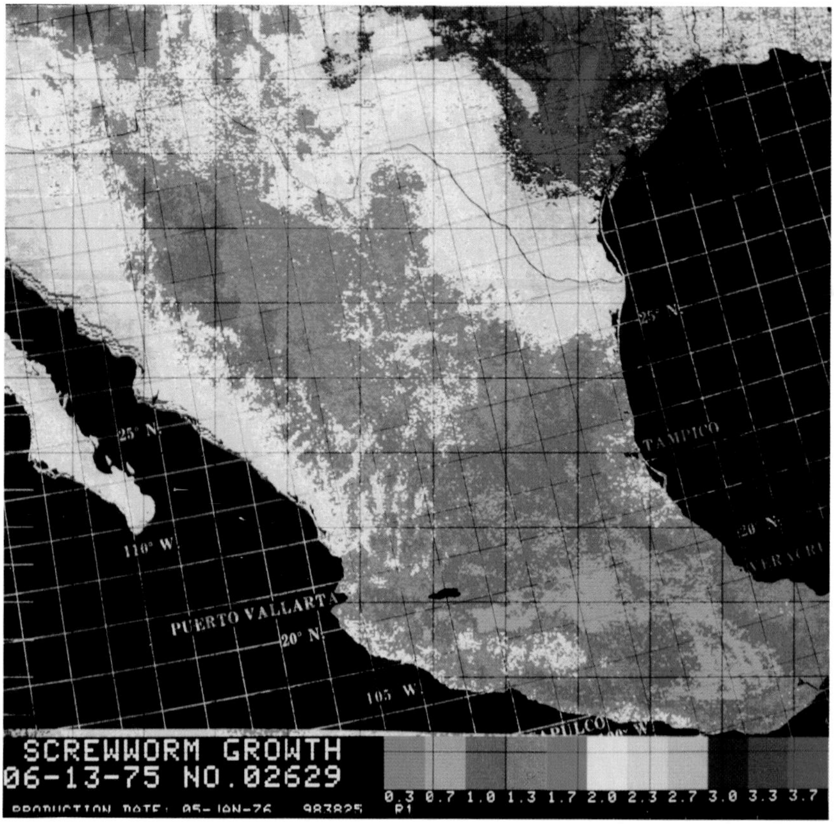

Fig. 28.4. This image of southern Texas, New Mexico, Arizona, and northern Mexico is a computer produced electronic false color image indicating best estimates of where screwworm populations were most active on June 13, 1975. Information in the image is based on environmental data received from the ITOS weather satellite on that date, and utilized basic growth information of that insect species. Growth index varies from light blue (declining populations) to bright red (areas likely to experience extremely rapid population growth).

to obtain so much data for so little.

Defining Precise Research Objectives. There are many misconceptions concerning remote sensing, and how it can be utilized. However, new technology does not accomplish everything in an effective way. In this case, remote sensors can give the health worker unique broad scale information never before available. The systems engineer and other members of the team must work with the health official to determine which objectives are feasible, desirable, or can be discarded as wasteful of computer time.

SUMMARY

Preliminary investigative work concerning the applications of remote sensing technology to classification of vegetation and terrain, which have implied biomass analysis and public health insect control significance, has been completed. Primary research emphasis has been placed on definition of environmental parameters conducive to the identification, growth and development of insect populations of importance to human and animal health, using aerial and space borne sensors. It appears feasible to utilize satellite imagery to classify into broad ecotypes the vegetation sometimes associated with insect development.

Satellite remote sensing has been used to measure temperature changes for northern Mexico on a twice daily basis. This program was designed to support the eradiction of the screwworm fly, Cochliomyia hominovorax, from that Republic. A computer system was designed to accept satellite data, fit it to an insect model, and produce imagery indicating estimates of where the screwworm fly can survive and grow, based entirely on weather and environmental consideration.

The use of remote sensing and computer systems in programs of biomass evaluation, eradication of some insects, and disease vector control is limited by the imagination of scientific investigators, and the willingness of administrators to accept such technology and put it to work for the benefit of mankind.

REFERENCES

(1) Cline, M.D., Barnett L. 1971. American Journal of Epidemiology.

(2) Penfound, William T. and Hathaway, Edward S. 1938. Plant Communities in the Marshlands of Southeastern Louisiana. Ecol. Monographs, vol. 8, no. 1, pp. 1-56, Jan. 1938.

(3) Michigan State University, Ecological Factors Affecting Tree Productivity: Report of Project 1180 Agricultural Experiment Sta.

(4) Philco-Ford Corp, 1973. Earth Resources Production Processing

Requirements for Aircraft Electronic Sensors. PHO-TR523, Feb. 1973.

(5) Oosting, Henry J. 1956. The Study of Plant Communities. San Francisco: W.H. Freeman & Co.

(6) World Meteorological Organization, United Nations. Weather and Animal Parasitic Disease, Report No. 159.

(7) The Martin Marietta Corp., NASA Contract NAS9-15598. The Applicability of Remote Sensing to Earth Biological Problems, Part I, (4 Insect Groups) MCR 79-598.

(8) Michigan State Univ. 1974-79. On Line Pest Management, Annual Reports.

(9) Vines, Robert A. 1960. Trees, Shrubs, and Woody Vines of the Southwest. Austin, Tex.: The University of Texas Press.

(10) Zaitzeff, E.M., Wilson C.L. and Ebert, D.H. 1970. MSDS: An Experimental 24-Channel Multispectral Scanner System. Bendix Technical Journal, vol. 3, pp. 20-32, Summer-Autumn 1970.

(11) Zaitzeff, E.M., Korb, C.L. and Wilson, C.L. 1971. MSDS: An Experimental 24-Channel Multispectral Scanner System. IEEE Transactions on Geoscience Electronics, vol. GE-9, pp. 114-120, July 1971.

(12) Viosca, Percy, Jr. 1928. Louisiana Wet Lands and the Value of Their Wild Life and Fishery Resources. Ecology, vol. IX, no. 2, pp. 216-229, Apr. 28, 1928.

(13) Marill, T. and Green, D.M. 1963. On the Effectiveness of Receptors in Recognition Systems. IEEE Transactions of Information Theory, vol. IT-9, no. 1, pp. 11-17, Jan. 1963.

(14) Eppler, W.G., Helmke, C.A., and Evans, R.H., 1971. Table Look-Up Approach to Pattern Recognition. In Proceedings of the Seventh International Symposium on Remote Sensing of Environment, vol. II, Willow Run Laboratories Rept. 10259-1-X, pp. 1415-1425, Aug. 1971, Ann Arbor: The University of Michigan.

(15) Cibula, Wm. G, 1976. Applications of Remotely Sensed Multi-Spectral Data to Automated Analysis of Marshland Vegetation, NASA Technical Note D-8139, Feb. 1976.

(16) Health Applications Office, 1973. The Use of Remote Sensing in Mosquito Control. MSC 07644, Feb. 1973, NASA Johnson Space Center, Houston, TX 77058.

(17) Barnes, C.M. and Cibula, Wm. G., 1979. Some Implications of Remote Sensing Technology In Insect Control Programs Including Mosquitoes. Mosquito News, July 1979.

Appendix - A Tribute to John McHale*

Shortly before his unexpected death last November, John McHale organized the International Conference on Bioresources for Development. At the opening session of the conference, Harlan Cleveland paid tribute to McHale with the following remarks.

Everyone in this room is acutely aware that John McHale, the restless mind and ambitious spirit who conceived this International Conference on Bioresources for Development, was quite unexpectedly stricken with a massive heart attack last week and taken from us quite literally at the height of his remarkable powers.

His close life companion, Magda Cordell McHale, his emotional and intellectual partner in every way, is recovering from the greatest shock in an eventful life that has never treated her gently. She is a strong person, but it would cruelly sap that strength for her to attend so soon even a conference that she herself organized. So in their joint absence - everything they have done has been a demonstration of jointness - we open this conference in celebration of John McHale.

We don't know very much about life after death, but we know enough to sense that in this place this morning, his spirit is patent and pervasive. It is not so much in his memory, therefore, but to honor him, that I ask you to rise, and stand for a moment to share in a moment of silence.

---

*From The Futurist 13, No. 1 (February 1979): 22.

The life and works of John McHale have touched all of us, and have profoundly influenced some of us. Artist and designer, sociologist and economist, analyst and historian of science, scholar of world resources and biospheric ecology and global development and planetary culture, deep student of the past, keen observer of the present, and prescient planner of the future--John McHale has been all of these. He was fun, too; he knew that truth comes in small paradoxical packages, and this far from dour Scot found especially in the ironies of human relations the raw material for his quiet sense of humor. But above all else, he has been an outstanding example in our time of a mind that brings expertnesses together to make something happen, the integrative mind.

It is not enough to describe him, as The Times of London did, as "a perfectly preserved, thinking, feeling, fully alive specimen of renaissance man." In the Renaissance there was so little to know; they thought that a Francois Rabelais could seriously aspire to learning all of it. John was a man of a new kind of renaissance, when the best thinkers focus on the interconnections among the exploding categories of knowledge, and search in the interstices for the elements of a new wisdom.

Our very presence in Houston today, though it was not so intended, is a living example of what John McHale meant to do . . . meant for us all to try to do. Our meeting bears the trademark of John and Magda McHale: it is a first of its kind. Their alert and ranging minds have always seemed to be out ahead of the crowd, exploring new art, new facts and trends, new potentials, new choices and alternatives for humankind.

So we all feel the sudden vacuum in this time and place. And we can all help fill it with integrative thought on this frontier of thinking they call bioresources.

Index

About the Contributors

ALEXANDER KING - Chairman of the Board of Trustees, International Federation of Institutes for Advanced Study (IFIAS), Paris, France.

HARLAN CLEVELAND - Director, Program in International Affairs, Aspen Institute for Humanistic Studies, Princeton, New Jersey.

GUY STREATFEILD - Vice Consul (Commercial), British Consulate General, Houston, Texas.

MOHAMED NABIL ALAA EL-DIN - Senior Researcher of Soil Microbiology, Institute of Soils and Water Research, Agricultural Research Center, Giza, Egypt.

ALEX G. ALEXANDER - Director and Principal Investigator, CEER-UPR Biomass Energy Program, Agricultural Experiment Station, University of Puerto Rico.

R. ANDERSON - International Federation of Institutes for Advanced Study, Karolinska Institutet, and the Medical Research Council, Stockholm, Sweden.

ANDREW J. BAKER - Chemical Engineer, Forest Products Laboratory, USDA Forest Service, Madison, Wisconsin 53705.

C. M. BARNES - Life Scientist with the Biomedical Applications Branch, Medical Sciences Division, Space and Life Sciences Directorate, L. B. Johnson Space Center, Houston, Texas.

K. BEHBEHANI - Kuwait Institute for Scientific Research.

PAUL F. BENTE, JR. - Executive Director, The Bio-Energy Council, Washington, D. C.

I. V. BEREZIN - Dean, Department of Chemistry, Moscow State University.

BERTRAND H. CHATEL - Chief, Technology Applications, Office for Science and Technology, United Nations.

INGEMAR FALKEHAG - Director of Renewing Systems, Inc., Mt. Pleasant, South Carolina.

I. Y. HAMDAN - Kuwait Institute for Scientific Research.

C-G. HEDEN - Intenational Federation of Institutes for Advanced Study, Karolinska Institutet and the Medical Research Council, Stockholm, Sweden.

J. HENRY - Consultant, The MITRE Corporation, McLean, Virginia.

N. HUSSAIN - Kuwait Institute for Scientific Research.

D. R. JACKSON - Battele Columbus Laboratories, Columbus, Ohio.

J. D. JOHNSON - Director, Office of Arid Lands Studies, University of Arizona, Tucson.

S. KRESOVICH - Battelle Combus Laboratories, Columbus, Ohio.

W. T. LAWHON, Battelle Columbus Laboratories, Columbus, Ohio.

BART LUCARELLI - Department of City and Regional Planning, University of California, Berkeley.

W. G. MC GINNIES - Director Emeritus, Office of Arid Lands Studies, University of Arizona, Tucson.

RICHARD L. MEIER, Professor of Environmental Design, Departments of City Planning, Architechture, and Landscape Architecture, University of California, Berkeley.

MURRAY MOO-YOUNG - Chemical Engineering Department, University of Waterloo, Canada.

HARRY W. PARKER - Professor of Chemical Engineering, Texas Tech University, Lubbock.

ARMAND F. PEREIRA - Escola Brasileira de Administracao Publica (ENAP) of Fundacao Getulio Vargas, Rio de Janeiro, Brazil.

RUSSELL W. PETERSON - President, National Audubon Society, New York.

J. R. PORTER - Professor of Microbiology, University of Iowa.

OSWALD A. ROELS - University of Texas Marine Science Institute, Port Aransas Marine Laboratory, Texas.

D. SALO - Group Leader, Biomass, Advanced Energy and Resource Systems.

M. SCHOLL - Department Head, Advanced Energy and Resource Systems.

C. A. SHACKLADY - United Nations University Program Coordinator, Institute for Animal Nutrition, The Netherlands.

A. SHAMS - Kuwait Institute for Scientific Research.

W. H. C. SIMMONDS - National Research Council of Canada.

MALCOLM SLESSER - Head, Systems Analysis Division, Joint Research Center, Inspra, Italy.

GEOFFREY STANFORD - Director, Greenhills Center and Experimental Station, Cedar Hill, Texas.

KEITH H. STEINKRAUS - Professor of Microbiology, Cornell University.

SEYMOUR WARKOV - Professor of Sociology, University of Connecticut, Storrs.

L. WILLIAMS - International Federation of Institutes for Advanced Study, Karolinska Institutet and the Medical Research Council, Stockholm, Sweden.

J. T. WORGAN - National College of Food Technology, University of Reading, England.

HOWARD E. WORNE - President, Worne Biochemicals Inc., Berlin, New Jersey.

JOHN I. ZERBE - Manager, Energy Research, Development and Application, Forest Products Laboratory, USDA Forest Service, Madison, Wisconsin.